SEARCHLIGHT ON PEACE PLANS

SEARCHLIGHT on PEACE PLANS

Choose Your Road to World Government

Edith Wynner and Georgia Lloyd

TO

THE PIONEERS FOR WORLD GOVERNMENT
— OF, BY, AND FOR THE PEOPLE —
AND TO THE MEN AND WOMEN WHO WISH
TO TURN OUR GLOBE INTO A SAFE AND HAPPY
HOME FOR ITS TWO BILLION INHABITANTS.

New York E. P. Dutton and Company, Inc. 1944

Copyright, 1944, by E. P. Dutton & Co., Inc.
All rights reserved. Printed in the U. S. A.

FIRST EDITION

¶ No part of this book may be reproduced in any form without permission in writing from the publisher, except by a reviewer who wishes to quote brief passages in connection with a review written for inclusion in magazine or newspaper or radio broadcast.

A WARTIME BOOK
THIS COMPLETE EDITION IS PRODUCED IN FULL COMPLIANCE WITH THE GOVERNMENT'S REGULATIONS FOR CONSERVING PAPER AND OTHER ESSENTIAL MATERIALS.

S. A. JACOBS, THE GOLDEN EAGLE PRESS
MOUNT VERNON, N. Y.

TABLE OF CONTENTS

☞ *Following years refer only to dates when works were published.*

ACKNOWLEDGMENTS xi

PART I: SEARCHLIGHT ON PEACE PLANS
Charting the Peace Plans; The Basic Issues 3

PART II: THEORETICAL PLANS
There Is Nothing New under the Sun — Old Plans to Unite Nations
Dating from 1306 to 1914 29

Pierre Dubois (1306) . . .	31	Baron Wiltrich Holbach (1773)	44
Dante Alighieri (about 1310) .	31	Richard Price (1776) . . .	44
George Podebrad, King of Bohemia (1464)	31	Pierre-André Gargaz (1779) . Johann August Schlettwein	45
Desiderius Erasmus (1514) .	32	(1780-84)	46
Pope Leo X and Cardinal Wolsey (1518)	32	Anonymous (1782) . . . Marie Jean Antoine Nicolas	47
François de la Noue (1587) .	33	Caritat, Marquis de Condorcet	
Eméric Crucé (1623) . . .	33	(1786)	48
Hugo Grotius (1625) . . .	34	Anonymous (1787) . . .	48
Campanella (1633) . . .	34	Palier de Saint-Germain (1788)	49
Maximilian de Béthune, Duc de Sully (1638)	34	Johann Gottfried Schindler (1788)	50
Johann Amos Comenius [Komensky] (1645-66) . .	35	Jean Baptiste du Val-de-Grâce, Baron de Clootz (1792) . .	51
Samuel Rachel (1676) . . .	35	Jeremy Bentham (1793) . .	51
William Penn (1693) . . .	36	Boissy-d'Anglas (1795) . .	52
John Bellers (1710) . . .	36	Johann Gottlieb Fichte (1795)	53
Charles Irenée Castel, Abbé de Saint-Pierre (1712) . . .	37	Immanuel Kant (1795) . . Carl Joseph August Hofheim	53
Giulio Alberoni (1736) . .	38	(1796)	54
Anonymous (1745) . . .	38	Josef Görres (1798) . . .	55
Johann Michael Von Loen (1747)	40	Anonymous (1800) . . . Andr. Moser (1800) . . .	56 56
Saintard (1756-57) . . .	41	Konrad Nägeli (1800) . . .	57
Ange Goudar (1757) . . .	41	Thomas Paine (1801) . . .	58
Johann Franz von Palthen (1758)	41	Karl Salomo Zachariä (1802) . Czar Alexander I (1804 and	59
Von Lilienfeld (1767) . . .	42	1815)	59

Table of Contents

Gondon (1807) 60
Anonymous (1808) . . . 61
Ph. A. Stapfer (1808) . . . 62
Eberhard Friedrich Georgii (1811) 62
Karl Christian Friedrich Krause (1811 and 1814) 63
Jean Baptiste Claude Isoard (about 1813) 65
Anonymous (1814) . . . 66
Alexander Lips (1814) . . 67
Dr. Arnold Mallinckrodt (1814) 67
Count Claude Henri de Saint-Simon (1814) 68
Rev. Noah Worcester (1814) . 69
Napoleon Bonaparte (1816) . 69
Count de Paoli Chagny (1818) 69
Emma Willard (1820 and 1864) 70
Conrad Friedrich von Schmidt-Phiseldek (1821) 71
Anonymous (1826) . . . 72
Simon Bolivar (1826) . . . 73
William Ladd (1828 and 1840) 73
Juan Francisco Sineriz (1839) 74
Victor Considérant (1840) . 75
Lieutenant Ferdinand Durand (1841) 75
P. R. Marchand (1842) . . 75
Elihu Burritt (1848) . . . 77
Charles Sumner (1849) . . 77
Prince Peter von Oldenburg (1863 and 1873) 78
Henry Richard (1873) . . . 79
Baroness Bertha Von Suttner (1889) 79
Jean de Bloch (1897) . . . 80
William T. Stead (about 1899) 80
Richard Bartholdt (1905) . . 81

PART III: THEORETICAL PLANS

Charts of Plans to Unite Nations since 1914 83

A. UNIVERSAL 83
Federal: 89
Alfred Owen Crozier (1915) . 90
Theodore Harris (1918) . . 94
Swiss Committee for the Preparation of the League of Nations (1918) 97
Raleigh Colston Minor (1918) 102
Lola Maverick Lloyd and Rosika Schwimmer (1924, 1937, 1938, 1942) 107
H. J. Paintin (1926) . . . 113
Women's Organization for World Order (1935, 1936, 1937, 1943) 116
Dr. S. J. Cantor (1939) . . . 120
W. L. Walton (1939) . . . 122
William C. Brewer (1940) . . 125
Hans Heymann (1941) . . 129
Oscar Newfang (1942) . . 132
Ruth Bryan Owen (1942) . . 137
Leslie Balogh Bain (1943) . . 140
Percy Bordwell (1943) . . 143
Edward J. Byng (1943) . . 148
John B. Corliss, Jr. (1943) . . 153
Eldon Griffin (1943) . . . 157
Max Habicht (1943) . . . 160
Richard Burton Johnson (1943) 163
Abe Rogow (1943) 167
John H. Rosser (1943) . . . 169
Wallace C. Speers (1943) . . 173
Jennie McMullin Turner (1943) 177
Michael Young (1944) . . . 180

Confederate: 189
German Government (1919) . 190
Frank Noel Keen (1934) . . 194

Table of Contents

C. E. M. Joad, C. D. Kimber, Miss F. L. Josephy, and K. Zilliacus (1942) 197
Ely Culbertson (1943) . . . 203
Gullie B. Goldin (1943) . . 213
William Hard (1943) . . . 216
Robert Morrison MacIver (1943) 218
Robert Arthur Merrill (1943) 221
Herbert F. Rudd (1943) . . 223

B. THE UNITED NATIONS 227
The Atlantic Charter [text] (1941) 230
The United Nations Agreement [text] (1942) 231
Example of Bilateral Lend-Lease Agreement [text] (1942) 232
Example of Bilateral Defensive Treaty of Alliance [text] (1942) 236
Moscow Conference Declarations [text] (1943) . . . 239
Cairo and Teheran Conference Declarations [text] (1943) 244
Agreement for United Nations Relief and Rehabilitation Administration (1943) . . . 246
General Marcel de Baer (1943) 251
Commission to Study the Organization of Peace (1943) 257
Walter Nash (1943) . . . 261
Harold E. Stassen (1943) . . 263
Michael Straight (1943) . . 266
Sumner Welles (1943) . . . 272

C. REGIONAL 275
José Weiss (1915) 277
Anonymous (1916) . . . 279
Carl Zimmermann (1917) . . 284

Aristide Briand (1930) . . . 287
Alfred M. Bingham (1940) . 289
W. Ivor Jennings (1940) . . 294
Oswald Dutch (1941) . . . 298
R. W. G. Mackay (1941) . . 302
Sir George Young (1941) . . 306
Abraham Weinfeld (1942) . 309
Richard N. Coudenhove-Kalergi (1943) 313
Dr. Leo Dub (1943) . . . 318
Offer of Union to France by Britain (1940) 320
Greek National Group (1931) 321
Constitution of a Balkan Union (1942) 324
Confederation of Poland and Czechoslovakia (1942) . . 325
Kazys Pakstas (1942) . . . 327
S. R. Chow (1942) 329
John Van Ess (1943) . . . 331

D. IDEOLOGICAL . . . 335
Crichton Clarke — Federal (1934) 337
Clarence K. Streit — Federal (1939 and 1941) 340
Walter A. Leach — Federal (1942) 344
Jeremiah S. Alguy — Confederate (1943) 346
Stephen King-Hall — Alliance (1942) 349
Clarence Budington Kelland — Alliance (1943) 351

E. COURT PLANS; ADVISORY DISARMAMENT CONFERENCE; INTERNATIONAL AIR FORCE 355
H. Francis Dyruff (1915) . . 358

viii   Table of Contents

Elijah W. Sells (1915) . . . 362
James T. Shotwell (1924 and 1936) 364
New Commonwealth (1939) . 367
F. SAMPLES OF WORLD PUBLIC WORKS PROJECTS 371
Herman Sörgel (1932) . . 373
Saco De Boer (1937) . . . 376

PART IV: PRACTICAL ATTEMPTS

Evolutionary Stages Toward a Governed World 1375 B.C. to 1918 . 379

Amenophis IV (Ikhnaton), Egypt (1375? B.C.) . . . 381
Boeotian League, Greece (776 B.C.) 381
Peloponnesian League, Greece (550 B.C.) 381
The Thessalian League, Greece (511 B.C.) 381
Confederacy of Delos, Greece (477 B.C.) 382
Aetolian League, Greece (426 B.C.) 382
Arkadian Union, Greece (370 B.C.) 383
Achaian League, Greece (274 B.C.) 383
Lykian League, Greece (168 B.C.) 383
The Roman Empire (27 B.C.) 384
Holy Roman Empire (800) . 384
Lombard Leagues, Italy (1093) 385
Rhenish Confederations, Germany (1254 to 1813) . . . 386
The Swiss Confederation (1291) 387
Hanseatic League, Germany (1367) 388
Great Peace Confederacy of the Iroquois, New York State (1457) 388
Union of Utrecht (1579) . . 389
New England Confederation (1643) 390
Albany Congress (1754) . . 391
United States of America (1778) 392
Congress of Vienna, Holy Alliance, Quadruple Alliance, and Concert of Europe (1815 to 1820) 393
German Confederation (1815) 395
International Legislation, Administrative Unions, and Technical Conferences (1864) . 395
The Dual Monarchy — Austria-Hungary (1867) 397
Inter-Parliamentary Union (1889) 398
Arbitration Treaties (1889 to 1914) 399
The Hague Conferences (1899 and 1907) 400
Pan-American Union (1890) . 401
Permanent Court of Arbitration (1901) 402
Central American Court of Justice (1908) 403
The Hague Congress of Women; The Ford Neutral Conference for Continuous Mediation; and The International Committee for Immediate Mediation (1915 to 1916) 403

Table of Contents

PART V: PRACTICAL ATTEMPTS

Charts of Confederate and Federal Constitutions 409

Constitution of the German Empire (1871) 416
Covenant of the League of Nations (1919) 420
Constitution of the International Labor Organization (1919) 426

American Constitutions
The Argentine Republic . . . 429
The United States of America . 435
The United States of Brazil . 440
The United States of Mexico . 449
The United States of Venezuela 457

British Constitutions
The Structure of the British Empire 465
The Commonwealth of Australia 466
The Dominion of Canada . . 471
The Union of South Africa . . 474

European Constitutions
The Swiss Confederation . . 480
The Union of Soviet Socialist Republics 486

DEFINITIONS OF TECHNICAL TERMS USED 493

INDEX 501

LIST OF ILLUSTRATIONS

Membership in World Government 15

How the Individual Controls Representation in World Government . . 17

Methods of Enforcement under World Government and Their Effect on the Individual 23

Map of the World of 1914 . . . . 84 and 85

Map of the World of 1938 . . . . 86 and 87

(*All by the Pictograph Corp.*)

ACKNOWLEDGMENTS

WE WISH to express our deep indebtedness and appreciation to all those whose help enabled us to prepare this book. First of all to Mme. Rosika Schwimmer for pointing out how much a book of this kind is needed and for inspiring us to write it. We are also grateful to her and to Miss Franciska Schwimmer for their encouragement, counsel, and guidance during the progress of this work.

The following assisted us with library research: Dr. Dora Edinger, Francis B. Riggs, Robert Heckert, Albert Herling, Tom Yamashita, William B. Lloyd, Jr., Miss Theresa Gay, Hugh Reichard, Miss Muriel Woodman, and Paul Berndt. Their research covered the New York Public Library, Woodrow Wilson Library (New York), Harvard University Library, Boston Public Library, Edwin Ginn Library of the Fletcher School of Law and Diplomacy (Medford, Mass.), Chicago Public Library, Library of International Relations (Chicago), University of Wisconsin Library, Hoover Library on War, Revolution, and Peace (Palo Alto, Calif.), Free Library of Philadelphia, Library Company of Philadelphia, Mercantile Library (Philadelphia), Pacifist Research Bureau (Philadelphia), and Antioch College Library.

We also wish to express our appreciation to Dr. L. S. Rowe of the Pan American Union for information and texts of some South American Federal Constitutions; to Mr. Filippus Mosèsco for translating the Constitution of Venezuela from Spanish into English; to Major Joseph Wheless for explaining technical provisions in the Mexican Constitution; to Robert W. Hill of the New York Public Library for permission to use the world government plans in the Schwimmer-Lloyd Collection; to Miss Harriet Van Wyck and Frank Barth of the Woodrow Wilson Library for special assistance in the use of the Library's current collection of postwar plans; to the British Information Services for supplying texts and information on the British Constitutions; and to the Australian and Soviet Consulates in New York for supplying texts of their nations' constitutions.

We are indebted to the following publishers for permission to quote from their books, magazines, and newspapers: The Curtis Publishing Company, John Day Co., Harper and Bros., *The New Yorker,* The *New York Herald Tribune,* and G. P. Putnam's Sons.

To the publishers mentioned in connection with each charted plan we wish to express our thanks for their cooperation in the use of their material.

PART I

SEARCHLIGHT ON PEACE PLANS

CHARTING THE PEACE PLANS
THE BASIC ISSUES

"It is too probable that no plan we propose will be adopted. Perhaps another dreadful conflict is to be sustained. If, to please the people, we offer what we ourselves disapprove, how can we afterward defend our work? Let us raise a standard to which the wise and the honest can repair. . . ."

GEORGE WASHINGTON *to the Constitutional Convention meeting in Philadelphia in 1787.*

"There are striking similarities between the disorganization of America in 1787 and the state of the world today, when in so many respects its economic body has outgrown its political breeches. The world for a long time has been in need of machinery to implement its pious intentions. After the war, the need will be more imperative than ever, if we are to avoid new wars, not to mention getting a quart of milk a day for everybody. This time, it is safe to predict, the problem will not be what Washington thought it was in 1787, namely, to persuade the people to accept what 'the wise and the honest' knew to be necessary. On the contrary, the job will be to extract from our political leaders a plan for cooperation strong and sound enough to satisfy the demands of the peoples of the world."

"Peace Is Not Automatic," editorial in *The Saturday Evening Post,* January 16, 1943.

"Mr. Edwin L. James told some journalism students recently that what this country needs is *one* peace plan. He sort of hinted at which one, just in passing. That's the trouble with the one-plan idea; it may not be the one you like. . . . How are we going to get one plan which truly represents Mr. James and us and a hundred and thirty million other planners? Well, we will get it in the usual manner — talk, talk, talk, everybody beating on the table and pacing up and down. It's going to be a colossal debate, but at least it'll be a debate and not a monologue."

The New Yorker, July 10, 1943.

"We would like to know what our government is doing about a peace plan. The papers say nothing about the Allied countries getting together to formulate a world policy of international trade, cooperation and friendship. Is there to be a federation of countries that will set up a police force that will police the world and preserve peace? Will the world disarm completely or will the victorious remain armed?

"Should peace come with the whole world mobilized, it is difficult to say what might happen if the mistakes of Versailles were duplicated at the peace table. We who are fighting do not have time to think of this, but as yet there has been no answer to the question which is larger than the war itself, for we hope to live permanently in a world at peace. . . ."

> First Lieutenant DONALD F. VAN BRUNT, U.S.A.A.C.
> from John Steinbeck's article in the *New York Herald Tribune*, August 10, 1943.

"I can assure you that *during your future lives it is almost certain that each one of you must face the situation that we face today.* (Italics ours. EDITORS.) It should be your earnest study to so order your lives now that when your country calls you will be able and anxious to answer that call and be mentally and physically prepared to give your utmost and thereby insure victory."

> Lieutenant General GEORGE S. PATTON, JR., to the *sixth grade class* of Pasadena Polytechnic Elementary School, in the *New York Herald Tribune*, July 17, 1943.

SEARCHLIGHT

on

PEACE PLANS

CHARTING THE PEACE PLANS

Two billion human beings are engulfed in blood, sweat, and tears, dazed and browbeaten into accepting periodic outbreaks of war, while common sense and the instinct of self-preservation intrude the suspicion that war is not inevitable — that peace can and must be organized. The foregoing quotations are characteristic of this conflict. The first is the voice of the American conscript soldier, and he speaks for the conscripts of all lands, who believe in and hope for a warless world. The second is the voice of the professional soldier, the same in all lands, for whom war is the culmination of his professional life, for whom preparation for war is the normal routine of peace. A "good peace" to him is one which leaves his country in the best military position for making a good showing in the next war.

Great masses of suffering mankind, however, agree with Lieutenant Van Brunt in believing peace is possible, and that it must be organized *now*. Mankind in the midst of war reaches hungrily for plans that profess peace as their aim.

Despite the fact that a people's peace is the hope and desire of countless men and women, they are overwhelmed and confused by the profusion of peace plans presented to them.

Because the general public has neither the time nor the facilities to study and analyze the many thousands of books and pamphlets which continue to be published, most people are limited to the consideration of peace plans whose authors are financially able to exploit their views by means of literature, meetings, banquets, newspaper advertisements, and the radio.

It seemed to us that a real need exists for a wider and more comprehensive presentation of plans for world organization. We, therefore, decided to analyze plans drafted since 1914 (the first phase of the present war) and to extract from them specific proposals, stripped of generalities, specious arguments, and the subtle influence of prominent supporters.

These proposals are presented in their bare essentials in the form of charts. In this way we hope to enable serious builders of peace to survey these peace plans so that they may decide intelligently what type of world organization they will support.

Thousands of books, pamphlets, and articles, many of which are duly listed in bibliographies, have something to say on war, postwar problems, and peace, but only a small proportion contains sufficient structural details of world organization to be suitable for charting under the specifications by which we tested each plan before including it in this survey.

To qualify as a chartable plan for supra-national organization, each proposal had to contain adequate structural details under the following headings.

1. TYPE: The plan should indicate whether an alliance, a league, a confederation, a federation or some other type of political organization among nations is proposed (see: *Definitions*). Some plans, however, are characterized by their authors, for instance, as federal when in fact they are confederate, or vice versa. Wherever we found such confusion we classified the plan according to the *actual* structure suggested.

2. MEMBERSHIP: Most planners are very specific about the nations to be included. *On the basis of membership proposed* we classified the plans charted as *universal*, with all nations of the world eligible; *regional*, determined by geographic location; *ideological*, based on similarity of ideas or forms of government.

3. ORGANS OF GOVERNMENT: Under this heading come the main structural pillars of world organization. To be chartable, each plan has to include proposals for some common *legislative or policymaking, executive or administrative,* and *judicial authority. Mere statements or discussions of the problem in general, or of some special phase, appeals for good-will, cooperation, or united action, or proposals of certain types of organization, without details of basic structure, could not be included.*

To throw some light on another possible source of confusion in the public mind about plans for world organization, we included the Kelland Plan, *The Zones of Safety,* and King-Hall's *Total Victory.* These are samples of a great many proposals whose authors do not present details for the structure of world organization, but only vague suggestions for alliances, associations, or agreements. These often involve serious obligations and responsibilities without the authors' devising machinery for carrying them out.

4. TRANSFERS OF JURISDICTION: This section deals with division of authority between member nations and the supra-national organization and is therefore of fundamental importance to specific plans. The process is popularly but mistakenly called "giving up sovereignty." Our phrasing is a more correct technical description of what would take place. The plans charted usually leave nations full sovereignty over national affairs, transferring by common consent only that part of national jurisdiction which the authors believe will enable the supra-national organization to deal with problems that go beyond national interests and concern also other nations and peoples.

5. METHODS OF ENFORCEMENT: Many planners make definite proposals for enforcement of the decisions of the supra-national authority. They specify whether enforcement is to operate on member nations as a whole or on individuals. Under this heading come suggestions for military and economic sanctions, provisions for an international army, navy, and air force, or for a police force operating only on individuals.

6. IMMEDIATE STEPS: These indicate the methods and means suggested for bringing the proposed organization into existence.

7. TERRITORIAL CHANGES: These include whatever boundary changes, disposition of empires, colonies, and mandates are suggested.

8. RATIFICATION: This outlines the procedure for securing formal agreement by governments or peoples to set up the new organization.

Many plans written during war present methods and terms for ending the war. We have listed such proposals under PREREQUISITES TO PEACE. Suggestions for dealing with the problems of transition from war to peace are listed under LIQUIDATION OF THE WAR. Data that do not fit other headings are listed under MISCELLANEOUS.

Examples of current books that we could not chart include Walter Lippmann's *U.S. Foreign Policy—Shield of the Republic* which advocates an alliance between Russia, China, Great Britain, and the United States operating according to enlightened self-interest. Mr. Lippmann does not suggest details of the joint machinery through which the alliance would function. Nathaniel Peffer's *Basis for Peace in the Far East* and Hallett Abend's *Pacific Charter — Our Destiny in Asia* discuss Far Eastern problems, and disposition of various colonies, and for some, international administration. Both advocate total crushing of Japan, and yet, paradoxically, both urge that Japan should have economic priority in Far Eastern markets after the war.

Wendell Willkie's *One World* pleads for global organization of peace, but suggests no details of structure or methods of achievement. *The Problems of Lasting Peace* by Herbert Hoover and Hugh Gibson provides discussion, a review of World War experience, and specific suggestions on liquidating the present war, but concrete recommendations on other essentials of world organization are lacking.

Robert Lee Humber's *Declaration of the Federation of the World*, adopted by a number of State legislatures in the United States, stresses the need for federal world government and expresses determination to secure it, but fails to present a blueprint.

Congressional resolutions, because they present insufficient details, were unsuitable for charting. The Fulbright Resolution (passed by the House, September 21, 1943) and the Connally Resolution (passed by the Senate, November 5, 1943) express overwhelming approval of efforts to set up some kind of postwar international organization to maintain peace but avoid detailed commitments. Earlier resolutions, outlining more specific courses of action, were introduced in the House by Rudolph G. Tenerowicz (House Joint Resolution 131, March 3, 1941) stressing neutral initiative in ending the war and organizing a world constitutional convention; and by Jennings Randolph (House Concurrent Resolution 5, January 7, 1943), asking the President to call an international convention to draft a constitution providing for international legislative, executive, and judicial machinery. In the Senate, the Ball-Hill-Burton-Hatch Resolution (Senate Resolution 114, March 16, 1943) proposes a continuing organization of the United Nations with authority to organize the transition from war to peace, and to assemble a United Nations military force to suppress attempted aggression by any nation.

War and peace aims, and peace terms, being usually vague and subject to constant revision, were consequently not charted.

In examining these plans we met with great surprises. Sometimes less than half a page of specific proposals emerged from four-hundred-page books, although they often provided stimulating discussion. Some plans, it seemed to us, were drafted to harness the world to serve mainly the interests of one nation or of a group of nations. After careful analysis, some of the most publicized books could not be charted at all because their authors' ideas canceled themselves out entirely. Their proposals, advocated in the beginning of a book, were discarded completely at the end. In many compilations of peace plans we found listings, consciously or unconsciously, favoring the type of plan appealing most to the compiler. In others, notwithstanding the absence of personal bias, we found that highly important plans had been omitted, due perhaps, to the technical difficulties involved in collecting the material, or because of plain intellectual fatigue.

In addition to the charts of plans since 1914, we have included, in brief outline, peace plans reaching back to the beginnings of civilization. At least since Ikhnaton, Pharaoh of Egypt (1375 B.C.), a chain of plans and practical attempts leads up to our time. This historical parade demonstrates the tragic futility of dreams and actions designed for mankind's peace and security as long as might supersedes right.

The numerous organizations active in postwar planning are included only when they stand committed to a plan specific enough to be charted. There are already three directories of organizations engaged in postwar planning which are published by the Twentieth Century Fund, the United Nations Information Center, and the Council on Foreign Relations.

The backgrounds of the various authors of world government plans are in themselves most interesting. Before 1914, for example, there were more active statesmen among planners than at any time since. The "people" are also well represented, proving that war has always been the concern of the common man.

We have included, for instance, a plan by Pierre-André Gargaz, who, while serving a sentence as a galley-slave, wrote *A Project of Universal Peace*. Benjamin Franklin, while in Passy, France, printed the plan for Gargaz in 1782, and also tried to obtain support for it in Europe.

In our own day, students, journalists, manual workers, physicians — men and women in every walk of life — have been deeply concerned with the abolition of war, and have tried their best to draft solutions. We find aeronautical engineers drawing plans for world government, asserting that this is an engineering job, and that social scientists are unable to accomplish anything because they are too conservative and backward in their outlook.

In the brief descriptions of the old plans (before 1914), we present a great many that are not mentioned in any English compilation we have examined. We are indebted for information on many of them to the two-volume work of Jacob Ter Meulen, published in German in The Hague in 1917 and 1929, which gives extensive quotations from the original German, French, Latin, English, and Spanish texts. Some of these plans are amusing, urging, for instance, political unions of Christian princes in order to achieve bigger and better wars to keep the Turks, or the Russians, or the French, or the English, or the Americans in their respective places or, to annihilate them altogether. Similar ideas are echoed in some present-day plans. There is hardly a feature in any current plan that cannot be found in the old plans.

We deeply regret that wartime conditions made it impossible to cover adequately peace plans from non-English-speaking countries, and we failed to find any Axis plans specific enough to be charted.

We have not included charts of the numerous plans antedating and similar to the Covenant of the League of Nations which were drafted by organizations such as the League to Enforce Peace, the Fabian Society, the Union for Democratic Control, and by many individual supporters of world organization, among them Lord Bryce, Paul Otlet, H. N. Brailsford, Sir Norman Angell, and Salvador de Madariaga. Texts of some of these plans are given in Theodore Marburg's *Development of the League of Nations Idea*. Their proposals for confederate world organization were realized in the Covenant of the League of Nations which we have charted.

Texts proposed by various governments for the League Covenant are given in David Hunter Miller's *The Drafting of the Covenant*.

Many of the plans provide guarantees of individual rights by the world organization. Among the strongest advocates of a World Bill of Rights is H. G. Wells, who has long advocated a federally organized socialist world state, but none of his many writings on the subject present chartable details. His book *The New World Order* urges the adoption of a universal charter of *The Rights of Man,* stating in simple terms the inalienable rights of all men and women to life, to protection of minors, to work, to earn money, to possess property, to move freely, to knowledge, to freedom of thought, discussion, and worship, to personal liberty, and to freedom from violence.

One of the most interesting proposals for a method of safeguarding individual rights was made by the Swedish Group of the Inter-Parliamentary Union in April, 1914 (see: *Recueil De Documents* 1914, published by Groupe Interparlementaire Suédois). Through its President, Edvard Wavrinsky, it suggested adapting to international usage the institution of the *Swedish Parliamentary Attorney General of Justice*. Although elected by Parliament, this officer is completely independent of all government bodies and functions exclusively as the champion of the public against abuses by the government or its officials. His duty is to safeguard all the general and personal privileges of the individual; to proceed either on his own initiative or on the complaints of individuals against officials guilty of breaches of duty; to supervise the state of justice throughout the nation; to determine whether the laws work adequately and justly in practice; and to receive and investigate the complaints of individuals. His annual report to Parliament records his investigations and prosecutions; his observations on the laws and their application; and suggestions for new legislation.

It was obviously impossible to include the 22,165 plans for peace submitted to the $100,000 Bok Peace Award contest of 1923. These plans are excellently classified and analyzed by Esther Everett Lape in *Ways to Peace* (Charles Scribner's Sons, 1924).

Even a superficial reading of the plans we have charted in this work shows that while some by themselves may be impracticable, yet here and there they have an original idea, a helpful suggestion as to representation, elections, structure, or any number of technical details which may turn out to be vastly important in resolving an international constitutional problem.

Many will ask, "Of what use are all these plans? They were not adopted when proposed. Why bother with them now?"

Generalities about the beauties of peace, the horrors of war, and the need for international cooperation are easily stated. Virtually everyone will agree with these platitudes. Yet preparations for war will continue in periods of peace, wars will persist in being horrible, and international cooperation will remain a favorite subject of postwar planning, *unless words lead finally to action.*

A specific plan for world government is to international cooperation what a model of the first airplane was to man's desire to fly. The model helped people visualize what a flying-machine would be like and served as an object for further experimentation and improvement.

When our Constitutional Convention met at Philadelphia in 1787, at least four different plans for constitutional revision were presented. These plans provoked discussion, counterproposals, and revisions, and the final product contains parts of all four. In addition to these plans, the delegates attempted to analyze former leagues and confederations of states, especially those of ancient Greece, to find out why these former attempts had failed. In retrospect, it is remarkable that the drafters of the American Constitution heeded the lessons of history and avoided repeating the failures of the past.

Unfortunately, statesmen and politicians since that time have not profited, in the main, by their example. Nor have those who say today: "It can't be done." Dean Tucker, around 1786, expressed the following opinion on the chances of union of the thirteen jealous, quarreling American States.

> As to the future grandeur of America, and its being a rising empire under one head, whether republican or monarchical, it is one of the idlest and most visionary notions that ever was conceived even by writers of romance. The mutual antipathies and clashing interests of the Americans, their differences of governments, habitudes, and manners, indicate that they will have no center of union.... They never can be united.... under any species of government whatever: a disunited people till the end of time, suspicious and distrustful of each other, they will be divided and subdivided into little commonwealths or principalities, according to natural boundaries....

Charting the Peace Plans

Many people are as skeptical now about the possibility of uniting the nations of the world as was Dean Tucker, in 1786, concerning the union of the States.

In writing his treatise on *Constitutions*, Aristotle (384-322 B.C.) is said to have studied 158 constitutions of the Greek City States of his time. Today there are more than 200 written constitutions in existence. At least 184 of them are constitutions of states, provinces, and cantons which operate within the framework of ten functioning regional federations: the Argentine Republic; and, respectively, the United States of America, of Brazil, of Mexico, and of Venezuela; the Commonwealth of Australia; the Dominion of Canada; the Union of South Africa; the Swiss Confederation; and the Union of Soviet Socialist Republics. These *ten federal constitutions*, together with the Covenant of the League of Nations, have been charted, because they contain the basic ingredients needed to write a new constitution for the world.

Few peace planners or the general public seem to realize that so many huge regional federations are already in existence. Federalism, although founded in diverse ways, has demonstrated its value as an efficient functioning system, together with its ability to adapt itself successfully among various peoples and in different regions.

Even experts often apply incorrectly and carelessly many of the technical terms appearing throughout this book. We include, therefore, simple definitions of their correct meaning.

The short section on some former leagues, federations, confederations, personal unions, and courts is included to indicate the practical evolution of *various types* of governmental organization between sovereign and independent units, and to emphasize that many peoples have contributed to this evolution.

Our aim has been to present an unbiased survey of plans for a governed world so that those who want supra-national organization may examine existing plans and support their choice with full knowledge of its advantages and disadvantages as compared with other possible methods.

THE BASIC ISSUES

MOST peace-planning today is *postwar* planning. Much of it is a form of escape from the terrors and frustrations of the present. During the last war there was a great deal of the same type of planning, and programs for a durable peace poured out by the ream. But when the war ended the military leaders of the victorious countries, together with the militarized civilian leaders, refused to make their exit and allow the peace-planners to take over.

German militarism was defeated and discredited, but not *militarism*. Therefore, militarism in defeating *German militarism* claimed that it was indispensable for the safety of mankind. As a *punitive* measure, Germany and her allies were disarmed. Military conscription was forbidden to them, with the pledge, however, that the victors would also disarm. Not only was this pledge not kept, but on the contrary the newly constituted nations at once introduced enforced military service, thereby encouraging the secret rearmament of the vanquished countries.

Despite the lesson that unilateral disarmament does not work, official plans for the postwar era now again demand it. This time the victors do not even propose ultimate universal disarmament, but increased and permanent militarism for themselves. After Allied victory, for example, only Axis militarism is to be totally crushed and the enemy nations are to be completely and permanently demilitarized. Disarmament is to be exacted from the defeated powers as the direst punishment and the lowest form of degradation which can be forced upon nations. If this is our concept of disarmament, can we blame the people on whom we want to impose it for having the same opinion about it? If disarmament brands some nations with the mark of degradation, they will struggle determinedly for the "high privilege" of being armed.

One assumption of the present period is that the world does not need political organization, but merely economic bureaus or controls. This is the economic approach to peace, advanced by many because it looks easier of accomplishment. Economic unions, bureaus, and agreements negotiated through international conventions, adhered to by varying groups of nations, are already functioning. The most successful one is the Universal Postal Union. These international bodies, however, are not coordinated. Their establishment took years of painstaking effort to secure national ratification of the conventions setting them up. Once a convention has been ratified, the same laborious process is required for every single amendment necessitated by changed conditions. If this method of uncoordinated economic bodies were applied in governing the United States, it would mean obtaining the consent of each of the forty-eight state governments to every law and amendment. Those who oppose the exclusively economic approach to peace insist that popular consent is necessary to set up even these economic unions or controls. The exercise of such popular control requires political machinery.

There are those who have faith in the continuance of various Allied boards now controlling shipping, food, and raw materials. They hope these will be retained to carry on the work of reconstruction when the fighting ends, and to serve as the nucleus of organized world cooperation. But others would like to know how solid is the ground on which these hopes rest? These war-time boards will certainly have acquired a mass of experience, but their members are only appointees of war-time leaders. Their allegiance, their official lives, depend on the will of national leaders acting generally not by legislative sanction but under extended war-time powers. In short, these boards operate in time of war without popular consent which would have to be granted for them to continue functioning after the war.

While there are enormous numbers of plans for peace, the major decisions which the people must make are relatively simple, and easy to define. They come under the following headings:

1. *How much of the world should be governed?* Shall we federate only Europe, or each continent separately, or parts of continents? Or shall we include the whole world? Most of the plans advocate universal world organization, but some propose complicated regional confederations or federations under it, and would keep the universal organization as weak as the League of Nations has been. Other plans exclude all-inclusive structure and advocate modest beginnings, that is, more diplomatic conferences, consultations, and military pacts.

Many of the planners question whether a world suffering death agonies in global war can afford to plan anything less than a global peace. Are millions of Chinese, Filipinos, Indians, Africans, to say nothing about Americans and Europeans, to continue to kill and be killed for the purpose of producing at the end of the slaughter perhaps a Czech-Polish Confederation or a Greek-Yugoslav Confederation — suspected both by Germany and Russia? Or is there to be a Federation of Europe including England, its dominions and colonies extending around the world, armed for "defense," as all regional groups are, facing the militarized continents of America and Asia? Many planners maintain that in such arrangements there lies no basis for peace; that such developments would surely be the curtain raisers for Act III of the war that actually began in 1914.

The plans present, roughly, three categories of membership. Some planners insist, whatever world organization is established, that all nations must be eligible to membership on equal terms. They are convinced that in a world technically and scientifically integrated, any nation potentially dangerous within the organization would be infinitely more dangerous if left outside of it. Disruptive and peace-menacing tendencies would be counteracted more easily within the world organization where grievances could be aired and constructive solutions sought.

Those who advocate regional unions of Europe, of Asia, of the Americas, or of parts of them maintain that many problems are peculiar to certain regions, and that only regional organization can or should cope with them. Sometimes these advocates accept the necessity of world organization within which various regional unions may be members, but their primary concern is regional organization, irrespective of what is planned for the world at large. Other regional planners, however, believe that world government must wait until further unification of the continents is achieved. Some of them concede that the possibility of intercontinental wars of hitherto unimagined magnitude looms large in such arrangements.

A third group believes similarity of concepts of political organization is the firmest foundation of union between nations. While ideological unions may be communist, fascist, or democratic, the only chartable plans we found propose unions of democracies. The proponents of this approach contend that within the foreseeable future no all-inclusive political union is possible. They would exclude most of the Latin American countries, many European nations, Russia, and the peoples of Asia. Several reasons are advanced for this exclusion: that these peoples are "politically immature"; that the huge populations of Asia would outnumber the peoples of the democracies and overwhelm them. They insist that every country must first become a democracy before it can safely be admitted to union with other democratic countries.

Advocates of all-inclusive organization find some common ground

MEMBERSHIP IN WORLD GOVERNMENT

UNIVERSAL:
- All nations and peoples eligible to immediate membership.

REGIONAL:
- Eligibility of nations to membership determined by geographical location.

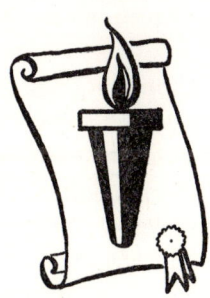

IDEOLOGICAL:
- Eligibility of nations to membership determined by similarity of ideals, national political institutions, or structure of government.

with those who propose regional unions when they suggest decentralized regional administrative headquarters under world organization. They believe, however, that new regional unions, unless subordinated to global organization, would be a greater menace to world peace than the present co-existence of large and small nations.

The gap between proposals for worldwide membership and those restricting effective union to democratic nations only, is difficult to bridge. Supporters of all-inclusive union believe the danger of counter-unions of the excluded nations far outweighs the difficulties of uniting all countries. They are skeptical about democracy evolving in undeveloped nations by spontaneous action from within, and believe that impartial assistance will be needed for their political reorganization, internal reconstruction, and the raising of their literacy level. Planners of global union believe that only international administration can provide this assistance.

The problem of union of large and small states has been solved by different compromises in the various existing federal unions. One instance of a successful compromise was the establishing of the Congress of the United States which provides equal representation of the states in the Senate, and representation on the basis of population in the House.

A compromise suggested by the Swiss at the time of the drafting of the League Covenant was to count the votes of the Assembly twice: once on the basis of equality of states, and a second time on the basis of population. Further suggestions would take as a basis of representation not only population but also other factors such as national resources, international trade, literacy, or the number of voters in national elections. Representation based partially on the extent of voting in national elections might stimulate nations with large sections of their population disfranchised to grant them voting privileges. Within the United States, for example, the whole country might be aroused to abolish poll taxes and other voting restrictions if thereby American representation in a world assembly could be increased.

2. *What structure shall we give the world government?* Shall we restore the League of Nations as it was? Shall we amend the Covenant? Shall we equip the League with an international army to enforce its decisions? Or shall we decide on another structure? Some maintain that structure is unimportant, that we must decide on *world cooperation* first, and work out the details later. Others maintain structure is all-important because several vital issues depend upon it, particularly the

HOW THE INDIVIDUAL CONTROLS REPRESENTATION IN WORLD GOVERNMENT

AGENCIES THROUGH WHICH THE ORGANIZATION FUNCTIONS

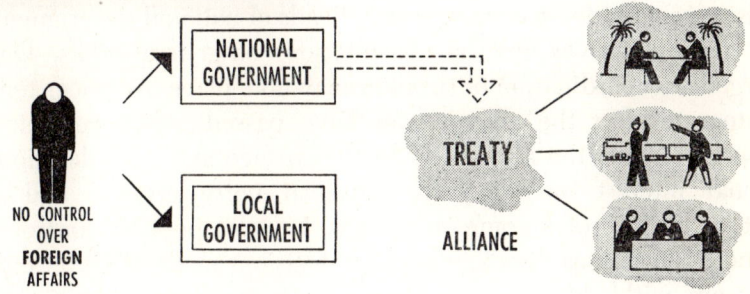

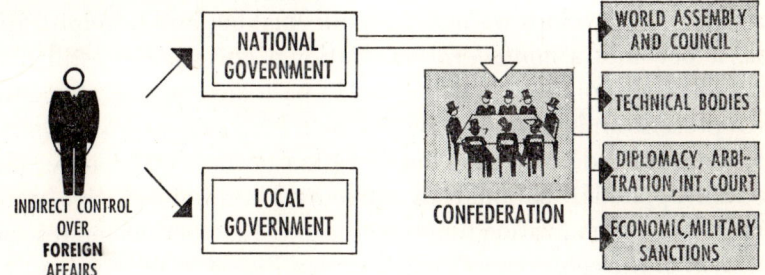

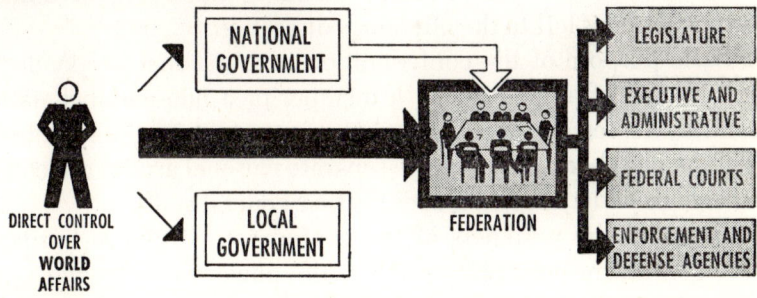

PICTOGRAPH CORPORATION

methods of enforcement — whether world law is to operate on whole nations or on individual world citizens.

In general, three structural types, short of a unified world state, are possible. The least defined of these is the *alliance* of which both the Axis and the United Nations are typical. In alliances there are practically no permanent common organs for policymaking and administration. Decisions are made by *conferences* of heads of national governments or their representatives and by consultations of general staffs. During emergencies coordination of supplies may take place. Alliances tend to disintegrate after the emergencies have passed, when suspicion of motives between the allies rises to the surface and considerations of national interest outweigh the artificial unity created and held together by fear of a common danger. Lack of popular control over alliances is a serious disadvantage, for decisions made at secret conferences are withheld from the people until resulting actions can no longer be affected by popular influence. The constant danger of counter-alliances is another factor which adds to the instability of this type of organization.

If an *alliance* develops permanent policymaking and administrative organs, it becomes a *confederation*. National governments still make ultimate decisions on policy. Delegates to periodic confederate conferences represent and reflect the views of their national governments; policies recommended by the confederation go into effect only when ratified and applied by national governments. The administrative branch of a confederate organization functions more as a secretarial and research department of the conferences and their committees than as an enforcement and administrative body. In a confederation there is no day-by-day law enforcement, usually a common function of local, state, and national governments. Violations of confederate agreements by nations may be called to the attention of the offending national governments, but further action is left to the offender's discretion.

The basic purpose of the confederation is to marshal preponderant strength in case of aggression by a member or a non-member nation. The military forces are organized either from contributions of armed forces of the member nations, or the separate national armies are coordinated through periodic conferences of their general staffs.

At this point, the weakness of the confederate structure burdened with the greatest responsibility of all — the power to make war — becomes most apparent. The confederation, dependent on its member nations both for military and financial support, is powerless to do more than criticize an act of aggression unless member governments declare war on the aggressor. While aggression is commonly understood to be any unprovoked act of hostility, especially invasion, the League of Nations after twenty years of effort was unable to define aggression. It found that the nation invading another country is not always the aggressor because the invading government may have had secret knowledge of military preparations against it and merely took the initiative to protect itself.

Once war has broken out and a sufficient number of nations consider themselves actually menaced, their war-time collaboration tends to revert to an alliance and the consequent abandonment of the confederation. There are several reasons for this. While a confederation is built on the theoretical *equality of all nations,* large or small, the great powers always seek to dominate its decisions, and reserve to themselves the power of veto on major decisions on the ground that in the event of war their contributions in men and money are proportionately greater than those of the smaller nations. On the other hand, the smaller nations can never feel certain that the great powers would actually come to the aid of a weaker confederate unless they consider their own vital interests endangered. Therefore, the smaller nations are reluctant to incur the antagonism of other nations, especially those in their immediate neighborhood, whose intentions may be anything but peaceful.

The difficulty lies in the fact that under confederate organization nations still reserve the right to wage so-called "defensive" wars and to be the sole judges of their armament needs. Since international inspection and control are never authorized, enforcement other than war cannot take place.

Nations organized under a *federal* structure depart from the confederate realm of unlimited though vague commitments as to future collaboration, and enter into specific contractual relationship. A redivision of authority takes place. The national governments transfer limited but specific powers and responsibilities to the federal authority, and enforcement in the federal sphere operates directly on individuals in the same way that national and local laws operate within their respective fields independently of one another. The individual is brought into direct relationship with the new governmental structure not only because its laws operate directly on him — not indirectly through national governments — but because the duties and responsibilities he assumes towards the new authority, such as direct election of representatives to the legislative branch, the payment of taxes, and observance of world laws, involve a constant relationship of benefits and obligations to which he is already accustomed locally and nationally.

Irrespective of the extent of membership proposed, the problem always arises whether an alliance, a confederation, or a federation should be set up. Under both the alliance and confederate types, unlimited obligations seem to be assumed by the participating nations; but, in times of crisis, reservations, interpretations, and the vague language of treaties and covenants are marshaled to prevent concerted action. There is always the danger of domination by the more powerful nations and the consequent mistrust and indifference of the others. Such difficulties seem to have been characteristic of alliances and confederations as far back in history as knowledge of them exists. These forms of association either disintegrated entirely or were welded into federal structures, some of them finally developing into unified nations.

Today's proponents of alliances and confederations maintain that nations are still unprepared for any larger transfer of sovereignty than is involved in these types of organization, and that the great powers should be entrusted with the task of maintaining world peace unhampered by the smaller nations. Conversely, spokesmen of the smaller nations assert that the inaction and vacillation of the great powers in the cases of Manchuria, Ethiopia, Austria, and Czechoslovakia furnish conclusive evidence that their unwillingness to prevent war was motivated by considerations of national interest, internal problems, or widespread apathy and indifference.

To reconcile the conflicting claims of large and small nations, most advocates of federal structure propose a bicameral legislature — comprising an upper chamber with equal representation, and a lower chamber with representation based on population, wealth, international trade, literacy, and extent of voting in national elections, or a combination of them.

Many planners also emphasize that in the world legislature unit voting by national delegations should be prohibited. Instead, all delegates should have the privilege of voting as individuals. Experience in federal legislative assemblies indicates that delegates usually vote according to interest groups within their states rather than on the basis of state loyalty, religion, or color. It may be expected that delegates voting as individuals in the supra-national legislature would collaborate across

The Basic Issues

national boundaries on most issues: liberals voting with liberals, radicals with radicals, and conservatives with conservatives.

Plans espousing a federal structure generally transfer certain minimum powers to the federation. These powers usually include conduct of foreign affairs, common citizenship, defense, taxation, regulation of trade between members and with non-members, and regulation of transportation and communications. A number of plans include public health and control of production and distribution of prime necessities. In all federal plans the member nations transfer their right to wage war. Supporters of federal plans assert that federal government leaves the maximum amount of autonomy to nations in their internal affairs, yet provides sufficient control over international affairs to enable the federal government to resolve by peaceful means conflicts which affect the whole world.

Proponents of federal structure are at odds among themselves on some problems involved in federal organization. Those who propose federal union of the democracies insist that member nations must guarantee a minimum of democratic rights to their citizens. Those who believe all nations should be eligible to membership in the federation insist that, inasmuch as the world organization is democratic in its own structure, with a uniform federally supervised system of federal elections, different systems of government within nations may be permitted. Participation in federal elections would encourage populations lacking democratic control over their own nations to strive for their rights. Such practical experiences could lead to the gradual peaceful extension of democracy to the whole world.

The German Constitution of 1871 furnishes an interesting example of greater democracy in the federal structure than in some of the member states (see: Chart p. 416). The Constitution established a mixed federal-confederate government formed by twenty-two states and three Hanseatic cities. Among its signatories were three Kings and several Grand Dukes. Certain of the states had absolute rulers; some granted to their subjects a form of limited franchise; and in others all male citizens could vote. But the Constitution of the German Confederation is explicit in providing for "general direct election by secret ballot" of representatives to the federal Reichstag by men over twenty-five irrespective of the existence or absence of popular elections within member states.

The American Constitution, on the other hand, leaves the regulation of all elections largely to each of the forty-eight states, some of which have disfranchised large sections of their populations by means of poll taxes, arbitrary literacy qualifications, and other discriminatory regulations. The difficulty of eliminating state restrictions through later federal legislation may be an argument in favor of federal regulation of international elections from the start.

3. *How shall we enforce world law?* This problem involves the most important decision of all. For on this issue world organization may stand or fall just as it contributed to the rejection of the Covenant by the United States in 1919, and to the gradual breakdown of the League of Nations in recent years. Enforcement of world law should be discussed along with consideration of the structure of world government.

Some plans advocate that the world get along without a legislature, without courts, equipped only with the biggest army, the biggest navy, and the biggest air force to punish law-breaking nations. Some plans frankly propose that such a world armed force be dominated by the more powerful nations. These plans often prove flattering and inviting to those who are citizens of the nations self-appointed to perform these policing operations. This punitive approach to peace, especially popular in time of war, is like trying to keep a volcano from erupting by putting a lid on the crater.

Prior to the establishment of the United States, peace planners were preoccupied in marshaling preponderant force against nations as a whole should they break the terms of the proposed compacts. Alliances, leagues, and confederations are all agreements *between governments, operating on national governments.* Under these types, nations as a whole would be punished for violations, something no individual nation would tolerate. Since the establishment of the American Federal System, peace planners have little excuse for continuing to propose such unsuccessful methods.

Many of those who contend that nations will not transfer control over a few well-defined spheres of government are often the strongest advocates of the greatest transfer of all: submission to armed force applied to whole nations.

This suggestion gains support in time of war when the cost of disarming aggressor nations and keeping them disarmed, and of suppressing future aggressor nations, seems like a cheap and easy solution. Many who propose world armed forces for this purpose do not seem to realize that their nation might some day be on the receiving end of international

METHODS OF ENFORCEMENT UNDER WORLD GOVERNMENT AND THEIR EFFECT ON THE INDIVIDUAL

THE LAW-BREAKING INDIVIDUAL   METHODS OF ENFORCEMENT

ALLIANCE

TREATY
ALLIANCE
→ NATIONAL GOVERNMENT
→ LOCAL GOVERNMENT

THE ALLIANCE OPERATES ONLY ON NATIONS

NO ENFORCEMENT OTHER THAN **WAR!**

CONFEDERATION

CONFEDERATION
- WORLD ASSEMBLY AND COUNCIL
- TECHNICAL BODIES
- DIPLOMACY, ARBITRATION, INT. COURT
- ECONOMIC, MILITARY SANCTIONS

→ NATIONAL GOVERNMENT
→ LOCAL GOVERNMENT

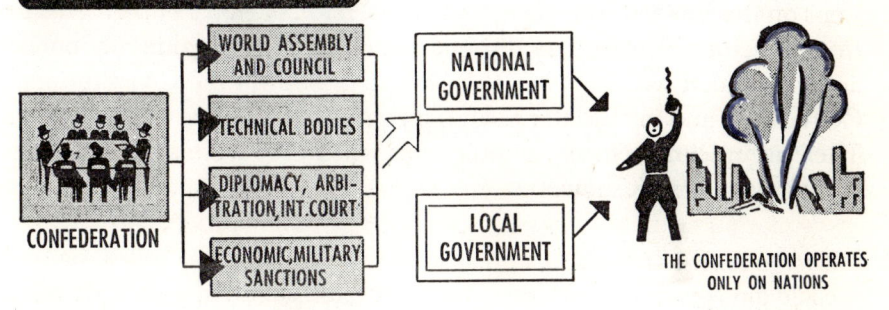

THE CONFEDERATION OPERATES ONLY ON NATIONS

ULTIMATE ENFORCEMENT **WAR!**

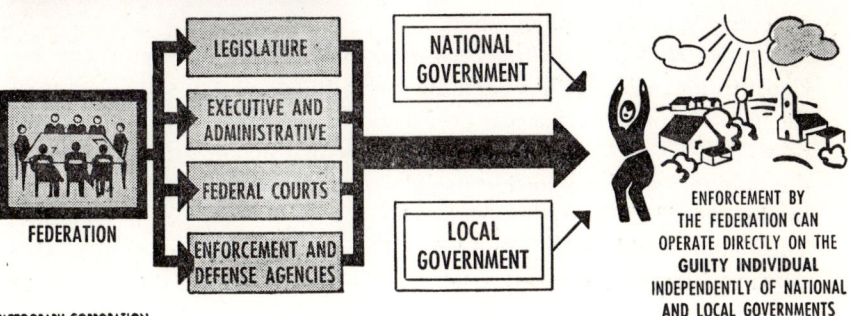

FEDERATION

FEDERATION
- LEGISLATURE
- EXECUTIVE AND ADMINISTRATIVE
- FEDERAL COURTS
- ENFORCEMENT AND DEFENSE AGENCIES

→ NATIONAL GOVERNMENT
→ LOCAL GOVERNMENT

ENFORCEMENT BY THE FEDERATION CAN OPERATE DIRECTLY ON THE **GUILTY INDIVIDUAL** INDEPENDENTLY OF NATIONAL AND LOCAL GOVERNMENTS

PICTOGRAPH CORPORATION

punishment. The peace treaties of 1919 dictated permanent disarmament of the defeated nations but unilateral or one-sided disarmament proved to be ineffectual. The historical records show that it is impossible to foresee future aggressions by nations large or small. Italy, a victorious ally, dissatisfied with her share of the spoils, at once began to rearm her former enemy, Hungary, secretly. Official investigations have revealed the encouragement given to the rearmament of Germany by powerful French, English, and American interests.

Both Italy and Japan, our allies in World War I, became two of the leading aggressor nations against us. Russia, the only nation expelled from the League of Nations for aggression against Finland, is now accepted as one of the leading non-aggression powers. Poland, having served as the spark for the present explosion, was herself an aggressor when she participated with Germany in the partition of Czechoslovakia.

Some planners maintain that peace cannot be safeguarded by coercion of nations. This problem was thoroughly debated in our own Constitutional Convention in 1787. The suggestion had many supporters, but its opponents won. The framers of the American Constitution had no illusions on the subject. In their judgment *coercion of states in their collective capacity* was war; they did not try to evade it by calling it "police action." War it was, and war they called it, both in the Constitutional Convention and in the later ratifying conventions of the various states. Their arguments seem as valid today as when they were uttered, as the following examples show.

> *George Mason* argued: ". . . . that such a Government was necessary as could directly operate on individuals, and would punish those only whose guilt required it."
>
> *James Madison,* in his Journal of the Convention, observed, "that the more he reflected upon the use of force, the more he doubted the practicability, the justice and the efficacy of it when applied to people collectively, and not individually."
>
> *Alexander Hamilton,* in the New York State Convention to ratify the Constitution, said: "It has been observed, to coerce the states is one of the maddest projects that was ever devised. . . . Can any reasonable man be well disposed towards a government which makes war and carnage the only means of supporting itself — a government that can exist only by the sword? Every such war must involve the innocent with the guilty. The single consideration should be sufficient to dispose every peaceable citizen against such a government. . . . What is the cure for this great evil?

The Basic Issues

Nothing, but to enable the national laws to operate on individuals, in the same manner as those of the states do."

Oliver Ellsworth, before the Connecticut State Convention to ratify the Constitution, said: "Hence we see how necessary for the Union is a coercive principle. No man pretends the contrary; we all see and feel this necessity. The only question is, shall it be a coercion of law or a coercion of arms? There is no other possible alternative. Where will those who oppose a coercion of law come out? Where will they end? A necessary consequence of their principles is a war of the States one against the other. I am for coercion by law — that coercion which acts only upon individuals. This Constitution does not attempt to coerce sovereign bodies, States, in their political capacity. No coercion is applicable to such bodies but that of an armed force. If we should attempt to execute the laws of the Union by sending an armed force against a delinquent State, it would involve the good and bad, the innocent and guilty in the same calamity.

"But the legal coercion singles out the guilty individual, and punishes him for breaking the laws of the Union. All men will see the reasonableness of this; they will acquiesce, and say, let the guilty suffer."

To have preponderant force the world government would either have to engage in a perpetual arms race with the member states, or depend on them for armed intervention when called upon. Either course would be disastrous to peace and unnecessary when all over the world the individual has already become accustomed to enforcement by local and national governments, and would quickly accept direct enforcement of world laws. At present, whenever local laws are broken by the individual, enforcement is exercised by the local authorities; whenever national laws are broken, enforcement is carried out by the nation; in the same way whenever world laws are broken, the world government could proceed directly against the guilty individual without the interference of national governments.

Another advantage that coercion of individuals has over coercion of nations as a whole is that the individual can be protected against abuse by the government through guarantees embodied in a World Bill of Rights and can appeal through federal courts against injustice. But what protection is there for the individual when collective punishment has been decreed and enforced against his nation? Moreover, what appeal is open to nations against possible injustice after their cities have been laid waste, and their populations slaughtered?

While member nations will object to the application of military coercion by any central government, they will continue to seek assurance that neighboring nations will not attempt violence against them. As a way out of this dilemma some plans propose that the world government should be given control over production and distribution of basic raw materials that might be used to manufacture armaments. These plans also suggest that the world organization assume immediate control over newly discovered elements, such as Uranium, to guarantee their use for mankind's benefit, and not its destruction. They maintain that with all nations represented on the control boards and inspection commissions, with violators punished as individuals wherever they are found, the world government would have no need of that super armament pile with which some planners would equip it.

There are also marked differences of opinion about the proper time to begin organizing world government. Many planners advocate a "cooling off" or transition period at the end of hostilities for reconstruction and policing of the defeated nations and of some of the disorganized countries liberated by the great powers. In the opinion of these planners world organization should be deferred until the restoration of normal conditions.

Others urge immediate provisional organization of a Council of all the United Nations authorized to make political settlements and to supervise the transition from war to peace, and to serve also as a foundation for the future world organization.

Some plans drafted during the first phase of the World War (1914–18) and some written now urge that an invitation be extended to all peoples to participate in the creation of world government as a basic condition for the cessation of hostilities. The authors of these plans do not believe that organization of world government can wait until after the war. They fear that after the cessation of hostilities, there will be no transition period because the suppressed controversies and the scramble for spoils will break open the deep cracks in the alliance of the United Nations. They believe that only by going directly to the heart of the issue without delay — safety organized for all under world government — can we prevent an endless disruptive wrangle over boundaries, over disposition of colonies and mandates, and over division of air power, shipping, and markets.

Some planners also express deep distrust of action by governments unless they are led and balanced by popular action representing all the peoples of the world. Those who lay principal stress on popular initiative

The Basic Issues

to set up provisional world government maintain that faith in the promises of governments, statesmen, diplomats, and politicians has reached the vanishing point. They fear that diplomatic considerations, expediency, and shifting temporary military advantages will continue to lead to compromising official commitments thereby crippling the organization of nations.

The issues before us involve not only the problem of the transition from war to peace, but also the transition from world chaos to world order. Here are the plans of the few who in every generation have not only hated war and have wished for peace, but in addition have grappled with the problem long enough to think through to possible solutions. They have faced the objective to be achieved, the difficulties to be overcome, and the available tools with which to work. Some wrote peace plans and let it go at that. A few others had the determination to work for the realization of their objectives. The lesson of their tragic failures should help today's planners of a better world to recognize and eliminate factors which frustrated the attempts of past generations.

Some planners have designed clever, elaborate structures with a fine eye to the expediencies of the particular time in which they lived. Some plans are naive, others are slavish imitations of national forms of government. Most of the war-time plans in every generation are predicated on the assumption of a peace dictated by one group of belligerents who are to establish their own brand of salvation.

Through all the plans there appears a strong belief that human ingenuity can — if it will — build a structure within which the whole human family can live, developing a civilization based on right instead of might.

Mankind's social, political, and economic experiences, and the imagination of thinkers and dreamers, suggest the structural outlines for the global home of the human family. These blueprints for world peace must come off the shelves. No house that remained but an architect's sketch ever sheltered a family from bad weather.

Unless we are resigned to the total destruction of life on this planet, we must make constructive decisions and implement them with immediate action.

We hope our survey will facilitate these decisions by helping men and women clarify in their own minds whether they wish to establish government for the whole world or only for parts of it; what system of government they will demand — an alliance, a confederation, or a federation; and what system of world law enforcement — an international army to operate on nations or police action operating on individuals.

Mankind is about to make its most fateful decision. The choice before us is chaos and destruction, or world order and the end of wars among nations. Men and women of all creeds and races have both the high privilege and the solemn duty to take the momentous steps that will lead to the creation of a united world — governed by law — whose citizens can find in it safety, justice, and equal opportunities for their fullest development.

PART II

THEORETICAL PLANS

THERE IS NOTHING NEW UNDER THE SUN — OLD PLANS TO UNITE NATIONS DATING FROM 1306 TO 1914

"... Peace is the richest of all gifts that Sovereigns can make to Nations.
 "Nevertheless, in order that it may be firm and lasting, it is absolutely necessary that its terms be just, that they cause no marked injury to anyone, that the honor of all be found thereby conserved, and that everyone may be able to glory in having consented cheerfully, and with full knowledge, to all the conditions inserted in the final Treaty."

PIERRE-ANDRÉ GARGAZ, *A Project of Universal and Perpetual Peace* (1782). Reprinted by George Simpson Eddy, New York, 1922.

Old Plans to Unite Nations—1306 to 1914

PIERRE DUBOIS
FRENCH JURIST AND POLITICIAN
1306

De Recuperatione Terrae Sanctae. (Of the Restoration of the Holy Land.)

Urged the absolute dictatorship of one Monarch, waging war until only one power was left in all Christendom in order to eliminate war between Christian nations. Then a *General Council* should be established representing all Christian States under the Presidency of the Pope, and to be policed by France. Other member nations also to contribute their armies to the *General Council,* and pledge to submit their differences to a *Tribunal* for arbitration; those dissatisfied with award of *Tribunal* to appeal to Pope. Failure to arbitrate or fulfill their engagements to be punished by Papal Excommunication. Members of the *Council* obliged to wage war against nations disturbing the peace.

DANTE ALIGHIERI
FLORENTINE POET
About 1310

De Monarchia. (*Of Monarchy.*)

Advocated restoration of the ancient Roman Empire, divinely ordained for the civilization of the world and the establishment of universal peace.

GEORGE PODEBRAD
KING OF BOHEMIA
1464

Project to organize a Holy War against the Turks by means of a series of pacts of perpetual friendship between the European princes, pledging absolute renunciation of war among themselves. The coalition to function through an assembly (*Congregatio*) of representatives of the Princes, meeting in turn in various cities; a *Judicium* to settle differences between the Princes, a member Prince and a non-member, or between non-members; a *Syndic* or *Fiscal Procurator* to receive contributions from the Princes, either a tenth of their entire income or the equivalent of three days' revenue. Non-payment to be punished by force of arms. The *Congregatio* to have full war powers: assign leadership; fix quotas of military and naval force; enlist the aid of non-members, etc. Antonius Marini of Grenoble assisted Podiebrad in trying to find support for the plan. His efforts resulted in friendship pacts with Hungary and France, but failed otherwise, probably because the plan was opposed by the Pope.

DESIDERIUS ERASMUS
DUTCH SCHOLAR
1514

From *Querela Pacis* and other writings.

Advocated arbitration by Popes, Abbots, Bishops, wise and just men especially summoned to settle disputes between Christian Princes "so that wars shall not breed wars."

"It is the true duty of Popes, Cardinals, Bishops, and Abbots to settle disputes between Christian Princes."

"One can hardly imagine an unfavorable peace which would not be preferable to the most favorable war."

POPE LEO X and CARDINAL WOLSEY
ITALIAN   ENGLISH
1518

Negotiated a *Treaty of Universal Peace*, with the object of a five-year truce among the European Princes, a defensive alliance against the Turks, and a treaty of assistance in the event one member Prince attacked another. Members to be the Pope, the Emperor of the Holy Roman Empire, the kings of France, England, and Spain, and their confederates. Other princes to join within eight months. Armed forces to be contributed by each member according to a quota. The Treaty was ratified by the Emperor, the Pope, and the King of Spain but never came into effect because war broke out between France and Spain.

FRANCOIS DE LA NOUE
French Nobleman
1587

Discours politiques et militaires. (Political and Military Discourses.)

(Written while he was imprisoned in the Castle of Limburg for having supported the Huguenots.) Proposed a *Union of European States* to fight against the Turks. Pope to initiate a wide membership; suggested a general conference to meet in Augsburg to discuss and settle European problems.

EMERIC CRUCE
French Monk
1623

Le Nouveau Cynée. (The New Cyneas.)

Suggested a permanent *Council of Ambassadors*, meeting in a neutral city to settle all differences between Princes by majority vote of the whole Council. Those refusing to accept the decisions of the Council to be disgraced. Member Princes to defend the Council against resistance by force of arms. Membership to be universal including the Pope, the Emperor of the Turks, the Jews, the Kings of Persia and China, the Grand Duke of Muscovy, and monarchs from India and Africa. A universal police, "useful equally to all nations and acceptable to those which have some light of reason and sentiment of humanity." The Council to exercise legislative power in order "to meet discontents half-way ... and appease them by gentle means, if it could be done, or in case of necessity by force." Crucé urged religious toleration, encouragement of scientific discoveries, and of commerce by safeguarding communication and transportation against pirates. Suggested Venice as the place of meeting.

HUGO GROTIUS
DUTCH JURIST
1625

De Jure Belli ac Pacis. (The Laws of War and Peace.)

Held that sovereign states should be bound by international law in the same way that individuals are bound by municipal law. The world being composed of societies and states as well as of individuals, the relations of all these groups should be governed by contract involving right, justice, obligation, and good faith. Grotius thought it necessary that the Christian Princes hold congresses to settle disputes enabling the disputants to keep the peace.

CAMPANELLA
ITALIAN
1633

Monarchia Messiae. (Messianic Monarchy.)

Advocated a universal monarchy to eliminate enmity, rivalry, and famine by relief of drought-stricken areas from the surplus of fertile regions, which would be possible if all stood united under one monarch.

MAXIMILIAN DE BETHUNE
DUC DE SULLY
FRENCH
1638

The Great Design of Henry IV of France, as attributed to him by Sully in his *Memoirs*.

Proposed as a condition of peace the redivision of Europe into fifteen states as nearly equal in territory and power as possible. With Russia and Turkey excluded from membership, there were to be six hereditary monarchs, five elective monarchs (elected by the hereditary ones); and four republics. The object was to eliminate the possibility of any single Power attempting to dominate Europe or to acquire non-

European dependencies. The fifteen States to be united in a *General Council* or *Senate* consisting of plenipotentiaries of all the States, nominated for three-year terms. The Council to be in constant session to clear up all civil, political, and religious disputes in Europe whether between members or non-members. The Council to have the power to form six inferior councils or subcommittees to sit for the convenience of different districts, but the full Council to be the final court of appeal. The Council to have at its disposal a permanent armed force contributed on a quota system as determined by the General Council. This armed force not to be used against member states. Conquest of parts of Asia and Africa to be undertaken, but new territories acquired to be formed into new kingdoms and admitted into the Federation instead of being parceled out among the original members. According to Sully this plan had the interest and support of Queen Elizabeth of England.

JOHANN AMOS COMENIUS (Komensky)
MORAVIAN BISHOP AND EDUCATOR
1645–66

De Rerum Humanarum emendatione consultatio catholica. (A Comprehensive Treatise on the Improvement of the State of Human Affairs.)

Maintained that all men were citizens of the world and that there was nothing to prevent their being assembled in one community under universal law. He advocated a universal educational system.

SAMUEL RACHEL
SCHLESWIG-HOLSTEIN
1676

Dissertationes de jure naturae et Gentium. (Essay on Natural and International Law.)

Urged establishment of a *College of Fecials* (Congress) to hear, investigate, and decide international disputes. Its membership to be universal, if possible, but to include at least all the Christian Princes. Armed force to be used against those disobeying or opposing decisions of the *Collegium*.

WILLIAM PENN
ENGLISH
1693

Toward the Present and Future Peace of Europe by the Establishment of an European Diet, Parliament, or Estates.

Penn suggested the establishment of a European *Diet* or *Parliament*, to meet annually, or once every two or three years, to which all disputes, not settled by direct negotiation, were to be submitted for decision. Deputies to be sent by each state in proportion to its power, revenues, exports, and imports. On this basis Germany to have twelve; France, Spain, Turkey, and Russia each ten; Italy, eight; England, six; Sweden, Poland, and the United Provinces (consisting of the present Netherlands and Belgium), each four; Portugal, Denmark, and Venice, each three; the Swiss Cantons, two; and Holstein and Courland, one.

Member states were to unite their military strength to compel a state to submit its dispute to the Diet and to comply with its decision as well as to pay for the cost of such military compulsion. The President of the Diet to be elected by rotation from among the delegates. All decisions to be made by a three-fourths vote with no abstention or neutrality permitted. Latin and French suggested as the international languages.

Among the savings to be made by the rulers through adoption of his plan, Penn included ". . . the great expense that frequent and splendid embassies require, and all their appendages of spies and intelligence . . ."

JOHN BELLERS
ENGLISH
1710

Some Reasons for a European State Proposed to the Powers of Europe.

Proposed that Europe be divided into 100 or more cantons, enabling every Sovereign State to send at least one member to an *Annual*

Congress and to make equal contributions in men, ships, or money to the joint armed forces of the Federation; remaining armed forces of the member states to be limited. Russia and Turkey to be included in the Federation. The *Congress* to settle disputes as to boundaries, and the rights of Princes and States, thus preventing future wars.

CHARLES IRENEE CASTEL
Abbé de Saint-Pierre
French
1712

Mémoires pour rendre la paix perpétuelle en Europe. (Project to Bring Perpetual Peace in Europe.)

Urged that the twenty-four states of Christian Europe form a *Grand Alliance* or *European Union*. Representation to be equal: one delegate, two substitutes, and two agents to meet as a *Senate of Peace* permanently stationed at Utrecht.

The *President* of the Senate, to be known as the *Prince of Peace,* to be changed each week; revenue to be determined monthly by the Senate in proportion to the revenues of the member states. In case of disputes between members, the Senate to appoint *Mediating Commissioners*. If these did not settle the dispute, arbitration by the Senate to be compulsory. Temporary award to be made by a plurality of votes, and a final award five years later by a three-fourths majority. Member states refusing to abide by the judgment of the Union, or entering into treaties contrary to its rules, or making preparations for war, to be brought to submission by the combined forces of the Union and made to pay the costs of the war. In addition, the surrender of two hundred of the principal ministers and officers of the offender to the Union could be demanded, to be punished by death or by life imprisonment as disturbers of the peace.

Each nation to provide an equal number of troops, with the Union helping smaller nations to pay the cost of their quota out of funds contributed to the *Union Treasurer* by the more powerful states. The *Generalissimo* of the Union Forces, appointed and removable by the Senate by plurality vote, to have supreme command over generals of member states.

No treaties of any kind to be made; no territorial changes to be permitted, except by three-fourths vote of the Senate. The fundamental agreement to create the Union may be changed by unanimous consent only. After about fourteen states join the Union, they can compel other states to become members by waging war against them until they join or are conquered.

In 1761 Jean Jacques Rousseau reedited the Abbé de Saint-Pierre's plan but feared it could not be adopted except "by violent means which would have staggered humanity." He believed privileges of the upper classes first should be limited.

GIULIO ALBERONI
Spanish Cardinal and Prime Minister
1736

Scheme for Reducing the Turkish Empire to the Obedience of Christian Princes; and for a Partition of the Conquests; Together with a Scheme for a Perpetual Dyet for Establishing the Public Tranquillity.

Proposed a close and disinterested *Union of the Christian Powers* as a preliminary condition to conquest of the Turkish Empire in Asia and Africa. A *Perpetual Dyet* of the ministers and deputies of all the sovereign princes and states on the model of the German Diet, meeting at Ratisbon to decide all disputes by majority vote within one year. Refusal to abide by decisions of the Dyet within six months to be punished by military measures. Member states and princes to furnish the Dyet with military and naval forces on a quota basis.

ANONYMOUS
French
1745

Projet d'un nouveau système de l'Europe, préférable au système de l'Équilibre entre la Maison de France et celle d'Autriche. (Project for a new European system, preferable to the balance of power system between France and Austria.)

Advocated a *Union* of all European states on the German model. Every state to keep its own form of government and internal autonomy. But no member of the Union to negotiate treaties without the approval of the Union expressed by a three-fourths vote. Those breaking this rule to be declared enemies of the Union.

Commerce to continue under existing regulations until all European states are members of the Union; new commercial regulations to be made by three-fourths vote as long as they are equal and reciprocal to all nations.

Disputes between states to be submitted to the Union which is to appoint *Mediators*. If these fail to conciliate the parties, the *Senate* of the Union to render a temporary decision by majority vote and after receiving instructions from each sovereign, to render a final verdict by three-fourths vote.

A State refusing to abide by the Senate's decision or refusing to carry it out is to be declared an enemy of the Union with war waged against it until it is disarmed and has carried out the ruling of the Senate. It would have to pay the costs of the war and could never be united with the country it had invaded.

After formation of the Union, any Sovereign of Europe refusing to enter it to be declared an enemy and war waged against him until he agreed to enter for the security of the community.

The Union to be established when all Sovereigns of Europe have agreed to join. They are to be represented by Plenipotentiaries meeting in a permanent Congress or Senate in a free and neutral city, such as Utrecht, Geneva, Cologne, or Aix la Chapelle, where they are to work together on important matters for the expansion and perpetuation of the Union.

The Union to have *Commissions* located on the various frontiers to settle differences between the subjects of the various states. Enforcement of these decisions to be pledged by the sovereigns.

The Senate to have complete sovereignty over the inhabitants of the *City of Peace* and to have representatives in all states.

The author argued that the existing balance of power arrangements of his day did not succeed in maintaining peace as treaties of peace provided merely a temporary armistice. He held that only an authority standing above the states, charged with upholding justice, could create peace.

JOHANN MICHAEL VON LOEN
GERMAN. COUNCILOR TO THE KING OF PRUSSIA
GOVERNOR OF THE PROVINCE TEKLENBURG-LINGEN
1747

Von einem beständigen Frieden in Europa. (Of a Perpetual Peace in Europe.) Chapter in his book, *Entwurf einer Staatskunst.* (Outline of Statecraft.)

Suggested a *Court of Peace* to have forty to fifty judges to be selected from among the leading men of each state with a thorough knowledge of natural and international law, and an expert knowledge of the European states and their political structure. They must know the leading languages, especially Latin.

Member states to send their representatives to the Court to lay their case before it. The judges to act with absolute impartiality, deciding by majority vote.

The Court to have jurisdiction over questions of royal succession and territorial disputes, as well as colonial questions and freedom of the seas.

The Court to have means of enforcing its judgment against disturbers of the peace who refuse to carry out its decisions.

SAINTARD
FRENCH RESIDENT IN SANTO DOMINGO
1756–57

Roman Politique sur l'état présent des affaires de l'Amérique.
(Political novel about the present state of affairs in America.)

Maintained that the establishment of peace in Europe would be achieved ultimately through freedom of commerce, and the resulting economic interdependence of peoples, rather than by a simple political act creating the Union.

Advocated a just division of colonial territory in North America as a condition of peace there.

ANGE GOUDAR
FRENCH WRITER
1757

La paix de l'Europe. (The Peace of Europe.)

Argued that peace, like war, was a matter of habit. To establish the peace habit, he suggested a twenty years' truce, to be negotiated through a *Congress* of the Ambassadors of all sovereigns of Europe. All Princes to guarantee the truce; no other matter to be discussed at this Congress. Any state violating the truce to be denounced by the *Congress*. Should the state persist in its aggression, the other sovereigns to wage war against it and force it to pay the costs of the conflict. Upon a second violation of the truce, it is to pay to the Congress a fine of forty million livres. Further violations to be punished by expulsion from the *League*.

JOHANN FRANZ VON PALTHEN
GERMAN COUNSELOR OF JUSTICE AND POET
1758

Projekt einen immerwährenden Frieden in Europa zu unterhalten.
(Project for Maintaining an Everlasting Peace in Europe.)

Urged the establishment of a general *Parliament* or *Tribunal* with all European states pledged to abide by its decisions, meeting in a centrally located city — Hamburg, Nüremberg, or Leipzig. The *Tribunal* to have eighty-eight members, with each state sending four representatives, except the German Empire, which was to have twenty. Membership to include Russia and Turkey. The *Tribunal* to elect four presidents and four vice-presidents from among its members. Representatives to be prominent persons, learned in history and natural, national, and international law.

The *Tribunal* to have jurisdiction over every type of dispute. Cases to be presented by attorneys of the disputing states. The official language to be Latin. In rendering decisions, fairness, rather than the letter of the law, to serve as a guide in each judgment.

The *Tribunal* to be divided into a *Senate* of fifteen to twenty judges, first, to decide cases; then, sitting together, to hear cases on appeal.

Neighboring states to place their armed forces at the disposal of the *Tribunal* to compel a state to submit to its jurisdiction and abide by its decision. Severe penalties to be imposed on offending states, in addition to making them pay all costs of enforcement.

VON LILIENFELD
LITHUANIAN NOBLEMAN AND OFFICER
1767

Neues Staats-Gebäude. (A New Structure of States.)

Proposed setting up of a *Court of Peace* to settle disputes between Christian Princes.

The Princes to send plenipotentiaries to a *Congress* called to establish eternal peace and disarmament between the Christian States of Europe. All former alliances to be abolished, and only established rights and just demands to be recognized. The *Congress* to arrange for future Congresses, make new laws, alter or improve old ones; set up the *Tribunal* or *Court of Peace;* determine the number and

Old Plans to Unite Nations—1306 to 1914

method of appointing judges; place of meeting, official language, preservation of archives, financing, and procedure; organize armed contingents to be at the disposal of the *Tribunal;* establish strength of the armed forces to be retained by each nation. The fundamental agreement creating the Union to be deposited with the archives of the *Tribunal.*

Every time a new government takes office, the ruler and his subjects to pledge their allegiance anew.

Russia to be among the twenty nations establishing the Union.

The *Tribunal* to have a President, eight Chief Councilors, twenty Councilors, and forty Assessors.

French suggested as the official language.

Candidates to the Court to be nominated by the member nations, the *Tribunal* choosing the new member from the list of candidates presented by the States.

The *Tribunal's* decisions, taken by majority vote, to be final. *Tribunal* subject to control only by the *Congress,* representing all the nations, which created it. International law to be codified in one short, clear book to serve for the guidance of all the member nations.

The *Tribunal* to concern itself directly with all disputes threatening peace, but not to interfere in the internal affairs of the states.

Sanctions against violators of its decisions to be applied as follows: (1) The Sovereign to be warned. (2) Strengthen the *Tribunal's* armed forces by calling on additional contingents from neighboring countries; break off diplomatic relations. (3) Declare that the rebellious ruler has forfeited his realm and offer his throne to a successor. A final measure to give weight to peaceful pressure would be the calling, if necessary, of the troops of the *Tribunal,* the native troops of the disciplined state, the requisitioned troops of the neighboring states, and the host of knights.

Member states to retain only a minimum number of troops.

(Von Lilienfeld completed his plan before he had read that of the Abbé de Saint-Pierre.)

BARON WILTRICH HOLBACH
FRENCH PHILOSOPHER
1773

La politique naturelle. (The Natural Law.)

"The law of the great society of the world obligates the rulers equally to the exercise of justice, peace, and good faith. But there exists no force or visible authority which can constrain the Princes or the peoples to observe the decrees. If all the rulers meeting together formed by common agreement a *Tribunal* where their quarrels could be brought and discussed; if their expressed wishes could be executed based on combined authority, as in each separate society, it would be to the interest of every ruler, who would be obligated to submit to the decisions of the *Tribunal*. The force exerted by the associated rulers would render these laws sacred and inviolate."

RICHARD PRICE
ENGLISH POLITICAL PHILOSOPHER
1776

Observations on the Nature of Civil Liberty, the Principles of Government, and the Justice and the Policy of the War with America.

Urged the formation of a general *confederacy* by the appointment of a *Senate* consisting of representatives from all the different states, to have the power "of managing all common concerns of the 'united states,' and of judging and deciding between them, as a common Arbiter or Umpire, in all disputes; having at the same time under its direction the common force of the states to support the decisions of the *Senate*."

PIERRE-ANDRE GARGAZ
FRENCH
1779

Printed in 1782 by Benjamin Franklin at Passy

Conciliateur de toutes les nations d'Europe, ou projet de paix perpétuelle entre tous les souverains de l'Europe et leurs voisins. (Conciliator of all the Nations of Europe or a Project of Universal and Perpetual Peace between all the Sovereigns of Europe and their Neighbors.)

Gargaz, a former schoolmaster of Thèze, in Provence, was falsely accused of murder and served twenty years as a galley-slave. During his servitude, he wrote a plan for universal and perpetual peace and sent his manuscript to Franklin in 1779, signing himself "Convict No. 1336." After his release, in 1781, he walked all the way to Passy, where Franklin printed his plan and gave him as many copies of it as he could carry. Gargaz sent copies of the plan to the brother of the King of France, to all the Ministers of State, and to twenty-nine Ambassadors in Paris. In 1786 he wrote to Thomas Jefferson, then American Minister to France, to urge the Americans to initiate the Union.

Gargaz proposed that each sovereign appoint, in addition to his regular Ambassadors, one *Mediator* to meet in a perpetual *Congress* at the City of Lyons. As soon as a minimum of ten Mediators were appointed (at least five representing hereditary sovereigns), they should meet and pass judgment by majority vote on all disputes between their sovereigns. In case of a tie, decision of the President (the Mediator representing the oldest hereditary monarch) is to prevail. Any sovereign breaking the peace, or refusing to abide by the decisions of the Congress to be deprived of his position by the combined force of all the other monarchs, and a Prince from another ruling house elected by the Congress to succeed him. The associated states to have complete freedom in all other respects: control of commerce and armament, except for an unfortified zone, to be maintained between all borders, and land and sea forces kept to a fixed quota. Gargaz advocated ambitious world-wide public works programs to be paid out of the sums to be saved through the adoption of his project; among them, road-building, irrigation, and flood control. He advocated the storing of surplus crops and their loan or outright gift to regions stricken with famine; the building of canals over the Isthmus of Panama and that of Suez (about sixty feet wide, thirty feet deep and forty leagues long); State supervision and support of children living in undesirable environments, and their removal and placement in proper foster homes.

1796–97

Gargaz published an addition to his plan, proposing the immediate establishment of a *Kollegium* of five citizens over forty years old to act as a *Court* to decide disputes between individuals and nations. The French Government to invite at the same time other nations to appoint five persons each to establish a *Congress of Free Masons*.

JOHANN AUGUST SCHLETTWEIN
GERMAN
1780–84

Die wichtigste Angelegenheit für Europa oder System eines festen Friedens unter den Europäischen Staaten. (The Most Important Issue for Europe, or a System of Firm Peace among the European States.)

Proposed that the European states hold an *International Congress* to establish a Union setting forth the rights and duties of all states, and guaranteeing freedom of commerce and of all the seas, rivers, and highways of the world.

All boundaries to remain as at the time of the establishment of the Congress: the states to drop forever any claims they may have had against one another. All agreements between states to be perpetual unless changed by unanimous consent.

All disputes between states to be submitted to mediation or to a court appointed by states not involved in any dispute.

Membership in the Union to be open also to non-Christian Nations, such as Turkey, provided they submit to Christian laws. If they refuse membership in the Union on these terms, their territory is to be divided among the Christian states.

The Union to guarantee the German Confederation and its constitution because this union of large and small states greatly influences the affairs of all Europe.

Revolutions within states to be suppressed with the aid of members of the Union as endangering the peace and existence of the Union. (Schlettwein refers to the French Revolution as proof of the need for such action. EDITORS.)

ANONYMOUS
1782

Project for a Holy Alliance.

Austria, France, Spain, and Portugal, joined by Prussia, Saxony, and Poland, are to form a grand alliance. The first four to decide all disputes; other nations obliged to accept their decisions.

Each of the four Great Powers to send representatives to an *Arbitral Court* situated in a centrally located city of Europe. The *Court* to decide disputes between states subject to the final decision of the four Great Powers.

The Secondary Powers must join the Alliance. Those refusing are to be forced to join, but the four Great Powers must not enlarge their territories at the expense of the smaller ones.

The armed forces of the Four Great Powers and contingents from the Secondary Powers to be used to defend Christian Europe.

MARIE JEAN ANTOINE NICOLAS CARITAT
Marquis de Condorcet
French Metaphysician
1786

De l'influence de la révolution d'Amérique sur l'Europe. (The Influence of the American Revolution on Europe.)

Proposed establishment of an *International Tribunal* to decide disputes between nations. Each nation is to retain its army and navy, and to enforce for itself the award of the Court.

Condorcet advocated the study of a world language in addition to the national, and a *World Institute of Learning* to encourage the establishment of a world language.

ANONYMOUS
German
1787

Eine Idee von der Möglichkeit Eines Allgemeinen und Ewigen Friedens in der Welt. (An Idea of the Possibility of a Universal and Eternal Peace in the World.)

The author proposes a *Union* to embrace the whole world on the model of the German Empire, with each nation retaining its own form of government and sovereignty. All disputes that might lead to war to be submitted to an *International Court;* war between nations prohibited in a solemn agreement.

The judges of the Court—numbering about a hundred—to be between the ages of 35 and 65, and learned, respected citizens of their native countries. They are to be paid adequate salaries and pensioned by their rulers on retirement. The judges are to be subject to recall at any time. Upon conviction of a judge for accepting a bribe punishment by death is decreed. The Praesidium of the *Court* to change each month.

The *Court* to have at its disposal armed forces and a fleet made up of international contingents. The member states to reduce their armaments to a point needed only for internal peace.

The *Court* to have the right of intervention to restore order in case of civil war within a nation. Frontiers and international arrangements existing at the time of union to be carefully codified, to serve as a guide for the *Court's* decisions. To settle difficult cases the *Court* may give itself a time limit up to ten years. The *Union* to be established as soon as three or four Great Powers desire it. States which refuse to become members to be declared enemies of the *Union*, but they are not under compulsion to join it.

PALIER DE SAINT-GERMAIN
Swiss
1788

Nouvel Essai sur le projet de la Paix perpétuelle. (A New Essay on the Project for Perpetual Peace.)

On the initiative of France all Christian sovereigns to unite in a perpetual association guaranteeing one another their possessions, territories, states, and rights. All disputes to be submitted to the mediation of other states through a *Permanent Tribunal* or *Council* to which each state is to send Plenipotentiaries. Christian states outside Europe also eligible to join.

In case of dispute between two states, each nominates two mediators from among states not involved. Each disputant state chooses one from the other state's nominees. If the mediators fail to agree or, if one of the parties refuses to accept the verdict, the case is to be appealed to the *Tribunal* for a final decision by majority vote.

If a state refuses to accept the judgment of the *Tribunal*, all the other states are to unite their strength to compel its submission, together with payment of necessary damages.

The states are to place at the disposal of the *Association* contingents of troops ready to march. Any state refusing to contribute its allotted share to be excluded from the benefits and protection of the *Association*. Some states may be permitted to furnish money in place of troops, but in that case they cannot be represented on the *Tribunal*.

Each member to have one vote in the *Kollegium* including the Federal Republics: Switzerland, the United Provinces, and the United States. The Chairmanship of the Congress to be changed every year, each outgoing President naming his successor.

The first Congress is to determine whether existing alliances and agreements between States are to be declared void; the size of the military contingents; freedom of the seas; whether the Ottoman Empire is to be informed, and other issues.

JOHANN GOTTFRIED SCHINDLER
GERMAN THEOLOGIAN AND UNIVERSITY RECTOR
1788
Published under the pseudonym *Schinly*.

Was ist den grössern Fürsten zu raten um das Wohl und Glück der Länder zu befördern. (What Advice Should be Given to the More Important Rulers to Promote the Welfare and Happiness of the Countries.)

Schindler proposed that Russia, Austria, Prussia, England, and France shall negotiate a treaty of perpetual peace. He maintained that if the powerful states united, the smaller ones would also join.

A Congress to be organized to which each state sends its leading men as representatives. The claims of the various states to be heard, then decided by majority vote. Each state to reduce its armaments by one-half. Any state waging war to be stopped by the united force of the other member states.

JEAN BAPTISTE DU VAL-DE-GRACE
BARON DE CLOOTZ
PRUSSIAN-FRENCH REVOLUTIONIST
1792

La République universelle ou adresse aux tyrannicides. (The Universal Republic, or An Address to the Destroyers of Tyranny.)

(This is the first plan to place human rights above *states'* rights. EDITORS.)

Advocated that all independent nations and boundaries should be abolished and a *World Republic of Man* established with Paris as its capital. Every people to have cultural autonomy. A legislative assembly of 1,500 to 2,000 members and an executive council elected by the Assembly and responsible to it. Each week or every two weeks another Chairman of the Council to be chosen.

The lower courts to be sufficient. A *Bill of Human Rights* to be the basis of the *Republic*.

To avoid misunderstanding as to the motives of France, the people were no longer to call themselves Frenchmen but *brothers*.

De Clootz presented this plan to the French National Assembly, which voted against it in 1792. A year later he was falsely charged with treason by his enemies and guillotined.

JEREMY BENTHAM
ENGLISH
1793

A *Plea for an Universal and Perpetual Peace,* and *Emancipate your Colonies.*

As a preliminary condition to peace Bentham urged agreement between France and England on the following basis: emancipation of their colonies; end of defensive and offensive treaties of alliance; end of preferential trade agreements; reduction of their armed forces to a fixed point; negotiation of perpetual treaties to maintain these agreements; creation of a *Common Court of Judicature* to resolve differences between nations; a *Congress* or *Diet* with advisory powers only, depending for enforcement on public opinion in each state supported by freedom of the press. As a last resort, decrees of the Court to be enforced by military contingents furnished by the member states.

BOISSY-D'ANGLAS
FRENCH. MEMBER OF THE NATIONAL ASSEMBLY
1795

Épitre du vieux cosmopolite Syrach à la convention national de France.
(Epistle of the old cosmopolite Syrach to the national convention of France.)

The European nations to unite in a *World Republic*. A broad agreement to be made, regulating relations between the states. Details to be left to them. Maritime regulations except for inland waters to be under the jurisdiction of the *Republic*. No state to be permitted to negotiate defensive or offensive alliances with other continents, without the knowledge of the rest of Europe. Commercial treaties permissible. Secret treaties to be forbidden.

International law to be codified and developed into a *European Constitution* as soon as an agreement is reached by a few of the leading Powers.

The *Constitution* to provide for the protection of the *Republic* against a state attacking a member state. The Great Powers to be forbidden to add to their territory, but small states allowed to federate.

Russia and Turkey as semi-Asiatic Powers not to be members of the General European Federation.

France and one other great power could initiate the Federation which was to be organized by a new diplomacy, operating not through secret agreements, but with full publicity.

Advocated a strong European fleet for defense in a probable war with America and Africa.

JOHANN GOTTLIEB FICHTE
GERMAN PHILOSOPHER
1795

Fichte proposed that a number of states form a *League* through a solemn binding agreement to defend one another's independence from attack, either by member or non-member states. The *Tribunal* set up by the League was to have jurisdiction not only over member states, but also over states not members but in alliance or treaty relationships with member states.

Fichte expected that the *League* would seldom need an army to enforce its decrees, and so it would be sufficient for the states, if necessary, to furnish military contingents to those members in need.

IMMANUEL KANT
GERMAN PHILOSOPHER
1795

Zum ewigen Frieden. (Perpetual Peace.)

Proposed *Preliminary Articles of Peace* creating a *Confederation of Nations* and outlawing secret reservations in treaties; acquisition of one state by another through inheritance, purchase, exchange, or donation, since a state is a society of human beings and not a piece of property. Standing armies to be abolished gradually; non-interference with the constitution and administration of another state except in case of civil war. Loans to be made only to encourage manufacture and commerce, none for military purposes.

Members of the *Confederation* to have a Republican form of government, with separation of the legislative, executive, and judicial branches. The *Confederation* to function through a permanent *Congress of States* attended by Ministers and Ambassadors to settle disputes between states without recourse to war. Members allowed to withdraw from the Confederation. Such a confederation to be established through a "covenant of peace" putting an end to war forever, rather than by a treaty of peace.

Kant urged world citizenship and freedom of movement based on a universal law of hospitality.

CARL JOSEPH AUGUST HOFHEIM
GERMAN
1796
Published under the pseudonym *Justus Sincerus Veridicus*.

Von der europäischen Republik. Plan zu einem ewigen Frieden nebst einem Abriss der Rechte der Völker und Staaten und einer Erklärung derselben. (Of the European Republic. Plan for Perpetual Peace, with a Sketch of the Rights of Peoples and States and a Declaration of these.)

Hofheim believed that Europe ought to set an example to the rest of the world by establishing an international organization to assure unrestricted commerce and freedom of the seas, and to set up the regulations and means whereby these rights are to be safeguarded.

The rulers of European states to send representatives to an *Assembly*, meeting in a neutral city, centrally located. The Assembly to codify existing international and natural law and to draw up a constitution. The constitution to specify the regulation of commerce and foreign affairs; set the number of troops allowed each nation; create an international fleet to guarantee freedom of sea travel; organize the *Perpetual Congress of Nations* and submit its work to the public opinion of Europe.

As soon as the constitution comes into effect, the Assembly is to dissolve, its place to be taken by a *Congress* (Kollegium) made up of representatives chosen by each state according to its own methods. Each state to send three representatives; one of each to serve in the legislative branch, one in the executive, and one in the judicial branch. Complete equality of large and small states, irrespective of their internal organization.

These deputies to function with complete independence of the governments that appointed them. They must not have served their government in any capacity whatever for nine years previous to their appointment, and after nine years of service in the Congress are ineligible for reappointment. Sessions not to last longer than three years and must be open to the public.

The judicial branch interprets cases brought before it; renders decisions under law and precedent. It makes recommendations to the legislature whenever it finds the law ambiguous or inequitable.

Hofheim stressed the importance of heads of nations taking an oath to the European Congress when they assume their office. He also urged the importance of creating a world outlook and sense of international obligation through the medium of newspapers, books, churches, and schools.

The Congress to deal only with matters of interest to all Europe, between states, or a whole people and its government. Congress may not interfere in the economy of any nation unless it affects the other nations or unless requested by that nation or a majority of its people. Should any member state attempt to set itself against the Union, the states nearest geographically to proceed against it with arms, if requested by the Congress.

JOSEF GORRES
GERMAN
1798

Der Allgemeine Frieden, ein Ideal. (Universal Peace, an Ideal.)

Hoped that Republican France, under the leadership of Napoleon, together with other nations liberated by France, would create the *World Republic*, including the United States of America.

Görres proposed a *popular convention* to determine the rights of states and to draw up a constitution; regulate the rules admitting states to the Republic and the rules whereby they might secede. Urged separation of Church and State; also free trade. The Government of the Republic also to serve as a *Court* for the settlement of disputes between states.

ANONYMOUS
1800

Patriotische Beiträge zum Ewigen Frieden. (Patriotic Contributions to Perpetual Peace.)

The writer proposed that states negotiate a solemn agreement consisting of six articles in which they bind themselves as follows:

1. Each state retains its rights and privileges.

2. Each state pledges not to attempt to add to its territory.

3. The states pledge to defend each of their fellow states and all of them together against attack either by a member or a non-member state.

4. All alliances, agreements, and secret treaties are declared void, and each state pledges to forbid the passage of troops through its territory and not to engage in war.

5. Each state retains the right of non-interference by others in its internal affairs.

6. No state to engage in hostile maneuvers, and the fleets and troops of the various states to consider each other friends.

In the event of foreign war the League is to preserve neutrality and thus also its right to carry on trade on all the seas.

ANDR. MOSER
GERMAN
1800
Published in Berne, Switzerland.

Gesunder Menschenverstand über die Kunst Völker zu beglücken. (Common Sense about the Art of Making Peoples Happy.)

Moser wanted society to establish democratic Republican systems. Arbitration courts to settle disputes between individuals; national

Peace Councils, and international courts to settle disputes between nations.

Nations not to go to war without first referring their disputes to a *Council* of the *National Arbitration Commissions*, which is to set a certain time limit for compliance with its award. All states to combine in waging war against the nation refusing to accept the decision of the *Council*.

If the opposing states decide finally to war with each other, they should abide by the outcome of one battle, or better still by individual combat.

KONRAD NAGELI
Swiss Priest
1800

Suggestions to be incorporated in the Revision of the Swiss Constitution:

Art. 161: "The people of the Swiss Republic desire furthermore that all sovereign nations join in establishing a *General Assembly* with one representative for every million of population. The *Assembly* should have power to decide matters beyond that of any single nation which would be of benefit to all nations, as, for example, the wiping out of smallpox; building of canals to unite the Atlantic and the Pacific, via Mexico; the Mediterranean and the Red Sea, via Suez; the Rhine and the Rhone; the Bodensee (Lake Constance), and the Danube."

Art. 663: "In addition, the people of the Swiss Republic wish that all nations would set up a *Peace Court* with one delegate for every million population. The *Court* should meet in the city of a small state. The delegates should divide into two courts to provide for appeal from one court to the other.

"The armed forces of all nations should be at the *Peace Court's* disposal in order to enforce its decisions."

THOMAS PAINE
1801
ENGLISH by birth;
AMERICAN by adoption;
FRENCH citizen by decree;
Deprived of the right to vote in New Rochelle, New York.

The Maritime Compact.

Paine urged the formation of an unarmed association of neutral nations to act together in time of war to resist the unjust restrictions of belligerents on neutral commerce. The *Association of Neutrals* to impose a boycott on the commerce of nations violating neutral rights until reparation is made. Immediately on the outbreak of war, all neutral nations, whether members of the Association or not, to appoint deputies to meet in *Congress* in a place centrally located to take note of violations of neutral rights. The ships of each member nation to carry the rainbow colored flag of the *Association of Neutrals*, together with their respective national flags.

The Association to have a *President* for a term of years, the office passing by rotation to each nation composing the Association. The first President to be the ruler, or his deputy, of the most northerly nation in the Association. Geographical situation of each to be determined by the latitude of the capital of each nation. Paine suggested that the Emperor Paul (of Russia) be the first President of the Association, and maintained that had it not been for the untimely death of the Emperor "a law of nations would have been proclaimed."

Paine who had submitted this plan to all Ministers of neutral nations, represented in Paris in 1800, pointed out that following the publication of his plan, Russia, Sweden, Denmark, Prussia, and parts of Spain, Portugal, and Naples shut their ports and important rivers to English ships and commerce.

Thomas Jefferson, to whom Paine had also sent his plan, had it published in 1801 by S. H. Smith (Washington, D. C.). Commenting on the plan, Jefferson wrote to Paine: "These papers contain precisely our principles, and I hope they will be generally recognized here.

Determined as we are to avoid, if possible, wasting the energies of our people in war and destruction, we shall avoid implicating ourselves with the powers of Europe, even in support of principles which we mean to pursue. They have so many other interests different from ours, that we must avoid being entangled in them. We believe we can enforce these principles by peaceable means, now that we are likely to have our public councils detached from foreign views. . . ."

KARL SALOMO ZACHARIA
1802

Janus.

Held that world organization must be founded on the freedom and equality of peoples. That it must be guaranteed in a book of world law, defining the rights of nations and of world citizenship. Zachariä proposed a permanent *Congress of Representatives of the European States*, to be developed into an international *Tribunal*.

CZAR ALEXANDER I
Russian
1804 and 1815

Alexander I participated in the various coalitions of nations trying to restrict the growth of French power under Napoleon; also made plans for the reconstruction of Europe and the organization of relations between states.

In secret instructions to Novosiltsov, he wrote, in 1804, "Why could one not submit to it (a treaty of peace) the positive right of nations, assure the privilege of neutrality, insert the obligation of never beginning war until all the resources which the mediations of a third party could offer have been exhausted, until the grievances have by this means been brought to light, and an effort to remove them has been made? On principles such as these one could proceed to a general pacification, and give birth to a league of which the stipulation would form, so to speak, a new code of the law of nations, which, sanctioned by the greater part of the nations of Europe, would, without difficulty, become the immutable ruler of Cabinets, while those who should try to infringe it would risk bringing upon themselves the forces of the new union."

After the final defeat of Napoleon in 1815, Alexander I organized the Holy Alliance between Russia, Austria, and Prussia, joined by most of the other European states, for mutual assistance and protection, pledging the rulers to conduct their social and political affairs on the basis of Christian principles.

GONDON
French
1807

Du droit public et du droit des gens ou principes d'association civile et politique; suivis d'un projet de paix générale et perpétuelle.
(Civil and International Law or Principles of Civil and Political Association, and a Project of Universal and Perpetual Peace.)

Proposed that a European Union should be set up with four separate organs of government.

(1) A *Kollegium* of the Princes and Rulers of the various states to exercise legislative power.

(2) A *Congress* to superintend the observance of the laws and to lay cases before the *Tribunal*. Each state to have one delegate and two substitutes.

(3) A *Tribunal* to decide disputes submitted to it by the *Congress*.

(4) A *Protector* to compel observance of the laws and obedience to the decisions of the *Tribunal* and to head the armed forces.

Latin to be the official language. Laws to be codified. Freedom of commerce and of the seas assured.

Monarchies to arrange their successions in such a way as to avoid

Old Plans to Unite Nations—1306 to 1914   61

disputes and conflicting claims. Use of mercenaries to be forbidden. Laws must be permanent, and provide equal justice for all.

The seat of the *Congress* to be in territory belonging to all the Nations.

The *Tribunal* to sit as a full chamber in disputes affecting all members.

In disputes affecting certain states, only those judges to sit who represent those states not involved.

The *Protector of Europe* and two substitutes to be elected for ten years by a majority vote of the *Congress* from a list to which each member nation nominates one person.

Armed forces at the disposal of the *Protector* to be made up of contingents provided by the various states. In strength the forces together must not exceed that of the strongest member state to prevent an arms race.

Gondon thought that under these circumstances each state could reduce its army to one-sixth of its former strength.

ANONYMOUS
By a 70-year-old GERMAN STATESMAN
1808

Gedanken über die Wiederherstellung des Gleichgewichts in Europa, zur Begründung eines dauerhafteren Friedens als bisher möglich gewesen. (Thoughts on the Reestablishment of the Balance of Power in Europe to Establish a More Permanent Peace than was Possible Heretofore.)

Proposed merely to lessen the probabilities of war by having about twenty European states negotiate an agreement to decide disputes by majority vote of the member states. Each state to have as many votes as the number of its troops or warships, determined according to an elaborate table. Small states could jointly raise the minimum of 20,000 troops.

The League to be served by a chancellor, assisted by sixteen or more advisers and assessors, and three secretaries, one proficient in German, one in French, and one in Latin.

The expenses of the Bureau to be assessed among the various states according to the number of their votes.

Any state disturbing the peace to be occupied by its nearest neighbor with troops and ships three times greater than the offender's, until the decisions of the League are carried out and the costs of occupation paid by the guilty state.

PH. A. STAPFER
SWISS PROFESSOR AND DIPLOMAT
1808

While Secretary to the Minister of the Government of Berne to France, Stapfer proposed to the French Government that differences between the two countries should be resolved by requesting the Dutch, Lombard, and Genoese Republics to establish a *Court* to settle these quarrels. He asserted that this would set an example to other nations and be the beginning of *World Union*. France rejected his proposal.

EBERHARD FRIEDRICH GEORGII
GERMAN
1811
Published anonymously.

De jure generis humani vel divisi in gentes vel in unam civitatem scilicet hunc orbem conjuncti sen de jure gentium et cosmopolitico. (Whether mankind is divided into many nations or united into a single state, it is evident this globe can be unified only under the universal laws of all humanity.)

Georgii suggested that all European peoples join in an agreement (at the end of the Napoleonic wars) pledging themselves not to seek to establish their rights through force, and creating a *Court of Nations* to decide disputes. Large and small states alike to be represented by one Senator each. The Senators to decide every case by majority vote.

The *Court* to have at its disposal an executive force of troops to carry out its decisions in case of resistance. The troops to be contributed by all states, but to be under the exclusive command of the *Court*.

The expenses of the *Court* to be assessed against the state adjudged guilty of breaking the peace.

A code of law to be established, binding on all peoples. This code also to define boundaries between states. Union of small states with larger ones permitted.

The *Court* not to interfere in purely internal affairs. Troops and fleets to be disarmed; recruiting of soldiers considered a breach of law. Grant of loans to depend on consent of the *Court*. The printing of paper money entirely prohibited to prevent secret rearmament. (The writer foresaw the possibility of other continental Courts united possibly under one World Court.)

KARL CHRISTIAN FRIEDRICH KRAUSE
GERMAN
1811 and 1814

Das Urbild der Menschheit. (The Prototype of Mankind.)

Believed that as mankind organized into families, tribes, cities, and nations, it would also organize into federations of Europe, Asia, and Africa; of America; of Australia; and these continental groupings would join in one *World Federation* with its center in Polynesia. For a time he hoped Napoleon would achieve the unification of Europe.

Entwurf eines Europäischen Staatenbundes. (Project of a European Confederation.)

In 1814 Krause urged a *Federation of European States* under German leadership. As a preliminary step, Germany should be divided into three parts: an eastern part under the Austrian Emperor; a northern part under Prussia; and a southern part under various Princes. The three parts to federate.

The *Federation* to consist of free and equal states conducting its affairs with full publicity. All states eligible to membership, irrespective of religion or form of government, and to be permitted to withdraw from the Union.

Member states to be equal within the Union, irrespective of population. The states to guarantee equal rights to other member states within their own territories, waters, inland seas, and the oceans within the jurisdiction of the Union. In the event of secession, a state must first fulfill obligations previously assumed.

Each state undertakes to submit all its disputes to the decision of the Union *Court*, and not to go to war with a non-member state on its own initiative. A state opposing the Court's decision to be expelled from the Union and treated as a non-member.

The member states undertake to defend the rights of all states, to protect each member state against violence, and to wage war and negotiate peace wholly through the Union.

The *Court* not to prescribe sanctions against a state, only the conditions and continuance of membership.

The *Union Council* to be the governing body. Each state to have only one representative in the person of its ruling prince, president, or appointed delegate. The Council to develop the organization of the Union; also propose, approve, and execute new laws.

Matters affecting all states to be decided by unanimous vote; affecting only a few states not to require unanimous vote; but in that case each state to use its own judgment in carrying out decisions, as long as the basic agreement of the Union is not impaired.

Failing a unanimous vote on an important issue, those voting favorably to decide whether the issue at stake is vital enough to demand that the dissenting members withdraw from the Union.

Non-member states to be informed immediately of the formation of the Union and of the Union's readiness to decide all outstanding disputes according to international law. No force to be used against non-members, nor wars of conquest, and the Union should be ready at all times to admit as members those states requesting it.

Berlin to be the capital, and German the official language.

JEAN BAPTISTE CLAUDE ISOARD
FRENCH
Published under the pseudonym *Delisle de Sales*
About 1813

De la paix de l'Europe et de ses bases. (The Foundations of Peace in Europe.)

Proposed that the international Congress at the end of the Napoleonic wars create a permanent *Tribunal*. He suggested that it may be best to divide Europe into several federations: Germany, the Scandinavian States with Russia and Poland; Italy; and Portugal, Spain, Holland, France, and England.

The *Tribunal* to be composed of representatives from all independent states in Europe. The Presidency of the *Tribunal* to be held, in turn, by the representatives of each nation. To provide for appeal to the full chamber, the *Tribunal* divides into two chambers.

Should any state try to break the peace, the *Tribunal* calls on all the Powers to unite their strength and come to the aid of the Confederation.

ANONYMOUS
1814

Vorschläge zu einer organischen Gesetzgebung für den Europäischen Staatenverein zur Begründung eines dauernden Weltfriedens. (Proposals for a Constitution of the European Union of States to Establish Lasting World Peace.)

Proposed the establishment of a permanent *Congress* to decide definitely the boundary of each state according to the languages and customs of peoples. On this basis, all frontiers to be guaranteed forever; federations of states to be forbidden.

Future boundary disputes to be settled by judges, each state nominating three.

The *Congress* must decide all other international rights, eliminating ancient customs. Among the new rights, freedom of navigation of rivers, harbors, and the seas must be assured; as well as fishing rights, free trade, abolition of slavery, freedom of religion (where not in conflict with existing law and custom), uniform weights, measures, and coinage.

The author was opposed to the republican form of government because of the excesses of the French Revolution and proposed that all princes become Constitutional Monarchs guaranteeing one another's constitutions.

Disputes between rulers and their people also to come within the jurisdiction of the *Congress*.

Each ruler to appoint one representative. The Presidency of the *Congress* to be changed each year by lot.

Each state is obligated to furnish 4,000 soldiers for every 500,000 of population to restrain a state from enlarging its territories by attacking another. In case of need, the quotas to be increased.

ALEXANDER LIPS
GERMAN (?)
PROFESSOR OF PHILOSOPHY
1814

Der allgemeine Friede oder wie heisst die Basis über welche allein ein dauernder Weltfriede gegründet werden kann. (Universal Peace or the Basis on which alone a durable World Peace can be established.)

Lips proposed a *Council of Europe* to meet in a new or a free city to which each nation would send one representative. The Chairmanship to be changed each year; the seat of the *Council* to be moved to another city every five years. The *Council* to codify international law to include also freedom of the seas; to provide for judicial procedure in the settlement of disputes and for an executive body to enforce decisions. The Executive to have at its disposal the national armed forces to compel the obedience of any state breaking the peace by non-compliance with the *Court's* verdict. This would be a just war.

The boundaries of each nation to be limited, not according to natural frontiers but on the basis of linguistic groupings.

The author hoped for the ultimate transfer of power from the Princes to representative assemblies in each country.

DR. ARNOLD MALLINCKRODT
GERMAN (?)
1814

Was thun bey Deutschlands, bey Europas Wiedergeburt. (What to do for Germany's and Europe's Reconstruction.)

Mallinckrodt proposed calling a *Congress* to a neutral centrally located city, to have full executive, legislative, and judicial powers; to codify international law for European states, guaranteeing first of all freedom of the seas and of navigation. (This he expected would be opposed by England and warned her against overweening ambition.)

Should war not disappear completely, regulations as to its conduct to be incorporated in the *International Code*. All states to disarm, giving up even their muskets.

There should be free trade, freedom of movement, and complete equality of states and of religion.

COUNT CLAUDE HENRI DE SAINT-SIMON
FRENCH
1814

De la réorganisation de la société européenne. (Concerning the reorganization of the European community.)

Proposed that all states follow England's example and become parliamentary monarchies; a European Parliament to be set up then with a hereditary European monarch.

Parliament should consist of two houses. The members of the lower house, chosen directly by the people, to represent the professions of business, scholarship, administration, and law. Members to be individuals possessing an international outlook. Each must have at least 25,000 francs annual income from property. Especially eminent men, although lacking the property qualification, may be chosen (but not more than twenty), and are to be paid as much as the income they require.

Members of the upper house to be appointed by each monarch from among his richest subjects in unlimited numbers. The seats to be hereditary. In the upper house, at least twenty distinguished men and their heirs may also be admitted without the property qualification.

The *Parliament* is to meet in a city and territory under its own jurisdiction. It is to deal with all matters of general European concern, decide all disputes, lay its own taxes, supervise education, undertake public works such as the building of canals, and assure freedom of thought and religion.

The Union to be initiated by England and France; other states joining them must be willing to assume part of England's public debt acquired in her struggle to liberate Europe (from Napoleon).

REV. NOAH WORCESTER
AMERICAN
SECRETARY, MASSACHUSETTS PEACE SOCIETY
1814

A Solemn Review of the Custom of War.

Advocated the organization of a *confederacy of nations* with a *high court of equity* to decide *international controversies.* The membership of the court to be made up of the most eminent persons from each nation. Compliance with its decisions to be a point of national honor.

NAPOLEON BONAPARTE
CORSICAN-FRENCH
1816

In his memoirs *Mémorial de Sainte-Hélène,* Napoleon maintained that the object of his campaigns was the creation of a *European Federation* under one Constitution, one *Court,* with a unified monetary system, weights, measures, etc. He wrote that a precondition of European Federation was the unification of France, Spain, Italy, and Germany. The first three were well on the way to becoming unified nations, but Germany's unification would take longer. When that too was accomplished, Europe would federate.

COUNT DE PAOLI CHAGNY
FRENCH
1818

Projet d'une Organisation Politique pour l'Europe. (Project of a Political Organization for Europe.)

Proposed the division of Europe into *three confederations*. One under the King of Prussia; one under the Emperor of Russia; and one under the Emperor of Austria. The three rulers to be the final court of appeal in disputes between states. The author realized that force would be effective only against the small states and that extraordinary measures would have to be taken against the Great Powers, but he doubted that the Monarchs would let matters come to such a point.

Territories reconquered from France to be administered as domains by a *Commission* of the *European Federation*.

Income from these territories to be used to pay the higher officers for the support of the armed forces quartered there, and to repay England and Austria for their expenses in the war against France. Each federation to regulate the strength of the armies of its members.

EMMA WILLARD
AMERICAN
1820 and 1864

Mrs. Willard, who as a pioneer for the education of women established the first female seminary, also published in 1820 a plan, *Universal Peace to Be Introduced by a Confederacy of Nations, Meeting at Jerusalem*. In 1864, she republished essentially the same plan under the title *Universal Peace*. She proposed that the nations establish a permanent judicial *tribunal*, and refer their disputes to it by mutual consent. The *tribunal* to be established in Jerusalem to prevent national jealousies. England and France to purchase Palestine from the Turks, and the Rothschilds to provide funds to build a railroad to the coast and to establish the seat of the *Permanent Peace Council*. France, England, Russia, and the United States to take the initiative in establishing the *Council*. After delegates of all nations are assembled, a code of international law should be evolved to bind all nations. The Jews to be assisted by the whole world to return to Jerusalem.

Mrs. Willard believed that the American Civil War could have been averted, if such a Council had been in existence to hear the grievances of the South.

CONRAD FRIEDRICH VON SCHMIDT-PHISELDEK
GERMAN — naturalized Danish citizen.
DIRECTOR OF ROYAL STATE BANK IN COPENHAGEN
1821

Europäischer Bund. (European Union.)

Proposed organization of a *European Federation*, the beginnings of which he saw in the establishment of the German Confederation and the Holy Alliance. But the new *Federation* should unite states, not Princes, in a free and equal Union for mutual defense.

Urged freedom of trade and movement, uniform coinage and reduction of state budgets through decreasing military expenditures, and conduct of foreign affairs by the Union. Colonies to become affiliated with the *Federation*, which should raise the level of native culture; regulate immigration; and prohibit the slave trade. Citizens of each state to be entitled to equal privileges and immunities of citizens in all states; rights of aliens to be safeguarded; protection against violation of civil rights; freedom of press and correspondence.

Only sovereign states to be members. Federations to be represented as if they were unified states.

Congress of the Union to determine whether to divide into two chambers; appointment of executive and presiding officers of Congress; and method of voting.

States to be represented not only in proportion to population, but also according to wealth and influence.

A judiciary body to be appointed by the *Congress* from its own membership in rotation. Each state to have only one vote in *Court*. *Jurisdiction* over disputes between member states; between citizens and a state charged with injustice, persecution, unlawful arrest, or expropriation of property. In this case, a member of the *Court* to serve as attorney for the plaintiff.

The author believed strongly that states would voluntarily obey the decisions of the *Court* because of a long tradition of obedience to law, and because no state would want to be the object of an unfavorable public opinion throughout Europe. This is why meetings of the *Assembly* must be public.

Should a state refuse to abide by the Court's decision, it is to be expelled from the Union. If it persists in hostile actions, the Union's armed forces to be used against it.

Armed forces of the Union to consist of contingents supplied by the member states, at the complete disposal and command of the Union and paid by it from sums assessed against the states.

The Union also to have a fleet similarly organized. Inland states to contribute money instead of ships.

The Union would protect Europe against the rising influence of the American States.

ANONYMOUS
1826

Nouveau Projet de paix perpétuelle entre tous les peuples de la chrétienté, basé sur une délimitation fixe et naturelle des territoires nationaux, et sur la propagation des sentimens religieux et philanthropiques.
(A New Project of perpetual peace among all the peoples of Christendom, based on fixed and naturally defined national territories and on the propagation of religious and philanthropic sentiments.)

The author proposed that the world be divided into *Three Confederations* united in one *Universal Assembly* under the presidency of the Pope. The capitals of the *Three Confederations* to be Rome, Nanking, and Mexico. Delegates to the *Universal Assembly* to be chosen for life in proportion to population. Representatives of states entitled to more than one delegate to be appointed by the following groups: the Catholic Church; the ruler, the Upper House, the Lower House, the national judiciary, the universities, commerce and crafts, heads of the army and navy, the National Council, and the municipal authorities.

The Roman Catholic religion to be official; no new religions to be founded, but those already established to be tolerated.

The Assembly to decide all disputes, foster commerce, assure freedom of the seas, abolish the slave trade, control infectious diseases, provide for monarchical succession, regulate immigration, and propagate Christianity.

Should a non-Christian ruler join the Confederation, his participation in the Assembly to be advisory until he has been converted to Christianity.

Contributions in money and troops by each state also determined by the Assembly.

SIMON BOLIVAR
VENEZUELAN
1826

Bolivar, in his invitation to the former Spanish colonies to send representatives to the Congress of Panama, suggested "a congress of plenipotentiaries from each state that should act as a *council* in great conflicts, to be appealed to in case of common danger, and be a faithful interpreter of public treaties when difficulties arise, and conciliate, in short, all our differences."

WILLIAM LADD
AMERICAN. SEA CAPTAIN
1828 and 1840

Essay on a Congress of Nations.

Proposed the establishment of a *Congress of Nations* and a *Court of Nations.* The Congress to be composed of representatives of Christian and civilized nations, each to have one vote, but any number of representatives; Congress to elect its own officers and establish its own by-laws. Decisions in matters of legislation to be unanimous, each law thus acquiring the force of a treaty. The Congress not to intervene in the internal affairs of nations. Its sole function to be the regulation of intercourse between nations in peace and war.

Court of Nations to be established by Congress; judges to hold office during good behavior. Decisions by majority vote. *Duties:* To offer advisory opinions in controversies voluntarily referred to it by the nations; to offer mediation in disputes threatening world peace; to suggest new legislation to the Congress. *Enforcement:* To be only by the force of public opinion.

JUAN FRANCISCO SINERIZ
SPANISH
1839

Constitucion Europea, con cuya observancia se evitaran las guerras civiles, las nacionales y las revoluciones, y con cuya sancion se consolidará una paz permanente en Europa. (A European Constitution, a structure by means of which civil and national wars may be avoided and a permanent peace in Europe safeguarded.)

Sineriz feared the American States would be united and Europe would lose her influential position. He urged a *European Confederation* with a *Supreme Court*. The *Confederation* to function as an offensive and defensive alliance against aggressors within or outside of the *Confederation*. States to disarm, but maintaining sufficient troops to keep internal order.

Any nation refusing to abide by the decision of the *Supreme Court* is considered to have declared war on all the powers. Its obedience to the *Court's* decision to be enforced by military means.

Members of the *Supreme Court* to be appointed half by the rulers, half by the people. *Court* to decide disputes between nations and between peoples and their governments.

VICTOR CONSIDERANT
FRENCH
1840

De la politique générale et du rôle de la France en Europe, etc.
(Politics in general and the role of France in Europe.)

Victor Considérant maintained that English and Russian politics menaced Europe's peace. England sought profit for herself from the disputes of other nations, and Russia was seeking to expand both East and West. He proposed, therefore, that to protect themselves all the small nations of Europe confederate with France under her leadership. Then England and Russia would realize that they would have to join the Confederation. A regular *Congress of Europe* to be organized to decide all commercial and industrial matters, encourage art and science, and develop a Code of Law and a unified administration.

LIEUTENANT FERDINAND DURAND
FRENCH
1841

Tendances pacifiques de la Société Européene. (Peaceful Tendencies in the European Community.)

Urged that a *Federation* be organized under French supremacy. Once Russia also joined, the armies to be demobilized and organized into labor corps to carry out socially useful and necessary public works.

P. R. MARCHAND
FRENCH
1842

Nouveau Projet de Traité de Paix perpétuelle. (A New Project for a Treaty of Perpetual Peace.)

Proposes the establishment of a *federation* between Russia, England, Austria, France, and Prussia with a *Congress* consisting of their representatives. Europe reorganized as follows: Poland to be made independent; a Greek-Turkish Empire organized under a Russian prince (the Sultan and his family to be pensioned); the boundaries of France extended to the Rhine, and Belgium to become a part of France; German unity to be strengthened by consolidation with Holland and Denmark; Italy to become a federation with Switzerland joined to her but retaining her own form of government; Spain and Portugal also to federate.

England to have supreme authority over the seas, but guaranteeing their freedom. Other nations can then dispense with their fleets enabling England to reduce hers; should England misuse her power, the other nations to protect themselves by instituting an economic boycott.

Each state to have one representative in the *Congress* with decisions made by majority vote. The Russian representative to be the permanent presiding officer. The representatives to be instructed by their individual governments; sessions to be public.

The Union's authority to extend to matters affecting all nations whether or not they are members. The Union to be supported either through contributions by nations in proportion to their population and wealth, or from a duty on imports into the Union. The states to supply troops in proportion to their power, *also for wars of conquest to be undertaken by the Union.*

Independent judges invested with authority to decide disputes between states, or between one state and the citizen of another, or between citizens of two states. In disputes over maritime matters, half the judges to be appointed by England and half by the *Congress*.

The states to retain control over commerce and their colonies although the *Congress* may assume administration of some colonies.

Congress to intervene in the affairs of a state in case of civil war or overthrow of the existing dynasty. Decisions of the *Congress* to be carried out by armed force whenever necessary. *Congress* also to regulate international transport, undertake useful public works, encourage free trade; establish uniform currency, weights and measures.

Seat of the *Congress* to be federal territory — Rome, Constantinople, or Alexandria.

The author considered intervention in South America to be necessary, and suggested replacing the republican forms of government with parliamentary monarchies.

ELIHU BURRITT
AMERICAN
1848

Proposed that the International Peace Congress in Brussels work for the creation of a *Congress of Nations* to establish a Code of International Law. Burritt suggested that the Congress consist of one representative for every million of population to meet at Frankfort or Brussels. The Congress to appoint a *Committee on International Law* composed of eminent statesmen and jurists of different countries to study existing international law in the light of current and future needs and recommend new statutes to be adopted by the Congress. These statutes were then to be referred to the various national legislatures for their discussion and adoption.

Upon ratification of the International Code, a *High Court of Nations* to be organized with three jurists from each nation appointed for life to compose the *Bench of Judges*. The Court to decide all disputes between member nations according to the International Code.

Burritt suggested that the *Congress* be dissolved as soon as the *Court* was organized.

CHARLES SUMNER
AMERICAN
UNITED STATES SENATOR
1849

The Abolition of the War System in the Commonwealth of Nations.

Advocated a *Congress of Nations* with a high court of judicature or arbitration. He established an annual prize at Harvard College for the best dissertation by a student on organizing peace among nations.

PRINCE PETER VON OLDENBURG
Russian Army General; Grandson of Czar Paul
1863 and 1873

Thoughts of a Russian Patriot — Accord Among All Governments in the Interest of Peace and Humanity.

Prince Oldenburg not only wrote a great deal about his plan for peace but worked actively to secure its adoption by the rulers of Europe. From 1863 he traveled from one royal court to another discussing his plan with Napoleon III of France, the King of Prussia, Queen Victoria of England, Czar Alexander III of Russia, and others. To preserve the peace of Europe he suggested that:

(1) The civilized nations renounce war in principle, and the governments guarantee each other's territories.

(2) An *International Arbitration Commission* be established to settle disputes between nations.

(3) The strength of the armed forces be limited through an *International Convention*.

After the Franco-Prussian War, Oldenburg worked even more energetically for adoption of his plan. President Thiers of France, whose support he sought in 1872, protested: "What do you wish us to do? We are weak, we are the defeated. But the moment the victors propose disarmament we are ready to start negotiations."

He also sought the support of Wilhelm I, Emperor of Germany, and of Chancellor Bismarck to whom he outlined his plan in 1873. Oldenburg argued that Prussia, having been victorious over Austria, Denmark, and France, was now assured of her position in Europe and could afford to initiate a movement for peace. He suggested that French dreams of revenge could best be prevented by a determined effort to secure Europe's peace. The Church, the monarchical system, and society in general would be strengthened through the resulting reduction in taxes, improvements in education, development of science, better conditions for the workers, and increased expenditures for social services.

Oldenburg's nephew, Prince Elimar von Oldenburg, a German General, shared his interest in peace efforts and objected to the military regulation forbidding members of the armed forces from participating in social movements. He believed it was a soldier's duty not only to defend his nation in time of war but even more to defend it by preventing war.

HENRY RICHARD
WELSH
1873

Introduced a motion in the House of Commons while a Member of Parliament, asking for "the establishment of a general and permanent system of *arbitration*." The motion was carried by a majority of ten. Similar resolutions were introduced in the parliaments of Canada, Italy, Belgium, Holland, Denmark, and the United States.

BARONESS BERTHA VON SUTTNER
AUSTRIAN
1889

Die Waffen Nieder. (Ground Arms.)

Her novel led to the foundation of the popular peace movement in Europe. It dramatized the need for arbitration, disarmament, and world organization. By 1907, the book had gone through thirty-eight editions. Baroness Suttner inspired Alfred Nobel to establish the Nobel Prizes. She was a tireless speaker, writer, and organizer of efforts to prevent war, to stop those that had broken out (the Boer War), and to organize a Union of European States.

JEAN DE BLOCH
Russian, born Polish.
Banker and Political Economist
1897

The War of the Future in its Technical, Economic, and Political Relations. (6 vols.)

Bloch was the first to point out the destructive nature of *modern* war, and to state that even a successful war would disorganize society completely, because:

(1) Implements of destruction in modern warfare are so deadly that an unprecedented mortality rate was inevitable.

(2) Mobilization for war of the whole male population would produce results destructive to the state and to the complex economy of modern society.

This study appeared first in Russian in 1897, and was immediately published in several languages: German, in 1899; French, and Polish in 1900; English, with a conversation between Bloch and W. T. Stead, and an introduction by Edwin D. Mead, in 1902.

This work made a profound impression on Czar Nicholas II of Russia, and on governmental and financial circles in Europe. It was one of the chief influences which impelled the Czar to call the first Hague Conference in 1899.

Bloch organized an anti-war exhibit for the Paris Exposition of 1900, and subsequently gave the collection, with funds for its upkeep, to Lucerne, Switzerland, as a permanent anti-war exhibit.

WILLIAM T. STEAD
English Journalist and Organizer
About 1899

Advocated gradual establishment of the *United States of Europe* under the leadership of England and Germany, finally embracing the world. In the meantime, Stead favored maintaining the Concert of Europe as the nucleus of a United States of Europe; establishing peace among the colored races of Asia, Polynesia, and Africa. He favored uniting all branches of the English-speaking race in an *Anglo-Saxon Bund* to spread Liberty, Civilization, and Christianity throughout the world; he advocated arbitration in general and of the Boer War in particular.

RICHARD BARTHOLDT
AMERICAN
1905

As member of the Congress of the United States and President of the American Group of the Inter-Parliamentary Union, Congressman Bartholdt urged the Union at its thirteenth conference, in Brussels in August, 1905, to adopt the recommendation of the American Group that the Second Hague Conference be urged to establish a *Union of Nations* with a *legislature,* a *judiciary,* and an *executive.* All nations joining the Union to be guaranteed their territorial and political integrity and local sovereignty, equal opportunities in international trade, and participation in the decisions of the *International Congress.*

Nations could withdraw from membership in the Union on three years' notice. National legislatures to have the right to veto acts of the International Congress, and no nation to be limited in its armaments.

Bartholdt suggested that the International Congress have two houses — a *Senate* with equal membership, and a *House* with membership in proportion to each nation's international commerce rather than population.

Bartholdt did not believe the Union should have military and naval power to enforce its decisions.

PART III

THEORETICAL PLANS

CHARTS OF PLANS TO UNITE NATIONS SINCE 1914

A. UNIVERSAL FEDERAL PLANS

"In the future days which we seek to make secure, we look forward to a world founded upon four essential human freedoms.

"The first is freedom of speech and expression — everywhere in the world.

"The second is freedom of every person to worship God in his own way — everywhere in the world.

"The third is freedom from want which, translated into world terms, means economic understanding which will secure to every nation a healthy peacetime life for its inhabitants — everywhere in the world.

"The fourth is freedom from fear which, translated into world terms, means a worldwide reduction of armaments to such a point and in such a thorough fashion that no nation will be in a position to commit an act of physical aggression against any neighbor — anywhere in the world.

"That is no vision of a distant millennium. It is a definite basis for a kind of world attainable in our own time and generation."
     FRANKLIN D. ROOSEVELT, Washington, January 6, 1941.

"Past failures have not dimmed our hopes that an effective world instrument to dispense and enforce justice will arise from the terrors, sufferings and sacrifices of this war; for such an international government, China, with all other liberty-loving nations, will gladly cede such of its sovereign powers as may be required." T. V. SOONG, China; New Haven, June 9, 1942.

"We have seen our globe in no time turned into one armed camp. We can transform it as quickly into a fit home for the human family."
    LOLA MAVERICK LLOYD and ROSIKA SCHWIMMER
      (*Chaos, War, or a New World Order*, 1942).

THE WORLD OF 1914

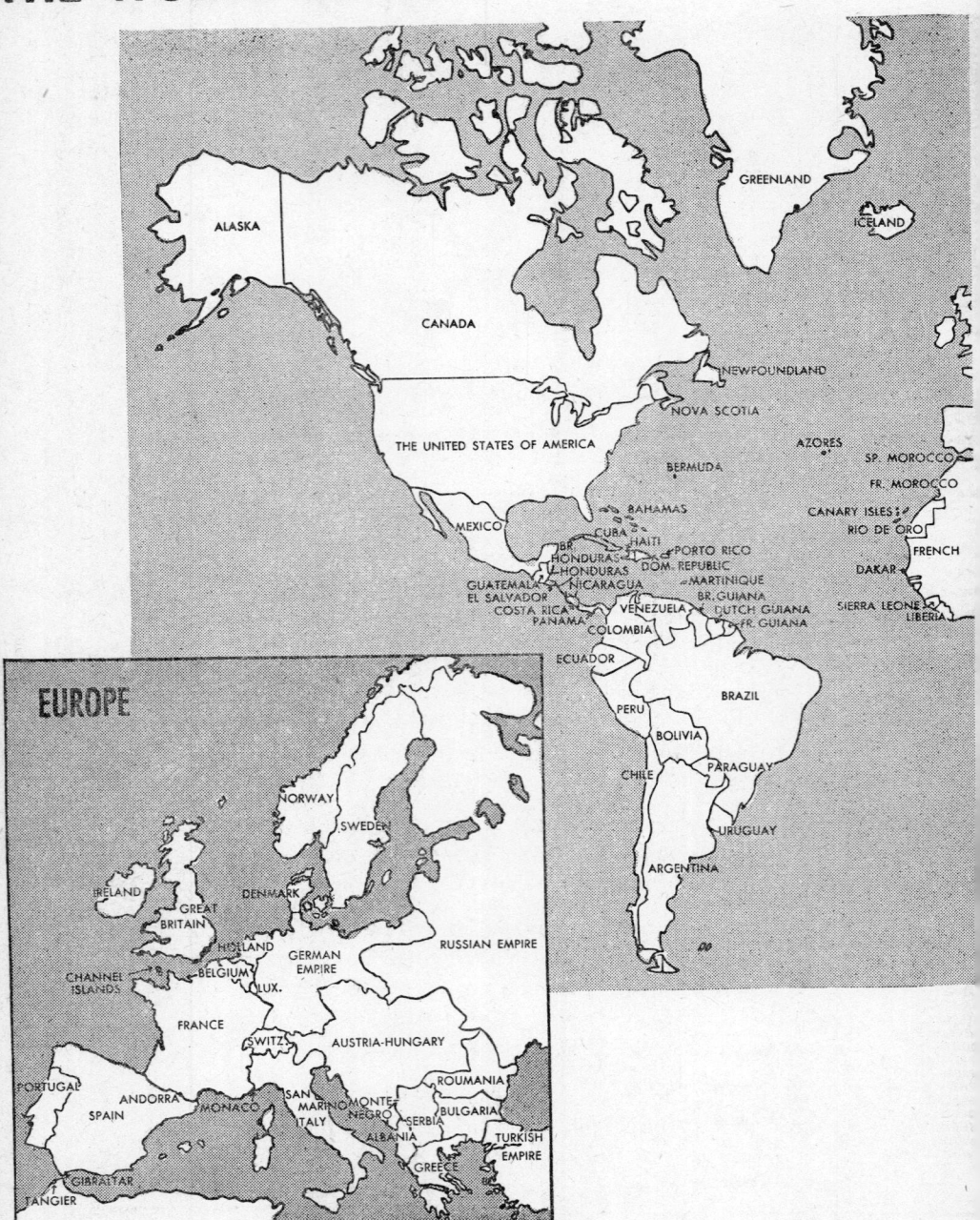

RUSSIAN EMPIRE

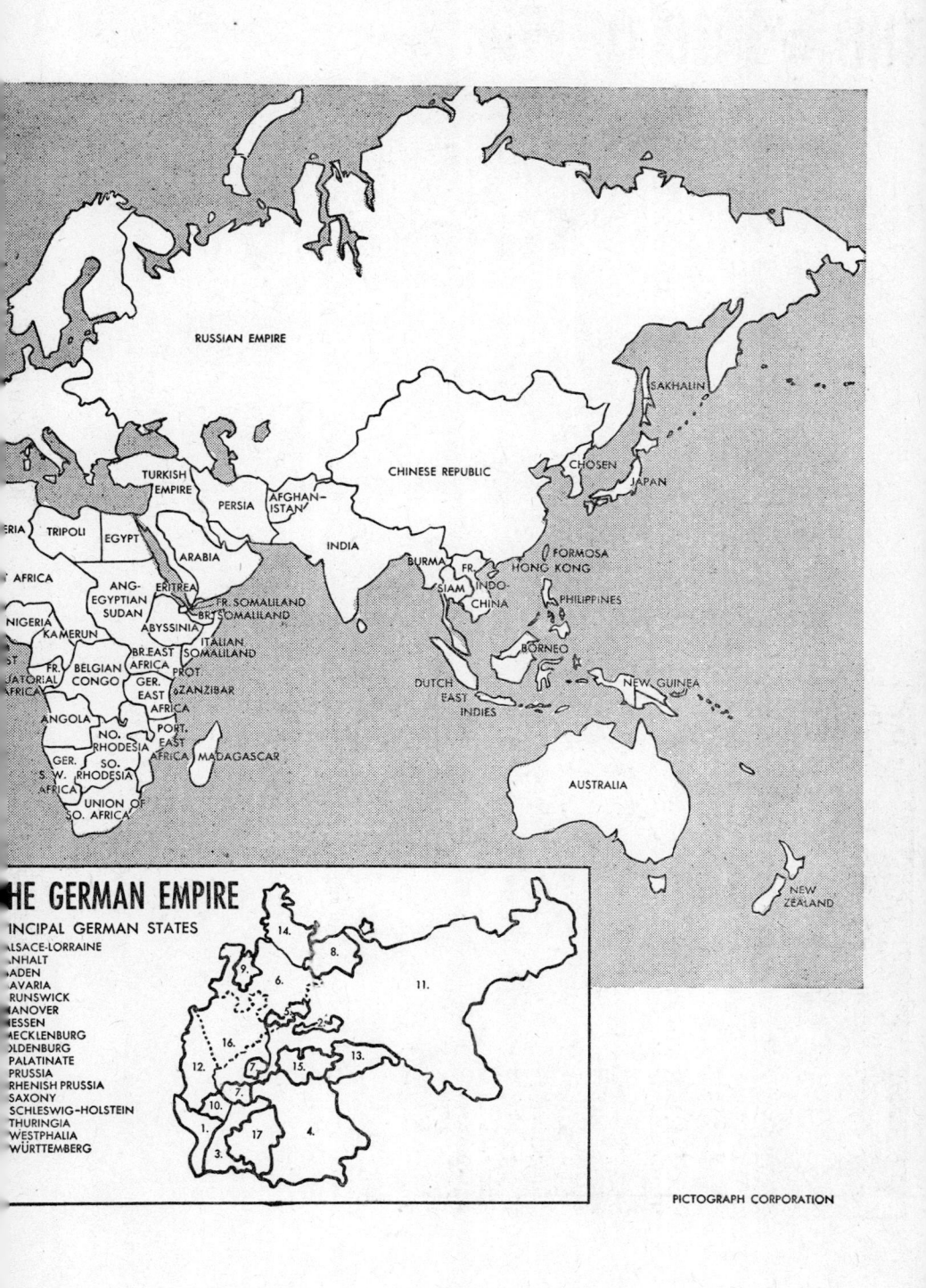

TURKISH EMPIRE
PERSIA
AFGHANISTAN
CHINESE REPUBLIC
CHOSEN
SAKHALIN
JAPAN

TRIPOLI
EGYPT
ARABIA
INDIA
BURMA
FR. SIAM
INDO-CHINA
FORMOSA
HONG KONG

AFRICA
ANG-EGYPTIAN SUDAN
ERITREA
FR. SOMALILAND
BR. SOMALILAND
ABYSSINIA
PHILIPPINES

NIGERIA
KAMERUN
BR. EAST AFRICA
ITALIAN SOMALILAND
PROT.
GER. EAST AFRICA
ZANZIBAR
BORNEO
DUTCH EAST INDIES
NEW GUINEA

FR. EQUATORIAL AFRICA
BELGIAN CONGO

ANGOLA
NO. RHODESIA
PORT. EAST AFRICA
MADAGASCAR
GER. S.W. AFRICA
SO. RHODESIA
AUSTRALIA

UNION OF SO. AFRICA

NEW ZEALAND

THE GERMAN EMPIRE

PRINCIPAL GERMAN STATES

ALSACE-LORRAINE
ANHALT
BADEN
BAVARIA
BRUNSWICK
HANOVER
HESSEN
MECKLENBURG
OLDENBURG
PALATINATE
PRUSSIA
RHENISH PRUSSIA
SAXONY
SCHLESWIG-HOLSTEIN
THURINGIA
WESTPHALIA
WÜRTTEMBERG

PICTOGRAPH CORPORATION

THE WORLD OF 1938

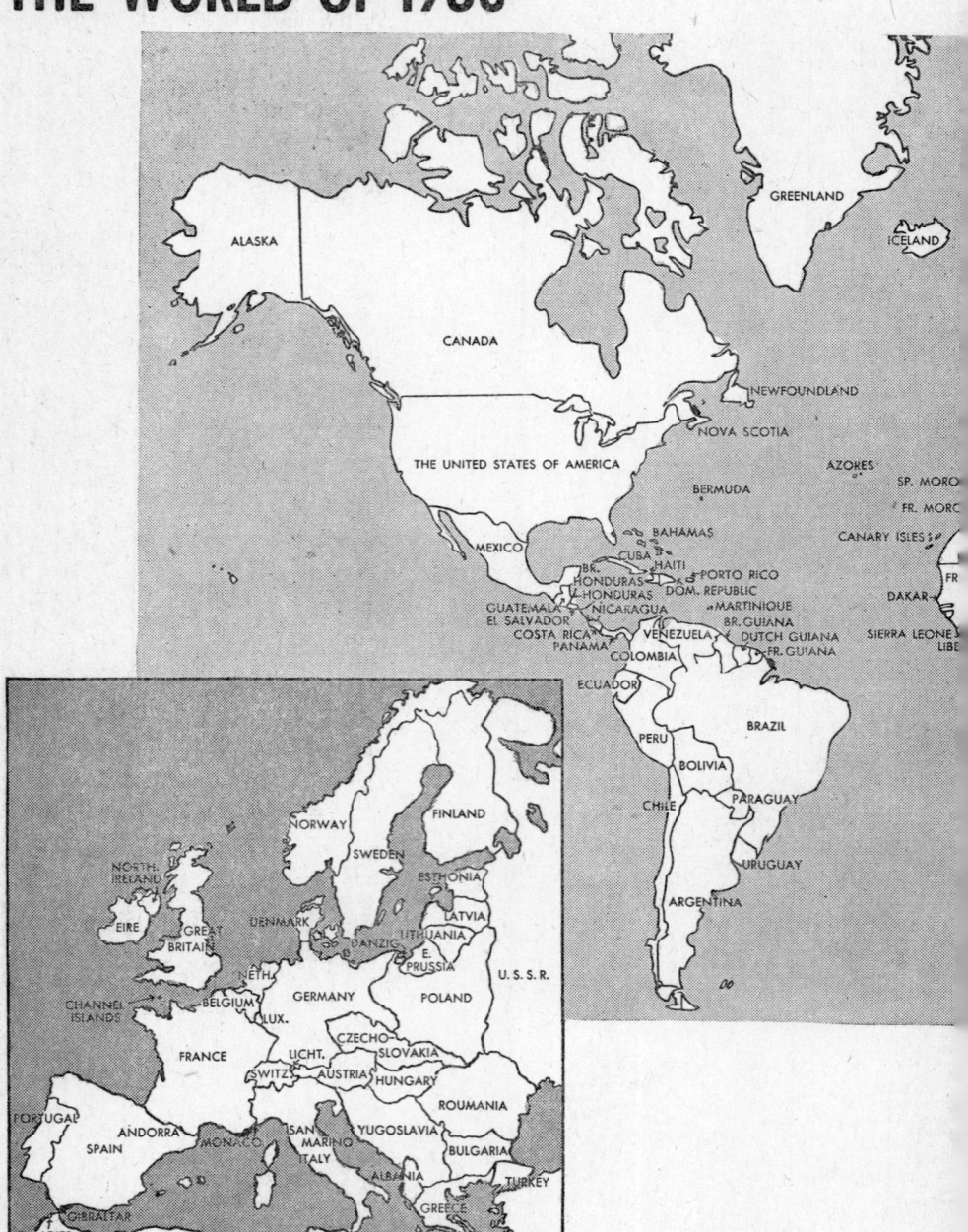

UNION OF SOVIET SOCIALIST REPUBLICS

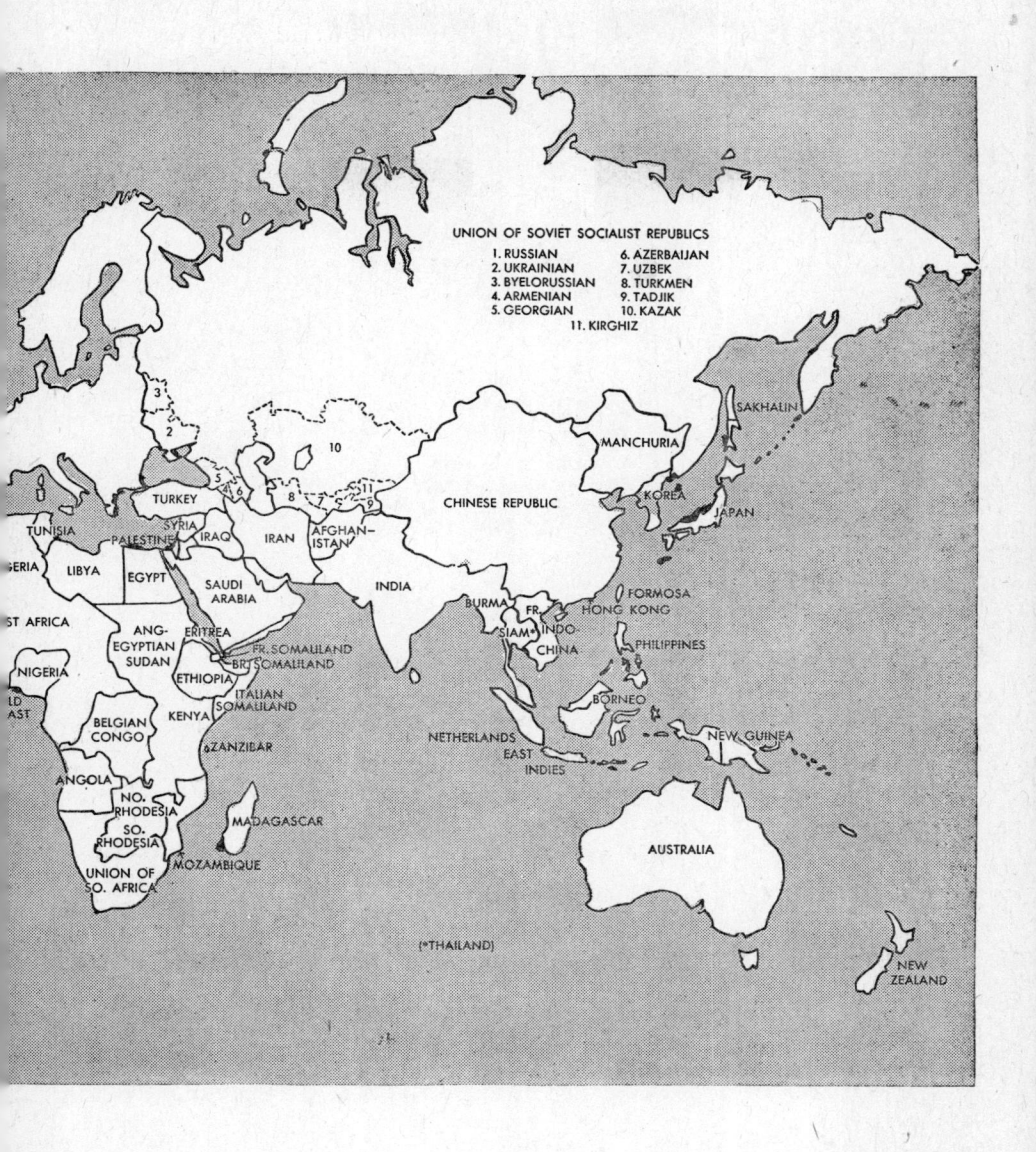

1. RUSSIAN
2. UKRAINIAN
3. BYELORUSSIAN
4. ARMENIAN
5. GEORGIAN
6. AZERBAIJAN
7. UZBEK
8. TURKMEN
9. TADJIK
10. KAZAK
11. KIRGHIZ

PICTOGRAPH CORPORATION

FEDERAL PLANS

It is interesting to find among the federal plans for world organization charted in this section, two plans written in 1918, using the title *United Nations*.

Of the women whose plans we charted, four propose federal structure with worldwide membership.

The Swiss Committee for the Preparation of the League of Nations (1918) was like a small constitutional convention. Its thirty-four members were of different nationalities and professions, several legislators being among them. Theirs is the only federal plan which proposes to abolish the Federal Defense Department as soon as universal membership is achieved. The plan recommends that for the first ten to twenty years after the war, only citizens of nations neutral during the war should head the federal departments to insure impartiality of administration.

Two federal plans (Minor's and Brewer's) provide for expulsion of member nations who do not live up to their constitutional obligations. In federal plans this suggestion is unusual. Existing federations do not permit either expulsion or secession. Minor also provides for return to the expelled nation of its share of the Union's assets.

Newfang revised the League Covenant to develop the League into a federal government.

Three war-time plans (Crozier, Swiss Committee, and Lloyd-Schwimmer) urge the establishment of world government by neutral, legislative, or popular unofficial action as the only secure basis for cessation of hostilities.

Three of the plans (Habicht, Lloyd-Schwimmer, Johnson) specifically oppose the military coercion of states, and provide for the enforcement of federal laws on individuals.

Byng's plan presents a detailed outline for a five-year transition period after the war.

Howard O. Eaton's *Proposed Constitution of the United Nations* (Federation: The Coming Structure of World Government, 1944; not charted here), follows closely the United States Constitution. However, he adds features of parliamentary forms of government by providing a Premier as the executive with Ministers of State and Finance. A vote of no confidence by absolute majority of Congress compels the Premier to resign. The United Nations are to initiate the Federation; non-belligerents may join immediately and keep their neutral status for the duration of the present war.

AUTHOR:
ALFRED OWEN CROZIER (American).

PROFESSION:
Attorney and Writer.

TITLE OF PLAN:
A Nation of Nations, the Way to Permanent Peace, a Supreme Constitution for the Government of Governments.

DATE: 1915.

PUBLISHER:
Stewart & Kidd Co., Cincinnati, Ohio.

TYPE:
FEDERAL: Some of its features modeled on Canadian, Australian Federal Constitutions.
NAME: Nation of Nations.

MEMBERSHIP:
UNIVERSAL: Any civilized nation with a population of two million or more. Nations not participating in proceedings settling World War and establishing Nation of Nations must apply for membership, but are to be accepted on equal terms.

ORGANS OF GOVERNMENT:
LEGISLATIVE: Bicameral: *Supreme Senate; Supreme Council.*
Supreme Senate: Seven-year term; candidate must have been a Cabinet Minister or President of his nation; representatives apportioned as follows:

1 for every nation with population of 20 million or less.
3 for every nation with population between 20 and 50 million.
5 for every nation with population of 50 million or over.

Sessions: Every two years or as often as President and Council request.

Duties: To make international laws for conduct of nations; elect President and three Vice-Presidents; elect one-half of membership of Supreme Council.

Decisions: Two-thirds vote necessary to veto President's orders on law enforcement or concerning the armed forces; override President's veto; impeach President, Vice-Presidents, Council Members, Ministers, Justices; concur in declaration of war. Three-fourths vote necessary to exercise supreme veto of any executive, administrative, or judicial decision by any branch of the Nation of Nations; require performance of given act by any department or employee; impeach Senators.

Ministers of Departments may participate in deliberations of Supreme Senate, but vote only if they are also Senators. Senators are elected by nations they represent.

Supreme Council: Seven-year staggered terms; fourteen regular members; two chosen each year: one by President with consent of Council (also removable by President and two-thirds vote of Council); one chosen by Senate (also removable by two-thirds vote of Senate). Additional members: three Vice-Presidents — ex-officio voting members; Ministers of Departments.

Duties: Appoints Ministers of Peace, Business, Justice, Laws, Finance, Human Welfare, Works and Waterways, Navy and War; fixes salaries of all officials; fills Presidential vacancies.

Exclusive authority: To make appropriations, incur liabilities, borrow money, issue currency, decide legal tender, issue and regulate credit, adopt sound banking and international exchange systems, negotiate treaties and agreements.

Decisions: Two-thirds vote necessary to remove Ministers; require President to perform any lawful act; share with President control of armed forces and law enforcement; override President's veto; ratify treaties.

Subject to veto by President and amendment or repeal by two-thirds vote of Senate, Council issues Supreme Orders with effect of, and Administrative Orders without effect of general law.

EXECUTIVE:

Supreme President and three Vice-Presidents: Elected by Supreme Senate for seven-year terms. *Duties:* Commander-in-chief of army and navy (subject to two-thirds veto of Council and Senate); appoints all officials with advice and consent of Supreme Council and may dismiss them without cause (except Supreme Justices) with consent of Supreme Council; declares war with two-thirds of Supreme Senate concurring.

JUDICIAL:

General Supreme Court: Fifteen Supreme Justices (not more than three from any one nation) appointed for life by President with consent of Supreme Council; removable without stated cause by two-thirds Senate vote, or by President if Council and majority of Senate approve.

Jurisdiction: Over questions involving the Constitution, international laws, treaties, or acts of the Nation of Nations. May act, *on request*, as final appeal from Supreme Courts of member nations, to compose differences between countries *voluntarily* submitting to a decision.

Powers: May create subordinate courts.

TRANSFERS OF JURISDICTION FROM MEMBER NATIONS TO THE NATION OF NATIONS:

Assumes authority over all member nations.

Apportions taxes between nations on basis of representation in Supreme Senate.

Exercises exclusive jurisdiction over all seas and waters more than three miles outside exterior boundaries or possessions of all organized sovereign nations.

Exercises exclusive control over all lands not yet owned.

Establishes and maintains self-government in backward areas.

Provides temporary administration to restore order in nations where civil government has ceased to exist.

Administers territory ceded to Nation of Nations by member nations, inhabitants thereof concurring by majority vote.

Regulates armaments and redistributes them.
Requires surrender to Nation of Nations by gift, grant, or lease one-half of naval and auxiliary vessels and one-half of every class of armament of each member nation.
Accepts voluntary enlistment of citizens of member nations for Nation of Nations armed forces.
Has right of investigation within member nations to safeguard proper performance of obligations to Nation of Nations.

NATIONS RETAIN:
Exclusive jurisdiction of all matters within their own territory and possessions as long as legal rights of other nations and citizens are not involved.
Regulation of imports if applied equally to all other member nations. Control over domestic, social, industrial, financial, commercial, revenue, and business affairs.

METHODS OF ENFORCEMENT:
Toward Member Nations: May be suspended, expelled, or otherwise dealt with when —

(1) guilty of one year's default of police power tax lawfully levied against it;
(2) neglects or refuses to be represented for two years;
(3) neglects or refuses to comply with Constitution, orders and laws of Nation of Nations; and
(4) threatens or engages in armed conflict with another nation without approval of Nation of Nations, unless it is defending itself against attack.

Nation of Nations obliged to assist member nations wrongfully attacked and to organize assistance of other member nations, without power, however, to compel their assistance.

IMMEDIATE STEPS:
United States initiative to bring about a suspension of hostilities followed by a peace agreement providing for the creation of a Government of Governments in which every nation will be equally represented. If European nations refuse to join, an American Nation of Nations should be created.

PREREQUISITES TO PEACE:
United States must keep out of the war whatever the cost or provocation in order to maintain civilization's one great remaining balance, and organize a world conference or congress to settle the issues of the war.

LIQUIDATION OF THE WAR:
Temporary international administration to restore order in nations where civil government has ceased to exist.

TERRITORIAL CHANGES:
International administration of backward areas; of areas not yet owned by any nation; exclusive jurisdiction of seas and waters three miles outside of national boundaries.

AUTHOR:
THEODORE HARRIS (American).

TITLE OF PLAN:
A Proposed Constitution for the United Nations of the World.

PAMPHLET

DATE: 1918.

PUBLISHER:
C. F. Ruckstuhl Inc., New York.

TYPE:
FEDERAL: Modeled on United States Constitution.
NAME: United Nations.

MEMBERSHIP:
UNIVERSAL: All nations with capacity for self-government.

ORGANS OF GOVERNMENT:
LEGISLATIVE: Bicameral *Congress: House* and *Senate.*

House: Four-year term; directly elected by voters qualified to vote for the most numerous branch of their national legislature; one representative for every two million of population or fraction thereof; representatives at least thirty years old and citizens for seven years of nations they are to represent. Vacancies filled by national executive. *Quorum:* Members from two-thirds of nations represented.

Senate: Eight-year term; ten Senators from each nation; elected by national legislatures. Expiration of term of office staggered; each Senator one vote; at least forty years old; nine years citizen of nation represented. Vice-President is President of the Senate, voting only in case of a tie. Senate has sole power to try impeachments — conviction by two-thirds vote. *Quorum:* Two-thirds of all Senators.

EXECUTIVE OR ADMINISTRATIVE:
President and *Vice-President* chosen by electors (appointed by national legislatures) equal to the number of representatives in United Nations Congress. Electors meeting in own nation vote on separate ballots for President and Vice-President, one of whom must be of a different nationality from that of the electors. Lists of all persons voted for with number of votes for each must be certified and sent to United Nations Congress. President of Senate before joint meeting of Congress counts votes for each office. Candidate receiving majority vote of all electors is President. If no candidate has majority, House chooses President by ballot from three highest on list: voting by national delegations, each delegation having one vote. If no majority for Vice-President, Senate chooses from two highest on list.

Duties of President: Commander-in-chief of army, navy, and of national militias when they are in United Nations service; makes treaties with two-thirds concurrence of Senate; appoints officers with consent of Senate; grants reprieves and pardons for offenses against United Nations.

JUDICIAL:
Supreme Court: Original Jurisdiction — in cases involving treaties, ambassadors, ministers, consuls; admiralty and maritime cases; also cases to which United Nations is party, or between two or more member nations, a nation and citizens of another nation, citizens of different nations, or a citizen of the United Nations and a foreign nation, or its citizens, or subjects; interpretation of United Nations Constitution. *Appellate jurisdiction* in other cases.

TRANSFERS OF JURISDICTION FROM MEMBER NATIONS TO THE UNITED NATIONS:
Congress has authority to levy and collect taxes, duties (except export duties), imposts, excises; provide for common defense and general welfare, but federal laws must apply equally to all nations; regulate commerce between member nations and with foreign nations; coin money, determine its value; create courts inferior to the Supreme Court; declare war; raise and support armies (but appropriations for this purpose cannot be made for a term longer than four years); maintain a navy; administer all property acquired from member nations.

No nation may keep troops or ships in peace time, declare war, or make treaties or alliances with foreign nations.

NATIONS RETAIN:
Equal suffrage in the Senate (Constitution cannot be amended in this respect).
Right to appoint officers of militia and supervise its training in accordance with disciplinary regulations of Congress.
Right to levy duties on imports to defray costs of inspection, subject to revision by Congress.

METHODS OF ENFORCEMENT:
Toward Non-Member Nations: Use of army and navy in case of hostilities. *Toward Member Nations:* In case of insurrection or disorder, federal troops can intervene only on request of national government. Individuals are protected by Bill of Rights modeled after that in United States Constitution.

RATIFICATION:
No provisions made.

AMENDMENT:
By two-thirds vote of both Houses of Congress, or legislative bodies of two-thirds of Member Nations may call a convention to propose amendments to be ratified by three-fourths of national legislatures, or by conventions in three-fourths of the nations.

MISCELLANEOUS:
Suggests that after the War Germany might be governed temporarily

as a federal territory until ability to govern herself has been proved. Suggests similar procedure be applied to China, Russia, and Mexico.

AUTHOR:
Swiss Committee for the Preparation of the League of Nations (34 members).

PROFESSIONS represented:
Three journalists; three lawyers; four ministers of religion; twelve national councilors; one ex-President of the National Council; one senator; four professors; one judge; one President of a peace organization; one public prosecutor; two representatives of local government.

TITLE OF PLAN:
Draft of the Constitution of a Universal League of Nations.

PAMPHLET

DATE: March 16, 1918.

PUBLISHER and supporting organization:
Swiss Committee for the Preparation of the League of Nations, Berne, Switzerland.

TYPE:
Federal: Modeled on Swiss Constitution.
Names used: Union of Nations, World Union of Nations, Universal Union of Nations.

MEMBERSHIP:
Universal.

ORGANS OF GOVERNMENT:
Legislative: Unicameral *World Council:* Five-year term; one delegate for every 500,000 persons entitled to vote; proportional system of voting, prescribed by member states with consent of World Council; equal, direct suffrage for men and women satisfying minimum

educational requirement fixed by World Council. *Delegates:* At least thirty years of age; citizens of state which elects them. *Duties:* Exercises supreme legislative, administrative, and legal functions; elects President and Vice-President who retain right to vote in Council; nominates naval and military commanders.

Decisions of Council: Elimination or alteration of old laws or creation of new ones requires unanimous vote. (*Unanimity rule proposed as temporary measure to dispel nations' fear of coercion.*) "Free Resolutions" (supported only by majority of Council) binding on League members whose national parliaments have ratified them; such regulations may be administered by Union if expense is refunded by participating nations.

EXECUTIVE OR ADMINISTRATIVE:

Committee of Elders: Members of longest service in Council; decide convocation and duration of meetings of World Council.

Business Committee: Draws agenda of Council.

Six Federal Departments: Appointed by Federal Council:

> *Home Office:* Education, press, reform, hygiene, and others.
> *Production and Trade:* Agriculture, industry, trade, consumer interests, transportation, communication, Federal Finance Office.
> *Colonies:* Education, production, defense.
> *Foreign Department:* Public law, intelligence service.
> *Federal Defense:* Land, naval, federal armament monopoly.
> *Justice:* Various courts — see judicial.

JUDICIAL:
Federal Tribunal: Offenses against federal laws; final court of appeal.

Court of Arbitration: Lawsuits between Federal States; States suing Federal Departments.

Court of Administration: Questions of jurisdiction between departments; misdemeanor of federal officials.

Federal Advocacy: Prosecution of offenses against federal laws; execution of sentences of federal criminal court.

Federal Criminal Court; Federal Divorce Court; Election Scrutiny Board: Examines disputed ballots (in federal elections) ex-officio or on appeal. *Professional Courts of Honor:* Pass judgment on insults and threats to institutions and organizations of Union in all countries or nations connected with it. Private appeals against decisions of various departments.

TRANSFERS OF JURISDICTION FROM MEMBER NATIONS TO THE UNION:

To *guarantee* members' frontiers, and their constitutions as far as they are not in conflict with Union Constitution.

To *defend* them against attack by non-members; restore order within a nation *on request of its representatives* in the World Council; Union to be reimbursed for expense of such intervention.

To *introduce* universal artificial language compulsory for all Union officials two years after adoption.

To *punish* those who orally, in writing, or otherwise insult or threaten Union, or its organizations.

To *impose* penalties for unfair commercial competition: subsidies, dumping.

To *control* communications: railway, naval, road, and air transportation open to all Union members.

To *administer* colonies through a Colonial Office; their right to self-determination safeguarded; existing colonial institutions and officials retained for ten years from date of adoption of Constitution.

All *Union members* to have equal rights in colonial territory; all colonial receipts to be used for development of colonies and expenses of Colonial Office.

To *maintain* Union army and navy (contributed by member nations in proportion to representation in Council) for defense against non-member nations; *as soon as membership is universal, Federal Defense Department to be abolished.*

Union supported by contributions of member states in proportion to representation in World Council.

Union Foreign Office to conduct members' dealings with non-members until membership is universal; no member nation to negotiate political treaties — all existing ones to be dissolved or adapted to Union's legal requirements.

RESTRICTIONS ON THE UNION:
Union can create administrative subdivisions as necessitated by growth,

but these must not violate unity of federal organization, its constitution, or equality of rights and duties of individual states.

RESTRICTIONS ON NATIONS:
Member nations prohibited from having heavy armament or maintaining military troops; police, fire-brigade, and local militia only for internal security. Federal Defense Department to standardize strength and training to prevent abuse.

NATIONS RETAIN:
Right to negotiate certain treaties with other member states as to judicial relations, poor-laws, extradition, etc., as long as no other member state is at disadvantage; treaties with non-members must be approved by World Council. National control of immigration must apply equally to all members. In event of disagreement, states pledge to submit to Union authorities, and to World Council as final court of appeal.

NATIONS GUARANTEE:
Freedom of language and religion to their people.

METHODS OF ENFORCEMENT:
Toward Individuals: Procedure through various Federal Courts.

Toward Member Nations: For failure to fulfill obligations — confiscation of customs duties, or coercive administration as determined by Council.

Toward Non-Member Nations: No coercion whatever; Union armed forces not to leave Federal territory unless threat of attack is proved. When universal membership has been achieved, defense sections of Constitution are to be repealed.

IMMEDIATE STEPS:
Inter-Parliamentary Conference, to be called to a neutral country, representing *legislative bodies* of all nations prepared in principle to create Union.

Duties: To draft *Provisional Constitution and Statutes* of Union to be submitted for ratification to national parliaments. Hostilities to cease between nations ratifying Constitution. When a sufficient number of nations ratify Constitution to assure its successful operation and permanence, Inter-Parliamentary Conference to constitute itself a *Provisional World Council.*

Duties: To organize elections to World Council in all countries entering the Union; arrange for seat of World Council and details for its meeting; disband upon first convention of elected World Council which must convene immediately after election.

PREREQUISITES TO PEACE:
Belligerents must abandon demands that can be satisfied only by crushing their opponents; they must attach greater importance to obtaining lasting peace than to military or material success; abandon forcible attempts at changing frontiers or forms of government, relying on democratizing influence of a legalized and efficiently protected community of nations; no attempts should be made to conquer nations not incorporated originally in the Union.

LIQUIDATION OF THE WAR:
World Council to appoint *Temporary Committee* to aid in restoration of districts damaged or destroyed by war. Subcommissions to determine sums necessary for restoration of economic life. Amounts to be assessed among individual nations in proportion to war-profit taxes raised by them.

TERRITORIAL CHANGES:
Colonies administered by Federal Colonial Office.
Ten years after establishment of Union, single provinces desiring separation from a nation can do so if 75 per cent of their inhabitants wish it because their economic and cultural development is being hindered; because States governing them will not rectify these grievances; and if they are able to assume their proportionate share of obligations of membership in the Union.

RATIFICATION:
By national parliaments.

MISCELLANEOUS:
During first ten to twenty years after Union Constitution has come into force, only subjects of nations neutral in the World War can be

directors or managers of Federal Departments. Exceptions permissible only on unanimous vote of Council.

Any nation can declare its adherence to Union conditional on entry of another nation into Union, but such reservations subject to time limit terminating before meeting of first elected World Council.

Suggest decentralization of the government by locating different Federal Departments in various neutral cities, temporarily at least. Until a universal artificial language is adopted, English, French, and German are to be used in all Federal transactions.

AUTHOR:
RALEIGH COLSTON MINOR (American).

PROFESSION:
Professor of Constitutional and International Law.

TITLE OF PLAN:
A Republic of Nations — A Study of the Organization of a Federal League of Nations.

DATE: May, 1918.

PUBLISHER:
Oxford University Press, American Branch, New York.

TYPE:
FEDERAL. NAME: United Nations.

MEMBERSHIP:
UNIVERSAL.

ORGANS OF GOVERNMENT:
LEGISLATIVE: Bicameral *Congress of the United Nations: Senate; House of Delegates.*

House of Delegates: One delegate for every four million of population; each nation at least one; method of election prescribed by national laws; national delegations to vote as a unit or as instructed. In deciding the basis of representation, the *whole number of white* persons are to be counted, and *one-third of all the others* except Japanese, who are to be counted as white.

Senate: Two Senators for each nation, elected according to national laws and to vote as national laws direct.

Congress is to be in perpetual session; no recess to exceed four months.

Quorum: A majority in each house. *Decisions:* By majority vote.

A Census is to be taken every ten years; the first, five years after the first session of Congress.

EXECUTIVE OR ADMINISTRATIVE:

Prime Minister: Elected by Congress as follows: Eight Senators and eight Delegates appointed by the respective houses, nominate for each house, three members for Prime Minister; the candidate receiving a majority of ballots of both houses becomes Prime Minister; if no candidate receives a majority, new nominating committees are appointed and the whole procedure is repeated. The Prime Minister may be recalled by majority vote of either house of Congress.

Powers: Negotiates treaties with non-member nations with advice and consent of two-thirds vote of Congress; appoints and removes officers and ambassadors of the United Nations; enforces its laws; grants pardons, etc.

Council of Ministers: Members of Congress and others appointed by the Prime Minister (no two Council Ministers shall be of the same nation); members of Congress serving as Ministers to receive compensation in addition to their salaries as Congressmen.

JUDICIAL:

Supreme Court: The executive authority of each member nation appoints an equal number of justices to the Court; the Court then divides by lot into three equal sections:

First Section: Jurisdiction in controversies affecting ambassadors or ministers, disputes between member nations, between the United Nations and a member nation, and between non-member nations with their consent.

Second Section: Final court of appeal in all civil cases between private persons.

Third Section: Hears and determines all criminal cases. The decision of any *Section* may be *appealed* to the three Sections sitting together.

Chief Justice: Presiding judge of the *First Section;* in case of a vacancy, all justices advance one degree in seniority.

General Jurisdiction: In all cases under the Constitution, laws, or treaties of the United Nations or treaties of member nations.

Power of Veto: Three-fourths vote of the Court can declare any law or treaty of the United Nations or of member nations unconstitutional.

TRANSFERS OF JURISDICTION FROM MEMBER NATIONS TO THE UNITED NATIONS:

Declare war; raise and support armies (but no appropriation for more than two years); provide and maintain a navy.

Call on armed forces of member nations to execute laws, suppress insurrections against the Government of the United Nations, and repel invasion.

Levy and collect taxes *on land* (sole form of taxation permitted the United Nations); pay debts of the United Nations; provide for their common defense, etc.

Issue currency, coin money, fix standards of weights and measures.

Borrow money through bond issues.

Regulate international commerce (laws not to be in force longer than ten years from passage).

Regulate international postal and other communications.

Provide for international patents and copyrights.

Constitute tribunals inferior to the Supreme Court.

Define and punish offenses committed on the high seas and against the Law of Nations.

Admit new states by three-fourths vote of both Houses of Congress.

Govern federal territory ceded by particular nations and territories purchased.

The Constitution, treaties, and laws of the United Nations are supreme.

RESTRICTIONS ON THE UNITED NATIONS:

Citizenship of the United Nations is to be restricted to persons born in the federal territory who have never been citizens of any nation, or citizens of member nations domiciled there at the time the district was ceded to the Union.

No crime of treason against the United Nations is to be recognized. The United Nations may not require member nations to reduce their troops below one-tenth of one per cent of their populations, nor their tonnage of ships below one per cent of their merchant fleets.

In case of internal dissension within a member nation, the United Nations is not to intervene, but must continue to recognize the de facto government until it is overthrown, when the new government is to be recognized.

NATIONS RETAIN:
Any member nation may veto a law passed by the United Nations Congress, if it believes the law violates its reserved-powers clause, by giving thirty days' notice through its delegation that it considers a veto. If the law is not vetoed within one year, it becomes binding. If vetoed, it may be voted again in each House and becomes binding if passed by a three-fourths vote.

Nations may regulate immigration and emigration.

May appoint officers and train national armed forces subject to United Nations regulations.

May secede after twenty-five years' membership and one year's notice, regaining complete sovereignty, territories, and adjustment of share of common property.

RESTRICTIONS ON MEMBER NATIONS:
May not enter into treaties on matters under the jurisdiction of the United Nations, or into alliance or confederation without consent of Congress.

May not levy a tax on commerce except what is necessary for enforcement of its inspection laws, subject to revision and control of Congress.

May not support an army in time of peace in excess of ten per cent of the troops and war vessels kept by the United Nations, or engage in war unless invaded, etc.

May not abridge the privileges and immunities of citizens of other states whether or not members of the United Nations.

INDIVIDUAL RIGHTS GUARANTEED:
Habeas corpus; freedom of religion, free speech; right of assembly and petition; equal protection under the law; speedy and public trial by jury.

METHODS OF ENFORCEMENT:
In the event a member nation refuses or neglects to fulfill its obligations under the Constitution and laws of the United Nations, Congress by three-fourths vote of both houses may decide on the following measures of enforcement:

1. Embargo a part or all of the nation's commerce with other nations.
2. Expel the nation from the Union, returning its common share of assets in it.

(The author is opposed to war as a disciplinary method, holding that it is contradictory to the fundamental principle of union — the preservation of peace.)

IMMEDIATE STEPS:
Calling a Conference of Nations to discuss the feasibility of some such plan of union.

RATIFICATION:
By approval of constitutional treaty-making power of each nation. Ratification of eight nations is sufficient to establish the Union, but five of them should be of the following: Austria-Hungary, France, Germany, Great Britain, Italy, Japan, Russia, and the United States.

AMENDMENT:
Must be proposed by two-thirds vote of both houses, passed by three-fourths vote in both houses, but only after four years from date proposed. Except that no nation may be deprived of its equal representation in the Senate, on the Supreme Court, proportional representation in the House, or of its right to veto an act of Congress, or to secede from the Union.

Charts of Plans to Unite Nations Since 1914

AUTHORS:
LOLA MAVERICK LLOYD (American); Feminist, pacifist leader.
ROSIKA SCHWIMMER (Stateless; born in Hungary); Journalist, lecturer, feminist, pacifist leader; first woman diplomat in modern history.

TITLE OF PLAN:
Chaos, War, or a New World Order. What We Must Do to Establish the All-inclusive, Non-military, Democratic Federation of Nations.

PAMPHLET:
and from Manuscript.

DATE: November 1942 (previous editions: 1924, 1937, 1938).

PUBLISHER:
The Campaign for World Government, Chicago, Illinois.

ORGANIZATIONAL BACKING (of the 1938 edition):
The Campaign for World Government; The Hungarian and Swedish Sections of the Women's International League for Peace and Freedom.

TYPE:
FEDERAL. NAME: Federation of Nations.

MEMBERSHIP:
UNIVERSAL: One class of membership for all.

ORGANS OF GOVERNMENT:
LEGISLATIVE: Unicameral *World Parliament:* Ten-year term.
Ten *Delegates* and ten *Alternates* from each nation; men and women equally eligible; subject to recall by own electorate; uniform election by Proportional Representation irrespective of system used in national elections. *Disqualification:* Government officials and high ranking officers of the armed forces may not serve as Delegates or Alternates; may be invited to serve as occasional experts without the right to vote on decisions. Votes of Delegates to count individually, not as national units. *Decisions:* By majority vote. Temporary or permanent vacancies to be filled by Alternates. *Sessions* first three months of every year,

to be prolonged or reassembled by vote of the delegates; all sessions public; official summary of proceedings to be furnished daily to the press. Elects its own president and vice-president; the *Executive Board* (of the Federation), *Administrative Commissions, Permanent, and Regional Secretaries.*

EXECUTIVE OR ADMINISTRATIVE:

Executive Board; Permanent Secretary; Regional Secretaries; Regional Headquarters established for administrative purposes on each continent. Direct telegraph, telephone, and radio communication between World Capital and the continental offices. Operation of a *Central Broadcasting Station.*

Federal Economic Commission: Five to ten members, assisted by non-voting experts. *Duties:* To prepare recommendations to the World Parliament for internationalization and control of worldwide communication and transportation systems; establishment of a uniform monetary system, weights, and measures; abolition of tariffs and customs and establishment of free trade and commerce; regulation of world finance.

International Raw Materials Commission: (To control production and distribution of raw materials and prime necessities.) All member nations represented, assisted by expert advisers. *Duties:* To provide all human beings with the prime necessities of food, shelter, housing, health, and clothing; to allocate quotas of surplus raw materials of oil, coal, ores; and of surplus foods such as meats and grain; to fix prices of raw materials fair to both producing and consuming nations; to organize transport and supply; to regulate industrial and agricultural production of prime necessities to prevent both underproduction and overproduction. Nations dissatisfied with their quota allotment may appeal to a special Federal Court whose decisions are to be final.

Health Commission: To plan adequate public health service with special emphasis on preventive measures; to support scientific and practical research into all hygienic problems.

Commission on Education: To supervise revision of textbooks from a world point of view, emphasizing moral, economic, scientific, and artistic contributions to mankind's progress by all nations, races, classes, creeds, and both sexes; to provide educational opportunities for all children; to organize worldwide campaign to wipe out adult illiteracy.

Federal Peace Guard: Representatives of all member nations.

Duties: To institute proceedings before a special Federal Court against individuals, groups, organizations, and publications which tend to incite war; to publish full details of the charges and defense in each case, including the full facts, clearing all those falsely accused; those bringing accusations out of spite to be fined in addition to being made to pay all expenses of the suit and to be publicly branded as denouncers. No anonymous reports to be accepted. Convictions according to federal laws.

JUDICIAL:
Legal Commission: Five to ten members. *Duties:* To prepare the *Code of International Law;* to recommend executive machinery and a system of courts to replace the present diplomatic intercourse between nations. Some suggested courts: *Federal Courts* to settle disputes between nations and to receive cases on appeal from inferior federal courts, and from national courts; *Arbitration Courts* to settle disputes that may lead to civil war; *Criminal Courts; International Press-Juries, Courts of Honor,* and similar forums to protect the honor of nations and individuals. To make recommendations for the scientific observation and treatment of criminals.

TRANSFERS OF JURISDICTION FROM MEMBER NATIONS TO THE FEDERATION:
Control worldwide transportation and communication systems.
Establish a uniform currency, weights, and measures; regulate world finance.
Grant world citizenship to each human being and regulate the rights and duties of world citizens.
Establish free trade and commerce.
Allocate quotas and fix prices of raw materials.
Regulate industrial and agricultural production of prime necessities.
Provide adequate public health service and legalization of birth control.
Supervise revision of textbooks to emphasize world citizenship.
Supervise repatriation and resettlement of refugees.

Develop sparsely settled regions to attract dislocated populations (no compulsory migration).

Admit colonies as independent nations into the Federation when the populations ask for self-government.

Administer colonies and mandates, with populations which do not think themselves ready for self-government, through federal civilian commissions.

Prohibit establishment of new monarchies or reestablishment of old ones (existing monarchies to continue if populations wish to retain them).

Safeguard historically truthful presentation of news.

NATIONS RETAIN:
Autonomy in all matters not regulated by federal laws.

METHODS OF ENFORCEMENT:
World law to operate on individual world citizens and not on nations as a whole. No provision for military coercion.

IMMEDIATE STEPS:
Establishment by at least ten world-minded men and women of different national origin and indisputable integrity of an unofficial, self-constituted *Provisional World Government,* to continue in permanent session with full publicity. *Basic Qualifications:* Theoretical knowledge and practical experience in organizing and administration; uncompromising stand for the all-inclusive, non-military character of the World Federation, democratic in its own structure, with its laws operating directly on individuals instead of on nations. Men and women of all nationalities, creeds, and races to be equally eligible to all elective and appointive positions and offices if otherwise qualified. *Headquarters:* To be located temporarily in the United States or in any country where headquarters and working funds are provided.

Immediate Duties: To inform the world, using all existing means of communication, *of the establishment of the Provisional World Government,* its aims of justice, freedom, and equal opportunity to all peoples; to *appeal simultaneously for cessation of hostilities everywhere,* with the assurance that no military conquest will be recognized; armed forces to remain temporarily in the positions held when hostilities ended; all manufacture of war materials to be suspended.

International Demarcation Line Commission: To establish demarcation lines between the enemy forces and supervise their observance; to encourage local reconstruction work to occupy the local population, the immobilized war workers, and the foreign armed forces until the *Federal Reconstruction Commission* can assume direction of this work.

Committee of Constitutional Experts: Men and women who have participated in the drafting of modern constitutions and legal experts.

Duties: To *draft a World Constitution* for submission to the Provisional World Government and adoption by simple majority vote; to publicize in all languages and by all possible means the text of the World Constitution, the announcements to be repeated until the response (not necessarily acceptance) proves its reception in all parts of the world.

PREREQUISITES TO PEACE:
Establishment of Provisional World Government to negotiate simultaneous cessation of hostilities; to establish demarcation lines between the enemy forces; supervise suspension of armament manufacture, and organize preliminary reconstruction and relief.

LIQUIDATION OF THE WAR:
Commissions with *emergency powers* established by the Provisional World Government:

World Reconstruction Commission: Two to five members from every cooperating nation acceptable to the Provisional World Government, plus special experts irrespective of nationality. *Duties:* To organize systematic demobilization of the millions of soldiers; to organize scrapping of all war material and its conversion to reconstruction work; to initiate creative public works on a worldwide scale to absorb the demobilized armed forces (including their highest ranking officers), and all able-bodied unemployed men and women.

"Save the Human Race" Commission: (Organized as above).

Duties: To rush food, medical supplies, clothing, and other prime necessities to every country where famine, undernourishment, and disease threaten the human race.

Claims and Complaints Commission: (Organized as above). To receive, investigate, and prepare for submission to courts, to be established under the World Constitution, claims, complaints, and accusations against individuals, groups, or nations.

TERRITORIAL CHANGES:
Planned liquidation, under world government, of empires, colonies, and mandates; self-government or temporary federal administration to be determined in every case by the local populations themselves.

RATIFICATION:
Ratification of the Constitution of the *Federation of Nations* by at least ten nations, irrespective of their size, geographical location, or form of government; *authorizes the Provisional World Government* to organize elections to the World Parliament.

MISCELLANEOUS:
The authors recommend English as the auxiliary world language to be taught in the schools of the non-English-speaking nations. To achieve worldwide bilinguality the English-speaking nations to agree on one auxiliary language to be taught in their schools.

The World Parliament is to count its official time from the year of its establishment as being the most important date in world history. Every nation, race, and religion is free to continue its traditional reckoning of time.

The authors also suggest complete separation of Church and State, with full freedom of worship to religious individuals and freedom of conscience to irreligious persons.

This plan was first drafted in 1924, and presented to the Women's International League for Peace and Freedom. The first three editions provided alternative action by governments or by the people. Between the 1937 edition, and the publication of the 1942 enlarged edition, the Campaign for World Government initiated and supported a great number of bills in Congress and in several state legislatures providing for governmental action to establish world government. As governmental action was not forthcoming, the 1942 edition of the plan stresses immediate popular initiative starting with the establishment of a Provisional World Government.

Charts of Plans to Unite Nations Since 1914

AUTHOR:
H. J. PAINTIN (English).

PROFESSION:
Publisher.

TITLE OF PLAN:
The League of Nations at the Bar of Public Opinion, and the Federation of Man.

DATE: 1926.

PUBLISHER:
Paintin & Simpson.

TYPE:
FEDERAL. NAME: Federation of Man.

MEMBERSHIP:
UNIVERSAL.

ORGANS OF GOVERNMENT:
LEGISLATIVE: Bicameral *Parliament: Senate; Lower House.*

Senate: Each nation to have at least one Senator; none to have more than twenty-five; number of Senators determined on basis of national revenue (other than rent), customs dues, profit from trading, etc. Also determines basis of tax assessment.

Lower House: One representative for every million of population; maximum twenty; qualifications of federal electors for Senate and House same as those prescribed in national elections.

EXECUTIVE OR ADMINISTRATIVE:
Supreme Executive Council: President and *Heads of the Departments;* Heads of Departments recommended by Senate, appointed by President and removable by him, stating his reasons to the Senate; Heads of Departments may sit in Lower House but not vote.

Ministry of International Defense: Organizes and maintains an International Force; provides protection against foreign aggression or invasion; patrols the high seas; maintains order and compels obedience to international law; protects means of international communications.

Information Bureau: Keeps a record of all laws, treaties, court decisions of all governments for the inspection of all.

Permanent Commission: Stabilizes national currencies to prevent violent fluctuations.

JUDICIAL:
Senate is Supreme Court of Appeal in disputes on international law and questions of jurisdiction.

Judicial Council or *Court of International Judicature:* Ten to fifteen judges and a president chosen by Senate; formulates own rules of procedure. *Quorum:* Ten. *Decisions:* By majority with each judge writing a written statement in each case. *Jurisdiction:* Cases under the Constitution and international law; may issue injunctions on complaint of one nation with grievance against another.

International Criminal Department: Right of free entry into any country, vessel or aircraft on warrant to investigate breaches of international law and arrest criminals.

Court of Equity: Decides disputes between subject nations and those exercising authority over them.

Additional Courts to Be Established: To assist in obtaining access to ice-free harbors, waterways, and canals; assure for inland nations suitable outlets to the sea, overseas communications, and uninterrupted supplies of necessities from other countries; provide for access to raw materials; adjust boundary disputes, etc.

TRANSFERS OF JURISDICTION FROM MEMBER NATIONS TO THE FEDERATION:
Sole right to raise, maintain, and control armed forces; license manufacture, possession and use of arms, warships, submarines, airplanes, poison gases.
Establish uniform navigation laws and regulate shipping.
Assure free and equal entry into all ports.
Establish uniform system of monetary standards, weights, and measures. Assure freedom of the seas; patrol all seas beyond three miles

of low-water line; all waterways leading from one nation to another, from one sea to another; and the air over them.

Collect taxes and other dues for defense, government, and other international purposes.

Supervise mandates; adjudicate claims for self-government; fix date terminating control by one country of territory outside its boundaries unless majority of adult population of not less than ten years' residence decides otherwise.

RESTRICTIONS ON NATIONS:

No nation may tax its subject people without allowing them representation.

Nations must protect foreigners within their territory.

Nations may not supply munitions to people engaged in civil war.

NATIONS RETAIN:

Right to determine their own form and system of government. Exclusive jurisdiction within their boundaries; Federation may not enter without nations' consent even to quell an armed force.

METHODS OF ENFORCEMENT:

As prescribed by the courts, operating on nations, groups, and individuals; International Force upholds law, protects means of communication and transportation, patrols the seas, and defends Federation against aggression.

Within one year of adoption of the Constitution, the Federation takes possession of and may destroy all fortifications and armaments within firing range of any international waterway or of another nation's territory.

IMMEDIATE STEPS:

The League Council is to instruct the Secretary-General of the League to establish an equitable proportion of representation for each nation and issue writs of election to each nation.

Temporary Basis of Representation:

Average number of electors to national parliaments in past ten years. Annual average amount of revenue from direct taxation in past ten years.

Average annual amount of international commerce within a similar period.

MISCELLANEOUS:
The law of libel is to be extended to include all written and printed matter tending to degrade a nation, its government, or its people in the opinion of other nations, governments, or peoples.

AUTHOR:
WOMEN'S ORGANIZATION FOR WORLD ORDER (Switzerland, Austria, Czechoslovakia, and Canada).

PROFESSIONS represented:
Social Workers, Physicians, Housewives, Writers, Attorneys, Scientists, Legislators, Teachers. (All women.)

Mimeographed 12 pages.

TITLE OF PLAN:
Protocol; A New Declaration of Human Rights.

DATE: 1935, 1936, 1937, 1943.

PUBLISHED in:
Vancouver, British Columbia, Canada.

TYPE:
FEDERAL. NAME: League of Nations.

MEMBERSHIP:
UNIVERSAL.

ORGANS OF GOVERNMENT:
LEGISLATIVE: Unicameral *World Parliament:* Equal proportion of delegates from each nation; direct election by universal suffrage and secret ballot; delegates subject to recall by their electorate. Delegations must have equal proportions of men and women. Only those trained for this office in *International Training Schools* may be candidates for election.

Executive or Administrative:

World Government: Chosen by World Parliament; equal proportion of men and women. Appoints an *official observer* for each nation.

Advisory Committee of Psychiatrists and Psychologists: Appointed by World Government. *Duties:* To attend all sessions of Parliament; to report their observations to the Government; to publicize their report.

Economic Bureau: To control industry to prevent the manufacture of armaments; to regulate international commerce; to internationalize transportation.

International Bureau of Health.

Education Department: To revise and coordinate school curricula every five years; to sponsor holiday exchange projects for students and teachers of all nations; to establish *International Training Schools* for candidates to the World Parliament in each nation, open to all its citizens.

World Press Service: To publish regular World Government reports.

Central Financial Institution: To establish a standard universal unit of currency; to facilitate exchange and credit; to control inflation and deflation; to provide credit to stimulate production for use; to regulate private lending institutions.

World Order Force: Composed of equal numbers of men and women of all nations voluntarily registered for this service; an equal proportion from each nation; to be stationed in all administrative centers under direct command of World Government.

Duties: To insure execution of world laws. Order Force to be equipped with latest technical means for restraining law-breakers without resort to physical destruction wherever possible. Such equipment to be in exclusive possession of the Order Force; its manufacture to be decentralized and assembled at the seat of the World Government.

Judicial:

World Court of Arbitration: Composed of equal proportion of men and women. *Jurisdiction:* Over all disputes between nations; over suits brought against national governments. Receives appeals from governments and individuals.

Control Commission: Appointed by Court to investigate governments charged with abusing their citizens. Commission to have access to all prisons and records of verdicts; to review methods of enforcement and punishment for crime.

All laws to be reviewed, revised, and simplified every five years.

TRANSFERS OF JURISDICTION FROM MEMBER NATIONS TO THE LEAGUE:

To disarm all nations; to assume sole control of armament manufacture.

To receive from all member nations an equal proportion of their national incomes.

To regulate international commerce; establish free trade.

To internationalize transportation.

To regulate public health.

To regulate education, especially the teaching of history and other subjects relating to world citizenship.

To plan production and distribution.

To establish an international unit of currency; to control inflation and deflation; to provide credit for stimulating production.

To grant world citizenship.

RESTRICTIONS ON NATIONS:

Nations refusing to enter the League are to be placed at the greatest possible disadvantage.

Nations resigning from League become its enemies.

No nation may exercise sovereignty over other peoples.

NATIONS RETAIN:

Light armed forces.

Right of appeal to World Court.

DEMOCRATIC RIGHTS:

Freedom of conscience; separation of Church and State.

Freedom of mind and body regardless of sex, race, and creed.

No person may be deprived of his national citizenship.

No person may be compelled to bear arms.

WOMEN'S RIGHTS:
  Men and women to have equal rights and duties; equal pay for equal work.
  Women to compose half of the delegates in representative political and economic bodies.

ECONOMIC RIGHTS:
  Freedom of choice as to occupation.
  Right to an adequate lifelong minimum maintenance.
  Right to acquire land for farming.

OBLIGATIONS OF INDIVIDUALS:
  Compulsory enrollment at end of educational and training period in a *Work Group* or the *World Order Force* for a limited number of years. (Goods and services produced by the obligatory work group to be distributed to the entire population in the form of minimum housing, food, clothing, culture, and medical aid according to the economic and cultural level of the people.)

HUMAN RELATIONS:
  Women to retain their maiden names and citizenship after marriage.
  Children born in or out of wedlock to have equal rights before the law and equal claims upon their parents.
  All children to have the right to take the name and citizenship of either parent.
  Both parents to have equal rights and duties towards their children.
  Divorce to be granted at the request of either party.
  Every person to receive information and instruction in birth control.
  Abortion to be illegal only when performed against the woman's will or by unqualified persons.
  Prostitution to be abolished by guaranteeing women economic security, by suppressing licensed prostitution, all forms of commercialized vice, and by educating men and women to a healthy conception of sexual life.
  Rape in or out of wedlock to be punished as a crime against personal freedom.
  Compulsory registration and treatment of venereal diseases.
  Sterilization of persons suffering from incurable hereditary diseases to be permissible with their own consent and on decision of a medical staff.

Euthanasia (death induced painlessly) for incurables and mentally defective infants by decision of a jury composed of physicians and relatives.

IMMEDIATE STEPS:
Women to exert immediate pressure on their governments in order to have each nation send also women delegates to the Peace Conference.

MISCELLANEOUS:
This plan is the result of study by three international congresses of women held in: Geneva, Switzerland, 1935, with eleven countries represented; Salzburg, Austria, 1936; and Bratislava, Czechoslovakia, 1937. It is known as the *Bratislava Protocols* and was completed in its present form by *The Seminar for International Affairs* in Vancouver, British Columbia, Canada. It is subject to further discussion and revision.

AUTHOR:
Dr. S. J. Cantor (Australian).

PROFESSION:
Director of a Mental Hospital.

TITLE OF PLAN:
The Constitution of a Commonwealth of Nations.

PAMPHLET

DATE: (1939?).

PUBLISHED by the author.

TYPE:
Federal. Name: Commonwealth of Nations.

MEMBERSHIP:
Limited to citizens of "civilized nations"; citizenship rights of "back-

ward nations or races," that are part of the Commonwealth, to be held in trust for them.

ORGANS OF GOVERNMENT:
LEGISLATIVE: Bicameral *Parliament: Council* (Upper House); *Assembly* (Lower House).

Council: Members to be apportioned on national basis to be determined by a formula, but total number not to exceed 200.

Assembly: One representative for every million of population.
Both Houses: Three-year terms; direct election by qualified citizens. Laws must be passed by both Houses and signed by President; Parliament may authorize the President to stop or prevent war or aggression.

EXECUTIVE OR ADMINISTRATIVE:
President; Vice-President: Three-year terms; both must be at least fifty years old; President may not be reelected, but elected from each nation in rotation.

Duties: Heads all executive departments; commands Commonwealth armed forces; appoints officers, judges.

Audit Office.

Civil Service or *Secretariat* (must swear allegiance to Commonwealth Constitution).

Central Commonwealth Bank.

JUDICIAL:
High Court of Justice of the Commonwealth.

Jurisdiction: May call disputants into court; empowered to enforce its decisions; may give advisory opinions.

TRANSFERS OF JURISDICTION FROM MEMBER NATIONS TO THE COMMONWEALTH:
Issue Commonwealth currency, establish a central bank.
Administer mandated territories, or delegate administration to nations now holding such authority.
Initiate world economic planning, if not in conflict with ordinary rights and privileges enjoyed by nations.

Bring about reduction in national armament.
Raise and support adequate Commonwealth Police Force.
Call on quotas of military, naval, and air forces of member nations to maintain "international discipline" and to preserve peace (these forces to be maintained at Commonwealth expense).
Initiate legal action against states or individuals for breaches of Commonwealth Law, for recovery of fines, and taxes.
Promote use of international auxiliary language such as Esperanto.

NATIONS RETAIN:
Member nations may form treaties and alliances for collective security against aggression, but they must be registered with Commonwealth President.
Constitution may not be amended to abrogate interests, rights, and privileges of more advanced member nations and capital powers.
Nations may secede from and reenter the Commonwealth.
Commonwealth must respect regional understandings such as Monroe Doctrine and Australian (white) Immigration Policy.

METHODS OF ENFORCEMENT:
Towards Member Nations and individuals: Administrative machinery and the Courts.

Towards Non-Member Nations: Military force.

IMMEDIATE STEPS:
Organization of a Governmental Conference as a result of a mandate of the people of the world expressed nationally or through representatives in an international conference.

AUTHOR:
W. L. WALTON (American).

TITLE OF PLAN:
Workable World Peace: The Practical Plan.

PAMPHLET

DATE: 1939.

Charts of Plans to Unite Nations Since 1914

PRINTED IN Grafton, South Dakota.

TYPE:
FEDERAL.

MEMBERSHIP:
UNIVERSAL.

ORGANS OF GOVERNMENT:
LEGISLATIVE: Unicameral *World Congress:* Five-year term; method of selection decided by each nation; total number of representatives about 150; retirement at sixty on half pay; decisions by majority vote.

Basis of representation: Population, area, education, and volume of overseas trade; one representative for every fifty million of population; plus one for every million square miles of territory; plus one for every billion dollars of overseas trade including exports and imports; every self-governing nation of one million population entitled to at least one representative.

Representation reduced ten per cent for every ten per cent of illiteracy below a standard of eighty per cent.

Self-governing territories of at least one million square miles, divided by sea from mother nations entitled to separate representation.

First allotment of representation to be based on taxes on travel and on overseas commerce as of 1938.

EXECUTIVE:
World Governor: Five-year term; elected by Congress by majority vote. (Supreme Court may appoint the World Governor if Congress fails to elect one.) Candidates thirty-five to fifty years old; may be reelected for second term by sixty per cent vote of Congress; for third term by seventy-five per cent vote; for fourth by eighty per cent vote; none may serve longer than twenty years.

Duties: Commander-in-Chief; appoints Cabinet; may veto legislation; two-thirds vote of Congress to override veto.

Cabinet: Secretaries of State, Treasury, Commerce, Law, Armed Forces, Peace, etc. *Secretary of Peace* arbitrates differences between nations when submitted.

Information Department: Congress elects a *Master of Information* for life; may be retired at half pay at sixty; provides all information requested by World Governor, Congress, and Supreme Court.

Council of Wisdom: Its members are all retired Masters of Information, World Governors, Supreme Court Justices, and Congressmen of ten years' service. *Duties:* To advise members of the Government.

JUDICIAL:
World Supreme Court: Nine judges; must have served on a high court in their own nations; Congress may increase number of judges by two-thirds vote but not by more than two every ten years; odd number must be retained.

Duties: To determine constitutionality of legislation within one year; three-fourths vote necessary to revoke a decision after rehearing; must set aside other business to render decision in case of a dispute; may render judgments even if a nation does not appear in its own defense.

TRANSFERS OF JURISDICTION FROM MEMBER NATIONS TO THE FEDERATION:
Right to acquire federal territory; maintain peace; purchase existing navies; prohibit certain types of armament; provide for defense; summon disputing nations to court; enforce Court's decisions; suppress piracy, immoral traffic; tax tonnage and passengers passing through federal domain.

NATIONS RETAIN:
Right of secession whereupon the services of all their citizens in any world office are automatically canceled.

METHODS OF ENFORCEMENT:
Towards Member Nations: Non-compliance with Court decisions results in suspension of nation's rights and ultimately military action against it.

IMMEDIATE STEPS:
Nations wishing to adhere to the Constitution should appoint one member to a *Formation Commission* to meet in New York City with full authority to set up World Government. Each nation appointing

a member to the Commission shall deposit twenty-five million dollars to be refunded when the World Treasury has an adequate surplus. *Duties:* Determines first allotment of representatives; purchases Azores or other islands for seat of government; salaries of Commissioners, $12,000 yearly. (The Commission, according to the author's time schedule, was to have completed its work by July, 1939, and representatives to Congress were to have been chosen by October, 1939.)

RATIFICATION:
Constitution in force when ratified by responsible governments representing two-thirds of the peoples of the world.

AMENDMENT:
By three-fourths vote of the World Congress upon the third reading not less than two nor more than three years from date of introduction.

MISCELLANEOUS:
Official language of the Federation: English.

AUTHOR:
WILLIAM C. BREWER (American).

PROFESSION:
Attorney.

TITLE OF PLAN:
Permanent Peace.

DATE: 1940.

PUBLISHER:
Dorrance, Philadelphia.

TYPE:
FEDERAL. NAME: World Alliance.
   Modeled on the Swiss and United States Constitutions.

MEMBERSHIP:
UNIVERSAL: All civilized nations enter on an equal basis; a permanent Union.

ORGANS OF GOVERNMENT:
LEGISLATIVE: Bicameral *World Congress: Assembly* and *Council.*

Assembly: Four-year term; representatives appointed by national governments; one representative for every nine million of population; ten is maximum number of representatives for any nation; each nation to have not less than one; representatives must be at least thirty years old; twelve years citizens of the country appointing them, and inhabitants thereof at least six years before appointment. Representatives may not be impeached, but Assembly, by two-thirds vote, may request a nation to recall its representative; nation failing to do so, Assembly may expel its representative by two-thirds vote.
Revenue bills must originate in Assembly.

Council: Six-year term chosen by the *Assembly* from its own membership (terms of one-third of the members expiring every two years); maximum membership seventy-five; not more than five from any single nation at one time. Council chooses its own President and other officers. President votes only in case of a tie.

Duties: May vote to expel a nation from protection, immunities, and privileges of membership by two-thirds vote, if policies or conduct of its leaders endanger world peace. Nation may be reinstated by two-thirds vote. Determines language to be used in proceedings. Official *Journal* must be published also in two other widely used languages. Fixes salaries, and appoints officers in proportion to qualified personnel in the population of each nation. Determines what constitutes treason against the Alliance. Bills left unsigned within ten-day period by Governor General may be reconsidered by two-thirds vote of House of origin and then passed by majority vote of both Houses.

EXECUTIVE OR ADMINISTRATIVE:
Governor General: Six-year term; appointed by Council and Assembly (ineligible for reappointment). *Duties:* Commander-in-Chief of Alliance forces; commissions all officers; in charge of executive and administrative affairs of Alliance; appoints *Cabinet* with advice and

consent of Council. Has no veto power; may express opinions on legislation.

Secretary General: Six-year term; appointed by Council; eligible to election as Governor General on concluding term of office.

Duties: In charge of diplomatic affairs of World Alliance; negotiations with member nations; jurisdiction over civil service and post-office.

Cabinet Members: Secretary General, Chief of International Police, Commander of International Marines, Director of the Information Service, Secretary of International Commerce, Attorney General, Secretary of the Treasury, and others created by Congress.

JUDICIAL:

World Supreme Court: Ten-year term; number of judges determined by Congress, appointed by Council with consent of Assembly. May be reappointed for another five years.

Jurisdiction: All cases arising under the Constitution; disputes between two or more nations; crimes against Alliance, established international law; cases involving officers of the Alliance; advisory opinions requested by either House; review of constitutionality of Congressional legislation. No suits permissible against World Alliance.

Public jury trial in criminal and civil cases.

Inferior Courts as established by Congress.

TRANSFERS OF JURISDICTION FROM MEMBER NATIONS TO THE ALLIANCE:

The World Alliance is charged only with the maintenance of peace, but it is the sole judge of what may jeopardize it. In order to fulfill its functions the Alliance has the right to levy and collect taxes, pay World Alliance debts; provide for protection and economic welfare of all nations; establish, define, and enforce international law; punish counterfeiting of a nation's currency outside its boundaries; define crimes and acts of individuals which may jeopardize world peace; provide for the arrest and punishment of spies, war agitators, and leaders of governments whose acts threaten world peace; govern tax evasion between nations by persons and corporations; provide for an international police force and marines to enforce laws, suppress insurrections, and repel invasions; erect forts, airfields; control federal property; provide for a census from time to time; declare war; supervise nations and territories incapable of self-government; mediate and conciliate disputes affecting international commerce and industry; supervise international communications; and collect international statistical information.

Nations may not keep troops or manufacture military weapons without consent of World Alliance Congress.

NATIONS RETAIN:
Right to establish and enforce immigration regulations, tariffs, and nationality; right to keep a militia; jurisdiction over oceans to 100 miles from their boundaries (to the middle of smaller bodies of water). Policies and regional understandings recognized at the establishment of the World Alliance to be guaranteed to all nations.

METHODS OF ENFORCEMENT:
Towards Member Nation (for policies and conduct endangering world peace):
1. Expulsion from the World Alliance by two-thirds vote of Congress.
2. Embargo, blockade.
3. Use of armed force furnished by member nations on quota basis; militia allowed member nations subject to emergency call.

Towards Individuals: Enforcement of laws by International Police.

Towards Non-Member Nations:
1. Use of embargo and blockade.
2. Military and Naval force.

RATIFICATION:
The World Alliance is established on ratification of its Constitution by three-fourths of the world's nations. Possible founders: United States, United Kingdom, Republic of Germany, Union of Soviet Socialist Republics, Republic of France, Italy, Japan, China, Netherlands, and Belgium.

AMENDMENT:
By two-thirds vote of both Houses; ratification by three-fourths of the nations.

MISCELLANEOUS:
The plan provides for a Bill of Rights similar to that in the United States Constitution. Established governments are to be protected against unreasonable demands of organized minorities, but willful oppression of peaceful minorities is not to be tolerated.

The author has faith in the German people, and believes that when conditions of slavery and inequality are removed, the democratic government in Germany will be re-created.

Seat of the World Alliance in The Hague or Geneva.

AUTHOR:
HANS HEYMANN (German).

PROFESSION:
Former economic adviser to the German Foreign Office under Weimar Republic; Research Professor, Rutgers University.

TITLE OF PLAN:
Plan for Permanent Peace.

DATE: 1941.

PUBLISHER:
Harper & Bros., New York.
(Plan for a Bank of Nations first published in 1922 in Berlin.)

TYPE:
FEDERAL. NAME: Federal World Authority (especially devoted to economic aspects of World Government).

MEMBERSHIP:
UNIVERSAL, with regional administration.

ORGANS OF GOVERNMENT:
LEGISLATIVE: Bicameral World Parliament: *World Council; World Assembly.*

EXECUTIVE OR ADMINISTRATIVE:
World Economic Council. World Economic Planning Board.

Bank of Nations: Under joint guarantee of all nations with 300 million currency units. *Board of Directors:* One government representative from each nation; the president (or his representative) of every central or leading bank; representatives of industry, trade, agriculture, banking, and labor. *Qualifications:* Competence in banking, commerce, and worldwide organization.

Permanent Advisory Committee: Specialists from all fields of economic activity.

Statistical Department; Research Department; World Building and Colonization Bank; National Branch Banks.

Regional Banks:

Western Hemisphere Bank: Empowered to sell and lend United States gold funds to central banks of foreign countries to redistribute idle gold hoard into international channels; empowered to create inter-American medium of exchange.

Europa Bank: To clear money; to create money and credit; to create European medium of exchange; to be located in Amsterdam, Zurich, London, or Paris.

Oriental Bank: To aid economic settlement of East Asiatic problems with international financial support; to create Oriental currency.

Functional Subsidiaries of Bank of Nations:

International Labor Migration Department: Supported by contributions from participating nations. *Duties:* To provide labor where needed with aid of centralized employment agency, cooperating with national labor organizations, employers' associations, and governments; to equip migrant labor groups with necessary means of transportation and tools for work; to stimulate and support great productive works; to develop backward countries with good prospects.

Department for Relief and Reparations: To handle investment of joint loans, reparations, and relief foundations to devastated nations for reconstruction and transformation of war industries into useful, peaceful work.

International Social Insurance Department: To establish uniform international standards and principles of social insurance in all countries.

International Unemployment Insurance Department: To help in cases of extraordinary national unemployment crises with contributions accumulated from national unemployment insurance funds, assessed in various countries.

International Labor Organization: To collaborate with all other administrative departments.

World Crop Insurance Department: To organize universal crop insurance; to assure continuous and equitable production for use; and to cover needs of working population.

World Index Office: To keep statistics and index figures on crop and agricultural conditions; to combine national index institutions.

International Raw Materials Clearing House and Reserve Board: To organize distribution of raw and subsidiary materials and of other natural products; to set aside in good years reserves of natural durable goods, such as cotton, corn, grain, sugar, and rubber, to be drawn upon in lean years.

World Army, Navy, and Air Force.

JUDICIAL:
  World Court of Justice.
  Court of Wisdom: Twenty members.
  International Arbitration Board for Trade Differences.

TRANSFERS OF JURISDICTION FROM MEMBER NATIONS TO THE WORLD AUTHORITY:
To introduce auxiliary medium of exchange through power to issue bank notes.
To grant short- and long-term credits on basis of sound collateral.
To establish branch banks in every member nation, with issuing and credit departments.

To establish subordinate national Construction Banks to finance new productive enterprises such as factories, soil reclamation, public utilities, maintain and enlarge existing trade and business; issue bonds free of interest for three- to ten-year periods to be held by Bank of Nations or its branches until end of interest-free period.
To grant long-term bank credits to Construction Banks.
To reconstruct and support national currencies.
To regulate various export-import boards, establish standards, rules, and modes of operation.
To control international cartels, trusts, and syndicates.

IMMEDIATE STEPS:
Creation of Office of Planning, Establishing, and Preserving Peace, possibly as a division of the United States Department of State.

PREREQUISITES TO PEACE:
Peace without domination by any power.

AUTHOR:
OSCAR NEWFANG (American).

PROFESSION:
Writer and credit manager.

TITLE OF PLAN:
World Government: A Suggested Formula for Use at the End of the War — A Suggested Revision of the Covenant to Develop the League into a World Federal Government.

DATE: 1942.

PUBLISHER:
Barnes & Noble Inc.

TYPE:
FEDERAL: Based on Covenant of the League of Nations.

Charts of Plans to Unite Nations Since 1914

MEMBERSHIP:
UNIVERSAL: All members and allies of the United Nations; all members and allies of the Axis Nations.

ORGANS OF GOVERNMENT:
LEGISLATIVE: Unicameral *Assembly:* Each member state entitled to not more than three representatives but only one vote.

Method of Voting: Votes of the representatives are to be counted first as units representing sovereign member states; second to be counted and multiplied by the population represented according to the last census.

Decisions: By majority of both counts of the vote.

The Assembly is to meet once a year in September.

EXECUTIVE OR ADMINISTRATIVE:
The Council: Representatives of the British Empire, France, Germany, Italy, Japan, U.S.S.R., United States, and the representatives of ten other member nations selected by the Assembly by majority vote. Each nation has one representative and one vote.

Quorum: Two-thirds of Council members.

Decision: By majority vote of quorum.

Duties: To deal with any matter within the jurisdiction of the League or affecting world peace.

Secretariat: Secretary-General appointed by Council with approval of majority of the Assembly. Under-Secretaries and staff appointed by Secretary-General with approval of Council; all positions open equally to men and women.

General Staff: One representative from each of the seven Great Powers plus officers appointed by Council.

Existing International Bureaus and Commissions to be placed under League Control.

JUDICIAL:
Permanent Court of International Justice: To exercise original and compulsory jurisdiction in disputes between member nations; between

a member nation and a citizen or citizens of another member nation, and of citizens of different member nations upon application of either party.

TRANSFERS OF JURISDICTION FROM MEMBER NATIONS TO THE LEAGUE:
The armed forces of each member nation are to be restricted to one-tenth of one per cent of its population; soldiers are to serve for ten-year terms.

The League is to have sole possession of all armed sea, air, and land craft, and of all guns over a caliber of 75 mm.

The League is to supervise and license all armament manufacture.

The League protects the territorial integrity and existing political independence of all members, and, on appeal from the existing head of any nation, against internal violence.

The League assumes the administration of non-self-governing colonies; regulates the free movement of labor, goods, money, and persons throughout League territory and navigable rivers.

Right of direct taxation of individuals, and collection of taxes by League officials.

Right to review, modify, or repeal treaties that have become obsolete or endanger peace.

Right to raise and maintain armed forces, and establish a world monetary and banking system.

The League can legislate on any other subject voted by majority of both counts of the Assembly as within its jurisdiction.

No member nation may enter into an alliance or treaty with a non-member nation, nor with a member nation without consent of the Assembly.

Covenant, laws of the Assembly, decisions of the Permanent Court of International Justice are supreme, abrogating laws of member nations or obligations between nations declared inconsistent by the Court.

NATIONS RETAIN:
Powers not granted to the League nor assumed by it by vote of the Assembly are reserved to the member nations and their citizens.

METHODS OF ENFORCEMENT:
Towards Member Nations (For resistance to Court's decision):
Expulsion from benefits of customs union and application of tariffs. Armed intervention only on request of national executive.

Towards Non-member Nations: Military defense against attack.

PREREQUISITES TO PEACE:
United Nations victory.

LIQUIDATION OF THE WAR:
MILITARY AND TERRITORIAL:
Armistice terms to include transfer to the Council of the League of Nations of all land, water, and air armaments, and as much of national military personnel as requested by the League; transfer of all non-self-governing colonies to League Mandatory Commission with equal access to all states; prepare colonies for self-government and admission as equal members of the League; transfer to League control, fortification and garrisoning of Gibraltar, Suez Canal, the Dardanelles, the Bosphorus, Singapore, the Panama Canal, Kiel Canal, Malta, Pantellaria, Perim, as well as bases at Cape Town and Magellan when requested by majority vote of Assembly. League armed forces to take oath of allegiance to the League; to be paid from League's Treasury; all belligerents and their allies to reduce their armed forces to one-tenth of one per cent of their population.

ECONOMIC:
Draft Conventions of the International Labor Office to become binding on all citizens without confirmation by national governments.

Convention to Establish a General Customs Union: Ratification by five Great Powers and by majority of other nations; membership open to all belligerents, their allies, and any other self-governing state; no increase of tariffs or trade restrictions between members after ratification of Convention; tariffs, quotas, monetary and other restrictions on imports, exports, capital transfers, or investments to be reduced or abolished after passage of time equal to the period they were in force before ratification. Fifty years after ratification, entire freedom of trade and investment throughout territory of the Customs Union.

ORGANS:

Tariff Commission: One member from each nation; decisions by majority vote.

Jurisdiction: Over all tariff rates; collection of customs duties; additional levies against non-members guilty of subsidies and dumping.

Enforcement: Towards non-member nations — application of highest tariff levied by any member of the Union.

Towards member nations (for refusal to conform to Commission's ruling): Expulsion from the Customs Union, and application of outside tariff rates by majority vote of members.

Surplus revenue from duties against non-member nations to be divided among member nations in proportion to population after deduction of operating expenses.

Customs Court: One member from each of the seven Great Powers; six additional members elected by them; each member one vote.

Jurisdiction: Receives appeals from rulings of Tariff Commission lodged by any member nation. Decisions final.

TERRITORIAL CHANGES:

International administration of important canals, straits, and waterways; and of non-self-governing colonies.

AMENDMENTS:

By majority vote of Council and majority of both votes in the Assembly, except that no member nation may be deprived of its equal vote in the first count of the Assembly votes.

MISCELLANEOUS:

The author has been advocating world government for the past twenty-four years and has a number of other books on the subject. In 1918 he addressed a pamphlet to all the Governments entitled: "A World Government Needed." Some of his other books are: "The United States of the World," 1930, and "World Federation," 1939.

Charts of Plans to Unite Nations Since 1914

AUTHOR:
RUTH BRYAN OWEN (Mrs. Borge Rohde), American.

PROFESSION:
Former Member of Congress; former Minister to Denmark; writer and lecturer.

TITLE OF PLAN:
Look Forward, Warrior.

DATE: 1942.

PUBLISHER:
Dodd, Mead & Co., New York.

TYPE:
FEDERAL: Based on the United States Constitution.
NAME: Constitution of the Union of Nations.

MEMBERSHIP:
UNIVERSAL.

ORGANS OF GOVERNMENT:
LEGISLATIVE: Bicameral *Congress: Senate* and *House of Representatives*.
House: Four-year term; elected by the people as prescribed by national governments; one representative for every twenty-five million of population; each nation to have at least one representative.

Duties: Sole power of impeachment; initiates revenue bills.

Senate: Four-year term; elected by the people as prescribed by national governments; two Senators from each nation (one-half of the Senate renewed every two years). Vice-President of the Union to be President of the Senate.

Duties: Sole power to try impeachments; two-thirds vote to convict.

Congress to meet at least once a year. *Quorum:* Majority of each House; expulsion of a member by two-thirds vote; to override President's veto of legislation: two-thirds vote.

EXECUTIVE OR ADMINISTRATIVE:

President; Vice-President: Both elected for four-year terms.

Method of Election: each nation appoints one elector; electors assemble and vote by ballot for two persons from a slate supplied by the Union Congress; each elector must vote for one person of a nationality other than his own. List of all persons voted for and number of votes for each to be sent to Union Congress, which counts the votes. Person having a majority of all the votes of the Electors is President; if more than one person has such a majority, election of the President is up to the House; if none has a majority, the House chooses a President from among the five highest on the list. The person with the next highest number of votes is to be Vice-President; if two or more have an equal number of votes, the election is up to the Senate.

Duties: President requests opinions from heads of departments; grants reprieves and pardons; nominates, with advice and consent of Senate, Judges of the World Court and officers of the Union; fills vacancies, etc. Convenes and adjourns Congress; commissions the Director of the Union Forces.

The President cannot succeed himself, and his successor cannot come from the same nation.

JUDICIAL:

World Court: Nominated by the President with advice and consent of the Senate.

Original Jurisdiction: Over disputes arising under the Constitution, international law, admiralty and maritime questions; over disputes to which the Union is a party; disputes between two or more nations; between a nation and citizens of another nation; between citizens of different nations; between a nation or its citizens, and a foreign nation, its citizens, or subjects.

Appellate Jurisdiction: Under regulations made by Congress. *Duties:* Directs the enforcement of laws of Congress by the Union Forces.

TRANSFERS OF JURISDICTION FROM MEMBER NATIONS TO THE UNION:

The Union Congress has the right to levy and collect taxes, pay debts, provide for the defense and general welfare of all nations, regulate commerce, promote progress of science; raise and support Union land, sea, and air forces; call out the militias of member nations to execute Union laws, suppress insurrections and repel invasion pending arrival of Union Forces; to make all laws necessary to carrying out the powers delegated to it.

RESTRICTIONS:
No direct taxes are to be levied unless in proportion to census to be taken every ten years.
No preference to be shown to ports of one nation over those of another.
No nation may engage in war or keep warships, warplanes, except by consent of Congress, or troops, except for the militia to keep internal order.

NATIONS RETAIN:
Powers not delegated to the Union, nor prohibited to the nations, are reserved to the nations or to the people.
Nations are to be protected against hostile entry of enemy forces or of the Union Force except upon a Court order and for armament inspection.
Right to equitable access to world markets and essential commodities.
Right to payment for bases furnished to International Armed Force.

METHODS OF ENFORCEMENT:
Union protects member nations against invasion and against domestic violence on request of the national legislature or the executive.
Citizens of each nation entitled to the privileges and immunities of citizens in other member nations.
Full faith and credit are to be given in each nation to the public acts, records, and judicial proceedings of every other nation.

IMMEDIATE STEPS:
Declaration of Interdependence by Representatives of the United Nations of the World in General Congress assembled.

The Constitution of the Union of Nations is to be drafted and submitted to the nations for ratification during the postwar period of economic adjustment and reconstruction.

PREREQUISITES TO PEACE:
Victory of the United Nations.

AUTHOR:
Leslie Balogh Bain (American).

PROFESSION:
Journalist.

TITLE OF PLAN:
Chaos or Peace.

DATE: 1943.

PUBLISHER:
M. S. Mill Co., Inc., New York.

TYPE:
Federal. Name: League of Nations.

MEMBERSHIP:
Universal.

ORGANS OF GOVERNMENT:

Legislative: Unicameral *World Assembly:* Membership of all United Nations and all enemy nations to be compulsory; neutral nations to be elected on application after proving their adherence to aims of Assembly. One representative for every ten million of population.

Permanent Political Committee: To formulate policies of the Assembly; to report on developments within member nations; to assist them to achieve political reforms; to maintain observers in all parts of world to guard against political movements endangering world peace.

Executive or Administrative:
Economic Committee: To regulate world trade, credit, and finance; to assure freedom of commerce and peaceful access to raw materials and resources.

International Economic Planning Board: To assist economically backward countries; to modernize economies of Africa, Asia, and South America; to work in cooperation with non-political national planning boards.

International Credit Bank: To grant credit to all needy nations for international purchases. Security to be based on soundness of national political and economic structure and ability to apply credit to socially useful purposes. Credit may not be used for armament, to finance privately owned monopolies, or to establish factories, mines, and transportation facilities whose profits are not under effective public control.

Permanent Labor Committee: To eliminate disparity in labor standards.

Colonial Commission: To investigate all colonial problems; to establish native governments in each colony ready to assume responsibilities of independence. Other colonies to remain under its custodianship with specific date set for their independence. Individual nations may not exploit colonies nor exercise mandates or protectorates over them.

Educational Committee: To supervise textbooks of member nations with power to enforce text revisions.

JUDICIAL:
Special Tribunal: To hear and determine disputes between member nations. Nations may appeal decisions to World Assembly.

TRANSFERS OF JURISDICTION FROM MEMBER NATIONS TO THE LEAGUE:
To enforce the peace treaties.
To regulate world trade, credit, and finance.
To assure freedom of commerce.
To raise economic standards.
To administer colonies.
To supervise and revise textbooks.
To prevent the rise of movements dangerous to world peace.

IMMEDIATE STEPS:
United Nations must establish a *Council* with jurisdiction over all political matters and subcommittees to deal with territorial and economic problems. The Council should proclaim the following war aims for the United Nations:

1. To wipe out fascism and imperialism all over the world.

2. To pledge reform of their own political and economic systems to prevent special groups from endangering democratic progress.
3. To retain political control over liberated territories until a more permanent international organization is established by the Peace Conference; and to permit no one to hold office in occupied territories who cannot prove past loyalty to democratic principles and antifascist activity at home or abroad.

TERRITORIAL CHANGES:
India, Dutch East Indies, Burma, Indo-China, Philippines, French and Spanish Morocco, Tunisia, Algeria, and Syria to receive immediate independence. An *Arab Federation* should be established, and the following federations organized in Europe:

The Union of Scandinavian States: Norway, Sweden, and Denmark; also Finland.

Federated States of Northern Europe: Esthonia, Latvia, Lithuania, East Prussia, and Poland.

Federated States of the Danubian Valley: Czechoslovakia, Hungary, Roumania, and parts of Yugoslavia north of Danube and Drava rivers.

Federated Balkan States: Serbia, Greece, Croatia, Dalmatia, Slovenia, Bulgaria, Bosnia, Herzegovina, Albania, and Montenegro.

These federations to be patterned on the United States union with common economy, defense, and foreign policies. All member states to retain political and cultural autonomy. Thorough-going land reforms to assure land to the peasants. These federations to be established by the United Nations by force, if necessary.

MISCELLANEOUS:
The author suggests the following measures to safeguard the democratic process against its present defects: Each political unit (state, county, town, village) to elect annually by proportional representation *Twelve Electoral Supervisors* who may hold no other political office.

Duties: To draw up a list of issues in their districts including those suggested by popular petition of at least one hundred signers. Each candidate to furnish written answers stating how he would deal with each issue if elected, adding additional problems with which he would deal. Each voter to receive lists of questions and each candidate's answers. Supervisors to maintain order during balloting. To ascertain that officials adhere to preelection pledges. To serve as jury, trying officials charged with serious breaches of office. Immediate removal from office on *unanimous conviction of guilt;* but official may be candidate at subsequent election. If only a *majority of Supervisors votes* official guilty, he must submit to a *recall election* with runner-up of last election as his rival candidate. If vote of Electoral Supervisors is equally divided or less than six vote the official guilty, he is freed of all charges.

Supervisors to attend monthly district meetings to discuss new issues with electorate; to decide by majority vote recommendations to officials concerned. Within thirty days officials must state their position on the new issues. Non-elective officials, other than aides of elected ones, must be under civil service.

Candidates for reelection must submit original answers to previous campaign issues, their record of official action, and answers to the new electoral questionnaire. Candidates of political parties to attach also party platforms to their questionnaire. All campaign documents to be printed at government expense.

Electoral Supervisors may be removed by petition of fifteen per cent of the registered voters presented to the highest district court. New elections of Supervisors must be called within thirty days.

In national elections party platforms to be equivalent of electoral questionnaire but they must deal with specific issues. Members of Parliament or Congress to assume duties of Electoral Supervisors towards Presidential and other national candidates. President may be removed *by unanimous vote* of national legislative body for serious breach of the party platform. *Two-thirds vote* of national legislative body sufficient to decree a national referendum; President and his party must then submit to recall election against defeated candidate and party of previous election.

AUTHOR:
Percy Bordwell (American).

PROFESSION:
Professor of Law.

TITLE OF PLAN:
A Constitution for the United Nations.

DATE: March, 1943.

PUBLISHED BY Iowa Law Review, Vol. 28, No. 3, March, 1943.

TYPE:
FEDERAL: Based on United States Constitution.
NAME: United Nations.

MEMBERSHIP:
United Nations at the start. (Aim: universal.)

ORGANS OF GOVERNMENT:
LEGISLATIVE: Unicameral *Assembly:* Three-year term; chosen by direct universal suffrage in proportion to population; one representative for every two and one-half million non-colonial inhabitants but no nation may have more than ten, nor less than one representative. *Qualifications:* At least twenty-five years old; seven years a citizen of the United Nations; inhabitant of nation from which elected. *Sessions:* Every three years. Chooses own Speaker and other officers. Determines own rules and procedure. *Quorum:* Majority of members. May override Council's veto by two-thirds vote and approval of majority of Council. If Council majority does not approve bill it must be passed again by Assembly in succeeding session. Sole power of impeachment by two-thirds vote of members present.

EXECUTIVE OR ADMINISTRATIVE:
Council: Three-year term; fifteen members chosen by Assembly from its own members. *Restriction:* Not more than one representative may be chosen from the same nation. Membership in Assembly continues. Vacancies filled by Assembly, or, if not in session, by Council. *Duties:* Chooses Chairman and Vice-Chairman for one-year term. (Chairman ineligible as Chairman or Vice-Chairman for following year, nor may same member serve as Vice-Chairman for two consecutive years.) Commands army and navy, and national militias when in service of United Nations; grants reprieves and pardons except in cases of impeachment; makes treaties by two-thirds vote; receives ambassadors and public ministers; appoints, with consent of Assembly, ambassa-

dors, public ministers, consuls (until United Nations is worldwide), judges of Supreme Court, and other United Nations officers; fills vacancies during Assembly recess to expire at end of next session; recommends measures for Assembly's consideration. Members of Council may be removed from office on impeachment along with all civil officers of United Nations on conviction of treason, bribery, or other high crimes and misdemeanors.

JUDICIAL:

Supreme Court: And such inferior courts as Assembly may establish; nine-year term in all cases; chosen by Council with consent of Assembly. *Jurisdiction:* Over cases arising under Constitution, laws of United Nations and its treaties; cases affecting ambassadors, consuls, admiralty and maritime jurisdiction; over controversies to which United Nations is party; between two or more nations; a nation and citizens of another nation; citizens of different nations; citizens of the same nation claiming lands under grants from different nations; between a nation or its citizens and foreign nations, citizens, or subjects. Sole power to try impeachments.

TRANSFERS OF JURISDICTION FROM MEMBER NATIONS TO THE UNITED NATIONS:

Provide for the common defense and general welfare.

Take the census.

Levy and collect uniform imposts, duties, and excises.

Pay debts; borrow and coin money; regulate its value; punish counterfeiting.

Regulate commerce with foreign nations (until worldwide), and among member nations.

Establish uniform rules of naturalization.

Fix standard of weights and measures; provide patents and copyrights.

Establish post-offices and post-roads.

Declare war; raise, support, and regulate the armed forces; prescribe the organization, arming, and disciplining of national militias; and regulate them when in United Nations service.

Control federal district and property.

Admit new nations.

Protect each nation against invasion, and on application of its executive authority, against domestic violence.

Constitution and laws of United Nations supreme law of land.

RESTRICTIONS ON THE FEDERAL GOVERNMENT:
Habeas Corpus may not be suspended, unless in cases of rebellion or invasion public safety requires it.

No ex-post-facto laws may be passed, nor income or inheritance taxes imposed, nor duties on exports from any member nation.

No religious test to be required for office under United Nations.

No person to be convicted of treason unless on testimony of two witnesses to the same overt act or on confession in open court.

NATIONS RETAIN:
Powers not delegated to the United Nations nor prohibited to nations are reserved to nations respectively or to the people.

Right to appoint officers of the militia and to train it according to regulations prescribed by Assembly.

Nations may not be deprived of territory or joined with other nations without consent of legislatures concerned as well as of Assembly.

OBLIGATIONS OF NATIONS:
Full faith and credit to be given in each nation to public acts, records, and judicial proceedings of every member nation.

Citizens of each nation to be entitled to all privileges and immunities of citizens in the several nations.

Extradition of fugitives from justice upon demand of executive authority of the nation where crime was committed.

RESTRICTIONS ON NATIONS:
No nation may coin money, pass any ex-post-facto law, or law impairing obligation of contracts.

No nation may, without consent of Assembly, levy duties on imports or exports except when absolutely necessary for executing inspection laws, net proceeds to go to United Nations treasury; nor keep troops or ships of war in time of peace except as worked out in cooperation with Government of United Nations; nor engage in war unless actually invaded.

No nation may deprive any person of life, liberty, or property without due process of law nor deny any person within its jurisdiction the equal protection of the laws; nor abridge right to vote on account of race, color, or sex.

DEMOCRATIC RIGHTS:
Freedom of religion, press, speech; right of people to assemble peacefully and petition for redress of grievances.

Security against unreasonable searches and seizures.

No person to be twice put in jeopardy of life or limb for the same offense or compelled to be a witness against himself, nor be deprived of life, liberty, or property without due process of law.

Right to public trial by impartial jury.

Bail may not be excessive, or punishment cruel or unusual.

Right to vote may not be abridged on account of race, color, or sex.

Slavery or involuntary servitude prohibited except as punishment for crime.

METHODS OF ENFORCEMENT:
Enforcement operates on individuals through courts.
Assembly may call forth militia to execute laws of the United Nations.

IMMEDIATE STEPS:
Speedy calling of a constitutional convention (upon termination of hostilities on Western Front) consisting of representatives of United Nations called into session by President of the United States.
Constitution would help in solving problems of Final Peace, but probably should not go into active operation until then.
In the United States adoption of a Constitution of the United Nations is within powers reserved to the people (not treaty-making power of President and Senate). Calling of a constitutional convention in the

United States would be necessary to accept or reject the United Nations Constitution.

RATIFICATION:
By China, Great Britain, the U.S.S.R., and the U. S. A. sufficient to establish United Nations (if these ratify, author expects that speedy acceptance by all the United Nations, neutrals, and eventually by defeated powers would follow).

AMENDMENT:
By two-thirds vote of Assembly or on application of two-thirds of the nations, a special convention may be called to propose amendments. In either case, ratification by legislatures of three-fourths of the nations or by conventions in three-fourths of the nations, whichever method Assembly proposes, is necessary.

AUTHOR:
EDWARD J. BYNG (English).

PROFESSION:
Journalist.

TITLE OF PLAN:
A Five-Year Peace Plan — A Schedule for Peace Building.

DATE: 1943.

PUBLISHER:
Coward-McCann Inc., New York.

TYPE:
FEDERAL: To be modeled on United States Constitution on basis of gradual development.

NAME: Union of Nations (French: Union des Nations; German: Völkerverein).

MEMBERSHIP:
Universal with subregional federations.

Charts of Plans to Unite Nations Since 1914

ORGANS OF GOVERNMENT:

LEGISLATIVE: Unicameral *Union Assembly:* Composed of delegates of member nations; meets at least once a year. *Duties:* Approves Union budget; ratifies treaties negotiated by Executive (*other political and economic decisions and agreements negotiated by Executive which are not formal treaties do not need Assembly ratification*); may discuss any question of policy, conflict between nations, etc., and pass resolutions on them, *but actual decisions reserved to the Executive;* appoints *standing committees* from among its members each year:

1. Political and Disarmament Committee.
2. Law and Arbitration Committee.
3. Administration, Mandates, and Colonies.
4. Economy, Trade, and Industry.
5. Labor, Employment, and Public Works.
6. Finance.
7. Education.
8. Interior Affairs, including Government of the Union District.

Duties of Committees: Meet every three months; keep in permanent touch with Executive and inform Assembly on current activities of Executive; pass resolutions but they are not binding on the Executive.

EXECUTIVE OR ADMINISTRATIVE:

President: Elected by the Assembly for seven-year term; cannot be reelected. (Proposes all-powerful Executive.)

Secretary-General: In charge of Union Administration; responsible to President; together with President represents Union at international functions outside Union territory.

Administrative Departments: Four Secretaries; sixteen Under-Secretaries. Departments with their subdivisions as follows:

1. *Political Department:* Policy, Disarmament and Policing, Law and Arbitration, Administration of Mandates and Colonies.
2. *Economic Department:* Trade; Industrial Planning and Production; Raw Materials and Agriculture; Communications; Labor, Employment, and Public Works; Hygiene; Finance; Statistics.
3. *Education:* Information; Leadership; Education.
4. *Interior:* Personnel and Interior Administration; Government of the Sovereign Union District.

JUDICIAL:

Permanent Court of International Justice: Eleven Judges; four Deputy Judges; elects its own President and Vice-President. (The Court should be moved from The Hague to the Seat of the Union.)

Jurisdiction: Interprets Union Constitution; passes on constitutionality of executive and legislative acts when requested; serves as Court of Appeal in arbitral and other Union decisions.

TRANSFERS OF JURISDICTION FROM MEMBER NATIONS TO THE UNION:

Creation of Sovereign Union District in Geneva through purchase of land on which Union buildings stand.

Union citizenship for officers and permanent employees of Union; on expiration of terms of office, employees may resume dormant national citizenship.

Grant of temporary or permanent Union citizenship to refugees.

Union conducts worldwide barter system, public works, population transfers, and worldwide educational program.

METHODS OF ENFORCEMENT:

United Nations imposes its settlement by armed force during five-year transition period. Thereafter, formal peace treaties to provide for disarmament and international armed force.

IMMEDIATE STEPS:

Two years after the armistice a Constituent Assembly of the Union is to be called.

PREREQUISITES TO PEACE:

United Nations victory and occupation of Europe.

LIQUIDATION OF THE WAR:

Five-year transition period set up after military occupation by United Nations troops of key cities, railway junctions, inland waterways of western, central, and eastern Europe; installation of "delousing" stations in eastern and southeastern Europe to prevent spread of typhus by returning soldiers; emergency air transport of dehydrated and concentrated foods, and vitamins to Europe pending food shipments by sea.

First Year:
1. United Nations Political, Economic, and Education Boards begin operation supervising worldwide barter trade; issue priorities for international transportation; planned relief of worldwide unemployment; removal from Germany of steel and aluminum industries; first stage of supra-national fight against unemployment; establishment of Open Door in Central African colonies.
2. *France* and *Italy* adopt modified versions of the United States Constitution.
3. Germany ruled by a Protectorate. Prussia divided between Bavaria, Saxony, the Hanseatic Cities, etc. Cancellation of citizenship of members of Nazi Party, military, semi-military, and reactionary civilian organizations; confiscation of most of their fortunes and all landed property to be used to compensate Nazi victims. Voting age of Germans to be raised to 24 years.

Second Year:
1. Creation of various federations and making of territorial adjustments.
2. Shogunate is reintroduced in Japan on a democratic basis (see: Miscellaneous).
3. Repatriation of civilians forcibly removed from their homes.
4. United Nations Economic Board initiates international public works program to combat world unemployment.
5. Education in democracy via radio and schools; establishment of *School of Democratic Leadership* at seat of United Nations.

Third Year:
The Constitution of the Union of Nations is adopted; the permanent government begins to operate; takes over direction of United Nations boards:
1. Conducts plebiscites, and on the basis of the results begins population transfers found to be necessary, or grants cantonal status to minorities within states.

2. Continues reconstruction program.
3. Begins worldwide revision of teaching of history.

Fourth Year:
1. Population transfers continued; also public works.
2. Initiation of worldwide legislation supervising stock and money exchanges; trusts, cartels, and patents.
3. Education Division initiates worldwide campaign against illiteracy, helps set up schools, etc.

Fifth Year:
1. Conclusion of population transfers.
2. Revision and readjustment of political and economic reconstruction policies on basis of four years' experience.
3. Germany adopts modified form of the United States Constitution and assumes control of its domestic and foreign affairs.
4. Development of additional public works to combat unemployment.

TERRITORIAL CHANGES:
Regional federations established under Allied guidance:
1. Danube, Balkan, Pan-Arab, Dutch East Indian federations.
2. United States of India to become a dominion in the British Commonwealth of Nations.
3. Senegal, Madagascar, Martinique-Guadeloupe, Tunisia, and French Indo-China become dominions within the French Empire on the model of the British Commonwealth.
4. Poland given a new access to the sea.
5. Ireland becomes a federation, with Ulster a member canton on the Swiss model.
6. Austria regains her independence and joins the Danube Federation.

MISCELLANEOUS:
The author suggests that the Union have its own flag and anthem to foster loyalty to its institutions.

The *Shogunate,* because it is familiar to the Japanese, is to be revived in the form of responsible parliamentary government with the *Shogun* as Minister, the Emperor remaining only as a figurehead.

AUTHOR:
John B. Corliss, Jr. (American).

TITLE OF PLAN:
The Greatest Project of All Time: A Federation of the Nations That Will Insure a Lasting Peace Between Them — Constitution of the World State.

DATE: 1943.

PAMPHLET
Published by:
The author, Detroit.

TYPE:
Federal: Based on United States Constitution.

MEMBERSHIP:
Universal: Axis nations and subjugated peoples to be under supervision of the World Congress.

ORGANS OF GOVERNMENT:
Legislative: Unicameral *Congress of Nations: Envoys* appointed for three-year term (one-third of Congress renewed each year) by Executive Authority of each nation and by consent of its legislative body or Senate if it has power of confirmation; vacancies filled by Executive. Number of envoys determined by population, literacy, cultural advance, and peaceful pursuit of self-government; one envoy for every two million population; where literacy is over ninety per cent, two envoys; twenty envoys is maximum; any island or dependency of less than 100,000 population may have self-government or be annexed to a neighboring nation by decision of Congress; reallotment of number of envoys by Congress every ten years, according to census.

First allotment of envoys as follows:
Two Envoys: Congo, Ethiopia, Afghanistan, Austria, Portugal, Greece, Morocco, Bulgaria, Anglo-Egyptian Sudan, Sweden, Chile, Cuba, Switzerland, Bolivia, Denmark, Ecuador, Finland, Iraq, Ireland, Madagascar, Norway, Syria and Lebanon, Venezuela, New Zealand, Tunisia, Uruguay.

Three Envoys: Indo-China, Korea, Nigeria, Egypt, French West Africa, Iran, Thailand, Burma, Colombia, Peru, Netherlands, Belgium, Algeria.

Four Envoys: Australia, Manchukuo, Poland, Spain, Mexico, Turkey, Yugoslavia, Philippine Islands, Hungary, Roumania, Argentina, Canada, Union of South Africa.

Five Envoys: Italy.

Six Envoys: Japan, Netherlands Indies, Brazil, France.

Nine Envoys: United Kingdom.

Eleven Envoys: Germany.

Twenty Envoys: China, India, U.S.S.R., United States.

Duties of Congress: To legislate on matters within the jurisdiction of the World State; fix salaries of all officers; decisions by majority vote, except that two-thirds vote required to expel an envoy.

Congress to meet every year in January on *different continents* in the following order: North America, Europe, Asia, South America, Africa, Australasia; and may establish an international capital on each continent.

EXECUTIVE:
President, Vice-President, Executive Council, Board of Administrators.

President and Vice-President: Elected for three-year term by the Congress by majority vote; if no candidate has a majority on the first ballot, the choice is made from the two highest; in case of a tie, the envoys vote by national delegations, each delegation having one vote.

Duties: Commander-in-Chief of World Army and Navy and of the Armed Forces of the member states; reports each year to Congress on world affairs; requires written reports from principal officers of the Departments; appoints higher officers with advice and consent of Congress; grants reprieves and pardons, except in cases of impeachment; signs legislation approved by Congress or may state his objections to it, returning it for reconsideration; if repassed, becomes law even without his signature.

Executive Council: Not over thirty members; not more than one from any nation, appointed by President. *Duties:* To formulate policies and action for efficient and economical administration of business of the World State for welfare of member nations and preservation of peace; to furnish Congress with information and recommend necessary legislation.

Board of Administrators for each Continent: Appointed by President. *Duties:* To administer, supervise, direct, control all projects, institutions, etc., established by Congress to promote employment, and welfare of the people.

JUDICIAL:

Supreme Court: Six Continental Appellate Courts; Inferior Courts established by Congress within member nations.

Original Jurisdiction: In all cases between a nation or nations and the World State; in all other cases appellate jurisdiction.

TEMPORARY:

International Court of Claims: To decide all claims between nations in existence before the establishment of the World State.

Code of Justice to be used by Supreme and Appellate Courts to be determined by Congress; Code of Justice used by Inferior Courts to be those of the nation in which the Court is stationed.

TRANSFERS OF JURISDICTION FROM MEMBER NATIONS TO THE WORLD STATE:

Admit nations to membership; levy and collect taxes, uniformly imposed; borrow money; regulate commerce, communications between nations; charter an International Bank; issue an international currency; promote progress of science and education; encourage free schools where illiteracy is prevalent; provide for Army, Navy, and Air Force to protect all nations, suppress rebellions within nations, patrol the seas; guarantee to each nation the right of the people to choose their form of government and officials; to exercise exclusive jurisdiction over the Federal District on each continent.

Congress may call a *Legislative Convention of the Nations* to submit to the national legislatures recommendations providing for uniform legislation throughout the World State.

RESTRICTIONS ON NATIONS:
Nations may not keep troops or warships without consent of Congress or engage in war, except in case of actual invasion; may levy duties on exports or imports only to the extent necessary to carry out inspection laws, and the net return must be paid to the World Treasury.

NATIONS RETAIN:
National legislatures to consent to any change in national territories. Nations may restrict imports to balance production and consumption of certain products within a nation.

Treaties in force before establishment of Federation remain in force unless in conflict with World Constitution.

Nations may prohibit or restrict immigration and prescribe qualifications for settlement.

Powers not delegated to the World State nor prohibited to the Nations are reserved to the Nations or to the people.

METHODS OF ENFORCEMENT:
Towards Individuals: Courts.

Towards Nations: Courts and Armed Forces.

IMMEDIATE STEPS:
United States Congress to provide by resolution for the translation of the proposed constitution and submission to the executive and legislative body of every nation, empire, dominion, province, colony, territory, possession, and dependency.

PREREQUISITES TO PEACE (in general):
Dissolution of all empires, international trade monopolies, diplomatic manipulation, and entangling alliances.

LIQUIDATION OF THE WAR:
Aggressor nations, their dependencies, and nations and people subjugated by them shall be held under the direction and control of the World State until they are qualified to join the Federation and their sovereignty and rights are restored to them.

TERRITORIAL CHANGES:
All dominions, provinces, colonies, territories, possessions, dependencies not contiguous to the mother country are freed from all allegiance or political connection, and may, as free units, join the World State.

RATIFICATION:
By the executive and legislative bodies of nations and territorial units qualified to join.

AMENDMENT:
By two-thirds vote of Congress, President, Vice-President, Executive Council, Administrative Boards, members of Supreme and Continental Appellate Courts in concurrent session, President presiding. Amendments may be proposed by Executive Council, Administrative Boards, Congress or by petition of 100 Envoys. Concurrent sessions for considering amendments are to be held once a year wherever Congress directs.

MISCELLANEOUS:
The author provides for a Bill of Rights similar to that in the United States Constitution.

AUTHOR:
ELDON GRIFFIN (American).

PROFESSION:
Writer; Asiatic Research Specialist; Oyster Farmer.

TITLE OF PLAN:
Clinching the Victory.

DATE: 1943.

PUBLISHER:
Wilberlilla Publishers, Seattle, Washington.

TYPE:
FEDERAL. NAME: United Nations World Government.

MEMBERSHIP:
UNIVERSAL.

ORGANS OF GOVERNMENT:
LEGISLATIVE: Unicameral Legislature: Direct election of representatives in proportion to population; supplementary representation from regional associations of nations. *Decisions:* By three-fifths or three-fourths vote of all members.

EXECUTIVE OR ADMINISTRATIVE:
Small Commission: Members to have staggered terms; rotating chairmanship.

Regional Commissions: Composed of representatives of governments of member nations; of occupational and interest groups; of elected representatives of the regional populations. *Personnel* to be multinational and multiracial; direct selection on competitive merit basis; candidates able to speak two or three languages; retirement with generous pensions.

Independent Board of Roving Critics: Ten- to twenty-year term. Composed of distinguished individuals of all ages. *Duties:* To locate and expose incipient trouble; to suggest remedying legislative and executive action. *Powers:* To attend all meetings and conferences; to examine all records; to criticize highest authorities.

International Police: Composed of volunteers. *Duties:* To check disorder; prevent military activity; safeguard elections; protect and restrain minorities. Empowered to determine what disturbances threaten general peace and which are of local nature. Use of neutral units suggested in the beginning.

JUDICIAL:
Central Supranational Court: Regional Courts. Minority of non-lawyers to be appointed to each bench.

Full-time Advisory Board: Composed of men and women of experience, as well as young persons, representing different interests. *Duties:* To participate in discussion of all cases in private sessions.

Direct communication between Courts and Legislative Bodies to correct injustices in laws and rulings and to enable the Courts to suggest new legislation.

TRANSFERS OF JURISDICTION FROM MEMBER NATIONS TO THE UNITED NATIONS:

To levy taxes.

To control military and naval installations at strategic points, such as Pearl Harbor, Corregidor, Panama Canal, Gibraltar, Singapore, Vladivostok.

To assume war debts of member nations.

To assume direct and exclusive administration of colonies unprepared for self-government.

IMMEDIATE STEPS:

Establishment of a *Peace Board* to be composed of already existing agencies with twenty-five million dollars at its disposal. Representatives of now hostile peoples to be added as soon as possible. *Duties:* To keep in touch with official action and popular reactions and aspirations; to assume leadership as military activities slow down; to substitute for a general peace conference; to revise all agreements negotiated by nations during the war that are inconsistent with the world settlement; to examine national archives for assurance that no secret pacts between nations exist.

Unification of all popular elements in all nations working for a better society.

PREREQUISITES TO PEACE:
United Nations victory.

LIQUIDATION OF THE WAR:

Long armistice. Twenty-five- to thirty-year training period of Axis nations in democratic processes. Restoration by Axis of undamaged property; repair of others; no cash indemnities to be exacted; no retribution. Axis military equipment to be surrendered to United Nations Government. There is to be no formal moralizing on war guilt; all national archives to be opened to scholars to deprive the issue of its inflammatory character.

Colonies belonging to members of the United Nations, temporarily occupied by the Axis, are not to be restored to their former possessors. Instead, polls to be taken by United Nations Government to determine local opinion on future status of colonies.

MISCELLANEOUS:
The United Nations Government to have at least four world headquarters to be used in rotation. Separate sets of archives to be maintained. Legislative and commission sessions to be held in different parts of the world.

AUTHOR:
MAX HABICHT (Swiss).

PROFESSION:
Former Member Legal Section League of Nations Secretariat.

TITLE OF PLAN:
Is an Enduring Peace Possible?

MANUSCRIPT

DATE: 1943.

TYPE:
FEDERAL.

MEMBERSHIP:
UNIVERSAL.

ORGANS OF GOVERNMENT:
LEGISLATIVE: Tricameral Parliament: *Senate; Chamber of Guilds; House of Deputies.*

Senate: 150 members (some seventy nations to nominate one, two, three, or four Senators); each nation to decide its own procedure of appointment.

Chamber of Guilds: 150 members representing international trade and labor unions, professional organizations, farmers, etc., nominated by each organization according to its own procedure.

House of Deputies: 500 representatives elected by popular vote; one for each one million adults over twenty-one, with eight years of compulsory schooling.

Decisions by majority vote in each of the three chambers; passage by Senate and House of Deputies, or Chamber of Guilds and House of Deputies required for legislation.

EXECUTIVE OR ADMINISTRATIVE:
World Council: Seven Councilors; five-year terms; elected by majority vote of all three Chambers in united session; reelection permissible; decisions by majority vote. *Duties:* To carry out the laws of the Federation.

Secretariat: Civil Service recruited from all nations. *Duties:* To assist World Parliament and Council.

JUDICIAL:
World Court: Fifteen Judges; nine-year terms; elected by majority vote of all three Chambers in joint session; reelection permissible.

Jurisdiction: In all disputes between member states upon the application of one party. Special jurisdiction between States and individuals if agreed upon in treaties or special agreements.

TRANSFERS OF JURISDICTION FROM MEMBER NATIONS TO THE FEDERATION:
The Constitution should transfer to the World Parliament all matters which are best regulated by world legislation. In the beginning these should include control of armaments, regulation of international air traffic, of navigation on international rivers and on the seas, etc. Additional transfers of jurisdiction by amendment of the Constitution.

METHODS OF ENFORCEMENT:
World law in every case is to be enforced against guilty individuals only, and not against states as a whole.

Enforcement must be carried out by professionals, not by the average citizen transformed into a soldier; police forces to be recruited, according to high standards, from all nations on voluntary basis and stationed all over the world; numbers and type of equipment will depend on amounts of military, naval, and air power allowed each state by the World Government.

IMMEDIATE STEPS:
A Constitutional Convention establishing a federation between the United States, the British Commonwealth, the U.S.S.R., and China would compel the rest of the world to join the federation in a relatively short time.

PREREQUISITES TO PEACE:
Popular education of the voters to an understanding that without properly organized world government there can be no world peace.

LIQUIDATION OF THE WAR:
Transition from war to peace should not last longer than five years. End of hostilities must be followed by joint action to prevent anarchy, hunger, and pestilence.
There should be no peace treaties.
A World Constitutional Convention should be called in which all nations can participate. The resulting written Constitution should be submitted to all nations for ratification.

TERRITORIAL CHANGES:
An attempt should be made to transfer dependent territories from national sovereignty to the World Federation for administration with the object of later liberation.

RATIFICATION:
Each nation to decide its own method of ratification and whether to submit the question of adherence to the World Federation to plebiscite.

MISCELLANEOUS:
Headquarters of the World Federation to be independent of any member of the Federation; present location of the League of Nations buildings should be enlarged by addition of Free Zone of Gex (French territory) to be equal in size to the District of Columbia.

AUTHOR:
RICHARD BURTON JOHNSON (American), Chairman of a small study group which included American-born Filipinos, Chinese, Japanese, and Negroes.

PROFESSION:
Teacher.

TITLE OF PLAN:
Armistice Terms; Emergency World Legislative Assembly; Universal Bill of Rights; A World Constitution.

Mimeographed 12 pages.

DATE: 1943.

ORGANIZATIONAL BACKING:
The World Party, Seattle, Washington.

TYPE:
FEDERAL. NAME: World Federation.

MEMBERSHIP:
UNIVERSAL.

ORGANS OF GOVERNMENT:
LEGISLATIVE: *The World Assembly:* Four-year term; terms of one-third of the delegates to expire every sixteen months; composed of delegates from each *National Assembly of Councils* (see: Miscellaneous) unless Continental Assemblies have been organized. World Assembly to divide its membership into *Councils* of fifteen to twenty-five delegates each. Each Council to elect one delegate to the *World Board*. World Assembly may create additional legislative, judicial, administrative, and executive bodies. *Decisions:* On rules of procedure and their amendment by two-thirds majority.

Before it can undertake legislation on matters of major importance, the World Assembly must have the two-thirds majority approval of two worldwide independently conducted public-opinion polls.

EXECUTIVE OR ADMINISTRATIVE:

World Board: Composed of delegates elected by Councils of the World Assembly. *Executive Administrator:* Appointed by World Board as its chairman.

Executive President: Appointed by World Board. *Duties:* To formulate general policies.

World Civil Service: Lists to be compiled on basis of merit; all civil service employees to retain political rights possessed by rest of population.

World Migration Commission: To prevent restrictions on freedom of movement and discrimination based on race, nationality, creed, age, or sex. Its rules and regulations to apply equally to all peoples.

World Trade Commission: To prevent restrictions on access to raw materials imposed by tariffs, quotas, imposts, duties, taxes, inspection fees, discriminatory freight rates, transportation charges, exclusion acts, and migration acts except those imposed equally on all nations and peoples by the World Assembly and the World Trade Commission.

Other Commissions to be established by the World Assembly.

TRANSFERS OF JURISDICTION FROM MEMBER NATIONS TO THE FEDERATION:

Control of trade, migration, postal system, transportation, communications, natural resources, production, consumption, distribution, exchange, public health, and education.

Establish a uniform monetary system, weights and measures, and a World Calendar.

Levy taxes.

Apply police powers operating on individuals only.

Define boundaries.

Prevent racial discrimination and crime.

Administer justice.

Provide emergency relief.

Establish a universal language.

NATIONS RETAIN:

Freedom of trade, of the seas, and of the air.

Equal access to world's resources and manufactured goods.

Internal autonomy over all matters except those transferred to the Federation.
Concurrent jurisdiction over matters in which the Federal power is limited.
Right to secede on one year's notice of cause.

INDIVIDUAL RIGHTS:
Right to life, sustenance, world citizenship, and political activity.
Freedom of movement and of conscience.
Freedom of every form of expression and of access to all mediums of expression; freedom of peaceable assembly.
Freedom of religion.
Prohibition of slavery and involuntary servitude.
Imprisonment for crime to attempt rehabilitation of the individual instead of his punishment.
Ex post facto laws to be prohibited.
Right of habeas corpus may not be abridged for any reason.
Security against search and seizure except on warrant showing due cause.
Private property to be taken for public use only after just compensation, except in cases when the majority of the population votes for socialization of private property.
Right to work may not be denied on account of race, creed, or nationality; nor for non-membership in a labor organization or guild until after sixty days of employment.
No person may be debarred from any place frequented or used by the general public, nor segregated in such places, on account of sex, age, race, creed, nationality, or literacy.
Men and women to have equal rights of suffrage, citizenship, labor, education, and equal pay for equal work.

METHODS OF ENFORCEMENT:
Police powers operating on individuals only.

PREREQUISITES TO PEACE:
Declaration of armistice on equal terms with equal representation of all belligerents and without victor or vanquished. No indemnities.
Armed forces to begin immediate reconstruction; demobilization to

be gradual. Complete immunity for military leaders, political leaders, members of the armed forces, and civilians for all acts connected with the war to the date of the armistice; liability for criminal acts to date from the declaration of armistice. Immediate relief of starving populations.

LIQUIDATION OF THE WAR:
Earliest possible establishment of *Emergency World Legislative Assembly:* Each nation to send fourteen delegates, each delegate representing one of the following groups: government, religion, education, labor, industry, world government or peace organizations, commerce, finance, health, agriculture, arts, science, armed forces, and one delegate-at-large. Each nation to have one vote for every ten million of population. *Duties:* To organize a *World Police Force* consisting of equal military contingents from each major belligerent nation; police powers to be used only against individuals. Police force to remove all vital gear from armed equipment such as warships, airplanes, tanks, guns, and small arms. Such vital parts to remain under jurisdiction of force pending disarmament legislation by the Permanent World Government.

To draft the *World Bill of Rights* and *World Constitution* to be submitted to popular ratification.

Emergency World Council: Composed of one delegate from each national delegation of the Emergency Assembly. *Duties:* To select temporary executive and administrative officers. All sessions of both bodies to be open to the press. Daily records of all sessions to be published and broadcast. Temporary capital of Assembly to be in the *Azores* or in *Bermuda*. The entire area to be under the jurisdiction of the Assembly until the seat of the Permanent World Government is selected.

RATIFICATION:
By simple majority of the total world population.

AMENDMENT:
By two-thirds popular majority determined by a public-opinion poll, plus a two-thirds majority vote of the World Assembly.

Charts of Plans to Unite Nations Since 1914

MISCELLANEOUS:
The author suggests the following worldwide political reorganization: The organization of *Local Councils* of twenty-five persons or less. Each *Local Council* to send one delegate to a *Community Assembly of Councils*, which sends one delegate to the *City-County Assembly of Councils*. These in turn are represented in the *Regional Assembly of Councils* which are represented in the *National Assembly of Councils*. All issues and suggestions originating in the lower assemblies must be carried forward by each higher assembly and resulting action reported in writing to the originating assembly. Each assembly to have its own constitution and field of jurisdiction.

AUTHOR:
ABE ROGOW (American).

PROFESSION:
Carpenter (member Carpenters' Union Local 383).

TITLE OF PLAN:
A Plan for Immediate and Lasting Peace.

PAMPHLET

DATE: 1943.

PUBLISHED for the author in Bayonne, New Jersey.

TYPE:
FEDERAL. NAME: League of States.

MEMBERSHIP:
UNIVERSAL — all nations must be members of the League; in addition they must join one of the *Eight Regional Federations* to which they belong by geographical location.

The *Regional Federations* are:
United States of Europe (Iceland included).
Union of Soviet Socialist Republics.

United States of South Asia (India, Burma, Philippines among those included).
The Mongolian Federation (China, Indo-China, Korea, and Japan).
The United States of Africa (All Africa to Suez and Madagascar).
The United States of Australia.
The United States of North America (United States and Canada).
The United States of South America (including Caribbean Islands, and Mexico).

ORGANS OF GOVERNMENT:
LEGISLATIVE: Unicameral *World Congress:* Every state represented.

JUDICIAL:
Supreme Tribunal: Settles differences among the states that cannot be resolved by the Federation Government; disputes between the Federations.

TRANSFERS OF JURISDICTION FROM MEMBER NATIONS TO THE LEAGUE:
Regulates tariffs between the Eight Federations.
Stops inter-Federation conflicts.
Patrols high seas, skyways, important waterways such as Panama, Suez, Gibraltar, Petsamo, the Dardanelles.
Governs backward peoples.
Governs seat of the League.

NATIONS RETAIN:
Right to frame their own laws and constitution; and to participate in setting up their Regional Federation after the model of the United States or of Switzerland.

IMMEDIATE STEPS:
United Nations should start immediately to organize the various Regional Federations to prove that the democracies are determined this time to straighten out the globe.

LIQUIDATION OF THE WAR:
The demobilized soldiers must be provided with constructive work in continental and world reconstruction.

Germany: For fifty to one hundred years should not be allowed to participate in state, federal, or world league elections; European Federation to appoint Governor for Germany, as well as Germany's representatives in the Federal Congress, and judges to the highest courts; federal supervision and direction of German school system for fifty years; only local police to be permitted; economic participation to be on an equal basis. Nazi leaders to be put to death; professional soldiers and lesser leaders exiled to Devil's Island. German labor gangs to be sent all over Europe to rebuild what has been destroyed; all stolen goods to be returned.

Japan to receive similar treatment. *Italian* leaders to be exiled to Devil's Island.

TERRITORIAL CHANGES:
Any economic, religious, or racial entity claiming sovereign independence as a state to be recognized irrespective of size after a plebiscite. If the group is so small that it could not exist separately economically and politically, resettlement may be arranged. Empires to be abolished. Jews may be settled in Palestine, or if Arabs refuse resettlement, possibly in Crimea.

Hawaii, to become capital of the League of States.

AUTHOR:
John H. Rosser (Australian).

TITLE OF PLAN:
World Charter — A Constitution for the Post-War World.

PAMPHLET

DATE: 1943.

PUBLISHED for the author by Morcoms Pty., Brisbane, Australia.

ORGANIZATIONAL BACKING:
The Council for Universal Peace and Security, Benowa, via Southport, Queensland.

TYPE:
FEDERAL. NAME: People's World Union.

MEMBERSHIP:
UNIVERSAL — the peoples of the world.

ORGANS OF GOVERNMENT:
LEGISLATIVE: Unicameral *Council:* Five-year term; one representative for every million population, directly elected by all citizens at least eighteen years of age (except criminals, feeble-minded, and peoples illiterate and not politically conscious); peoples illiterate, but politically conscious, as in India, to vote according to electoral plan determined by their literate leaders.
Powers: Exercises full law-making power, appoints executive and judiciary. Representatives subject to recall by their electorate.

EXECUTIVE OR ADMINISTRATIVE:
President and *Cabinet:* Selected by Council.
President and Cabinet retain powers until formation of a new Executive by the newly elected People's Council. President convenes People's Council.

Members of the Cabinet:
Minister for *Education* and two Assistant Ministers.
Minister for *War* and two Assistant Ministers.
Minister for *Customs* and two Assistant Ministers.
Minister for *People's Rights* and two Assistant Ministers.
Minister for *Development of Backward Peoples* and two Assistant Ministers.
Minister for *Public Honesty* and two Assistant Ministers.
Attorney-General — Five-year term.

JUDICIAL:
International Court of Justice: Created by Council.
Jurisdiction: Over disputes between the nations of the world and the World Union; interprets laws of the Council; determines whether democratic rights are maintained by the nations; tries warmakers, war-advocates, makers of false public statements.

TRANSFERS OF JURISDICTION FROM MEMBER NATIONS TO THE WORLD UNION:

The People's World Union shall:

Control and direct armed forces of world; conscript all citizens and property for defense of Union, its member nations, and people.

Control and collect tariffs to supply its revenues.

Issue uniform currency.

Control, and direct if necessary, education of backward and semi-literate peoples; direct their industrial development; prevent their exploitation for profit by companies, or citizens of other nations.

Create credit to extent of resources under its control for development of backward areas.

Direct teaching of history of civilization, of social science, and of biological science among all peoples.

Introduce democratic rights by referendum in nations where they do not exist or are not carried out; or by supporting the people of a nation prevented by force from exercising such rights.

Direct teaching of common language among all people.

Prevent formation, or continuance, of Interstate Trusts, Combines, Cartels, Banks, Insurance and Trading Companies.

Reduce tariffs gradually between nations until only those levied by World Union remain.

Intervene in nations where disorder has broken out to prevent illegal use of force or rioting; maintain order with Union army or police force; hold referendum to determine how the people wish to be governed.

Assume administration of any area of a nation where more than a half million citizens are illiterate unless the nation begins immediately to apply Union educational program.

Probe false statements of press or politicians, and publicize court judgments on such statements.

NATIONS UNDERTAKE:

To allow their people freedom of speech and organization and enjoyment of democratic rights.

To take referendum of their people when requested by Council.
To use educational curriculum laid down by Council.

RESTRICTIONS ON NATIONS:
They may not exceed in area one-fourth of the earth's land surface.
They may not impose customs or tariffs except under direction of the Union Council, nor start, continue, or control industries among races more backward than themselves.
They may not raise militia or armed forces without consent of Council.
They may not permit organization of secret societies, nor drilling of large bodies of men.
They may not manufacture munitions.
They may not have a police force above the number permitted by the Council.

DEMOCRATIC RIGHTS:
All peoples of the world are citizens of the People's World Union.
Each human being entitled to citizenship of the nation in which he is born.
Freedom to travel anywhere assured to all law-abiding, literate people.
Right to free education to the limit of individual ability.
Right to work and payment for work.
Right of assembly, worship, speech, writing, and publication at own expense.
Right of travel and settlement subject to laws of the nations concerned.
Right to free medical attention as provided by nation, and to aid in sickness and old age.

IMMEDIATE STEPS:
Development of local *People's Councils* as the base of international political organization, meeting regularly to discuss government policy; after establishment of World Union, local councils to initiate recall of representatives. Plan stresses popular initiative to create world government.

RATIFICATION:
By referendum of the people of the world.

Charts of Plans to Unite Nations Since 1914

AMENDMENT:
Amendment of the Constitution and the grant of additional powers to the World Union by referendum of the people of the world.

The Constitution must be resubmitted to the people of the world every eighteen years for revision and ratification by referendum.

MISCELLANEOUS:
The seat of the World Union is to be located in Japan, England, Australia, or New Zealand whichever country first revises its industrial and social organization, basing them on common ownership. If none of these industrially developed nations will adapt their social organization, a backward island such as Madagascar or New Guinea to become the seat of the Union.

Union laws to be published in the language of each nation and in the common language of the Union.

AUTHOR:
Wallace C. Speers (American).

PROFESSION:
Business executive.

TITLE OF PLAN:
Coorder Nations — A Proposal for World Coordination.

DATE: June, 1943 (revised).

PAMPHLET

PUBLISHED by the author.

TYPE:
Federal. Name: World State.

MEMBERSHIP:
Universal: All nations to be invited immediately to join the World State.

Three Classes of Membership with advancement from the two limited classes to full participation on fulfillment of definite conditions.

Class A: All members of the United Nations; all nations advanced from Class B who have signed a *Bill of Duties* ratified by majority vote of their nationals, who have repaid Lend-Lease Aid, and are able to assist the World State instead of receiving assistance from it.

Class B: Nations without representation in World Parliament assigned to this group by World Senate on basis of advanced state of self-government, industrialization, rising standards of living, partial repayment of Lend-Lease Aid, ratification of *Bill of Rights* by majority vote of their nationals.

Class C: All Axis nations; all colonies remaining under jurisdiction of nations now controlling them; colonies not under national jurisdiction at end of war under World Senate jurisdiction. No representation in World Parliament.

ORGANS OF GOVERNMENT:
LEGISLATIVE: Bicameral — *Senate; House of Representatives.*
Senate: Three-year term; one member from each A nation; Senate elects President of World State; sole power to declare war by majority vote.

House of Representatives: Two-year term; one representative for each ten million inhabitants of A nations; proportionate fractional vote for representatives of populations under ten million. House initiates all legislation.

Members of Senate and House elected or appointed on same day in each nation according to national procedure. First duty of Senate and House to draft detailed World Constitution with Bill of World Rights and Bill of World Duties. Two-thirds vote of both Houses to override presidential veto, and to pass World Constitution.

EXECUTIVE OR ADMINISTRATIVE:
President: Three-year term; elected by Senate from its own membership; may not succeed himself; may veto all legislation; automatically removed from office if both houses override his veto.

World Armed Forces: Stationed in A nations; seventy-five per cent composed of nationals of nation in which forces are stationed; twenty-five

Charts of Plans to Unite Nations Since 1914 175

per cent of nationals of other A nations. *Duties:* To patrol the world; to prevent secret preparation of heavy armament.

War Council: Fifteen Senators elected by Senate; fifteen Supreme Military Commanding Officers (not more than one from any A nation) selected by House. *Duties:* To determine strategic location of world army.

Educational Council: Fifteen educators appointed by Senate. *Duties:* To assign *Educational Forces* to positions in C nations to provide primary education and social, economic, and political instruction; to assign educators to B nations in consultation with their national educational authorities; educational forces to prevent instruction or indoctrination in any nation contrary to provisions of World Constitution.

Economic Committee: Appointed by Senate. *Duties:* To administer World Lend-Lease (Peace Loans) to assist in rehabilitation (these loans not to be repaid); to assure supply of raw materials to all nations; to purchase raw materials for nations unable to pay for them in open market, subject to repayment in kind, or in gold plus interest charge.

JUDICIAL:
Supreme Council: Fifteen members elected by Senate from among existing and former heads of governments of class A nations. *Duties:* To determine legality of all legislation under World Constitution.

TRANSFERS OF JURISDICTION FROM MEMBER NATIONS TO THE WORLD STATE:

To maintain a World Army for protection of member nations.

To declare war against any aggressor nation.

To provide economic and educational aid to class C and B nations through World Lend-Lease (Peace Loans).

To organize tariff union between all member nations with five per cent yearly tariff reduction to bring about free trade in twenty years.

To organize progressive reduction of restrictions on immigration and emigration as living standards are raised in undeveloped areas.

To receive social security funds accumulated by A nations to finance World Lend-Lease.

To levy interest charges on loans to nations; and proportionate direct tax on each A nation.

NATIONS UNDERTAKE:
To guarantee absolute freedom of worship to all their people.

RESTRICTIONS ON NATIONS:
Class B and C nations to have no vote in World Parliament; they may not produce or own heavy armament; their nationals may not enlist in the World Army.

Class A nations may not own heavy arms, but may produce them for use of World Army.

NATIONS RETAIN:
Light arms for police protection.

Right to impose immigration and emigration restrictions for interim postwar period.

RESTRICTIONS ON DEMOCRATIC RIGHTS:
One year's compulsory training and service in class A nations of all men and women on reaching twenty-one years of age either in World Army, Navy, Air, or Educational Forces.

METHODS OF ENFORCEMENT:
Towards Nations: Use of World Armed Forces to suppress a nation declared an aggressor by majority vote of World Senate; such nation to be reclassified as a C nation.

LIQUIDATION OF THE WAR:
No peace treaty at end of war; three years' armistice.

United Nations to disarm Axis nations and keep them disarmed; to patrol world, guaranteeing safety to all nations; to assure freedom to disorganized nations to adopt their own form of government; to provide military patroling of nations, undergoing internal revolutions, to assure freedom of thought and action but to prevent violence and destruction.

Organization of the World State.

RATIFICATION:
World Constitution to be submitted to each nation for ratification after passage in World Senate and House. Constitution with the tabulated votes of national ratifications to be submitted to Supreme Council which is to interpret the results and make its recommendations to House for changes in World Constitution expressed by popular demand. Both Senate and House must then pass revised Constitution by two-thirds vote before it comes into force.

AMENDMENT:
By same method.

MISCELLANEOUS:
Capital of World State to be located for four-year periods in each A nation on land donated for such purpose. First capital of World State to be in the United States of America.

AUTHOR:
JENNIE McMULLIN TURNER (American).

PROFESSION:
Supervisor of General Adult Education, State of Wisconsin.

TITLE OF PLAN:
Proposed Constitution of the United Nations.

DATE: 1943.

MANUSCRIPT

TYPE:
FEDERAL: Based on United States Constitution but modified to provide for responsible parliamentary government.

NAME: United Nations.

MEMBERSHIP:
UNIVERSAL.

ORGANS OF GOVERNMENT:

LEGISLATIVE: Unicameral *Congress* — One representative from each nation; plus one representative for every ten million population eligible to vote in United Nations elections; after first ten-year period Congress to determine basis of representation in proportion to number of *active international citizens,* qualified by a university education or its equivalent; but total number of representatives shall not exceed four times the number of nations represented. Representatives to be elected at-large within the nations on non-partisan ballots.

EXECUTIVE OR ADMINISTRATIVE:

Prime Minister: Elected by Congress by majority vote after each general election, either from its own membership or outside it; subject to recall by majority vote.

Duties: Acts as Chairman of Cabinet.
Appoints members of Cabinet with consent of Congress.
Attends Congress sessions and answers questions regarding administration of United Nations affairs.
Acts as head of International Police Force.

Cabinet: Made up of Ministers of administrative departments established by Congress. Serves as Planning Board, presenting plans and proposed legislation to Congress.

President: Elected by majority vote of Congress after each general election. *Duties:* To represent the United Nations at social affairs and functions.

JUDICIAL:

Supreme Court: Jurisdiction extends to all cases arising under Constitution and laws of United Nations; to controversies to which United Nations is party, and between two or more nations if referred to the Court by Congress; between citizens of different nations; between a nation or its citizens and foreign nations, their citizens, or subjects.

Powers: The Supreme Court may veto national laws found unconstitutional, but may not veto United Nations laws; it should report to Congress on any law it considers in violation of the Constitution, and make recommendations at least once a year as to changes in legislation.

TRANSFERS OF JURISDICTION FROM MEMBER NATIONS TO THE UNITED NATIONS:

To regulate trade and commerce among the nations, assuring access by all to natural resources.

To borrow money; assume debts of the United Nations incurred in the war.

To make binding or optional regulations regarding money and banking, weights and measures.

To create and maintain United Nations Force (Police Force or Peace Force).

To admit nations or territories into the United Nations by majority vote of Congress.

To administer all former mandates as United Nations territory.

To acquire by gift or purchase territory suitable for international parks and air fields.

To provide for peaceful separation or union of nations or territories with other nations.

To settle boundary and other disputes between nations through judicial process.

To establish, operate or regulate international postal and express systems.

To build roads with consent of nations traversed; to regulate, own, and operate travel and transportation systems by land, sea, and air, traversing nations only by their consent.

To regulate and conduct elections for United Nations officials within nations.

To regulate international citizenship by providing for *resident* and *active* citizenship. (Active citizens are those with four years' college education or its equivalent.)

To negotiate with nations not yet members of the United Nations.

To levy and collect taxes to provide for the foregoing.

Congress may recommend regulations of migration and travel to be binding only on nations formally accepting them.

NATIONS RETAIN:
Powers not delegated to the United Nations by the Constitution nor prohibited to the nations are reserved to the nations or to the people.

METHODS OF ENFORCEMENT:
In addition to its functions in upholding United Nations laws, the United Nations Force is to be trained in languages, history; government and social sciences; also trained to organize community enterprises, disaster relief, etc.

IMMEDIATE STEPS:
Passage of Joint Resolution in Congress proposing the following amendment to Article I, Section 8, of the United States Constitution: The Congress shall have Power:
> To join with other nations of the world in establishing a world federation which shall provide a law-making, executive, and judicial machinery through which the nations may settle their differences peacefully and work toward justice for all and for the general welfare.

PREREQUISITES TO PEACE:
The United States must convince the world that this time it means to take part in world organization.

TERRITORIAL CHANGES:
Mandates to become United Nations territory.
Other territorial changes to be regulated by the United Nations in accordance with expressed wishes of the people.
Suggests Honolulu as the capital.

AUTHOR:
MICHAEL YOUNG (British).

PROFESSION:
Journalist.

TITLE OF PLAN:
The World Settlement from *The Trial of Adolf Hitler*.

DATE: 1944.

PUBLISHER:
E. P. Dutton & Co., Inc., New York.

TYPE:
FEDERAL. NAME: World Association of Free People.

MEMBERSHIP:
UNIVERSAL: All nations to be equal members irrespective of their size, population, industrial, or agricultural development.

ORGANS OF GOVERNMENT:
LEGISLATIVE: *Annual Convention:* Composed of popularly elected representatives of associated peoples. *Duties:* To approve or reject legislation formulated by Governing Council.

EXECUTIVE OR ADMINISTRATIVE:
Governing Council: Two-year term; composed at first of men and women elected by the peoples of the United States, Great Britain, the Soviet Union, and China. *Chairman:* Elected annually from among their number by members of the Council. *Duties of Council:* To formulate world legislation for submission to Annual Convention; to appoint administrative Commissions, High Commissioners; to direct the World Police.

Judicial Commission: Composed of world's leading jurists. *Duties:* To draft procedure, rules, and code of civil, criminal, and military law for use of High Tribunal of Justice.

Financial Commission: To manage and control World Bank.

World Bank: To serve as clearing house and lending agency. *Duties:* To advance funds, raw materials, livestock, and other supplies on long-range terms to rehabilitate European and Asiatic nations; to maintain credit and debit accounts of supporter and borrower nations; to manage and supervise international transactions of associated nations.

Commissioners of Labor: To supervise German labor battalions engaged in reconstruction work in devastated areas.

Theoretical Plans

Educational Commission: Composed of American, English, and Russian scholars. *Duties:* To devise new educational system and textbooks for defeated nations.

World Police: Composed of *Military High Command, Naval High Command,* and *Air Force High Command.*

JUDICIAL:
High Tribunal of Justice: Six-year term; one-third of terms to expire every second year; composed of twelve judges elected by the national legislative bodies from among justices with ten years' experience on highest national judicial bodies; one from each of the following nations or regions: the United States, Great Britain, Canada, Australia and New Zealand, the Union of South Africa, the Soviet Union, France, the Moslem countries of the Middle East, India, China, Latin America, and one from the newly created Republic of Judea (consisting of Kenya and Italian Somaliland). *Jurisdiction:* To decide disputes between nations. Its jurisdiction to be compulsory and its decisions final and binding.

TRANSFERS OF JURISDICTION FROM MEMBER PEOPLES TO THE ASSOCIATION:
To preserve peace.
To fix quotas of national armies, navies, and air forces.
To own and control raw materials and plants manufacturing armaments (armament and airplanes to be manufactured only in the United States, Great Britain and the Dominions, the Soviet Union, China, and certain nations of the Western Hemisphere).
To supervise and regulate air transport and shipping.
To bring about equitable distribution of world's resources.
To determine boundaries between associated nations.
To administer German and Italian colonies.

RESTRICTIONS ON NATIONS:
May not resort to war for any reason.
May not negotiate alliances, balance-of-power agreements or unions.
Must submit disputes to High Tribunal of Justice.

NATIONS RETAIN:
Right to choose their own form of government as long as it provides for elections by secret ballot.

Right to enact and enforce own national laws, maintain law and order, levy and apportion taxes.

DEMOCRATIC RIGHTS:
The absolute sovereignty of the people is recognized.

METHODS OF ENFORCEMENT:
Governing Council to refer breaches of world law to *High Tribunal of Justice* for adjudication. *World Police* to compel execution of Court decision, if necessary.

IMMEDIATE STEPS:
Meeting in Assembly at Vatican City of popularly elected representatives of the common people of the United States, Great Britain, the Soviet Union, and China to organize the World Association of Free People.

PREREQUISITES TO PEACE:
United Nations victory.

LIQUIDATION OF THE WAR:
Germany to be divided into a number of independent republics. Their boundaries to be fixed and guarded by the World Police for fifty years. *High Commissioner* of Association of Free People to reside in Berlin, with final authority over all matters pertaining to peace in the Germanic States. Allied army of occupation to be composed of American, British, and Russian troops commanded by a military commission. Reeducation of German youth to be under supervision of the *Association*.

No reparations to be exacted, but battalions of several million demobilized German soldiers to be sent to devastated nations to assist in reconstruction work. Workers to be fed, clothed, housed, and paid a small sum fixed by the *Governing Council* and advanced by the *World Bank*.

Japan to be expelled from all occupied and conquered territory. Fifty-year military occupation by army composed of Chinese, Formosans, and Manchurians. *High Commissioner* and *World Police* to exercise general supervision. Constitutional monarchy to be established with responsible government composed of Japanese and Chinese administrators. Japan to be reduced to an agricultural nation: merchant shipping and all forms of manufacturing to be forbidden. Youth may not engage in military drill. Educational system to be reformed under Chinese teachers.

Italy to become a democratic republic. No reparations or other punitive measures. Token army of occupation for a short period. *High Commissioner* to be stationed in Rome. *World Police* to exercise nominal supervision.

Bulgaria, Roumania, and *Hungary* to be under twenty-five year military occupation and protective custody of Association.

Yugoslavia, Greece, and *Albania* to abolish their monarchic systems.

France to grant independence to *Syria* and *Lebanon* under temporary and nominal French supervision. *Morocco, Algeria,* and *Tunisia* to become sovereign independent states with France permitted to keep military bases and troops within their territories. France to transfer French *Indo-China* to China. May retain *African* and *American colonies* with political concessions granted to natives.

Palestine to become a *Free State* under supervision of the Association without direct control by Jews or Arabs.

Kenya and *Italian Somaliland* to be established as *Republic of Judea* for settlement of expatriated Jews. American people to contribute financial support, agricultural tools, seeds, livestock, and machinery necessary for settlement.

Liberia to receive economic assistance to make it self-supporting.

British Crown Colonies to be granted home rule with resident governors appointed by the King, but subject to removal by two-thirds popular vote.

India to be granted Dominion status for a twenty-five year period; thereafter nation-wide referendum to determine continuance as member of British Commonwealth or withdrawal and full independence. *Special Commission* of the Association to bring about cooperation between Princes' States and the Provinces.

China to become a Federated Republic patterned after the Soviet and United States Constitutions.

Other British, French, and Dutch colonial possessions to continue for twenty-five year period under former political and economic control; their economic development to be planned and aided by lend-lease with native populations educated for home rule. At end of preparatory period colonies to decide their future status.

German and *Italian colonies* to be administered by *Regional Commissions* of the Association and prepared for eventual self-government.

TERRITORIAL CHANGES:
Headquarters of the governing organs of the Association of Free People to be distributed as follows:

Governing Council in Washington, D. C.

High Tribunal of Justice in London, England.

World Bank in Basle, Switzerland.

Military High Command of World Police in Berlin, Germany.

Naval High Command of World Police in Tokyo, Japan.

Air Force High Command of World Police in Rome, Italy.

Germany to be reorganized into the following independent republics: Bavaria, Württemberg, Mecklenburg, Baden, Saxony, Thuringia, Hesse, Oldenburg, Brunswick, Anhalt, Lippe, Schaumburg-Lippe; Prussia to be divided into three states: Eastern, Western, and Southern Prussia; Berlin and surrounding area to form a separate state.

PART III

THEORETICAL PLANS

CHARTS OF PLANS TO UNITE NATIONS SINCE 1914

A. UNIVERSAL CONFEDERATE PLANS

"Let me, however, make this clear, in case there should be any mistake about it in any quarter: we mean to hold our own. I have not become the King's first minister in order to preside over the liquidation of the British Empire. For that task, if ever it were prescribed, someone else would have to be found and, under a democracy, I suppose the nation would have to be consulted."
     Prime Minister WINSTON CHURCHILL, November 10, 1942.

"We want France to recover everything that belongs to her. For us the end of the war means restoration both of complete integrity to our home country, the empire and the French heritage, and of the nation's absolute sovereignty over her own destinies."
     General CHARLES DE GAULLE, London, June 24, 1942.

"But it is not enough merely to make safe the freedom of those peoples who are still free, or even to restore freedom to the nations which have been conquered. If we want to lay the whole of the foundation which I believe is necessary in order for the world to have peace, then the peoples now living in mandates and colonies — of whatever nation — must also see that there will be room in the structure which we are building for them to attain eventual freedom. Otherwise we will be leaving outside our structure hundreds of millions of people who may eventually come to believe that their only hope of realizing their aspirations is through war. And our structure of world peace will be subject to constant threat."

Wendell L. Willkie, New York, November 17, 1943.

"That is the goal of India — a united, free, democratic country, closely associated in a world federation with other free nations."

Jawaharlal Nehru in *Toward Freedom*, 1942.

"If we are honestly determined to banish once and for all the Imperialist idea and all it means, we must rid ourselves of the prejudices in which it has such fertile roots. We must rid ourselves of the idea that there exists, or can exist, an inherently superior person — superior nation — or superior race."

Walter Nash, New Zealand; Washington, September 3, 1942.

CONFEDERATE PLANS

COMPARISON of the German Government's proposals for the establishment of a League of Nations with that of the actual League Covenant (see p. 420) helps to explain the German Delegation's bitter denunciation (see p. 411) of the Covenant in 1919.

Keen was among the first to suggest specific revisions of the League Covenant. These include representation in the Assembly in proportion to population, and the addition of an Equity Tribunal.

The League of Nations Association of London, in its *Draft Pact for the Future International Authority* (International Conciliation, February, 1944; not charted here), retains most of the provisions of the present Covenant. A Defense Committee to prevent or stop aggression is added, composed largely of the Permanent Members of the Council. It is to have the assistance and advice of a General Staff. Subcommittees are to be organized to deal with aggression occurring in special regional areas. Except in cases of emergency, the Defense Committee is to act with the approval of a majority of the Council and Assembly.

Philip C. Nash also adapts the Covenant in his draft of *The Constitution of the United Nations of the World* (An Adventure in World Order, 1944; not charted here). His suggestions approach federal organization. Representation in the Assembly is to be based on population, with China, Great Britain, India, the Soviet Union, and the United States limited to twenty delegates each. Other nations are to have one delegate for each six million of population including colonies and mandates. Every nation is to have at least one delegate. Members of the Assembly are to be paid by the United Nations, and funds raised by direct taxation. The author suggests as one source of world revenue, the addition of one-half cent to all postage rates. He proposes an Executive Board of eight members, elected by Assembly and Council. Four of them are to be citizens of the United States, China, Great Britain, and the Soviet Union. He plans an International Police Force which is to have half the strength of the largest national force. The United Nations is given the right to inspect all national armaments.

In their joint plan, Joad, Kimber, Josephy, and Zilliacus suggest a

World Confederation with a *tricameral* legislature and with a strong Federal Union of Democracies within the Confederation to function as its military enforcement agent.

Culbertson sets up eleven regional confederations under his World Confederation. His detailed proposal for a Quota Armed Force provides for fifty-five per cent military control by Russia, Great Britain, and the United States. He would have the United States and Great Britain alone, or together with Russia and China, set up a Provisional Government during the war to act as a Supreme War and Peace Council.

Merrill also suggests regional confederations within the World Confederation.

AUTHOR:
THE GERMAN GOVERNMENT.

TITLE OF PLAN:
Proposals of the German Government for the Establishment of a League of Nations.

DATE: May 9, 1919.

PUBLISHED IN:
The Drafting of the Covenant, Vol. II. (Document 35)
By David Hunter Miller.

PUBLISHER: G. P. Putnam's Sons, New York, 1928.

TYPE:
CONFEDERATE. NAME: League of Nations.

MEMBERSHIP:
UNIVERSAL: All belligerent states; all neutral nations; all others by two-thirds vote of original members; the Vatican may become a member.

ORGANS OF GOVERNMENT:
LEGISLATIVE: Bicameral — *Congress of States; International Parliament.*

Congress of States: Each member nation to have one to three representatives voting as a unit; Congress to meet at least once in three years. *Decisions:* By two-thirds majority of nations represented. Elects *Permanent Committee* to carry on in intervals between sessions.

International Parliament: One representative for every million of population, but not more than ten to any nation; elected by national parliaments. (Basis of representation may be changed with consent of Congress of States.) *Duties:* Legislates changes in the Constitution, international law; establishes the budget; appoints new bodies of the League. Meets at the same time as the Congress of States.

EXECUTIVE OR ADMINISTRATIVE:
International Administrative Bureau: Unites all existing international bureaus and unions; controls all future bureaus and international institutions of law, economics, and finance.

Chancery: Appointed by Permanent Committee of Congress of States; common bureau of all official League bodies. *Duties:* Publishes all resolutions and communications of the League and submits them to member nations for publication in the national press and submission to national legislatures; publishes texts of all international treaties.

International Labor Bureau: Supervises development of international labor law.

International Colonial Office: Branches in every colony. *Duties:* To supervise freedom of trade; prohibit militarization of natives; promote health, education, freedom of conscience of natives; protect natives against slavery, forced labor, expropriation, alcohol, munitions traffic, etc.

International Sea Police: Regulates sea traffic under control of League and of maritime nations of League; no other armed vessels to be permitted to navigate.

JUDICIAL:
Permanent International Tribunal: Nine-year terms; members elected by Congress of States; each nation nominates one to four candidates, at least one of a different nationality; each national delegation in the

Congress of States votes for fifteen from the total list; those receiving the highest number of votes elected as judges.

Procedure: Each party to a dispute selects one judge; the full Tribunal elects the third, if the parties do not agree on a choice.

Jurisdiction: Over legal disputes between nations (any member nation may bring a complaint to the Tribunal which must be answered by the opposite party); in suits of private persons against foreign nations or heads of nations; in disputes between subjects of different nations when national courts are incompetent to judge; subjects of different national members of the League if the dispute concerns interpretation of national treaties.

International Mediation Office: Fifteen members; ten substitutes. Each nation appoints four electors; all the electors decide by majority vote on fifteen members and ten substitutes.

Procedure: Each party to a dispute chooses two members, and the fifth who serves as President is appointed by the Mediation Office in full session if the parties cannot agree on a choice. Members of the Mediation Office may not hold any other office under the League or in their own nation.

Jurisdiction: In case of international tension, Mediation Office offers its services to the nations concerned. These are obliged to discuss their dispute before the Mediation Office and offer terms of settlement. Both the Permanent International Tribunal and the Mediation Office settle all disputes not resolved by diplomacy and for which special mode of arbitration has not been agreed upon.

TRANSFERS OF JURISDICTION FROM MEMBER NATIONS TO THE LEAGUE:
Limitation of armaments on land and in the air consonant with national safety.
Limitation of sea forces to defense of coasts.
Control of adherence to disarmament agreements.
Policing of sea traffic.
Publication of armament figures.
Regulation of free air traffic.
Assure freedom of communications by cable or wireless.

Prohibit imposition of transit duties on goods from or to a member nation passing through territories of other member nations.

Prevent import, export, or transit prohibitions by member nations unless for reasons of public safety, health, or internal economic legislation.

Tariffs and duties imposed by member nations must apply uniformly to all member nations.

Negotiate agreements between member nations, assuring nationals of all in the territory of another the greatest possible equality with their own citizens in personal liberty, freedom of conscience, of residence, settlement, and judicial protection.

RESTRICTIONS ON NATIONS:

Protection of minorities in their rights to their own language, school, church, art, science, and press.

Financial support of the League according to the standard fixed by the International Postal Union.

Member nations prohibited from concluding separate treaties, except arbitration treaties; all secret treaties void.

Member nations are obliged to suppress through legal and administrative authorities, libels on other nations expressed in speech, writing, or illustration; violations and rectifications to be decided by Permanent International Tribunal.

METHODS OF ENFORCEMENT:

If a nation should refuse to carry out decisions, resolutions, or orders of an official body of the League, or violates the Constitution of the League, the *Mediation Office* in full session decides on enforcement by one or all of the following methods:

1. Breaking off diplomatic relations by all other nations.
2. Limiting or breaking economic relations; import and export prohibitions; unequal customs treatment; prohibition on traffic of goods, persons, transmission of news; confiscation of ships.
3. Authorizing the imposition of military measures by the injured nation alone or together with other nations.
4. Imposing payment of the costs and damages of enforcement on the offending nation.

Theoretical Plans

AUTHOR:
Frank Noel Keen (English).

PROFESSION:
Attorney; authority on international law.

TITLE OF PLAN:
A Better League of Nations — The Draft of a Revised Covenant for the League of Nations.

DATE: 1934.

PUBLISHER:
George Allen & Unwin Ltd., London.

TYPE:
Confederation. Based on Covenant of League of Nations — revised.

MEMBERSHIP:
Universal: Association of fully self-governing nations, Dominions, and Colonies.

ORGANS OF GOVERNMENT:
Legislative: Bicameral — *Assembly and Council.*

Assembly: Each member nation *three representatives* but number of votes cast in Assembly determined on basis of population:

    15 million or less — 1 vote in Assembly.
    Over 15 million — 2 votes in Assembly.
    Over 25 million — 3 votes in Assembly.
    40 million — 4 votes in Assembly.

Council — Permanent Members: British Empire, France, Italy, Japan, Germany. Non-Permanent Members: Nine member nations selected by the Assembly from time to time. Each member nation *one representative* and *one vote*. Council is subject to control of the Assembly.

Legislative Commission: Fifteen Commissioners elected by Council and Assembly for one year from list of persons nominated by member nations, each nominating four. Assembly can prescribe rules regulating Commission's procedure.

Decisions of all three bodies by majority vote except when three-fourths majority is specified.

Legislative Procedure: Proposals must be initiated by a member nation, or by the Council to the Assembly; then referred by Assembly to Legislative Commission for report and recommendation. If recommended by Legislative Commission, must be approved by three-fourths vote of *Assembly* and *ratified by member nations* exercising three-fourths of the voting strength in the Assembly before becoming law.

EXECUTIVE OR ADMINISTRATIVE:
Secretariat: Secretary-General appointed by Council with approval of Assembly.

Secretaries: Appointed by Secretary-General with approval of Council. Staff: By same procedure.

JUDICIAL:
The Permanent Court of International Justice: Elected by Council and Assembly (they may refer any question to Court for an *advisory* opinion).

Jurisdiction: Interpretation of treaties, questions of international law; extent of reparations for breach of international law referred to it by Council.

Equity Tribunal: Seven Commissioners elected by Council and Assembly from list of persons nominated by member nations, each nominating four for one year. Decisions by majority vote. Assembly to make rules regulating procedure of Tribunal. *Jurisdiction:* Over any matter not referred to the Court; reports its recommendations to *Council* which acts to enforce them.

TRANSFERS OF JURISDICTION FROM MEMBER NATIONS TO THE LEAGUE:
Authority to *make* international law; to repeal, vary, or amend existing international law covering money, central banking, weights, measures, traffic by land, water, air, or submarine; passport, postal,

telegraph, telephone, and wireless arrangements; auxiliary language; international military, naval, and air forces; daylight saving; measurement of time; crime, disease; public works.

Reduction and *limitation* of national armaments and international trading in arms.

Reduction and *limitation* of import and export tariffs; currency exchange restrictions, etc.

To declare Conventions adopted by International Labor Organization binding on all member nations.

Set up and *administer* regional arrangements to carry out foregoing.

Expenses paid by member nations in proportion decided by Assembly.

Existing International Bureaus to be placed under League direction.

NATIONS UNDERTAKE:
To guarantee to preserve peace and maintain order within their borders; guarantee security of life, person, property, and personal liberty; ensure prompt, efficient, and impartial administration of justice.

To administer *colonies* for benefit of natives; forego establishment of fortifications, military or naval bases, or military training of natives except for defense.

To take a world census every fifth year.

METHODS OF ENFORCEMENT:
Towards Members (in case of breach of world law):
　1. Financial pressure.
　2. Economic boycott.
　3. War by means of land, sea or air forces, or all combined.
　4. Costs of enforcement to be repaid League by offending member.

Towards Non-Members:
　1. Invited to accept membership in League for purposes of settling dispute.
　2. If membership refused, Council can act to prevent hostilities and settle dispute.

Charts of Plans to Unite Nations Since 1914

AMENDMENT:
By three-fourths vote of the Assembly and ratification by member nations having three-fourths of the voting power in the Assembly.

MISCELLANEOUS:
Earlier suggestions by the author on this subject: The World in Alliance—a Plan for Preventing Future War, 1915, London, Walter Southwood & Co. Ltd. Suggested: International Parliament; Code of Law; Machinery for Enforcement; Armed Quotas from member nations.

Real Security Against War, 1929, London, Williams & Norgate Ltd. Suggested: Three new Articles to the League Covenant.

AUTHORS:
C. E. M. JOAD (English), C. D. KIMBER (English), MISS F. L. JOSEPHY (English), K. ZILLIACUS.

PROFESSIONS:
Writers and editors.

TITLE OF PLAN:
Federation — Peace Aim — War Weapon.

PAMPHLET

DATE: September, 1942.

PUBLISHER:
Federal Union, London.

TYPE AND MEMBERSHIP:
Two Organizations:
    1. Confederation — worldwide, based on the former League of Nations.
Name: World Confederation.

    2. Federal — ideological — close union of democracies within the World Confederation.
Name: Federal Union of Democracies.

ORGANS OF GOVERNMENT OF THE WORLD CONFEDERATION:

LEGISLATIVE: Tricameral — *Assembly; Council; International Consultative Parliament.*

Assembly: Decisions by majority vote with nations retaining the right to refuse to carry out decisions with which they are not in agreement (substituted for right of veto in present League Covenant).

Council: Decisions by majority vote with nations retaining right to refrain from cooperation in decisions with which they do not agree. Two-thirds majority vote of Assembly and Council necessary to declare a nation guilty of aggression.

International Consultative Parliament: Composed of delegations elected by proportional representation from national legislatures of all member nations; each representative one vote (apportionment according to scale used by Interparliamentary Union); reports and resolutions by majority vote; national governments obliged to submit Parliament reports to national legislatures and hold debates on them.

EXECUTIVE OR ADMINISTRATIVE:
Council: Also functions as executive of the World Confederation.
Economic Planning Board.
International Bank and Investment Board.

JUDICIAL:
Permanent Court of International Justice.

Organs of Government of the Federal Union of Democracies not specified.

TRANSFERS OF JURISDICTION FROM MEMBER NATIONS TO THE WORLD CONFEDERATION:

The League of Nations, the International Labor Office, and the Permanent Court of International Justice are to be combined under a single Constitution to form the World Confederation, financed by a single budget subject to authority of Council and Assembly.

Confederation assumes greater obligations regarding access to raw materials, reduction of trade barriers, international control of transport and communications, public health and social questions, cooperation in education than the League of Nations had.

Inspection and supervision of war industries throughout the world.

Members undertake never to resort to war or use force, and to refer all disputes not settled within one year by other means to Permanent Court of International Justice; members undertake to break off all economic and financial relations with a nation declared guilty of aggression by two-thirds vote of Assembly and Council.

Refusal to comply with this obligation makes nation liable to treatment as accessory to the aggression.

Only the *Federal Union of Democracies* and the Permanent Members of the Council may keep armed forces over the quota permitted to preserve internal order. The Union of Democracies and the Permanent Members of the Council decide on joint military action by agreement, maintain joint staff consultations, and permanent economic and political cooperation.

Regional agreements permissible.

TRANSFERS OF JURISDICTION FROM MEMBER NATIONS TO THE FEDERAL UNION OF DEMOCRACIES:
The purpose of the Democratic Union is to uphold its military obligations to the World Confederation and progressively to absorb the members of the World Confederation into the Democratic Federal Union.

Union (and Permanent Members of Council of the World Confederation, such as Russia and China, which are not to be members of the Union) to have sole possession of military air, naval, and land equipment with obligation to uphold world law and order acting through machinery of the World Confederation.

Union represents its members as a unit in the World Confederation and is permanent member of the Council; votes in Council, Assembly, and Committees of Confederation in proportion to its share of the total budget and population.

Federal control and eventual administration of colonial policy aiming to improve social and educational standards, training for self-government, progressive emancipation, and ultimate membership in the Union.

Federal control of interstate transport and communications; monopoly of civil aviation.

Federal defense system with Union War Office, Admiralty, Air Ministry, army, and navy.

Federal control of interstate trade, leading to a customs union within a specified time; monetary union; international bank and investment board; common economic planning, allocation of raw materials, location of industry, control of migration.

Democratically elected Federal Parliament and Government. Charter of Human Rights to include civil liberties, free elections, free education, right to employment and leisure, minimum living standard; free care of the sick, the aged, and those incapacitated.

Common citizenship.

METHODS OF ENFORCEMENT:
Armed force to uphold world law and prevent aggression on decision of the World Confederation.

IMMEDIATE STEPS:
The United Nations is to appoint a *Reconstruction Commission* to draft a Treaty setting up both the *World Confederation of States* and the Constitution of the *Union of Democracies*. Those members of the United Nations in control of their own territories, and able to do so, should initiate the Union of Democracies at once in order to come to the Peace Conference equipped with a draft of a constitution and a skeleton framework of organization.

PREREQUISITES TO PEACE:
Allied victory; occupation of strategic points in Axis territory; immediate disarmament of Axis adequate to rule out resumption of fighting.

Reconstruction Commission to control all disputed territory; to direct conversion to reconstruction of Axis war industries; distribution of food relief to Axis peoples to avert famine, but no resumption of

Charts of Plans to Unite Nations Since 1914 201

economic relations; no representation on Reconstruction Commission until proper government exists; no fascist, militarist, or Junker to remain in control of or with influence on the government.

LIQUIDATION OF THE WAR:
As soon as acceptable governments are established in the former Axis countries, they are to be represented on the *Reconstruction Commission* and to assume full share in responsibilities and benefits of international relief and reconstruction.

AXIS NATIONS:
Axis countries must return or replace what they actually stole from the occupied countries; their production must supply goods and services to help rebuild roads, railways, factories, towns and villages in accordance with an international economic plan making provision for future needs instead of in spirit of retribution for past wrongs.

"FREE GROUPS":
Various "free groups" from nations unable to have governmental representation are to be represented on the *Reconstruction Commission,* but only if they are likely to have influence in the postwar life of their countries and in the Provisional Governments established after the Axis defeat.

ECONOMIC:
Transfer of wartime economic machinery, adjusted to reconstruction purposes, to the *Reconstruction Commission,* such as *Shipping Adjustments Board, Raw Materials, and Munitions Assignments Board;* preservation of continental transport and economic planning developed in Europe for purposes of peaceful continental cooperation.

POLITICAL:
Restoration of constitutional governments in occupied countries; disarmament of defeated nations and maintenance of order; setting up of *International Consultative Parliament,* made up of all-party delegations elected by national legislatures, to draft a Federal Constitution; delegates to vote individually by majority vote; draft constitution to be referred to *Reconstruction Commission* for submission to ratification of the people wherever stable governments have been reestablished. The *Reconstruction Commission* then becomes the *Peace*

Conference proper. *Duties:* To negotiate the final terms of the peace settlement; to reach agreement on the Constitution, membership of the *Union of Democracies* and of the *World Confederation;* to organize economic cooperation; to regulate world's armaments and war industries.

TERRITORIAL CHANGES:
Political independence to be restored to *India* and *Burma.*

Return to *China* of various concessions; offer to share control of Singapore through Pacific War Council.

Japan to return all conquests acquired since 1931; her industries to make good vast damage done by her; she is to become a member of the World Confederation at the Peace Conference.

Italy may become a member both of the Union of Democracies and the World Confederation.

Hungary, Roumania, and *Bulgaria* may join Central European or Balkan regional federations and enter Union of Democracies as a unit. *Germany* may become a member of Union of Democracies at Peace Conference if by that time an acceptable government has been established; would have full rights in Union but may not contribute to Union forces nor share in their control until so decided by Union Parliament.

RATIFICATION:
By national legislatures.

MISCELLANEOUS:
The authors are against full military occupation of Axis nations to compel political and social changes because this would be opposed by soldiers anxious to be demobilized, by American and British public opinion, and probably by Soviet policy.

They advocate unified international policies in the teaching of history, international relations, and ethnology (the study of the origin of races).

Charts of Plans to Unite Nations Since 1914

AUTHOR:
ELY CULBERTSON (American).

PROFESSION:
Expert and Writer on Contract Bridge.

TITLE OF PLAN:
Total Peace — What Makes Wars and How to Organize Peace.

DATE: 1943.

PUBLISHER:
Doubleday, Doran and Co., Inc., Garden City, New York.

ORGANIZATIONAL BACKING:
The World Federation, Inc., New York.

TYPE:
CONFEDERATION. NAMES USED: Peace Trust; Peace Pool; Defensive Alliance; World Federation. (*Note:* Wherever the author uses *World Federation,* we have used *Confederation* to avoid confusion with full federal plans. EDITORS.)

MEMBERSHIP:
UNIVERSAL: World divided into eleven regional confederations united under a world confederation. (See composition of regional confederations in separate regional section.)

Explanation of terms: Initiating State — the most populous nation in each Regional Confederation; *Non-Initiating States* — the nations in each Regional Confederation with populations smaller than those of the Initiating State.

ORGANS OF GOVERNMENT OF THE WORLD CONFEDERATION:
LEGISLATIVE: Bicameral — *World Trustees; World Senate;* both have six-year terms; not renewable.

World Trustees: Thirteen — one from each Initiating State selected with approval of its legislature; two at-large from Non-Initiating States. *Decisions:* By nine out of thirteen votes. *World Senate:* Sixty-six members, six from each Regional Confederation, representing capital, labor, agriculture, science, education, arts, *appointed by President* with *approval of Senate* of each *Regional Confederation*. One-third of Senate renewed every two years. *Decisions:* By majority vote.

EXECUTIVE OR ADMINISTRATIVE:

World President: Six-year term; not renewable; chosen, with one exception, from each Initiating State (the most populous nation in each Regional Confederation) in turn. (First World President selected by U. S. Senate with approval of presidents of majority of member nations of American Regional Confederation, or by majority vote of American Regional Senate with approval of Regional President; second World President from British Regional Confederation; third, elected by member nations which are not Initiating States; thereafter each Regional Confederation chooses World President in turn, by majority vote of all its voting inhabitants or by majority vote of Regional Senate and approval of Regional President.)

World Bank: Receives money dues from member nations.

World Commodity Corporation: Receives dues paid in goods and raw materials by member nations.

Cabinet: Advises World President.

Quota Armed Force of Mobile Corps and National Contingents (see special section for details).

The World Armament Trust: Maintains staff of inspectors to supervise compliance with provisions of quota distributions of military strength; purchases plants to produce heavy armaments for the World Confederation in Initiating and Non-Initiating States in proportion to the quota assigned to each nation.

JUDICIAL:

World Supreme Court: Thirteen Justices, one from each Regional Confederation, appointed for life by Regional President with approval of Regional Senate; two at-large from Non-Initiating States. *Powers:* Final interpreter of World Confederation Constitution; issues *Writ of Economic Sanctions* in case of non-payment of dues to World Con-

Charts of Plans to Unite Nations Since 1914

federation by member nations, *Writ of War Emergency* in case of armed resistance to the Confederation; serves as *Council of Impeachment* with any four Chief Justices of the Regional Supreme Courts upon complaints against highest officials of World Confederation. *Decisions:* By nine out of thirteen votes.

World Equity Court: Thirteen members, one from each Initiating State, two at-large from non-initiating member nations. *Powers:* Deals directly or through appointed arbitrators with all treaties; economic, political, or territorial disputes between nations or Regions, or involving World Confederation. *Decisions:* By nine out of thirteen votes.

Regional Supreme Courts, Regional Equity Courts with similar organization but intra-regional jurisdiction.

Branches of *World Court:* To be established in each member nation, plus inspectors to enforce prohibitions on manufacture and transport of heavy weapons by private organizations or state officials.*

Lower Equity Courts: To settle disputes between citizens or corporations of different Regions, or between citizens and corporations and governments of member nations.*

TRANSFERS OF JURISDICTION FROM MEMBER NATIONS TO THE WORLD CONFEDERATION:
Defense of member nations against armed aggression.
Enforcement of quota force distribution of military power, of treaties and agreements between member nations, Regional Confederations, and the World Confederation.
Administration of World Armament Trust; ownership of all heavy armament.
Administration and command of armed forces.
Arbitration of economic, political, and territorial disputes between member nations and Regions.
Supervision of rights of Pooled Colonies to self-rule and fair treatment.
Granting to member nations right to extraterritorial rail or auto roads across territories of other member nations.
Administration of international communications, allocation of radio wave lengths.

* These are Federal features.

Administration of territories under jurisdiction of World Confederation; conduct of plebiscites.

World Confederation supported by dues from member nations in proportion to national wealth or annual income, or rental value of land. World Confederation *can impose no tax* except on imports and exports in case of non-payment of dues, and only to extent of amount due.

World Quota Force financed as follows: Each *Initiating State* pays amount equal to quota assigned to it plus one-twenty-second of Mobile Corps requirements; all *Non-Initiating States* pay remainder of expenses of Mobile Corps in proportion to number of their nationals serving in the Corps. In addition, the United States pays half the cost of the Malaysian Contingent; Great Britain pays half of the Indian Contingent.

Negotiation of treaties with each nation necessary for grant of additional authority to establish World Bank, World Commodity Corporation; to establish international universities and research institutions; to deal with unemployment, health, immigration, conservation, currency, relief of distressed and undeveloped peoples, education for world citizenship, world language, adoption of a World Bill of Rights.

RESTRICTIONS ON NATIONS:
Nations may not withdraw nor be expelled.*

Member nations may not negotiate a separate peace.

Membership of Germany and Japan to be compulsory.

Special Restrictions applied to Germany and Japan for twenty-four years: Their National Contingents to be recruited and commanded by International Mobile Corps; these contingents may not be stationed in Germany or Japan; may not manufacture heavy weapons for World Armament Trust; their Trustees and Justices subject to approval of other World Trustees; colonies of Germanic Confederation to be administered by World Confederation.

NATIONS RETAIN:
All other rights, including that of choosing their own forms of government; impose taxes, tariffs, trade laws; make and alter treaties; recruit,

* These are Federal features.

train, and command their National Contingents except in case of aggression anywhere in the world.

Nations and Regional Confederations may adopt their own method of popular election of World Trustees, Senators, and Justices.

Netherlands retains sovereign rights, except military control, in Netherlands East Indies.

France retains sovereignty, except military control, over Indo-China.

Belgium retains preferred status in administration of Belgian Congo.

METHODS OF ENFORCEMENT:

Towards officials and employees of World Confederation: Impeachment and penalties.*

Towards Individuals: Heavy penalties for violation of quota force distribution of military power.*

Towards Member Nations: Military Sanctions — To enforce quota force distribution of military power; to prevent manufacture or transport of heavy armaments; to stop armed aggression.

Economic Sanctions — For non-payment of dues to World Confederation; for violation of treaties, decisions of World Equity Court, ill-treatment of colonies, non-acceptance of results of plebiscites.

Towards Non-Member Nations: (1) When they would have been *Non-Initiating States:* The World Confederation forbids them to possess, manufacture, or transport heavy weapons and guarantees them against foreign aggression. (2) When they could have been *Initiating States:* The World Confederation negotiates a *Quota Limitation Treaty* with them limiting their armed forces and heavy armaments according to an assigned quota and providing for inspection by the World Confederation; if nations refuse to stay within their quotas, armed forces of World Confederation to increase in proportion to those of non-member nations.

IMMEDIATE STEPS:

United States and Great Britain alone, or with Russia and China, can initiate World Confederation and establish its Provisional Govern-

* These are federal features.

ment. Each Initiating State creating World Confederation appoints one *Temporary World Trustee* with full power to act. *Council of Temporary World Trustees* functions as *Provisional Government of World Confederation.* (President of United States or his representative is ex-officio member of Provisional Government, with deciding vote in case of a tie; seat of Provisional Government in United States with extra-territorial status.) *Provisional Government* acts as *Supreme War and Peace Council* in cooperation with allies.

Duties: To assume war expenses of all member nations (all loans and lend-lease to be cleared through it; repayment guaranteed by member nations in proportion to their wealth and annual national income); to make treaty of peace with Axis; to bring relief to nations liberated from Axis occupation; to reestablish sovereignty of liberated nations within one year; to establish the World Quota Force.

PREREQUISITES TO PEACE:

War to end without a Peace Conference when Axis nations agree to join World Confederation, subscribe to its Constitution and comply with following terms:

1. Cessation of hostilities; elimination of Nazi, Fascist, and feudal Japanese dictatorships.
2. Disarmament and demobilization of existing armed forces to allotted share of world quota of armed force.
3. *Evacuation* and resettlement of territories not part of their countries.
4. *Restoration* over ten-year period, under World Confederation supervision, of expropriations and loot from occupied countries.
5. *Surrender* for judgment by special tribunal, selected by World Supreme Court, of officials and officers directly responsible for gross violations of rules of war, of Axis as well as member states of World Confederation. Tribunal to impose any penalty, including death.

LIQUIDATION OF THE WAR:

During two-year *Armistice or Transitional Period,* the *Provisional Government* must organize the following:

1. *Economic Agencies* for emergency relief of all peoples, including former enemies.

Charts of Plans to Unite Nations Since 1914

2. Representative governments in defeated and liberated countries. (Within one year of cessation of hostilities, Constitutional Conventions must be called in each country to form new national governments under supervision of *Joint Commission* composed as follows: One-half of membership representing World Confederation, one-half representing de facto governments, one representative of a neutral country to vote only in case of tie.)
3. *Quota Armed Force* of World Confederation and *World Armament Trust,* supervised by one *Quota Commission* for each Initiating State composed as follows: One-half appointees of Provisional Government, one-half appointees of Government of Initiating State. *Mobile Corps Quota Commission* composed as follows: One representative from each Non-Initiating State, equal number of representatives of Provisional Government. *Duties:* To demobilize and disarm existing forces of *Non-Initiating States;* recruit volunteers on quota force basis to make up Mobile Corps.
4. Permanent Government of World Confederation and of Regional Confederations.

TERRITORIAL CHANGES:
1. Withdrawal by Axis nations from occupied territory.
2. Transfer of certain colonies from present national owners to some of the Regional Confederations. Compensation to former owner nations. (See p. 211)
3. Pooling of colonies belonging to members of Regional Confederations; supervision of administration by World Confederation.
4. Transfer of Mohammedan and Christian populations from Palestine to other Middle East territory; creation of a Jewish State in Palestine.
5. Sealed Roads across territory of one state to give access-to-sea outlet to another state on extraterritorial basis.
6. International administration and policing of important straits, canals, and waterways.
7. Acquisition by the United States of the islands mandated to Japan by the League of Nations, of fortified bases in the Western Hemisphere, leased bases in the Philippine Islands, Netherlands

East Indies, Indo-China, Thailand, Hainan, Formosa, Korea, and bases on various strategic islands in the Pacific.

RATIFICATION:

Test of admission: Willingness to abide by World Confederation constitution. Ratification by nation's constitutional authorities.

Amendment of Constitution: By vote of nine World Trustees, thirty-four World Senators, and ratification of seven Regional Confederations by vote of nine Regional Trustees and thirty-one Regional Senators in each region.

Amendment of quotas assigned to National Contingents or to Mobile Corps only by unanimous vote of World Trustees, plus ratification by at least nine Trustees of all Regional Confederations.

MISCELLANEOUS:

Non-Initiating States elect at-large World Trustees and Justices of World Supreme Court and of World Equity Court by means of a World Electoral Convention of thirteen members. Electors chosen by Regional Trustees of Non-Initiating States in proportion to population (the more populous nations to be limited to a maximum of fifteen million inhabitants for the purpose of this apportionment). If Regional Confederations not fully organized, heads of Non-Initiating States jointly choose Trustees and Justices to World Confederation.

Capital of World Confederation to be established every six years in *Initiating State* from which World President is chosen; grounds to have extraterritorial status and to be endowed as world universities when capital moves to other Initiating States.

REGIONAL CONFEDERATIONS:

(Government of Regional Confederations modeled on World Confederation.)

Pan-American: United States and all Latin American Republics, plus Western Hemisphere territories now held by non-American States; Japanese mandated islands; Kuril Islands.

British: United Kingdom, Dominions, Italian East Africa, Mozambique, Djibouti.

Charts of Plans to Unite Nations Since 1914

Latin-European: France, Italy, Spain, Belgium, Portugal, British Northwest African colonies.

Germanic: Germany, Austria, Belgian Congo, Angola, Southern Sudan.

Middle European: Poland, Lithuania, Czechoslovakia, Roumania, Hungary, Yugoslavia, Bulgaria, Albania, Greece.

Middle Eastern: Turkey, Iran, Iraq, Syria, Palestine, United Arabia, Afghanistan, Egypt, including Northern Sudan.

Russian: U.S.S.R., including autonomous states of Esthonia, Latvia, part of Bessarabia, strategic frontier with Finland, parts of Polish Ukraine (subject to plebiscite).

Chinese: China, including Manchuria, Formosa, all former foreign concessions or possessions.

Japanese: Japan (frontiers of 1894, plus southern Sakhalin).

Malaysian: (Autonomous) Philippines and Thailand; Netherlands East Indies; Indo-China; small Pacific Islands outside Western Hemisphere, except British and French possessions. *The whole Regional Confederation to be under the military control of the United States.*

Indian: (Autonomous) Hindu State, Mohammedan State, Princes' States. *The Indian Regional Confederation to be under the military control of Great Britain.*

Unattached Bloc:
Netherlands, Denmark, Norway, Sweden, and Finland may join Germanic or British Regional Confederation.
Irish Free State may join British or Latin-European Confederation.
Korea may join Japanese or Chinese Confederation.

Two-Way States:
Belgium, Switzerland, and Luxembourg belong to both Regional Confederations between which they are situated and have equal rights in both.

TRANSFERS OF JURISDICTION FROM MEMBER NATIONS TO THE REGIONAL CONFEDERATIONS:

Administration and development of any Pooled Colonies belonging to the Regional Confederation.

Legislation and *administration* of preferential economic agreements between member nations of the same Regional Confederation.

Levy of limited tariffs on trade between member nations to support Regional Confederation.

Negotiation of treaties with individual member nations regulating immigration from other Regional Confederations, imports and exports.

QUOTA ARMED FORCE:

Composition: Twelve separate armies: Eleven *National Contingents*, one *Mobile Corps* (made up of international contingents).

National Contingents: Consist of officers and men of each Initiating State, *stationed only in country of origin,* except United States and British Contingents which are also stationed in respective strategic zones in Malaysian and Indian Confederations. In time of war, National Contingents come automatically under command of World Confederation President without consent of nation of origin, but no part of armed force required to engage in war against its country of origin. Term of enlistment six years, not renewable; ex-soldiers have preference rating in World and Regional Confederation Civil Service.

Mobile Corps: Recruited from all member nations *other than* Initiating States; stationed in strategic areas purchased or leased by World Confederation; always under training and command of World Confederation of which soldiers are citizens during enlistment; country of origin no control; enlistment six years, not renewable; ex-soldiers receive preferential civil service rating in World and Regional Confederations.

QUOTA ARMED FORCE DISTRIBUTION:

National Contingents of Initiating States:
   20% United States.
   15% Britain, including Dominions.
   15% Russia.
    6% each of the following: France, China.

3% India (under British command), Germany, Poland, Turkey.
2% Malaysia (under American command).
2% Japan.

International Mobile Corps: Made up by all member Non-Initiating States not listed above: 22 per cent.

EDITORS' REMARKS:
The United States, Britain, and Russia together control fifty per cent of the world's armed force; with British control of the Indian armed force, and United States control of the Malaysian, these three nations actually control fifty-five per cent of the world's military force.

AUTHOR:
GULLIE B. GOLDIN (American).

PROFESSION:
Attorney.

TITLE OF PLAN:
The Coming Peace Settlement with Germany — A Study.

DATE: 1943.

PUBLISHER:
The Reklam Press, New York.

TYPE:
CONFEDERATE. NAME: Charter of Nations; Constitution of the Nations.

MEMBERSHIP:
UNIVERSAL — initiated by members of the United Nations and neutrals.

ORGANS OF GOVERNMENT:
LEGISLATIVE: Unicameral *Congress of the Nations:* Composed of delegates selected by member nations for a fixed term. Number of votes of each nation to be determined by size of its electorate or its population minus illiterates and backward peoples. Votes of nations to in-

crease in proportion to extent to which decisions would vitally affect their sovereignty (enactment may be prevented even if desired by a majority of other nations). *Duties:* To adopt general decrees within limits of Constitution; to examine and determine controversies between nations. *Sessions:* Should be continuous or, at least, frequent.

Standing Committees on armament, trade, finance.

EXECUTIVE OR ADMINISTRATIVE:
High Commissioner of the Nations: To propagate purposes and activities of agencies of the Congress of Nations in schools, through the radio, and other means.

International Guard.

JUDICIAL:
High Court of the Nations: Final court of review over Congress decisions in special controversies between nations; may suggest reconsideration by Congress; hears and determines disputes submitted to it by consent of nations involved; advises Congress on broad matters affecting the nations.

METHODS OF ENFORCEMENT:
Suspension of economic privileges and rights.
Nations to pledge certain assets, such as foreign investments, trade balances, or foreign possessions to an international bank or other agency as security for observance of their obligations under the Charter.

IMMEDIATE STEPS:
Calling of a *Convention* to formulate a *Constitution of the Nations* to be submitted to all of them for ratification. Nations initiating the Convention to determine membership, procedure, quorum, and ratification.

LIQUIDATION OF THE WAR:
United Nations to issue a *Provisional Peace Mandate* to the defeated nations specifying terms to be imposed on them until the permanent peace settlement; to appoint a *Committee of the Provisional Peace Mandate:* To administer its terms, supervise surrender of armament by the defeated, and to direct their military occupation.

Charts of Plans to Unite Nations Since 1914   215

Terms to be imposed on Germany:

(1) All armaments and armament-producing facilities to be destroyed or removed.

(2) Dissolution of all military units, schools, training centers, fraternal organizations, and bases; and destruction of military books and publications.

(3) Abolition of Nazi political, economic, and social institutions, political organizations, youth movements, Nazi law, science, and art; burning of Nazi books, publications, literature, emblems, and symbols.

Germany may retain small internal police force under strict supervision of United Nations.

Italian military power to be restrained but not destroyed.

German and *Italian* children to be reeducated under United Nations guardianship.

Germany and *Italy* to restore all lands seized by them; all machinery, tools, and art objects acquired illegally or by unfair pressure. Property that cannot be returned to be repaid at fair value except property destroyed in general conduct of the war. Material losses suffered by Jews through acts of persecution to be assessed and repaid. Germany and Italy must pledge to Jews equal protection before the law. If Palestine becomes the Jewish National Home, defeated nations to contribute to its budget in goods and services.

No general indemnity or reparations to be exacted for general war losses.

Germany and *Italy* may be placed under temporary United Nations protectorate; plebiscite to determine permanent form of government, but no government may be based on Nazi and Fascist ideology.

Treatment of War Criminals: (1) Those responsible for the war. (2) Those committing illegal acts during the war.

(1) *International High Court:* Composed of representatives of the Great Powers and of smaller nations which have been victims of Nazi aggression; representatives of German and Italian people with or without voting rights may also be added. *Duties:* To

determine guilt or non-guilt of Nazi and Fascist leaders; to pass sentence of death or of life imprisonment in an international penitentiary.

(2) *Departments of International High Court:* To be established in nations in which war crimes were committed; majority of court to be composed of that country's nationals; guilt or innocence and sentences to be determined according to national laws and customs.

Enforcement of Peace Terms: United Nations to establish international military zones within Germany and elsewhere, maintaining them indefinitely. Violation of peace terms such as manufacture of armament, continued after reasonable notice, to be punished by bombing.

Committee of the Permanent Peace Settlement: Composed of members of the United Nations representing capital, labor, agriculture, management, and various social interests. Defeated nations are not to be represented but are to cooperate in ascertaining facts and reaching tentative findings. *Duties:* To propose preliminary terms of the permanent peace settlement to be submitted for review to whatever United Nations political authority has been established.

Terms, with revisions by United Nations, to be submitted to *Peace Conference* representing all nations, including the defeated.

United Nations should not retain territory gained during the war nor seek territorial concessions from the defeated, except what is necessary to maintain air, military, and naval bases to enforce the settlement and maintain world peace.

AUTHOR:
WILLIAM HARD (American).

PROFESSION:
Writer.

TITLE OF PLAN:
American Internationalism.

DATE: December, 1943.

PUBLISHER:
Reader's Digest, Pleasantville, New York.

TYPE:
CONFEDERATE economic conference modeled after the International Labor Organization. NAME: World Union.

MEMBERSHIP:
UNIVERSAL.

ORGANS OF GOVERNMENT:
LEGISLATIVE:
Continuous Conference: Delegates from each nation representing government, finance, export-import industries, labor, and agriculture. *Duties:* To study economic problems; to transmit its conclusions and try to secure adoption of its recommendations by member governments on the following: export-import taxes, quotas, access to raw materials; investments in undeveloped countries; freedom of the air for commercial flying; stability of national currencies; worldwide action to combat depression.

TRANSFERS OF JURISDICTION FROM MEMBER NATIONS TO THE WORLD UNION:
None.

NATIONS UNDERTAKE:
Obligation of continuous consultation.

NATIONS RETAIN:
Complete freedom of action by individual governments to meet emergencies in any manner they determine.

Right to negotiate special agreements for certain purposes and limited in duration.

METHODS OF ENFORCEMENT:
There must be no power of compulsion by the World Union.

AUTHOR:
Robert Morrison MacIver (Scotsman).

PROFESSION:
Professor of Political Philosophy and Sociology.

TITLE OF PLAN:
Towards an Abiding Peace.

DATE: 1943.

PUBLISHER:
The Macmillan Co., New York.

TYPE:
Confederate. Name: Confederation of Nations.

MEMBERSHIP:
Universal.

ORGANS OF GOVERNMENT:
Legislative: Unicameral *Assembly of the Nations:* Equal representation of all nations. Popular election of candidates wherever system of national government permits; nominations by appropriate organizations.
Representatives to report publicly to national legislatures on their work in the Assembly.
Assembly to meet every second year at different national capital.
Powers: To vote the budget; apportion costs among the member nations; receive reports from executive and administrative divisions; modify or annul executive action; appoint members of permanent *International Economic, Labor,* and *Health Commissions.*

Executive or Administrative:
International Executive: Cabinet or Council of eleven members, representing the following nations or nation-groups:
United States.
Latin America.
Great Britain and the Dominions.

Russia.
Eastern Europe: Poland, Czechoslovakia, Greece, Yugoslavia, Hungary, Roumania, Bulgaria, Albania.
Central Europe: Germany, Austria, Switzerland, Italy.
Western Europe: France, Belgium, Holland, Spain, Norway, Sweden, Denmark, Finland.
Islamic States: Turkey, Palestine, Egypt, Iraq, Iran, and possibly Mohammedan India.
China and Korea.
Japan: With Thailand, Indo-China, etc.
India.

Council members chosen for five-year terms; eligible for reappointment; chairman chosen in rotation from each great territorial group; decisions by majority vote. *Duties:* Overall administration of affairs of Confederation of Nations; carry out laws and regulations approved by the Assembly; work of the Council prepared by committees for geographical areas.

Office of Armament Control: Supervise and control production of munitions; prevent violations.

Office of International Police: Control of world armed force subject to Assembly regulations.

JUDICIAL:
International Court: Elected by Executive and Assembly from list of candidates nominated by national governments.
Jurisdiction: Over disputes between nations; interpretation of Constitution and law of nations.

International Equity Commission: Eleven members — one from each geographical division; ten-year terms; not eligible for reappointment. (Position of Commissioner-in-Equity to be highest honor bestowed on an individual by nations and nation-groups.) The Commission functions on its own initiative or in response to appeals.

Duties:
1. To make proposals to nations, nation-groups, or the Confederate Assembly for settlement of disputes between nations or nation-groups not settled by International Court or arbitration.

2. To propose admission of non-self-governing territories as member nations of the Confederation and of the territorial divisions.
3. To propose transfers of territory and populations, and to receive requests for such transfers.
4. To propose equitable treatment of non-self-governing peoples, protection of minority groups in accordance with the Constitution of the Confederation on appeal from such groups.
5. To suggest proposals for advancement of the international order; adjustment to changing conditions, industrial changes, population movements, developments in communication, and transportation, etc.

TRANSFERS OF JURISDICTION FROM MEMBER NATIONS TO THE CONFEDERATION:
Entire abolition of national armaments within fifteen to twenty years; until then reduction to an assigned minimum.

International Armed Force to uphold the law made up of unit contributions from each nation in accordance with its resources and size; troops to owe allegiance to world authority, but would not be called on to act against their own nation.

Administration of internationalized areas, possessions, channels, routes, means of transportation and communication.

Supervision and control of armament production.

Removal of major barriers to world trade; assurance of equal access to raw materials.

Control of exchange rates between various currencies; assurance of international flow of capital.

METHODS OF ENFORCEMENT:
International Armed Force to uphold law and protect member nations.

IMMEDIATE STEPS:
Establishment of the *International Executive* right after the armistice by representatives of the United States, the British Commonwealth, Russia, China, and Latin America. Representatives of the Near East, Eastern Europe, Western Europe, the Islamic States, Central Europe, Japan, and India should be added as soon as orderly conditions are reestablished.

Renunciation by the President of the United States of further participation in domestic politics (except for formal responsibilities of his office) to devote himself to international affairs together with Wendell Willkie as an equal partner in the negotiations.

PREREQUISITES TO PEACE:
Clean-cut victory by the Allied Powers.

LIQUIDATION OF THE WAR:
No indemnities, reparations, or imposition of democracy by force.
Return of recoverable goods by the Axis countries.
United Nations to restore civic order and economic normality in liberated and occupied areas; no humiliation of defeated peoples; no foreign control of German heavy industry.
Definitive determination of boundaries.
International revision of history and social science texts.

TERRITORIAL CHANGES:
Esthonia and Latvia should be restored to Russia.
Lithuania should become a province of Poland.
Restoration of all conquered and ceded territory to China.
Japanese and Italian colonies and former Mandates to be transferred to control of an International Commission, including at least some of the colonies of members of the United Nations. (If this is not done, provision should be made for returning the colonies to Germany, Italy, and Japan in fifteen years.)
India should be granted independence.
Transfer to ultimate international control of Gibraltar, Suez Canal, Panama Canal, and the Dardanelles.

AUTHOR:
Robert Arthur Merrill.

TITLE OF PLAN:
Geopolirea Union.

PAMPHLET

DATE: May, 1943.

PUBLISHED by the author at Denver, Colorado.

TYPE:
CONFEDERATION. NAME: Geopolirea Union.

MEMBERSHIP:
UNIVERSAL — The world is divided into twelve Geopolitical Confederations united under one World Confederation. The democracies are distributed among the twelve regional confederations and have larger representation on the Regional Councils than the other members.

Geopolitical Areas with their respective capitals:

Mediterranean	Barcelona
North European	Copenhagen
East European	Budapest
Eurasian	Riga
Tri-Continent	Baghdad
North Pacific	Peking
Malaysian	Batavia
South Central	Benares
South Atlantic	Natal
Caribbean	Panama
North Atlantic	Rochester
South Pacific	Hobart

ORGANS OF GOVERNMENT:

LEGISLATIVE: Unicameral *Chamber of Deputies:* Not more than 1,000 members; considers rules and regulations proposed by World Council; Committees of the Chamber may sit in on Council meetings with right of debate but not of vote.

EXECUTIVE OR ADMINISTRATIVE:

World Council of Geopolireas: Equal representation from each of the twelve Geopolireas; six from each; six-year terms; one-third of the Council renewed every two years; representatives ineligible for reelection except after a lapse of six years. Council selects *Premier* to serve as *General Manager* or *Director General* of the Council.

Cabinet: Appointed by the Premier with approval of the Council. (Neither the Premier nor the Cabinet is to be a member of the Council.) Members of the Cabinet may be nominated also by the Presidents of International Professional Associations of Labor, Agriculture, Industry, Banking, Engineering, and others. *Duties:* Makes recommendations through Premier to World Council and Chamber of Deputies.

TRANSFERS OF JURISDICTION FROM MEMBER NATIONS TO THE UNION:
Worldwide distribution of surplus agricultural products.
Worldwide system of credits.
Unemployed to be formed into Labor Battalions of 800 men; each Geopolirea to create work for them; Battalions not to have military training but may be directed by Reserve Army officers.

METHODS OF ENFORCEMENT:
Geopolice: Armed force of each Geopolirea to be divided into twenty-two units; each area to have approximately the same number of armed forces; eleven units of the Geopolice always stationed within the Geopolirea; eleven, on duty in other Geopolireas, one unit in each. Thus each Geopolirea to be policed by twenty-two units at all times. Each unit to be on duty six months abroad, and six at home. About 100,000 men in each Geopolirea. Civilian reserve forces to have supplemental basic training.

MISCELLANEOUS:
Formation of first two Geopolireas permits establishment of World Council.

Geneva suggested as capital of Geopolirea Union.

AUTHOR:
Herbert F. Rudd (American).

PROFESSION:
Professor of Philosophy and History of East Asia.

Theoretical Plans

TITLE OF PLAN:
World Organization: Some Facts and a Practical Proposal.

DATE: 1943.

Mimeographed 23 pages.

PUBLISHED by the author in Durham, New Hampshire.

TYPE:
CONFEDERATE.

MEMBERSHIP:
UNIVERSAL.

ORGANS OF GOVERNMENT:
LEGISLATIVE: Unicameral *International Congress:* Four hundred members selected as follows:

(1) One hundred delegates apportioned among the nations on the basis of their proportion of the world total of foreign trade and extent of participation in international organizations, such as the Universal Postal Union, League of Nations, International Labor Organization, and Permanent Court of International Justice.

(2) One hundred delegates apportioned among the nations on the basis of their proportion of the world total of industrial development in steel, chemical, and electrical production.

(3) One hundred delegates apportioned among the nations on the basis of their proportion of the total world death rate and literate population as an index of the number of people sharing the privileges of a progressive democratic society.

(4) One hundred delegates apportioned among the nations on the basis of their proportion of the total world population.

On this basis approximate national representation would be:

Charts of Plans to Unite Nations Since 1914

Nation: *Number of Delegates:*

Nation	Number of Delegates
United States	72
Great Britain without colonies	30
Australia, Canada, New Zealand, and Union of South Africa	16
France without colonies	15
Belgium, Luxembourg, Switzerland, and Netherlands	16
Norway, Sweden, and Denmark	9
Russia	35
Germany	38
Japan	17
Italy	13
China	25
India	25
Nine other East Asia Peoples	19
Ten other European Nations	24
Latin American Nations	19
Ten Near East Nations	7

(The British Commonwealth, Soviet Russia, the United States, and China would have 178 delegates or almost half of the total membership of 400 delegates.)

National representation to be increased in proportion to rise in trade, industrial development, literacy, lowered death rate and population growth. *Decisions:* On administrative acts carrying out delegated functions by two-thirds vote of delegates.

EXECUTIVE OR ADMINISTRATIVE:
Administrative and Secretarial Personnel.

International Police Force: Composed of volunteers from member nations in proportion to national representation in Congress. Approximately 1,000 soldiers for each representative in Congress. Total: 400,000. Force to be controlled and directed by the Congress.

JUDICIAL:
International Court: Its judgments to be final in legal matters.

TRANSFERS OF JURISDICTION FROM MEMBER NATIONS TO THE WORLD ORGANIZATION:
To determine maximum quota of military forces to be retained by member nations.

To levy taxes on member nations in proportion to their representation in Congress.
To prohibit dangerous and destructive acts by any nation towards other nations and peoples.
To integrate international trade, transportation, and communication.
To supervise labor and health conditions.
To support and direct international cultural, educational, and relief projects.

RESTRICTIONS ON NATIONS:
Decisions ratified by two-thirds of the member nations to be binding on all nations.

NATIONS RETAIN:
Minimum military establishment.
Right to negotiate bilateral treaties and regional agreements dealing with local or special interests not prejudicial to the interests of other nations.

NATIONS UNDERTAKE:
To assist the Congress with their troops when called upon.

PREREQUISITES TO PEACE:
United Nations victory, with total defeat of Axis Powers.

IMMEDIATE STEPS:
Adoption of this plan as a tentative basis for appointment of delegates to an *International Constitutional Convention* with all members of the United Nations as well as neutral nations invited to send delegates. *Duties:* To work out details of representation in the Permanent Congress, the constitution, legal and administrative functions of the international organization; its jurisdiction, administrative personnel, method of appointment; judicial bodies, military or police forces; and under what conditions and how rapidly Germany and Japan are to be represented. *Decisions:* By two-thirds vote of delegates.

RATIFICATION:
By two-thirds of the national governments in existence.

AMENDMENT:
By two-thirds vote of Congress, to be ratified by two-thirds of the member nations.

PART III

THEORETICAL PLANS

CHARTS OF PLANS TO UNITE NATIONS SINCE 1914

B. The United Nations

"Winning the war will be futile if we do not throughout the period of its winning keep our people prepared to make a lasting and worthy peace. This time the peace must be global, the same as the war has become global."

    Franklin D. Roosevelt, Washington, September 24, 1942.

.... "You ask, what is our aim? I can answer in one word: It is victory, victory at all costs, victory in spite of all terror, victory however long and hard the road may be; for without victory, there is no survival. Let that be realized; no survival for the British Empire, no survival for all that the British Empire has stood for, no survival for the urge and impulse of the ages, that mankind will move forward towards its goal. . . ."

    Winston Churchill, London, May 13, 1940.

"It is not our aim to destroy Germany, for it is impossible to destroy Germany, just as it is impossible to destroy Russia, but the Hitlerite state can and should be destroyed, and our first task, in fact, is to destroy the Hitlerite state and its inspirers.

... "It is not our aim to destroy all military force in Germany, for every literate person will understand that this is not only impossible in regard to Germany, as it is in regard to Russia, but it is also inadvisable from the point of view of the future. But Hitler's army can and should be destroyed."

JOSEPH STALIN to the *Moscow Soviet,* November 6, 1942.

"There will be neither peace, nor hope, nor future for any of us unless we honestly aim at political, social and economic justice for all peoples of the world great and small. But I feel confident that we of the United Nations can achieve that aim only by starting at once to organize an international order embracing all peoples to enforce peace and justice among them. To make that start we must begin today and not tomorrow to apply these principles among ourselves even at some sacrifice to the absolute powers of our individual countries.

"China has no desire to replace Western imperialism in Asia with an Oriental imperialism or isolationism of its own or of anyone else. We hold that we must advance from the narrow idea of exclusive alliances and regional blocs, which in the end make for bigger and better wars, to effective organization for world unity."

CHIANG KAI-SHEK to the *New York Herald Tribune* Forum, November, 1942.

UNITED NATIONS PLANS

STASSEN proposes that the present United Nations be reorganized after the war with an elected representative assembly which appoints the Executive Council of seven members. He provides for land, naval, and air forces recruited from member nations on a quota basis.

Welles and Straight both suggest regional councils within the United Nations — Britain, the U.S.S.R., China, and the United States acting as the Executive. Straight devotes a great deal of attention to the problems of worldwide liquidation of the war, necessary supplies, and their possible sources. He proposes that most of the wartime boards and economic controls continue to function in the postwar period.

Full-scale participation of all the United Nations so far has taken place in two conferences held in 1943, one on the problem of refugees at Hamilton, Bermuda, April, 1943; the other on the problem of food at Hot Springs, Virginia, May, 1943. Both conferences made numerous recommendations and resolutions. No action has followed. But continuing committees and later conferences were suggested to make further studies.

To cope with the problem of providing an international auxiliary medium of exchange, and to facilitate settling of exchange balances between nations, the British propose a detailed plan for an International Clearing Union (published April 7, 1943), while the American Treasury Plan (published April 6, 1943) suggests a World Stabilization Fund subscribed by member nations with national currency values fixed in terms of gold. The United States Treasury Department has also presented outlines for a proposed *United Nations Bank of Reconstruction and Development* with capital funds of ten billion dollars subscribed by member nations. Its purpose would be to provide long-term capital, supplementing private investments, to develop the productive resources of member nations. Canadian experts have drafted proposals for an International Exchange Union (published June 9, 1943).

In addition to these banking proposals, none of which has yet received official governmental approval, a more political agency is established in the *United Nations Relief and Rehabilitation Administration* which provides for a policy-making Council of representatives of each member government, and for a Central Committee representing the Four Great Powers. The Council appoints a Director General, advisory Regional

Councils, and technical committees. The Administration is given wide powers within the appropriations granted by the member governments, but methods of enforcing its decisions in case of resistance are not specified, nor is the jurisdiction of any court, before which it can sue or be sued, indicated.

PRINCIPAL OFFICIAL UNITED NATIONS TREATIES, AGREEMENTS, AND DECLARATIONS

THE ATLANTIC CHARTER'S EIGHT POINTS

THE PRESIDENT of the United States of America and the Prime Minister, Mr. Churchill, representing his Majesty's Government in the United Kingdom, being met together, deem it right to make known certain common principles in the national policies of their respective countries on which they base their hopes for a better future for the world.

1. Their countries seek no aggrandizement, territorial or other.

2. They desire to see no territorial changes that do not accord with the freely expressed wishes of the peoples concerned.

3. They respect the right of all peoples to choose the form of government under which they will live; and they wish to see sovereign rights and self-government restored to those who have been forcibly deprived of them.

4. They will endeavor, with due respect for their existing obligations, to further the enjoyment by all States, great or small, victor or vanquished, of access, on equal terms, to the trade and to the raw materials of the world which are needed for their economic prosperity.

5. They desire to bring about the fullest collaboration between all nations in the economic field with the object of securing, for all, improved labor standards, economic advancement and social security.

6. After the final destruction of the Nazi tyranny, they hope to see established a peace which will afford to all nations the means of dwelling in safety within their own boundaries, and which will afford assurance that all the men in all the lands may live out their lives in freedom from fear and want.

7. Such a peace should enable all men to traverse the high seas and oceans without hindrance.

8. They believe that all of the nations of the world, for realistic as well as spiritual reasons, must come to the abandonment of the use of force. Since no future peace can be maintained if land, sea or air armaments continue to be employed by nations which threaten, or may threaten, aggression outside of their frontiers, they believe, pending the establishment of a wider and permanent system of general security, that the disarmament of such nations is essential. They will likewise aid and encourage all other practicable measures which will lighten for peace-loving peoples the crushing burden of armaments.

FRANKLIN D. ROOSEVELT
WINSTON S. CHURCHILL

August 14, 1941.

THE UNITED NATIONS AGREEMENT

PROCLAIMED AT WASHINGTON, JANUARY 2, 1942.

Declaration by United Nations:

A joint declaration by the United States of America, the United Kingdom of Great Britain and Northern Ireland, and the Union of Soviet Socialist Republics, China, Australia, Belgium, Canada, Costa Rica, Cuba, Czechoslovakia, Dominican Republic, El Salvador, Greece, Guatemala, Haiti, Honduras, India, Luxembourg, Netherlands, New Zealand, Nicaragua, Norway, Panama, Poland, South Africa, Yugoslavia.

The governments signatory hereto,

Having subscribed to a common program of purposes and principles embodied in the joint declaration of the President of the United States of

America and the Prime Minister of the United Kingdom of Great Britain and Northern Ireland dated August 14, 1941, known as the Atlantic Charter,

Being convinced that complete victory over their enemies is essential to defend life, liberty, independence, and religious freedom, and to preserve human rights and justice in their own lands as well as in other lands, and that they are now engaged in a common struggle against savage and brutal forces seeking to subjugate the world, Declare:

(1) Each government pledges itself to employ its full resources, military or economic, against those members of the Tripartite Pact and its adherents with which such government is at war.

(2) Each government pledges itself to cooperate with the governments signatory hereto and not to make a separate armistice or peace with the enemies.

The foregoing declaration may be adhered to by other nations which are, or which may be, rendering material assistance and contributions in the struggle for victory over Hitlerism.

Done at Washington,
January First, 1942.

Example of bilateral lend-lease agreement as negotiated between the United States and other members of the United Nations.

Text of the Anglo-American agreement signed in Washington on February 23, 1942, by Sumner Welles, Acting Secretary of State and Viscount Halifax, the British Ambassador:

AGREEMENT BETWEEN THE GOVERNMENTS OF THE UNITED STATES OF AMERICA AND OF THE UNITED KINGDOM ON THE PRINCIPLES APPLYING TO MUTUAL AID IN THE PROSECUTION OF THE WAR AGAINST AGGRESSION, AUTHORIZED AND PROVIDED FOR BY THE ACT OF MARCH 11, 1941.

Whereas the Governments of the United States of America and the United Kingdom of Great Britain and Northern Ireland declare that they are engaged in a cooperative undertaking, together with every other nation or people of like mind, to the end of laying the bases of a just and enduring world peace securing order under law to themselves and all nations:

And whereas the President of the United States of America has determined, pursuant to the Act of Congress of March 11, 1941, that the defense of the United Kingdom against aggression is vital to the defense of the United States of America;

And whereas the United States of America has extended and is continuing to extend to the United Kingdom aid in resisting aggression;

And whereas it is expedient that the final determination of the terms and conditions upon which the Government of the United Kingdom receives such aid and of the benefits to be received by the United States of America in return therefore should be deferred until the extent of the defense aid is known and until the progress of events makes clearer the final terms and conditions and benefits which will be in the mutual interests of the United States of America and the United Kingdom and will promote the establishment and maintenance of world peace;

And whereas the Governments of the United States of America and the United Kingdom are mutually desirous of concluding now a preliminary agreement in regard to the provision of defense aid and in regard to certain considerations which shall be taken into account in determining such terms and conditions and the making of such an agreement has been in all respects duly authorized, and all acts, conditions and formalities which it may have been necessary to perform, fulfill or execute prior to the making of such an agreement in conformity with the laws either of the United States of America or of the United Kingdom have been performed, fulfilled or executed as required;

The undersigned, being duly authorized by their respective Governments for that purpose, have agreed as follows:

ARTICLE I

The Government of the United States of America will continue to supply the Government of the United Kingdom with such defense articles, defense services and defense information as the President shall authorize to be transferred or provided.

ARTICLE II

The Government of the United Kingdom will continue to contribute to the defense of the United States of America and the strengthening thereof and will provide such articles, services, facilities or information as it may be in a position to supply.

ARTICLE III

The Government of the United Kingdom will not without the consent of the President of the United States of America transfer title to, or possession of, any defense article or defense information transferred to it under the act or permit the use thereof by anyone not an officer, employee, or agent of the Government of the United Kingdom.

ARTICLE IV

If, as a result of the transfer to the Government of the United Kingdom of any defense article or defense information, it becomes necessary for that government to take any action or make any payment in order fully to protect any of the rights of a citizen of the United States of America who has patent rights in and to any such defense article or information, the Government of the United Kingdom will take such action or make such payment when requested to do so by the President of the United States of America.

ARTICLE V

The Government of the United Kingdom will return to the United States of America at the end of the present emergency, as determined by the President, such defense articles transferred under this agreement as shall not have been destroyed, lost or consumed and as shall be determined by the President to be useful in the defense of the United States of America or of the Western Hemisphere or to be otherwise of use to the United States of America.

ARTICLE VI

In the final determination of the benefits to be provided to the United States of America by the Government of the United Kingdom full cognizance shall be taken of all property, services, information, facilities, or other benefits or considerations provided by the Government of the United Kingdom subsequent to March 11, 1941, and accepted or acknowledged by the President on behalf of the United States of America.

ARTICLE VII

In the final determination of the benefits to be provided to the United States of America by the Government of the United Kingdom in return for aid furnished under the Act of Congress of March 11, 1941, the terms and conditions thereof shall be such as not to burden commerce between the two countries, but to promote mutually advantageous economic relations between them and the betterment of worldwide economic relations. To that end, they shall include provision for agreed action by the United States of America and the United Kingdom, open to participation by all other countries of like mind, directed to the expansion, by appropriate international and domestic measures, of production, employment, and the exchange and consumption of goods, which are the material foundations of the liberty and welfare of all peoples; to the elimination of all forms of discriminatory treatment in international commerce, and to the reduction of tariffs and other trade barriers; and in general, to the attainment of all the economic objectives set forth in the Joint Declaration made on August 12, 1941, by the President of the United States of America and the Prime Minister of the United Kingdom.

At an early convenient date, conversations shall be begun between the two governments with a view to determining, in the light of governing economic conditions, the best means of attaining the above-stated objectives by their own agreed action and of seeking the agreed action of other like-minded governments.

ARTICLE VIII

This agreement shall take effect as from this day's date. It shall continue in force until a date to be agreed upon by the two governments.

Signed and sealed at Washington in duplicate this 23d day of February, 1942.

Example of bilateral defensive treaty of alliance as negotiated between the Soviet Union and other members of the United Nations.

Text of the Anglo-Russian treaty, May 26, 1942.

His Majesty, the King of Great Britain, Ireland and British Dominions Beyond the Seas, Emperor of India, and the Presidium of the Supreme Council of the Union of Soviet Socialist Republics;

Desiring to confirm the stipulations of the agreement between His Majesty's Government in the United Kingdom and the Government of the Union of Soviet Socialist Republics for joint action in the war against Germany signed at Moscow July 12, 1941, and to replace them by formal treaty;

Desiring to contribute after the war to the maintenance of peace and to the prevention of further aggression by Germany or the states associated with her in acts of aggression in Europe;

Desiring, moreover, to give expression to their intention to collaborate closely with one another as well as with the other United Nations at the peace settlement and during the ensuing period of reconstruction on a basis of the principles enunciated in the declaration made August 14, 1941, by the President of the United States of America and the Prime Minister of Great Britain, to which the Government of the Union of Soviet Socialist Republics has adhered;

Desiring finally to provide for mutual assistance in the event of attack upon either high contracting party by Germany or any of the states associated with her in acts of aggression in Europe;

Have decided to conclude a treaty for that purpose and have appointed as their plenipotentiaries;

His Majesty King of Great Britain, Ireland and the British Dominions Beyond the Seas, Emperor of India, for the United Kingdom of Great Britain and Northern Ireland:

The Right Hon. Anthony Eden, M.P., His Majesty's principal Secretary of State for Foreign Affairs;

The Presidium of the Supreme Council of the Union of Soviet Socialist Republics:

M. Viacheslav Mikhailovich Molotov, People's Commissar for Foreign Affairs,

Who, having communicated their full powers, found in good and due form, have agreed as follows:

PART I, ARTICLE 1

In virtue of the alliance established between the United Kingdom and the Union of Soviet Socialist Republics, the high contracting parties mutually undertake to afford one another military and other assistance and support of all kinds in war against Germany and all those states which are associated with her in acts of aggression in Europe.

ARTICLE 2

The high contracting parties undertake not to enter into any negotiations with the Hitlerite Government or any other government in Germany that does not clearly renounce all aggression intentions, and not to negotiate or conclude except by mutual consent any armistice or peace treaty with Germany or any other state associated with her in acts of aggression in Europe.

PART II, ARTICLE 3

(1) The high contracting parties declare their desire to unite with other like-minded states in adopting proposals for common action to preserve peace and resist aggression in the postwar period.

(2) Pending adoption of such proposals they will, after termination of hostilities, take all measures in their power to render impossible the repetition of aggression and violation of peace by Germany or any of the states associated with her in acts of aggression in Europe.

ARTICLE 4

Should either of the high contracting parties during the postwar period become involved in hostilities with Germany or any of the states mentioned in Article 3, Section 2, in consequence of the attack by that state against that party, the other high contracting party will at once give to the contracting party so involved in hostilities all military and other support and assistance in his power.

This article shall remain in force until the high contracting parties, by mutual agreement, shall recognize that it is superseded by adoption of proposals contemplated in Article 3, Section 1. In default of adoption of such proposals it shall remain in force for a period of twenty years and thereafter until terminated by either high contracting party as provided in Article 8.

ARTICLE 5

The high contracting parties, having regard to the interests of security of each of them, agree to work together in close and friendly collaboration after reestablishment of peace for the organization of security and economic prosperity in Europe.

They will take into account the interests of the United Nations in these objects and they will act in accordance with the two principles of not seeking territorial aggrandizement for themselves and of non-interference in the internal affairs of other states.

ARTICLE 6

The high contracting parties agree to render one another all possible economic assistance after the war.

ARTICLE 7

Each high contracting party undertakes not to conclude any alliance and not to take part in any coalition directed against the other high contracting party.

ARTICLE 8

The present treaty is subject to ratification in the shortest possible time, and instruments of ratification shall be exchanged in Moscow as soon as possible.

It comes into force immediately on the exchange of instruments of ratification and shall thereupon replace the agreement between the Government of the Union of Soviet Socialist Republics and His Majesty's Government in the United Kingdom signed at Moscow July 12, 1941.

Part I of the present treaty shall remain in force until the reestablishment of peace between the high contracting parties and Germany and the powers associated with her in acts of aggression in Europe.

Part II of the present treaty shall remain in force for a period of twenty years. Thereafter, unless twelve months' notice has been given by either party to terminate the treaty at the end of the said period of twenty years, it shall continue in force until twelve months after either high contracting party shall have given notice to the other in writing of his intention to terminate it.

In witness whereof the above-named plenipotentiaries have signed the present treaty and have affixed thereto their seals.

Done in duplicate in London on the twenty-sixth day of May, 1942, in the Russian and English languages, both texts being equally authentic.

MOSCOW CONFERENCE DECLARATIONS
November 1, 1943

Four-Nation Declaration

The Governments of the United States of America, United Kingdom, the Soviet Union and China:

United in their determination, in accordance with the declaration by the United Nations of January 1, 1942, and subsequent declarations, to continue hostilities against those Axis powers with which they respectively are at war until such powers have laid down their arms on the basis of unconditional surrender;

Conscious of their responsibility to secure the liberation of themselves and the peoples allied with them from the menace of aggression;

Recognizing the necessity of insuring a rapid and orderly transition from war to peace and of establishing and maintaining international peace and security with the least diversion of the world's human and economic resources for armaments;

Jointly declare:

1. That their united action, pledged for the prosecution of the war against their respective enemies, will be continued for the organization and maintenance of peace and security.

2. That those of them at war with a common enemy will act together in all matters relating to the surrender and disarmament of that enemy.

3. That they will take all measures deemed by them to be necessary to provide against any violation of the terms imposed upon the enemy.

4. That they recognize the necessity of establishing at the earliest practicable date a general international organization, based on the principle of the sovereign equality of all peace-loving states, and open to membership by all such states, large and small, for the maintenance of international peace and security.

5. That for the purpose of maintaining international peace and security pending the reestablishment of law and order and the inauguration of a system of general security, they will consult with one another and, as occasion requires, with other members of the United Nations with a view to joint action on behalf of the community of nations.

6. That after the termination of hostilities they will not employ their military forces within the territories of other states except for the purposes envisaged in this declaration and after joint consultation.

7. That they will confer and cooperate with one another and with other members of the United Nations to bring about a practicable general agreement with respect to the regulation of armaments in the postwar period.

Declaration on Italy

The foreign secretaries of the United States, United Kingdom and Soviet Union have established that their three governments are in complete agreement that Allied policy toward Italy must be based upon the fundamental principle that Fascism and all its evil influence and configuration shall be completely destroyed, and that the Italian people shall be given every opportunity to establish governmental and other institutions based upon democratic principles.

The foreign secretaries of the United States and United Kingdom declare that the action of their governments from the inception of the invasion of Italian territory, in so far as paramount military requirements have permitted, has been based upon this policy.

In furtherance of this policy in the future the foreign secretaries of the three governments are agreed that the following measures are important and should be put into effect.

1. It is essential that the Italian Government should be made more democratic by inclusion of representatives of those sections of the Italian people who have always opposed Fascism.

2. Freedom of speech, of religious worship, of political belief, of press and of public meeting shall be restored in full measure to the Italian people, who shall also be entitled to form anti-Fascist political groups.

3. All institutions and organizations created by the Fascist regime shall be suppressed.

4. All Fascist or pro-Fascist elements shall be removed from the administration and from institutions and organizations of a public character.

5. All political prisoners of the Fascist regime shall be released and accorded full amnesty.

6. Democratic organs of local government shall be created.

7. Fascist chiefs and army generals known or suspected to be war criminals shall be arrested and handed over to justice.

In making this declaration the three foreign secretaries recognize that so long as active military operations continue in Italy the time at which it is possible to give full effect to the principles stated above will be determined by the Commander-in-Chief on the basis of instructions received through the combined chiefs of staff.

The three governments, parties to this declaration, will, at the request of any one of them, consult on this matter. It is further understood that nothing in this resolution is to operate against the right of the Italian people ultimately to choose their own form of government.

Declaration on Austria

The Governments of the United Kingdom, the Soviet Union and the United States of America are agreed that Austria, the first free country to fall a victim to Hitlerite aggression, shall be liberated from German domination.

They regard the annexation imposed on Austria by Germany on March 15, 1938, as null and void. They consider themselves as in no way bound by any changes effected in Austria since that date. They declare that they wish to see reestablished a free and independent Austria, and thereby to open the way for the Austrian people themselves, as well as those neighboring states which will be faced with similar problems, to find that political and economic security which is the only basis for lasting peace.

Austria is reminded, however, that she has a responsibility, which she cannot evade, for participation in the war at the side of Hitlerite Germany, and that in the final settlement account will inevitably be taken of her own contribution to her liberation.

Statement on Atrocities

Signed by President Roosevelt, Prime Minister Churchill and Premier Stalin.

The United Kingdom, the United States and the Soviet Union have received from many quarters evidence of atrocities, massacres and cold-blooded mass executions which are being perpetrated by Hitlerite forces in many of the countries they have overrun and from which they are now being expelled. The brutalities of Nazi domination are no new thing, and all peoples or territories in their grip have suffered from the worst form of government by terror. What is new is that many of these territories are now being redeemed by the advancing armies of the liberating powers, and that in their desperation the recoiling Hitlerites and Huns are redoubling their ruthless cruelties. This is now evidenced with particular clearness by monstrous crimes on the territory of the Soviet Union which is being liberated from Hitlerites and on French and Italian territory.

Accordingly, the aforesaid three Allied powers, speaking in the interests of the thirty-two United Nations, hereby solemnly declare and give full warning of their declaration as follows:

At the time of granting of any armistice to any government which may be set up in Germany, those German officers and men and members of the Nazi Party who have been responsible for or have taken a consenting part in the above atrocities, massacres and executions will be sent back to the countries in which their abominable deeds were done in order that they may be judged and punished according to the laws of these liberated countries and of free governments which will be erected therein. Lists will be compiled in all possible detail from all these countries, having regard especially to invaded parts of the Soviet Union, to Poland and Czechoslovakia, to Yugoslavia and Greece including Crete and other islands, to Norway, Denmark, Netherlands, Belgium, Luxembourg, France and Italy.

Thus, Germans who take part in wholesale shooting of Polish officers or in the execution of French, Dutch, Belgian or Norwegian hostages or of Cretan peasants, or who have shared in slaughters inflicted on the people of Poland or in territories of the Soviet Union which are now being swept clear of the enemy, will know they will be brought back to the scene of their crimes and judged on the spot by the peoples whom they have outraged.

Let those who have hitherto not imbrued their hands with innocent blood beware lest they join the ranks of the guilty, for most assuredly the three Allied powers will pursue them to the uttermost ends of the earth and will deliver them to their accusers in order that justice may be done.

The above declaration is without prejudice to the case of German criminals, whose offenses have no particular geographical localization and who will be punished by joint decision of the Governments of the Allies.

Editors' Note

The Moscow Conference of Foreign Secretaries: of the United States, Cordell Hull; of the United Kingdom, Anthony Eden; of the Soviet Union, V. M. Molotov (October 19 to 30, 1943) agreed to establish in London a *European Advisory Commission* of representatives of the United Kingdom, the United States, and the Soviet Union, to make recommendations to the three Governments on European problems arising as the war develops. The Conference also decided to establish an *Advisory Council on Italy* to be composed of representatives of the United Kingdom, the United States, the Soviet Union, the French Committee of National Liberation, Greece, and Yugoslavia to deal with day-to-day problems other than military preparations and to make recommendations for coordinated allied policy with regard to Italy.

Other matters were left to be considered by special commissions or diplomacy. Further consultations between the three Governments to be continued through diplomacy.

Official Announcement on the Conference of President Roosevelt, Generalissimo Chiang Kai-shek and Prime Minister Churchill, together with their respective military and diplomatic advisers, in Cairo, December 1, 1943.

The several military missions have agreed upon future military operations against Japan.

The three great Allies expressed their resolve to bring unrelenting pressure against their brutal enemies by sea, land and air. (As issued at Washington the communiqué added: "This great pressure is already rising.")

The three great Allies are fighting this war to restrain and punish the aggression of Japan.

They covet no gain for themselves and have no thought of territorial expansion.

It is their purpose that Japan shall be stripped of all the islands in the Pacific which she has seized or occupied since the beginning of the first world war in 1914, and that all the territories Japan has stolen from the Chinese, such as Manchuria, Formosa and the Pescadores, shall be restored to the Republic of China.

Japan also will be expelled from all other territories which she has taken by violence and greed.

The aforesaid three great powers, mindful of the enslavement of the people of Korea, are determined that in due course Korea shall become free and independent.

With these objects in view, the three Allies, in harmony with those of the United Nations at war with Japan, will continue to persevere in the serious and prolonged operations necessary to procure the unconditional surrender of Japan.

THE TEHERAN DECLARATION

WE, the President of the United States of America, the Prime Minister of Great Britain and the Premier of the Soviet Union, have met these four days past in this capital of our ally, Iran, and have shaped and confirmed our common policy. We expressed our determination that our nations shall work together in the war and in the peace that will follow.

As to the war, our military staffs have joined in our roundtable discussions and we have concerted our plans for the destruction of the German forces. We have reached complete agreement as to the scope and timing of operations which will be undertaken from east, west and south.

The common understanding which we have here reached guarantees that victory will be ours.

And as to the peace, we are sure that our concord will make it an enduring peace. We recognize fully the supreme responsibility resting upon us and all the United Nations to make a peace which will command the good-will of the overwhelming masses of the peoples of the world and banish the scourge and terror of war for many generations.

With our diplomatic advisers we have surveyed the problems of the future. We shall seek the cooperation and active participation of all nations, large and small, whose peoples in heart and mind are dedicated, as are our own peoples, to the elimination of tyranny and slavery, oppression and intolerance. We will welcome them as they may choose to come into a world family of democratic nations.

No power on earth can prevent our destroying the German armies by land, their U-boats by sea, and their war plants from the air. Our attacks will be relentless and increasing.

From these friendly conferences we look with confidence to the day when all the peoples of the world may live free lives untouched by tyranny and according to their varying desires and their own consciences.

We came here with hope and determination. We leave here friends in fact, in spirit, and in purpose.

Signed at Teheran, December 1, 1943.

ROOSEVELT
STALIN
CHURCHILL

TEXT OF DECLARATION ON IRAN

THE PRESIDENT of the United States of America, the Premier of the Union of Soviet Socialist Republics and the Prime Minister of the United Kingdom, having consulted with each other and with the Prime Minister of

Iran, desire to declare the mutual agreement of their three governments regarding their relations with Iran.

The Governments of the United States of America, the Union of Soviet Socialist Republics, and the United Kingdom recognize the assistance which Iran has given in the prosecution of the war against the common enemy, particularly by facilitating transportation of supplies from overseas to the Soviet Union.

The three governments realize that the war has caused special economic difficulties for Iran, and they are agreed that they will continue to make available to the Government of Iran such economic assistance as may be possible, having regard to the heavy demands made upon them by their worldwide military operations and to the worldwide shortage of transport, raw material, and supplies for civilian consumption.

With respect to the postwar period, the Governments of the United States of America, the Union of Soviet Socialist Republics, and the United Kingdom are in accord with the Government of Iran that any economic problem confronting Iran at the close of hostilities should receive full consideration along with those of the other members of the United Nations by conferences of international agencies held or created to deal with international economic matters.

The Governments of the United States of America, the Union of Soviet Socialist Republics, and the United Kingdom are at one with the Government of Iran in their desire for the maintenance of the independence, sovereignty, and territorial integrity of Iran. They count upon the participation of Iran, together with all other peace-loving nations, in the establishment of international peace, security, and prosperity after the war in accordance with the principles of the Atlantic Charter, to which all four governments have continued to subscribe.

TITLE:
Agreement for United Nations Relief and Rehabilitation Administration

DATE: September 20, 1943.

RELEASED BY:
Department of State of the United States.

Charts of Plans to Unite Nations Since 1914

SOURCE: *New York Times*, September 24, 1943.

TYPE:
CONFEDERATE specialized agency, modeled on League of Nations Covenant.

MEMBERSHIP:
Governments or Authorities of the United Nations signing the agreement (forty-four members of the United Nations signed the agreement November 9, 1943).

ORGANS OF GOVERNMENT:
LEGISLATIVE: *The Council:* One representative and several alternates from each member government; one representative selected by Council to preside at each session; determines own rules of procedure.
Decisions: By majority vote unless otherwise decided by Council.
Sessions: At least twice a year convened by *Central Committee;* special sessions may be convened by Central Committee whenever necessary or within thirty days on request of one-third of Council members.

Duties: Policy-making body of Administration; approves budget; determines each member government's share of proportionate expense of Administration; establishes standing regional committees and other standing committees, technical committees on nutrition, health, agriculture, transport, repatriation, and finance to advise it and Central Committee; appoints Council members and alternates to various committees; may authorize Central Committee to make emergency appointments between sessions.

The Central Committee: Representatives of China, Union of Soviet Socialist Republics, United Kingdom, United States of America. *Director General* presides at meetings but may not vote.

Duties: Makes emergency policy decisions between Council sessions (subject to reconsideration by Council) but such decisions must be communicated to each member government immediately; makes emergency appointments between Council sessions; *may prevent publication of portions of Director General's report if in interest of United Nations.* Governments not represented on Central Committee may have their representatives participate in its meetings to discuss action of special interest to such governments.

The Committee on Supplies: Council representatives or alternates of member governments likely to be principal suppliers of relief and rehabilitation; members appointed by Council.

Duties: To consider, formulate, and recommend to Council and Central Committee policies to assure provision of needed supplies; to meet from time to time with Central Committee to review policy on supplies.

The Committee of the Council for Europe: (Replaces Inter-Allied Committee on European Post-War Relief established September 24, 1941; takes over its records.) All Council representatives or alternates representing European member governments and representatives of governments directly concerned with relief and rehabilitation in Europe; appointed by Council; may request establishment of regional subcommittees of the technical standing committees.

The Committee of the Council for the Far East: All Council representatives or alternates representing member governments of Far Eastern territories and representatives of other member governments directly concerned with relief and rehabilitation in the Far East; appointed by Council.

Duties of both Regional Committees: To meet within their respective areas; to consider, and recommend to Council and Central Committee relief and rehabilitation policies for regional areas.

EXECUTIVE OR ADMINISTRATIVE:

Director General: Appointed by Council on unanimous nomination of Central Committee; removable by Council on unanimous request of Central Committee.

Duties: Appoints Deputy Directors General, officers, experts, headquarters and field staff; delegates necessary authority to them; supplies secretariat, staff, and facilities required by Council and its Committees, including regional and subcommittees; presides at meetings of Central Committee but may not vote; distributes reports and recommendations of committees and transmits them with his comments to Council and Central Committee; has full power and authority

… to carry out relief operations within limits of resources and broad policies established by Council or Central Committee; prepares immediate plans together with military and other United Nations authorities for emergency civilian relief in occupied areas; procures and assembles necessary supplies; selects emergency organization; consults and collaborates with existing United Nations authorities in procuring, transporting, and distributing supplies and services, using existing facilities when practicable; regulates foreign voluntary relief agencies; submits annual and supplementary budgets to Council; negotiates with member governments providing supplies and resources; accounts for all contributions; reports periodically to Central Committee and to Council on Administration activities.

JUDICIAL:
None provided.

TRANSFERS OF JURISDICTION FROM MEMBER NATIONS TO THE ADMINISTRATION:
The Administration has power —

To acquire, hold, and convey property.
To enter into contracts; to undertake obligations.
To designate or create agencies and to review their activities.
To manage undertakings.
To perform any legal act appropriate to its objects and purposes.
To plan, coordinate, and administer relief of war victims in areas under United Nations control.
To provide food, fuel, clothing, shelter, and other basic necessities; medical and other essential services.
To facilitate adequate provision of relief, production, transportation, and servicing of relief articles and measures.
To formulate and recommend measures for individual or joint action by any or all member governments for coordination of purchasing, use of ships, and other procurement activities in period following cessation of hostilities.
To administer measures of coordination authorized by member governments.
To study, formulate, and recommend for individual or joint action

of member governments measures within its field proposed by any member government.

To accept new members.

RESTRICTIONS ON THE ADMINISTRATION:

During hostilities or other military necessities in any area, Administration activities subject to consent and control of military command; the necessity for such restrictions to be determined at the discretion of the military commander.

Relief activities within territory of a member government to be determined after consultation and with the consent of such government.

MEMBER GOVERNMENTS UNDERTAKE:

To pay travel and other expenses of members of Council and Committees.

To contribute their share of administrative expenses promptly, subject to requirements of national constitutional procedure.

To make purchases for relief and rehabilitation outside own territories during war only after consultation with Director General and as far as possible through United Nations agencies.

To contribute supplies and resources for relief to the extent authorized by national constitutional bodies.

MEMBER GOVERNMENTS RETAIN:

Right to withdraw from Administration six months after signing of agreement; withdrawal to be effective twelve months after notice of withdrawal to Director General if all financial, supply, and other obligations accepted or undertaken are fulfilled.

Right to request Council to prevent publication of such parts of Director General's reports as affect member government's interests.

RATIFICATION:

Agreement comes into force for each member of United Nations when signed by its government, unless otherwise specified by the signatory government.

AMENDMENT:

Involving New Obligations: By two-thirds vote of Council; effective for each member government ratifying it.

Modifying Provisions Affecting the Council and Director General: By two-thirds vote of Council including votes of all members of Central Committee.

Other Amendments: By two-thirds vote of Council.

AUTHOR:
GENERAL MARCEL DE BAER (Belgian).

PROFESSION:
Justice of the Court of Appeals of Brussels; Chief Justice of the Belgian Courts in Great Britain; Professor of Law; Member United Nations Commission for the Investigation of War Crimes.

TITLE OF PLAN:
Draft Convention for the Creation of an International Criminal Court. Mimeographed.

DATE: November, 1943.

PUBLISHER AND SUPPORTING ORGANIZATION:
Commission for Questions Concerned with the Liquidation of the War of the London International Assembly, London. (An unofficial organization, independent of all government control, of representatives of about fifteen of the United Nations. One of its objects is to consider principles of postwar policy and their application to national and international affairs. From time to time the Assembly recommends specific courses of action or policy to the governments.—EDITORS.)

TYPE:
International Criminal Court. Jurisdiction only over individuals and not over nations.

MEMBERSHIP:
During the War: Members of the United Nations; if Court continued, other nations ratifying Convention to be added to membership.

STRUCTURE:
Judicial:

International Criminal Court: Seven-year term; thirty-five judges; number may be increased; to be appointed within two months of ratification of Convention by member nations; term of office of five judges to expire each year. Vacancies to be filled by reelection or election of new judges by Court from list of candidates nominated by member nations (each nation nominating not more than three persons who need not be its nationals). First panel of judges to be appointed from among authorities on criminal law, members or former members of highest national judicial bodies or qualified for such appointment, or recognized authorities on criminal and international law; should know English. Court to represent principal legal systems of world and provide fair representation of nations occupied by Axis.

President and Vice-President: Two-year term; elected by Court; may be reelected.

Court may sit in several divisions of three, five, seven, or more members; at least seven judges present to try cases submitted for revision. Judges not eligible in cases where previously engaged in a private capacity, except by Court permission. Court to determine questions as to its jurisdiction during hearing of cases.

Decisions: On procedure — by majority of judges present. In deciding a case: by majority vote of judges present, stating reason for the decision; no dissenting opinion to be revealed.

Until Convention defining main principles of international criminal law and fixing penalties has been established, Court to decide cases on basis of: International custom, treaties, conventions, declarations, and general principles of criminal law recognized by members of United Nations. Judicial decisions and doctrines of highly qualified jurists to be subsidiary means of determining rules of law.

Executive or Administrative:

Registrar: Appointed by Court. *Duties:* In charge of *Registry of Court* and its archives.

United Nations Procurator General: Three-year term; qualifications and appointment same as for judges; reappointment by Court. May appoint any number of *Deputies* to assist him. *Removal from Office:*

Judges, the Procurator General and his Deputies may be removed from office by two-thirds vote of all these officers on request of any one of them.

Duties: To receive complaints; to make preliminary investigations; to collect evidence; describe the charges; prepare cases for prosecution; call witnesses; summon persons accused by a member nation to appear before Court; to demand arrest and handing over of accused persons; decide whether persons committed for trial are to be placed in custody; to accuse persons of war crimes and bring them before Court; prosecute any case sent to Court by *United Nations Commission for the Investigation of War Crimes;* to ensure carrying out of Court's decisions and orders in name of United Nations; request member nations to arrest accused persons within their territories; to issue warrants for arrest by *International Constabulary* of accused persons in Axis territory.

International Constabulary: Personnel nominated by member nations. *Duties:* To carry out orders of Court and of Procurator General with right to request assistance of local police.

TRANSFERS OF JURISDICTION FROM MEMBER NATIONS TO THE COURT:
(International Criminal Court to belong to all nations; persons tried before it not to be considered extradited.)

To try persons for outrages violating general principles of criminal law recognized by civilized nations, and crimes committed in wartime or connected with the preparation and waging of war, or committed to prevent restoration of peace.
To try persons, irrespective of rank or position, accused of ordering the commission of crime; of direct participation, aid, encouragement, or conspiracy in crime; heads of national governments to be included.
To determine whether persons accused by member nations are to be tried.
To determine whether accused shall be placed in confinement or allowed liberty.
To determine what witnesses and experts are to be summoned and heard.

To dispatch *letters of request* to member nations.
To pass sentence of fine, confiscation, imprisonment, or death.
To determine disposition of fines collected.

RESTRICTIONS ON COURT:
No case to be brought before International Criminal Court if domestic courts of any of the United Nations have jurisdiction over accused and are willing to exercise it. If domestic courts of two or more member nations have jurisdiction over accused the case may be brought before International Criminal Court by agreement of nations involved.

RIGHTS OF NATIONS:
To commit persons accused of war crimes to trial before International Criminal Court.
To request Procurator General to summon an accused person to appear before Court.
To intervene in a case: inspect the files, submit statements, and participate in verbal proceedings.
To apply for revision of sentence; Court to give its reasons for grant or refusal of revision.

NATIONS UNDERTAKE:
To assist International Criminal Court and Procurator General in discharge of their duties.
To adjust national legislation to meet requirements of this Convention.
To contribute to a common fund for expenses of Court including salaries, pensions, fees of counsel assigned to defend accused, etc.
To submit disputes over interpretation of application of Convention, if not settled by diplomatic negotiations, to *Permanent Court of International Justice* or to *Permanent Court of Arbitration*.
To grant members of Court diplomatic passports, privileges, and immunities when engaged in business of Court.
To hand accused persons residing within their territories to prosecuting agencies of Court when requested to do so.
To give Court every assistance in securing the presence of witnesses.
To provide suitable place of internment with staff for custody of accused persons if Court meets in their territory.

INDIVIDUAL RIGHTS GUARANTEED:
Court to consider charges only against person committed to it for trial.
Court may not try accused for any offenses except those for which he has been committed.
No accused person to be tried unless present.
No person tried by International Criminal Court may be tried for the same offense by a national court. (But a person tried by the court of an Axis nation, even if convicted, may be tried for the same offense by the International Criminal Court.)
Accused to have right of defense by counsel, admitted to plead before Court. (If accused does not choose own counsel, Court to assign one for his defense.)
Accused and his counsel to have right to inspect files, statements, and evidence in the case. Documents to be translated into language of accused on his request.
Except when Court decides otherwise, no examination, nor hearing of witnesses or experts may take place unless accused and counsel are present.
Trials to be public unless Court for special reasons decides on closed session. Decisions to be passed at public sessions.
Persons convicted to have right to apply for revision of sentence.
No person to be tried before the International Criminal Court for any act unless it is declared criminal by law of nation of the accused, or by law of the place of his residence at time the act was committed, and only if such law is in accord with general principles of criminal law recognized by United Nations.

METHODS OF ENFORCEMENT:
Court to determine whether persons adjudged guilty of war crimes are to pay damages and costs of proceedings; whether property unlawfully taken is to be returned to its rightful owner, or confiscated by the Court.
Sentences involving imprisonment to be enforced by member nations chosen by Court; nations may not refuse Court's request if trial of convicted persons was asked by them.
If capital punishment is illegal in nation chosen by Court to execute death sentence, nation may substitute most severe penalty provided by national law. Right of pardon to be exercised by nation charged with enforcement of penalty.

IMMEDIATE STEPS:
United Nations to establish *International Criminal Court for the Trial of Persons Accused of War Crimes*, during the war.

LIQUIDATION OF THE WAR:
Upon unconditional surrender of Axis countries, war to be terminated by United Nations with a *Declaration of Peace* providing for full occupation and administration of the defeated by an *Inter-Allied Council* with full legislative, executive, and judicial power.
Duties: To provide relief; to disarm the Axis nations; to punish war criminals; to prepare machinery of world organization. Axis nations to be invited to cooperate after resuming full control of their own governments at end of transitional period.

RATIFICATION:
Convention establishing Court to come into force provisionally on signing by seven nations. Instruments of ratification to be deposited with *Secretary General of League of Nations* who is to notify all League members and all nations signing the Convention. Government first signing Convention to convene initial meeting of all ratifying nations.

WITHDRAWAL:
Notice of withdrawal to be sent to *Secretary General of League of Nations* who is to notify all League members and nations signing the Convention. Withdrawal to take effect one year after notice given, but cases referred to Court previous to withdrawal are to be heard and obligations to enforce sentences fulfilled unless Court appoints another member nation to execute them.

MISCELLANEOUS:
Headquarters of the Court to be in London, but decision to meet elsewhere optional.
Official Language: English.

In arguing for the early establishment of such a Court the author says: "... in default of organized justice in which the peoples can have absolute trust, the victimized populations will take reprisals into their own hands, and, as always when the mob breaks loose, their vengeance will fall mainly on the innocent, leaving the real criminals to escape."

AUTHOR:
COMMISSION TO STUDY THE ORGANIZATION OF PEACE (American).

TITLE OF PLAN:
The United Nations and the Organization of Peace.
   Fundamentals of the International Organization.
   Security and World Organization.
   The Economic Organization of Welfare.

DATE: February and November, 1943.

PAMPHLETS

PUBLISHED BY:
The Commission to Study the Organization of Peace, New York.

TYPE:
CONFEDERATE. NAME: United Nations.

MEMBERSHIP:
Present United Nations, neutrals and enemy peoples to be added as early as practicable.

ORGANS OF GOVERNMENT:
LEGISLATIVE: *General International Assembly:* Open eventually to delegates of all nations.

EXECUTIVE OR ADMINISTRATIVE:
Executive Council: Composed of a limited number of nations.

Duties: To restore and maintain peace; to take quick decisions in case of threat of aggression. (See Chart of League Covenant, p. 421.)

Secretariat: To study international problems; to provide information and secretarial services.

Economic, Financial, and Transit Organization: Modeled after International Labor Organization (See Chart, p. 427) with representatives from governments and economic interests. The following subordinate Departments suggested:

International Clearing Union: To keep national currency exchange rates stable.

Economic Development Authority: (To work through Regional Authorities.) To aid economic development and investment through international public works; to control and develop river systems.

United Nations Commodity Corporation: To coordinate purchases; to accumulate materials for war and for reconstruction; to absorb world surpluses, releasing them when needed.

United Nations Shipping Administration: To coordinate transit.

United Nations Economic Council: To coordinate governing bodies of technical institutions through joint meetings, at least, of their Directors.

International Armaments Control Commission: To inspect observance of disarmament.

United Nations Colonial Authority: To study colonial problems; to develop trusteeship policy; to inspect national colonial administration.

United Nations Authority for Relief and Rehabilitation: To estimate needs; to plan production; to determine transportation and distribution priorities; to provide police protection; to rebuild ports and railways; to resume agricultural production.

International Refugee and Migration Agency.

International Labor Organization: To be strengthened and linked with the United Nations.

Advisory Committee on Social Questions, Opium Advisory Committee, and *Health Organization* to be taken over from League of Nations.

Permanent International Office of Education: To develop mutual understanding and loyalty to idea of international cooperation with power of inspection to prevent use of education for inculcation of war-like attitudes.

International Air Force: At first formed of squadrons ceded to it by principal United Nations. Later permanent force to be recruited from volunteers swearing allegiance to United Nations. To be supported by national military and naval contingents and by economic sanctions.

Equipment: Bomber and fighter planes; cargo planes to carry freight; troop carriers; submarines to protect air bases. *General Staff:* At first composed of combined military staffs of United Nations carrying out decisions of their governments. *Departments: Laboratories, Procurement Office, Inspection Force.*

Special Conference: Representing member nations. To regulate organization, recruitment, and discipline of Air Force; organization and procedure of military tribunals; to revise regulations when necessary.

JUDICIAL:
Permanent Court of International Justice: To have compulsory jurisdiction and subordinate and regional courts; also international criminal jurisdiction.

Permanent Commission on Human Rights: Composed of jurists of high standing. *Duties:* To deal with protection of human rights on basis of minimum standards; to reformulate periodically individual rights recognized under international law. Enforcement of respect for such rights left to member nations.

TRANSFERS OF JURISDICTION FROM MEMBER NATIONS TO THE UNITED NATIONS:
To promulgate Bill of Human Rights amplifying Atlantic Charter.
To develop international colonial policy.
To regulate economic intercourse.
To negotiate with member nations to permit travel and residence of refugees.
To organize international system of grants-in-aid to raise health standards.
To control about fifty strategic bases in various parts of the world in addition to training bases located in different member nations.
To levy taxes on international postal charges and on commercial use of international bases for support of International Air Force.

NATIONS RETAIN:
Freedom to develop their own culture, political philosophy, and economic system with due regard to international law and world welfare.

RESTRICTIONS ON NATIONS:
No withdrawal from United Nations.
National form of government cannot be independent of international law or free to operate against world government.

METHODS OF ENFORCEMENT:
Toward Nations: If they violate disarmament provisions, threaten war, or initiate hostilities, and disobey Council orders to suspend these aggressive actions, Council may declare them guilty of aggression, authorizing initial action by International Air Force. Actual suppression of armed aggression by cooperative military action agreed on by member nations.

IMMEDIATE STEPS:
United Nations Conference should establish planning commissions and administrative agencies to deal with occupied areas, colonies, relief, rehabilitation, migration and refugees, social, economic reconstruction, and education.

Agreement by China, Great Britain, the Soviet Union, and the United States to make the United Nations into an effective organization with other nations participating in its councils.

PREREQUISITES TO PEACE:
United Nations victory.

LIQUIDATION OF THE WAR:
United Nations to guarantee maintenance of order in disorganized areas in enemy and liberated territories; to provide for resettlement, transportation, health, and employment; to intervene to restore order in event of contests for national power between rival factions.

Axis nations to be disarmed and policed; their heavy industries, propaganda, and education to be supervised; property and civil rights of the dispossessed to be restored. War criminals to be brought to trial under accepted legal precedents. Racial and other discriminatory legislation to be repealed.

Control of epidemics and tropical diseases.

AUTHOR:
WALTER NASH (New Zealand).

PROFESSION:
Former Minister of Finance and Deputy Prime Minister of New Zealand. At present Minister to the United States.

TITLE OF PLAN:
New Zealand — A Working Democracy.

DATE: 1943.

PUBLISHER:
Duell, Sloan, and Pearce, New York.

TYPE:
CONFEDERATE. NAME: United Nations.

MEMBERSHIP:
Members of the United Nations.

ORGANS OF GOVERNMENT:
LEGISLATIVE: *United Nations War Council:* Composed of representatives of the Soviet Union, China, the United States, the British Commonwealth, and India (if and when she gives full support to the war). *Duties:* To determine major policies.

Regional War Councils: Composed of representatives of other member nations according to their vital interests in each war area, but subordinate to the United Nations War Council.

EXECUTIVE OR ADMINISTRATIVE:
United Nations Military Council: Composed of representatives of the Soviet Union, China, the United States, the British Commonwealth, and India (if and when she gives full support to the war). *Duties:* To determine military operations along general policies decided by War Council.

Production and Assignment Council: Subordinate to Military Council. *Duties:* To supervise production of munitions, equipment, and their allocation.

Combined Raw Materials Board: To determine requirements and distribute available stocks to peacetime industry of member nations.

Combined Production and Resources Board: To regulate maximum production of essential commodities, equipment, and services; to make them available to member nations in greatest need.

Combined Food Board: To regulate distribution of food to starving peoples of Europe and Asia; to establish worldwide standard of good nutrition.

Shipping Adjustment Board: To allocate ships.

World Reconstruction and Development Council: To be subordinate to future supreme United Nations political body.

Duties: To prepare economic, financial, and social rehabilitation of the world when fighting ceases; to work out peacetime supply, adjust stocks and surpluses; to continue world Lend-Lease method of transferring plant equipment and raw materials to nations needing them most.

Regional Reconstruction and Development Councils: To carry out measures agreed on by World Reconstruction and Development Council.

TRANSFERS OF JURISDICTION FROM MEMBER NATIONS TO THE UNITED NATIONS:
To determine major policies of war and peace.
To regulate production and distribution of munitions, raw materials, and food.
To allocate shipping.
To organize reconstruction.
To use air, military, and naval bases to maintain peace.
To maintain freedom of air transport with right of through traffic over national territory by all member nations.
To establish an international force.

METHODS OF ENFORCEMENT:
Economic sanctions to be immediate and automatic, involving complete boycott. Member nations applying sanctions to be prepared to use military force.

IMMEDIATE STEPS:
Calling of early meeting of all members of the United Nations to emphasize their existence as a body and determination to continue the united struggle against hunger, pestilence, unemployment, and insecurity.

LIQUIDATION OF THE WAR:
Storing and conservation of products for relief of peoples in need. Planned demobilization of armed forces on basis of national rehabilitation, reconstruction, and expansion. Pooling of shipping facilities to return soldiers to their homes. World resources to be used for reconstruction to the same extent they have been used for war. Complete disarmament of aggressor nations.

Colonies to have full self-government wherever possible; all other colonies to be under trusteeship administration of the United Nations.

MISCELLANEOUS:
The author describes at length New Zealand's program of postwar reconstruction including the following measures: At least half of the demobilized soldiers are to be employed immediately on land improvement, road building, hydroelectric power projects, irrigation, and flood control. Adequate loans made to those interested in farming; free-interest loans for purchase of tools and to set up small businesses; subsidized vocational retraining and continuance of professional education.

AUTHOR:
Harold E. Stassen (American).

PROFESSION:
Ex-Governor of State of Minnesota.

TITLE OF PLAN:
We Need a World Government.[1] Blueprint for a World Government.[2]

ARTICLES:
Giving tentative proposals for international organization.

Theoretical Plans

DATE: May 22, 1943.[1]
May 23, 1943.[2]

PUBLISHED IN:
[1]*The Saturday Evening Post.* [2]*The New York Times Magazine.*

TYPE:
FEDERAL. **NAME:** United Nations of the World.

MEMBERSHIP:
Present *United Nations* to be continuing organization of the United Nations of the World; membership qualifications for other nations to be clearly defined and admission always kept open.

ORGANS OF GOVERNMENT:
LEGISLATIVE: Unicameral Congress or Parliament: *Assembly*.
Assembly: Representatives apportioned in proportion to population, industrial development, resources, degree of literacy; election according to methods used in each nation in choosing members for its own legislative bodies. (In federations and commonwealths like the American and British, some representatives may be elected on a nationwide basis and some from the individual states or groups of states.)
Decisions: By two-thirds or three-fourths vote.

EXECUTIVE OR ADMINISTRATIVE:
Chairman; United Nations Council.

Chairman: Selected by United Nations Assembly.
Council: Seven members selected by Chairman from the Assembly, subject to consent of Assembly. Each member of the Council directs one of the administrative departments.

United Nations Legion or Keep the Peace Force: Air, naval, and land units; volunteers recruited on quota basis from member nations.
Duties: Enforce Code of Justice; support United Nations administration of airways, seaways; insure disarmament of outlaws and aggressors.

JUDICIAL:
United Nations Court: Judges nominated by Supreme Courts of member nations.

TRANSFERS OF JURISDICTION FROM MEMBER NATIONS TO THE UNITED NATIONS:
Temporary administration of Axis, backward, or disputed territories.
Levy of low and equitable duty on trade between nations for revenue.
Maintenance of a police force.
Regulation of international airways, air tariffs, safety controls, co-ordination of weather data, maintenance of radio beams, communications and accessible airports.
Supervision of sea gateways.
Stimulation of trade by reduction of barriers, clearing of banking and exchange regulations through United Nations, agreement by nations not to raise tariff barriers without consent of United Nations.
Promotion of health and literacy.
Enforcement of a basic Code of Justice.

NATIONS RETAIN:
Armed forces to back up United Nations force and to safeguard against a breakdown or perversion of the United Nations government.
Powers not delegated to the United Nations.

DEMOCRATIC RIGHTS:
Protection of minorities and of religious freedom.
Abolition of slavery.

METHODS OF ENFORCEMENT:
Towards Non-member Nations, aggressors, and outlaws: United Nations Legion assisted by member nations' armed forces if necessary.

IMMEDIATE STEPS:
American leadership must begin to explore, examine, and prepare the means and the methods of active United States collaboration in world organization after the war.

PREREQUISITES TO PEACE:
United Nations victory.

LIQUIDATION OF THE WAR:
United Nations administration of Axis nations including their disarma-

ment; maintenance of order in their territories; legal punishment of their criminal leaders.

Temporary United Nations administration of liberated nations until they are able to choose their own government; United Nations administrators to be barred from citizenship in the nations they administer and from holding office there after local autonomy has been restored.

United Nations administration of underdeveloped and disputed areas.

AUTHOR:
Michael Straight (American).

PROFESSION:
Journalist.

TITLE OF PLAN:
Make This the Last War — The Future of the United Nations.

DATE: 1943.

PUBLISHER:
Harcourt, Brace & Co. Inc., New York.

TYPE:
Confederate: Economic and Social Union operating through various international Boards. Based on the United Nations as a nucleus.
Name: United Nations of the World.

MEMBERSHIP:
Aims at universality after the war. During the war: Present membership of United Nations. Provides for postwar Federated Europe, Federated Indonesia, and others within the United Nations, and a series of interlocking military defense pacts.

ORGANS OF GOVERNMENT:
Legislative: *Assembly of the United Nations:* To be developed from the Supreme Council of the United Nations and the Regional Councils

for the Pacific, the Americas, Europe, Russia, India, the Middle East, functioning during the war.

EXECUTIVE OR ADMINISTRATIVE:

Supreme Council of the United Nations: United States, United Kingdom, Russia, and China; to function as an executive body in constant session.

Regional Councils: For the Pacific, the Americas, Europe, Russia, India, the Middle East.

Combined Chiefs of Staffs: (Leaders of the future world army which is to be the only armed force.) *Subordinate Boards:* Joint Planning; Joint Intelligence; Joint Allocations.

Relief and Reconstruction Council of the United Nations:
Central Committee: Britain, China, Russia, and United States.
Regional Committees: To be fully representative of the regions.

Duties:
1. Prepare detailed estimates of immediate postwar requirements of Russia, Europe, Middle East, Africa, and Asia for housing, food, medical, industrial, and agricultural rehabilitation.
2. Train large staffs of civilian administrators of representative nationalities at a United Nations University.
3. Must work in close collaboration with existing Boards, first in an advisory capacity, then, as war comes to an end, assuming central direction of reconstruction.
4. Merges with Economics, Finance, and Transit Committees, and Rationing Survey of League of Nations.

Planning Council of the United Nations: Made up of popularly represented national charter committees whose function it is to educate public opinion. To be merged with International Labor Office.

United Nations Shipping Administration: To coordinate all shipping in the relief period.

United Nations Farm Board (former Combined Food Board): To represent all primary producing nations.

United Nations Combined Raw Materials Board: To purchase and distribute raw materials from primary producing countries.

United Nations Combined Production and Resources Board: To direct flow of industrial products.

United Nations Reconstruction Finance Corporation: To direct world investments to regions requiring development.

JUDICIAL:
Disputes between members of the United Nations to be referred to judicial arbitration.

TRANSFERS OF JURISDICTION FROM MEMBER NATIONS TO THE UNITED NATIONS:
To prepare estimates of postwar requirements.
To train staff of civilian administrators.
To collaborate with existing United Nations Boards.
To direct postwar reconstruction.
To coordinate shipping for purposes of relief.
To purchase and distribute raw materials.
To direct world investments.

NATIONS UNDERTAKE:
To observe basic democratic forms and not deny them to others.
To subordinate their armed forces to the armed forces of the United Nations.
To teach values of humanism and world unity in their schools.
To be prepared for a general delegation of powers and acceptance of responsibilities.

METHODS OF ENFORCEMENT:
Negotiation of binding military alliances for a twenty-year period pending the establishment of a world organization and a world army. Each member must pledge to come to the aid of any other member *threatened by aggression or rebellion.*

On the model of the Anglo-Soviet Pact, the United States should negotiate military alliances with Russia, China, Britain, India, and with the European Council of Free Governments.

IMMEDIATE STEPS:
Promulgation of a *World Charter* guaranteeing all peoples basic

political, economic, and social rights; collective rights of free association; full national representation; full equality with other peoples; right to full national development and freedom from exploitation.
Supplementary *Regional Charters* should be guaranteed by all of the United Nations in terms of local conditions.
Establishment of a National Government in India, led by an Indian Prime Minister responsible to a temporary Governor-General and a Commander-in-chief of the United Nations.

Britain, Russia, and the United States should sign a treaty with China renouncing claims to all commercial property in China, giving full equality to the Chinese people, prohibiting restoration of Western imperialism in China and offering to mediate the civil war between the Chinese Nationalist Party and the Communists.

Britain, the United States, and Russia should sign a treaty with Egypt and the Middle East countries, recognizing their full independence; prohibiting the use of ports and garrisons by troops other than those of the future world organization of which they are to be members.

Joint declarations by Belgium, Holland, Britain, and the United States renouncing claims of exclusive domination over dependent countries, and pledging United Nations administration to bring them into the society of nations as equal members within a fixed time limit.

Russia, Britain, and the United States must conclude agreements with the governments-in-exile and the various underground movements in Europe regarding basic principles guiding the political settlement.

PREREQUISITES TO PEACE:
United Nations victory.

LIQUIDATION OF THE WAR:
Joint machinery of the United Nations must be retained for adequate postwar relief and rehabilitation program.

Europe:

1. Relief of hunger, clothing, and fuel needs.
2. Medical control of epidemics, tuberculosis, and nutritional diseases.

3. Controlled repatriation of the following *approximate* number of persons:
     12 million soldiers
     5 million forced settlers and conscripted workers
     5 to 12 million refugees
     50 million Soviet citizens returning to Western Russia
  4. Reorganization of transportation by rebuilding dock facilities, storage houses, and railway lines
  5. Industrial and agricultural rehabilitation: seed, timber, livestock, farm machinery, raw materials, and machine tools

Sources of Supply:
New Zealand: Dairy products.
Australia: Wool and grain.
Canada: Grain.
Argentina: Meat and wheat.

Conditions:
  1. Relief must be non-political.
  2. Europe must be regarded as one administrative area.
  3. All means of transportation to be regarded as common property of Europe.
  4. Industrial reconstruction of Europe as a single unit.
  5. Cooperation of trade-union committees, cooperatives, fishermen's associations, marketing centers of peasants, block organizations of city people.
  6. Germans to be incited to break up the landed estates and destroy the trusts by social revolution.
  7. Preparation of constitutional assemblies to elect both national governments and representatives to a *European Federal Assembly.*

ASIA:

Needs: Grain, rice, fertilizer, fuel, medical supplies, raw materials, new roads, railways, shipping, textile, and farm machinery.

Sources of Supply:
India: Grain.
Japan: Textiles.

United States: Machinery — surplus from armament industry to be converted to produce civilian supplies.

Japan: Americans of Japanese descent should be trained to administer Japan temporarily and to foment a democratic revolution.

Nationalization of Asia's resources to be administered with the aid of a *World Civil Service* to prevent commercial exploitation.

UNITED STATES:
1. Government direction of reconversion.
2. Aid to unemployed and demobilized soldiers until conversion is finished (there may be approximately twenty million unemployed).
3. Maintain priorities and allocations system.
4. Organize labor supply.
5. Public-works program to occupy workers temporarily unemployed during retooling of factories.
6. Large-scale training program for demobilized soldiers and new workers.
7. Maintenance of price control and rationing during worldwide relief and rehabilitation program.
8. Retaining of wartime tax revenues.
9. Retaining of wartime community welfare services under Office of Civilian Defense.

TERRITORIAL CHANGES:
1. Formosa and Manchuria to be returned to China.
2. Indo-China and Korea to be trained for self-government by United Nations Civil Service Administration.
3. Formation of an Indonesian Union with Burma, Malaya, Thailand, and the Indies, aided by United Nations Civil Service Administration.
4. Africa: Colonial administrators must be replaced by United Nations Civil Service; white settlers may remain temporarily as technical advisers and permanently as citizens, but only if they accept equal status with the natives.

AUTHOR:
SUMNER WELLES (American).

PROFESSION:
Former Under-Secretary of State of the United States.

SOURCE:
Address before Foreign Policy Association and article in the *New York Herald Tribune,* October 17, 1943 and January 26, 1944.

TYPE:
1. Four-Power Agreement to keep the peace.
2. United Nations Executive Council to coordinate regional organizations patterned after Pan-American system.

MEMBERSHIP:
United Nations at the start (aim: universal).

ORGANS OF GOVERNMENT:
LEGISLATIVE AND EXECUTIVE:
  Executive Council of the United Nations: Composed of Permanent Delegates from the United Kingdom, the Soviet Union, China, and the United States. Other major powers, willing and able to employ force to keep peace throughout world, to be added as Permanent Members. Additional representation to be assigned to regional systems of the Americas, Europe, the Near East, Far East, and the British Commonwealth.

  Decisions: By two-thirds vote of Delegates including approval of Permanent Members.

  Suggested Methods of Electing Regional Delegates: Appointed in rotation by each member nation of the regional organization or elected by all member nations of region from lists of nominees proposed by all member governments.

  Security Commission: Composed of military, naval, and air experts appointed by major powers. *Duties:* To carry out Council decisions requiring use of armed forces.

JUDICIAL:
World Court.

TRANSFERS OF JURISDICTION FROM MEMBER NATIONS TO THE UNITED NATIONS:
To resolve political and other questions which do not involve military conduct of war or limit decisions on military strategy nor impair provisions of Four-Power Agreement.
To supervise international agencies such as International Labor Office and Food and Agriculture Committee.
To organize additional United Nations agencies.
To formulate recommendations to be submitted to United Nations on World Court and other necessary permanent international bodies.
To deal with any matter affecting the peace of the world.

RESTRICTIONS ON NATIONS:
As condition of admittance to international organization, nations must show that their national constitutions guarantee their citizens freedom of religion, of speech, and of information.

Nations administering colonies to be responsible to world public opinion for preparing them for self-government as soon as they are capable of it.

METHODS OF ENFORCEMENT:
Each regional organization primarily responsible for maintaining peace in its region.

If war within the region threatens world peace, wider action is necessary.

IMMEDIATE STEPS:
Agreement between British, Soviet, Chinese, and United States Governments jointly to keep the peace of the world in the postwar period in accord and in conjunction with some of the Latin American Governments, the Fourth French Republic, and other qualified members of the United Nations; to define the nature and method of providing armed contributions for this common effort; to agree now upon machinery to be set up by common consent to provide for progressive reduction of armaments among themselves and other nations; to agree

upon common policy toward Germany and other conquered Axis powers to render them permanently incapable of renewing their assaults; to agree that they will not take independent action affecting sovereign rights of any other nation without consent of other three powers; to agree that they will further and perfect, as rapidly as post-war conditions permit, establishment of universal world organization into which proposed Four-Power Agreement would be merged.

Establishment of *Executive Council* to represent all the United Nations.

LIQUIDATION OF THE WAR:
Transition period to allow for readjustments and cooling of passions of war before attempt to set up permanent world organization.

PART III

THEORETICAL PLANS

CHARTS OF PLANS TO UNITE NATIONS SINCE 1914

C. Regional

... "There must be no return to the prewar habit of placating a strong aggressor with the sacrifice of a small nation, and the danger of such a return is a strong argument for creating confederations capable of holding their own against any aggressor.

"These confederations could have the necessary financial, economic, and industrial strength to provide themselves with well-prepared and well-armed forces and a sufficiently strong Air Force, controlled by a new organized system of European security. They could be economically better balanced than the separate small states, and politically they could have a more real sense of security and a greater absence of fear regarding their national existence than was the case under the Versailles settlement.

... "We regard confederations in Europe as an element in some sort of world commonwealth. Indeed, without this broad framework we cannot contemplate a regional confederation."

EDUARD BENES, Czechoslovakia; London, April 28, 1942.

"The future of Europe depends on its readiness to organize a union of nations, where each must be willing to sacrifice some part of its economic, political, and military independence for the good of the community as a whole."

JOSEPH BECH, Luxembourg; Washington, June 3, 1942.

... "We must hope and pray that the unity of the three leading victorious powers will be worthy of their supreme responsibility and that they will think not only of their own welfare but of the welfare and future of all. One can imagine that under a world institution embodying or representing the United Nations, and some day all the nations, there should come into being a Council of Europe and a Council of Asia.

"We must try — I am speaking, of course, only for ourselves — to make the Council of Europe, or whatever it may be called, into a really effective league, with all strongest forces concerned woven into its texture, with a high court to adjust disputes and with forces, armed forces, national or international or both, held ready to enforce these decisions and to prevent renewed aggression and preparation of future wars.

"Anyone can see that this council, when created, must eventually embrace the whole of Europe, and that all the main branches of the European family must some day be partners in it."

WINSTON CHURCHILL, March 21, 1943.

REGIONAL PLANS

THREE plans advocating European federation written in 1915, 1916, 1917 (Weiss, Anonymous, Zimmermann) suggest establishment of the federation during the war as a basis for cessation of hostilities. Weiss proposed that the Allies set up a Provisional Federal Government empowered to conduct and conclude the war, and to induce the German people to convert or overthrow their government by offering them admission to the European Federation on equal terms. Anonymous suggested that the non-European neutrals organize a Temporary Court of Arbitration to conclude the war, conduct plebiscites, and organize the first elections to the European Diet. Zimmermann urged that neutrals take the initiative in organizing the United States of Europe, and that the European Constitution be presented to the belligerents as a neutral peace proposal.

Both Jennings and Mackay would exclude Russia from a United States of Europe but would include the British Dominions if they wish to join. Jennings would have the Queen of the Netherlands appoint the first Acting President. Mackay wants the victorious allies to show generosity toward the Axis people in making peace.

Young wants a federated Europe, and suggests that England, France, and Germany each become federalized as subregional federations within the European Federation. He wants India to join an Asiatic Federation.

The three official proposals — Churchill's offer of Union to France (June, 1940), Confederation of Poland and Czechoslovakia, Confederation of Greece and Yugoslavia — are tentative outlines for possible action.

The Constitutional Commission of The Danubian Club of London, in its report of July, 1943 (not charted here), recommends a *Central and South-East European Union* to be composed of Albania, Austria, Bulgaria, Czechoslovakia, Greece, Hungary, Poland, Roumania, and Yugoslavia. Full federal organization is proposed.

AUTHOR:
JOSÉ WEISS (Alsatian; naturalized in England).

PROFESSION:
Landscape painter; also aviation pioneer; his glider model preserved in South Kensington Museum.

TITLE OF PLAN:
The Alternative: Armed Peace or Federation.

PAMPHLET

DATE: 1915.

PUBLISHED:
By the author in London.

TYPE:
FEDERAL. NAME: United States of Europe.

MEMBERSHIP:
REGIONAL at first, limited to Europe and the self-governing British Dominions; after the war, the American Nations, Japan, and the Chinese Republic may be included.

ORGANS OF GOVERNMENT:
LEGISLATIVE: *Parliament:* Elected.
EXECUTIVE: Appointed by Parliament; more than one.
Federal Army: Composed of volunteers.

TRANSFERS OF JURISDICTION FROM MEMBER NATIONS TO THE UNION:
War and Navy Departments of member nations pass to the Union; member states protected against attack from without by non-members or from anti-constitutional or revolutionary factions from within.
Authority over all international disputes, international trade, communication, finance, labor problems, crime, possibly tariffs.
Exclusive right to possess and manufacture arms.
Financed by contributions from each state.

NATIONS RETAIN:
Complete autonomy over internal affairs.

IMMEDIATE STEPS:
Establishment of a *Provisional Federal Government* or *Executive* to

meet temporarily at Le Havre, by Britain, France, Russia, Belgium, Canada, Australia, South Africa, and Egypt.

Duties: To try to induce the German people to convert or to overthrow their government *by offering them admission into the European Federation on terms of equality;* to negotiate with a reconstituted German Government; to conduct and conclude the war (individual governments to have no hand in the peace negotiations).

Organize elections as soon as possible of representatives to the first *Federal Parliament* to which the Provisional Government assigns its powers. The first Federal Parliament then appoints the first permanent *Federal Executive.*

AUTHOR:
Anonymous.

TITLE OF PLAN:
Suggestions for a Constitution of United States of Europe.

MANUSCRIPT

DATE: February 18, 1916.

Submitted to the Ford Neutral Conference for Continuous Mediation, Stockholm.

TYPE:
Confederate: Based on the Constitution of Switzerland.
Name: United States of Europe.

MEMBERSHIP:
Regional: European nations including Austria, Hungary, Germany, Norway, Sweden, Denmark, Holland, Belgium, Great Britain and Ireland, France, Portugal, Spain, Monaco, San Marino, Italy, Liechtenstein, Albania, Greece, Bulgaria, Roumania, Poland, Finland, Russia. (Special status for Switzerland. See Miscellaneous.)

ORGANS OF GOVERNMENT:

LEGISLATIVE: Bicameral *Confederal Diet: Upper House; Lower House;* representatives appointed or elected according to constitutional provisions in each nation.

Upper House: Two representatives from each nation with a population of 500,000 or more; one from each of the others.

Lower House: One representative for every 500,000 population; each nation entitled to at least one.

EXECUTIVE OR ADMINISTRATIVE:
Confederal Council: Five-year terms; seven members elected by *Confederal Diet.*

Confederal President: Member of Council elected by Diet to be Chairman of Council; may not be reelected for two years in succession.

Special Provision: In time of war the President (or any other member of the Council by two-thirds majority of Upper House) may be declared *Dictator* by the Diet for one year at a time but not in excess of the President's original term as member of the Council.

Confederal Military Department: Supervises military establishments of all nations; reports to Diet in order to maintain balance of military forces within and without the Confederacy.

Interstate Commission: Appointed by Confederal Council; supervises operation of Confederate laws regulating interstate commerce and state legislation affecting equality of other nations.

JUDICIAL:
Confederal Court of Justice: Appointed by Upper House; appointments may be canceled by unanimous vote of Confederal Council, reaffirmed by two-thirds majority of Confederal Diet.

TRANSFERS OF JURISDICTION FROM MEMBER NATIONS TO THE UNION:
Regulates military appropriations and armaments of member nations. Supervises interstate commerce: uniform import and export duties and privileges for all nations.

Charts of Plans to Unite Nations Since 1914

Ratifies treaties negotiated by member nations with non-member nations.

Final authority over all colonies and dependencies of member nations: all colonial disputes must be settled by arbiters chosen by the litigants or by the Confederal Court of Justice; rights, privileges, import and export duties must apply equally to all member nations and colonies other than the owning nation; proposed changes in status of colonies and dependencies must be submitted to plebiscite of two-thirds majority of votes of inhabitants entitled to vote by standards determined by Confederal Diet; subject to veto by two-thirds majority of Upper House.

Exclusive jurisdiction over:
The Capital District.
The following straits and fortifications: Straits of Dover, Gibraltar and Ceuta, Aden; Suez and Kaiser Wilhelm Canals; the Dardanelles, Marmora Sea, the Bosphorus, Trieste and its district; Constantinople; Scutari in Asia Minor (to be seat of World Court of Arbitration).
Railroad and other travel routes between the chief cities of the Western coast to cities in the East, Siberia, and Norway; from Algiers to Zanzibar; and from Cape Town to Cairo.
Assumes debts of member nations proportionate to value of lands, fortifications, and railroads taken from them.

NATIONS RETAIN:
Their armed forces subject to regulation by the Confederal Diet.

METHODS OF ENFORCEMENT:
Towards Non-Member Nations: Arbitration of disputes through *World Court of Arbitration;* appeals and retrials permitted until a decision is reached satisfying the litigants, or until a decision on appeal upholds the findings of one of the first two decisions of the Court *when it becomes binding on the United States of Europe.*

IMMEDIATE STEPS:
Appeal to all European countries *to agree in principle* to this program.
Appeal to *non-European neutral governments* to send delegates to a *Temporary Court of Arbitration* to meet at The Hague.

Duties: The Court declares further hostilities suspended and recog-

nizes the belligerents as temporary administrators of territories occupied by them at the time. Pending organization of the Confederation of Europe, officers of the Court are to report on the administration of such occupied territories, their reports to be held for future investigation by the Confederal Council.

PREREQUISITES TO PEACE:
Initiative by non-European neutrals to set up *Temporary Court of Arbitration* to negotiate a cessation of hostilities, supervise administration of occupied territories, conduct plebiscites in disputed areas, apportion indemnity claims, organize elections to first Confederal Diet.

LIQUIDATION OF THE WAR:
The *Temporary Court of Arbitration* conducts plebiscites in Germany and Austria-Hungary to determine whether the people wish to enter the Confederation united under their present nationality, or whether they wish to form new nations under the Confederation; if the people choose separation, the Court calls constituent assemblies setting up temporary administrations for the new nations.

The Court conducts plebiscites in territories occupied by hostile forces or which were battlegrounds during the war to determine which adjacent nation the people wish to join; conducts plebiscites in war-stricken colonial areas, effecting transfers according to wishes of colonial population.

The Court considers indemnity claims, apportioning them among the belligerents and the newly constituted nations.

The Court supervises elections and appointments to the Confederal Diet. When these have been completed, the functions and authority of the Temporary Court of Arbitration are ended and the Confederal Diet begins to operate electing the first Confederal Council.

TERRITORIAL CHANGES:
All territorial changes to be determined by plebiscites conducted by the Temporary Court of Arbitration. Suggested changes:
Asiatic Russia and Algiers to become colonies of the United States of Europe.
Plebiscites in Austria to determine whether Bohemia and Moravia

are to enter the Confederation as *Czechland* instead of as a part of Austria.

Plebiscites in Germany to determine whether German people wish to enter the Confederation as a unit or divided into the following federations:

Swabian Federation: Baden, Hohenzollern, Württemberg, Bavaria.
Saxon Federation: Kingdom of Saxony, Thuringia, Anhalt, Province of Saxony, Brunswick, and others.
Rhenan Federation: Prussia, Lippe, and others.
Friesland: All land north of Rhenan and Saxon Federations between Holland, the Elbe, and Mecklenburg.
Baltland Federation: All the rest of Germany.

Other possible changes to be determined by plebiscite: creation of a *West Balkan Federation* with Dalmatia as a basis; creation of *Ruthenia* with Bukovina and Bessarabia as joint bases; creation of *Dunaland* with Livonia and Courland as joint bases.

RATIFICATION:

Agreement in principle by European nations to form the Confederation; organization of elections to the first Confederal Diet by the Temporary Court of Arbitration.

MISCELLANEOUS:

Existing constitutions are to be interfered with as little as possible.

Seat of the Confederal Government is to be the Canton of Zug in Switzerland, to be administered by a Board appointed by the Council; confederate institutions may be maintained in any Swiss Canton but not more than one-tenth of the area of any one canton may be occupied, and confederate property is to be taxable by the cantonal treasury subject to approval of the Confederal Council.

The Swiss Cantons are to have no representation in the Upper House; but each canton to have one representative in the Lower House; cantons to be autonomous but new cantonal laws and constitutions subject to veto of Confederal Diet; cantonal militias subject to Confederal Military Department. Ministers and ambassadors of Confederal Government also represent Swiss Cantons in foreign countries; intercantonal disputes subject to Court appointed by Confederal Council.

AUTHOR:
Carl Zimmermann.

TITLE OF PLAN:
The United States of Europe. From: *Der Völkerbund — Beiträge zur Errichtung der Weltdemokratie.*

PAMPHLET

DATE: August, 1917.

PUBLISHED (in German):
By the Swiss Committee for the Preparation of the League of Peoples, Basle, Switzerland.

TYPE:
Federal: Based on Swiss Constitution.
Name: United States of Europe.

MEMBERSHIP:
Regional: Europe.

ORGANS OF GOVERNMENT:
Legislative: Unicameral *European Council:* Ten-year term; one representative for each one-half, three-fourths, or one million population, elected by uniform simple system of proportional voting; vacancies filled by the next highest candidate.
Popular initiative and referendum on all basic issues.
President of the Council, elected each year by the Council from its own members; also represents the Union as *President.*
The Council discharges all legislative and administrative functions.

Executive or Administrative:
Administrative Departments: Consisting of experts and civil service personnel; prepare material for the Council and carry out its decisions.

Department of the Interior: Defends Union and its members against public defamation; publishes Union newspaper and distributes it free to every citizen to develop consciousness of European citizenship; directs compulsory labor service replacing military conscription.

Department for Production and Trade: (1) *Transport and Communications Division;* (2) *Treasury Department;* secures acceptance of its recommendations by the member nations.

Colonial Department: Assures equal access to colonies by all Union members; promotes self-government of colonies and their admission as members of the Union; conserves colonial resources, preventing exploitation and speculation.

Department of Foreign Affairs: Unifies foreign ministries of member nations in dealing with non-members such as the American States and Asia.

Department of Defense: Provides for defense of Union coasts and borders; controls manufacture and distribution of munitions; supervises and provides for uniform training of national civilian relief corps and police forces.

Department of Justice: Prepares new laws; applies them after passage; prosecutes violations of Union laws.

JUDICIAL:
Union Court: Decides disputes between nations; final appeal to European Council; decides cases referred to it by the Departments.

Administrative Court: Exercises jurisdiction over Union personnel and decides disputes over administrative jurisdiction.

Professional Courts of Honor.

TRANSFERS OF JURISDICTION FROM MEMBER NATIONS TO THE UNION:
Assures equal treatment of all members in commerce.
Prohibits dumping, subsidies, and trusts.
Conducts impartial investigation of war guilt.
Directs European reconstruction, demobilization, exchange of prisoners.
Administers all colonies.
Conducts foreign relations.
Defends coasts and borders of the Union.

METHODS OF ENFORCEMENT:

Towards Member Nations: Three-fourths or four-fifths vote of Council necessary to impose military measures against a member nation.

Towards Non-Member Nations: Military and naval defense.

IMMEDIATE STEPS:

Organization of the *General Committee for Establishing the European Union of States:* Twelve prominent individuals from *neutral* nations.

Duties:
  (1) To call on experts to draft details of the European Constitution, and of the Federal Departments and Emergency Boards. The draft constitution is to be presented as a *Neutral Peace Proposal*.
  (2) To organize neutral popular support for the proposal.
  (3) To organize the European Council.
  (4) To organize the various administrative departments.
  (5) Each Parliament ratifying the Neutral Peace Proposal appoints one of its members to the *Central Committee Preparing the Union* to organize the election of representatives to the European Council.

As soon as a sufficient number of nations have ratified the Constitution of the European Union and elected their representatives, the European Council meets and organizes its various departments on the basis of the General Committee's unofficial recommendations and preparations.

Ratification of the Constitution by the belligerents ends hostilities between them.

PREREQUISITES TO PEACE:

The organization of the European Union and ratification of its Constitution as a basis for cessation of hostilities and permanent peace.

The belligerents must abandon demands that involve the crushing of their opponents, the forcible alteration of frontiers and of forms of government.

The Union must guarantee each member nation internal autonomy and external security.

LIQUIDATION OF THE WAR:
The transition from war to peace to be carried out by the following Boards headed by neutrals and located in neutral cities:

Board of Investigation: Collects relevant data on the causes, origins, and originators of the war; renders an impartial verdict. All groups must assist the Board in its work and refrain from interfering or attempting to influence its judgment.

Board of Reconstruction: Helps restore civilian enterprises wiped out in the war; one-half the cost to be supplied by the nation; one-half by the Union. (The Union contribution to be distributed among all member nations over a twenty-year period.) Author assumes that Japan and the American States would also contribute to reconstruction.

Board for Transitional Problems: Organizes demobilization of soldiers, exchange of prisoners, exchange of labor, raw materials, transportation facilities, fuel, machinery, and other necessities.
Advises revision of national constitutions to conform with Union Constitution.

TERRITORIAL CHANGES:
Alsace-Lorraine is to have autonomy within the European Union.
All disputed territories and dependent nationalities are also to have autonomy within the Union.

RATIFICATION:
By national parliaments.

AUTHOR:
ARISTIDE BRIAND (French).

PROFESSION:
Foreign Minister of France.

TITLE:
Memorandum on the Organization of a Regime of European Federal Union.

DATE: May 17, 1930.

SOURCE:
International Conciliation, June, 1930.

TYPE:
CONFEDERATE — Within framework of League of Nations.
NAME: European Association, or Union.

MEMBERSHIP:
REGIONAL: European members of the League of Nations.

ORGANS OF GOVERNMENT:
LEGISLATIVE: *European Conference:* Representatives of all European Governments who are members of the League of Nations.
President of Conference elected annually.

EXECUTIVE OR ADMINISTRATIVE:
Permanent Political Committee: Limited to a certain number of member governments. Each representative to be *President* in rotation. *Sessions* to coincide with meeting of League of Nations Council. European or non-European Governments, non-members of League, to be invited to take part in questions of interest to them.

Secretariat.

JUDICIAL:
European system of arbitration and security.

TRANSFERS OF JURISDICTION FROM MEMBER NATIONS TO THE EUROPEAN ASSOCIATION:
To expand markets.
To intensify and improve industrial production.
To guarantee against labor crises.
To study ways of setting up *Federal European Union,* and political, economic, and social questions.
To set up technical committees.
To establish a European system of arbitration and security.
To control industrial unions and cartels.
To provide progressive lowering of tariffs.
To coordinate public works, communications, and transit.

To develop economically backward regions of Europe.
To provide uniform labor legislation.
To coordinate health services.
(General subordination of economic problems to the political.)

MISCELLANEOUS:
Twenty-five nations replied to the Memorandum. *Sixteen governments* (Belgium, Bulgaria, Denmark, Germany, Great Britain, Irish Free State, Italy, Latvia, Lithuania, Netherlands, Norway, Poland, Portugal, Spain, Sweden, and Switzerland) doubted the need of setting up a separate European Association, fearing it would undermine the universality and influence of the League of Nations, and would revive the danger of alliances; many pointed out they had close ties with non-European nations; most nations opposed barring any nation merely because of non-membership in the League.

Five governments (Albania, Austria, Esthonia, Hungary, Roumania) stressed the need of dealing with economic problems before trying to settle political ones.

Four governments (Czechoslovakia, Greece, Yugoslavia [Luxembourg reserving her neutrality]) approved the proposal.

AUTHOR:
ALFRED M. BINGHAM (American).

PROFESSION:
Writer; former State Senator.

TITLE OF PLAN:
The United States of Europe.

DATE: 1940.

PUBLISHER:
Duell, Sloan and Pearce, New York.

TYPE:
FEDERAL. NAME: United States of Europe.

MEMBERSHIP:

REGIONAL: All Europe, including England, Iceland, Turkey; also Syria, Palestine, Egypt, and North Africa. Soviet Union excluded.

ORGANS OF GOVERNMENT:

LEGISLATIVE: *Tricameral — Council of States; European Assembly; Council of Nationalities.*

Council of States: Nations to be represented according to population and military position at end of war. *Decisions:* By majority vote.

European Assembly: All Europe to be divided into 100 electoral districts of one to five million inhabitants; each district to send from one to five representatives; proportional representation to be used in districts electing more than one representative; otherwise member nations to determine method of election.

Council of Nationalities: Representation in proportion to population of every ethnic group. (See: Chart of Soviet Constitution.) Participation in legislation limited to nationality problems.

EXECUTIVE OR ADMINISTRATIVE:
Dominant group of nations within Council of States to function as Executive.

Department of Foreign Relations: To represent European Federation in foreign capitals.

European Arms Control Commission: To supervise disarmament of member nations; to inspect their arsenals and arms factories.

European Colonial Administration: To supervise Mandate administration by member nations; to replace gradually national colonial administrators with graduates from international school of colonial administration without regard to nationality.

European Investment Bank: To finance vast public works program to provide transition from war to peace; to maintain adequate volume of long-term investments; to maintain balance between savings and investments.

European Reconstruction Agency: To provide money and labor to rebuild destroyed areas; to finance housing and public works program until private investment able to absorb labor supply; to borrow funds from individuals and governments to finance its activities.

JUDICIAL:

Courts of Migration: With power to issue writs of habeas corpus to assure migration with their families and property of persons fleeing from racial, national, religious, or political persecution.

European Supreme Court: To decide constitutionality of acts of member nations.

Federal Legislative Bodies: To decide political disputes.

Permanent Court of Arbitration and *Permanent Court of International Justice:* To decide judicial disputes.

TRANSFERS OF JURISDICTION FROM MEMBER NATIONS TO THE FEDERATION:

To represent the Federation in the Council of the League of Nations.
To grant cultural and administrative autonomy either as a federal territory or as part of a larger state to any area demanding such status through an internationally supervised plebiscite.
To maintain a European army at least as powerful as half of all national armies to be stationed at strategic points such as the Rhine, the Carpathian Mountains, and Alpine passes.
To assume command of all national navies including that of Great Britain.
To supervise disarmament of member nations; to license arms manufacture; to inspect arms factories and arsenals.
To control forts, barracks, arsenals, and strategic seaways such as Gibraltar and Suez.
To supervise colonial administration of member nations.
To internationalize all commercial air transport.
To levy taxes least in conflict with those of national and local governments.
To grant federal citizenship.
To protect national minorities.
To provide minimum safeguards against persecution.
To establish capital city, federal flag, coinage, and postage.
To operate a broadcasting chain.

To supervise newspapers and textbooks.
To establish international universities and staff college for international civil servants.
To organize leisure-time activities through youth hostels, European excursions, and scout movements.

NATIONS RETAIN:
Right to operate coast guard and patrol boats.
Right to restrict freedom of migration until living standards are more nearly equal.
Right to maintain diplomatic representation in each other's capitals and abroad.
Right to organize regional federations within the European Federation.
Right to separate representation in the Assembly of the League of Nations.
The British Commonwealth to retain a special naval contingent if the Dominions do not become part of the European Federation.

RESTRICTIONS ON NATIONS:
National areas not to be fortified.
No secession from the Federation.
British Commonwealth to abandon imperial trade preferences.

INDIVIDUAL RIGHTS:
Freedom of worship.
Freedom to migrate with property.

METHODS OF ENFORCEMENT:
Towards Member Nations: Use of European army in case of revolt within a nation, or an attack on another member nation; withdrawal of federal aid and patronage; ban on essential raw materials.

Towards Non-Member Nations: Use of European army to defend the Federation against threat.

PREREQUISITES TO PEACE:
Allies to define terms on which they would be willing to negotiate peace with Germany; neutrals to press for peace constantly; coopera-

Charts of Plans to Unite Nations Since 1914

tion and good-will of a responsible German Government necessary to creation of an intelligent settlement.

Decisive Allied military victory desirable only if present Allied Governments were replaced by progressive coalition governments of liberals, socialists, and labor elements pledged to an intelligent reorganization of the world.

LIQUIDATION OF THE WAR:
Preliminary Conference of all belligerent governments to bring about cessation of hostilities and to agree on temporary terms.

Conference of all nations, including neutrals, to draft a permanent settlement. Conference to be held in a neutral city. Funds for reconstruction should equal those spent for war.

Organization of a European Constitutional Convention, of military and naval disarmament conferences, of a financial and economic conference, and of a general conference to coordinate these decisions and to settle colonial and other worldwide issues. Popularly elected delegates and representatives of business, labor, and other groups should meet in assemblies connected with the various conferences at least in an advisory capacity to minimize influence of generals and diplomats.

TERRITORIAL CHANGES:
Possible organization of a north and a south German Confederation entering the United States of Europe separately. Token restoration of independence to Poles, Czechs, and Slovaks.

India, French Indo-China, parts of Netherlands East Indies, and Philippines to be consulted on whether they wish to be under international supervision.

American and European possessions in Western Hemisphere to be mandated to a Pan-American Colonial Administration.
European capital to be north of Basle on Rhine at junction of France, Germany, and Switzerland.

MISCELLANEOUS:
The *League of Nations*, the *International Labor Organization*, the *Bank for International Settlements* to be continued. The League to be

universal in membership to provide regular conference, coordination of international administrative agencies, and of economic planning, and reconstruction.

Bank for International Settlements: To act as clearing house for world's monetary transactions; to integrate various monetary systems; to introduce a managed international currency not based on gold.

The following agencies to be established on a worldwide scale:

Commission on Migration and Population Problems: To conduct research and publicize the problem; to advise League, European Federation, and their member nations; to serve as forum for airing grievances; to organize interchange of populations where no other solution is possible.

World Investment Commission: To supply information about foreign investment opportunities; to charter international corporations under its own jurisdiction; to coordinate and supervise regional investment agencies.

World Trade Commission — Cartels Division: To register and approve cartel agreements on prices, production and market quotas if labor and consumer interests are also adequately represented; prices not to be fixed too high; production and market quotas to be fair to all nations. *Raw Materials Division:* To supervise raw materials; to assure conservation of scarce resources and intelligent exploitation; to guarantee adequate supplies to all nations. *Tariff Division:* To undertake gradual lowering of tariffs through bilateral, multilateral, and regional agreements.

World Trade Commission: To enforce its decisions through threat of withholding international banking and investment facilities.

AUTHOR:
W. IVOR JENNINGS (English).

PROFESSION:
Attorney. Reader in English Law in University of London.

TITLE OF PLAN:
A Federation for Western Europe.

DATE: 1940.

PUBLISHER:
The Macmillan Co., Cambridge, England.

TYPE:
FEDERAL. NAME: Federation of Western Europe.

MEMBERSHIP:
REGIONAL: *Western Europe* — Germany, Belgium, Denmark, Eire, Finland, French Republic, United Kingdom and Northern Ireland, Iceland, Luxembourg, Netherlands, Norway, Sweden, Switzerland; also *Canada, Australia, Union of South Africa, New Zealand, Newfoundland, and Southern Rhodesia.*

ORGANS OF GOVERNMENT:
LEGISLATIVE: Bicameral — *The People's House; The States' House;* legislation by majority vote of both houses, except that revenue bills passed by People's House and signed by President become law within three months of passage by People's House even without approval of States' House. First meeting of the Federal Legislature to be set by Proclamation of Acting President; Federal Legislature may be dissolved by Presidential proclamation ordering new elections.

People's House: One delegate for every 500,000 federal electors; Federal Legislature to determine qualifications for voting, electoral areas, and method of election. (Until Federal Legislature provides otherwise, electoral requirements for the most numerous branch of the national legislature shall prevail.)

States' House:
9 members each: Germany.
7 members each: France, United Kingdom and Northern Ireland.
5 members each: Australia, Belgium, Canada, Denmark, Eire, Finland, Netherlands, New Zealand, Norway, Union of South Africa, Sweden, Switzerland.
3 members each: Iceland, Luxembourg, Newfoundland, Southern Rhodesia.

EXECUTIVE OR ADMINISTRATIVE:
Queen of Netherlands appoints *first Acting President* of the Federation;

thereafter the two Houses in joint session elect *President* for three-year term; may be reelected; in case of incapacity, Chief Justice of Supreme Court becomes Acting President; exercises powers at request of Council of Ministers.

Prime Minister: Appointed by President; dismissable by resolution of People's House.

Council of Ministers: Appointed by President at request of Prime Minister.

Prime Minister and Ministers must become members of the Federal Legislature within six months of their appointment.

Colonial Commission: Six-year term; may be reappointed; candidates nominated by two Houses by joint resolution; appointed by President and removable by him on resolution of both Houses.

Duties: To supervise administration of colonies by the nations and make recommendations for assistance and development.

(Member nations may transfer their dependencies to the Federation.)

Judicial:

Federal Supreme Court: Justices appointed for life by President on nomination of *Judiciary Commission;* may be retired by law; removed by President on resolution of both Houses.

Original Jurisdiction: In disputes between two or more federated nations; between a federated nation and the Federation; other matters prescribed by the legislature.

Appellate Jursidiction: Over interpretation of the Constitution.

Judiciary Commission: Three-year term; members appointed by States' House from among persons holding high judicial office in the Federation or in a federated nation; may be reappointed.

TRANSFERS OF JURISDICTION FROM MEMBER NATIONS TO THE FEDERATION:

Exclusive Jurisdiction:

Control of navigation and shipping except on inland waterways of nations.

Control of traffic by air.

Control of migration.

Licensing of armament manufacture.

Command of the armed forces.

Guarantees territorial integrity of each nation; protects its democratic system and assists each nation to maintain public order.

Issues passports to Federal citizens and to Federal-protected persons (persons belonging to the dependency of a federated nation), and protects them outside the Federation.

Admits new nations by two-thirds vote of each House; ratification by legislatures of two-thirds of federated nations.

Concurrent Jurisdiction (Ten years after establishment of the Federation):

Regulates trade between federated nations, foreign nations, and territories.

Regulates communication, currency, coinage, banking, interstate payments, copyrights, weights and measures.

National laws may be vetoed by the Federal President.

Citizens of one federated nation to have all the rights and duties of citizens in other federated nations except that political rights are dependent on residence requirements.

Rights and privileges granted by a nation to another nation must apply equally to all nations.

METHODS OF ENFORCEMENT:

On a date fixed by the Federal Legislature, the federated nations are to transfer their armed forces or a part of them to the Federation. Within one year, the forces not transferred are to be disbanded; the federated nations are to maintain no armed force except a police force.

Enforcement of federal law to operate on individuals.

Federal armed forces exist for defense against non-members.

RATIFICATION:

When four nations (of those enumerated) have given notice of ratification, the Federation is established. Notice of ratification to be sent to the Queen of the Netherlands.

AMENDMENT:

May be proposed by either House; must be passed by two-thirds of the members in each House and by majority vote of the legislatures in two-thirds of the federated nations.

MISCELLANEOUS:
Nations may not secede or be expelled from the Federation except by an amendment to the Constitution.

AUTHOR:
Oswald Dutch (English?) (pseudonym).

TITLE OF PLAN:
Economic Peace Aims: A Basis for Discussion.

DATE: 1941.

PUBLISHED BY:
Edward Arnold & Co., London.

TYPE:
Federal. Name: Commonwealth of Europe.

MEMBERSHIP:
Regional: Limited to European peoples having independent governments until 1938; *England's* relation to Europe similar to her relationship to her Dominions; *Russia* is to be excluded as long as she maintains inflexible Bolshevist system.
Other nations may cooperate with European Commonwealth through the *World Economic Plan,* and agree to principles of general disarmament, freedom of movement, and international scientific development.

ORGANS OF GOVERNMENT:
Legislative: Unicameral *Parliament:* One representative for every two million population; minimum of four representatives to each nation except Liechtenstein, Monaco, Andorra, San Marino, Danzig, and possibly Luxembourg.
Decisions: By majority vote; two-thirds vote required to decide questions of outstanding importance.

Executive or Administrative:
President: One-year term; chosen from leading representatives of mem-

ber nations (King of Norway, for instance, may also be President of the Union).

Ministry of Home Affairs: To include Departments of Home Security, Administration, Judiciary, Transport and Shipping.

Ministry of Public Welfare: To include Departments of Public Health, Leisure, Arts and Sciences, Political Education.

Continental Office of Coordination: To enforce adoption by member nations of uniform principles in Legal Codes, Labor, Education, and Communication, within five years from establishment of Commonwealth.

JUDICIAL:
Arbitration Court: Composed especially for each dispute; each party to the dispute chooses one representative, who together then choose a neutral chairman; the President or Prime Minister of the Commonwealth casts the deciding vote if a speedy decision is not reached.

Special Court of Arbitration for the Settlement of International Disputes: Decides frontier and trade disputes and questions of jurisdiction between the national parliaments and the Commonwealth during the transition period.

TRANSFERS OF JURISDICTION FROM MEMBER NATIONS TO THE COMMONWEALTH:

Special Position of England: While not a member of the Commonwealth, is entitled to send representatives to its Parliament, fill certain posts in the Commonwealth Government, and share responsibility for continental defense, finance, and economic problems.

The Commonwealth determines foreign policy, negotiates treaties, provides for continental defense, supervises disarmament, issues a common currency, assures freedom of commerce and migration, assumes debts of member nations; assures all individuals equal treatment and protection and citizenship after five years' work in any member nation; may veto or confirm national laws extending to interstate relations; assures nations cultural coadministration over their respective minorities even in other nations.

NATIONS RETAIN:
National autonomy; may restrict non-European (Asiatic) immigration.

RESTRICTIONS ON NATIONS:
Must provide for office of Prime Minister, Ministers of Home Affairs, Public Welfare, Finance, Education, and Procuration of Work.

METHODS OF ENFORCEMENT:
Towards Member Nations: Continental Army of Defense, made up of soldiers, sailors, and airmen from each nation in proportion to its representation in Parliament, paid by the Commonwealth, enlisted for five, ten-year periods, stationed only on frontiers; conscription abolished.

Towards Non-Member Nations: Cooperation between British and Commonwealth navies; strength of Commonwealth navy to be in fixed ratio to British and American navies.

IMMEDIATE STEPS:
Board of Reconstruction must be set up and ready to function when Allies take over Berlin; details must be told to all the peoples before the war ends.

PREREQUISITES TO PEACE:
Total British-American victory.

LIQUIDATION OF THE WAR:
Europe:

No reparations; no long-drawn-out peace negotiations; if reconstruction program is well prepared, armies of occupation may be withdrawn after a few weeks.

Court of Arbitration; Continental Office of Coordination; transitional organs of government through which Great Britain and the United States control European reconstruction.

Board of Reconstruction: Assumes control of all non-military matters.
Duties: Establishes a common currency, organizes demobilization, transport, and rebuilding. Sets up temporary administrative departments of the future European Commonwealth: Foreign Relations, Defense, Finance, Economy, European Bank of Issue, and Procuration of Work.

WORLDWIDE:

International Commission for the Procuration of Work: Chairman and four members (carefully selected persons of industrial and financial experience to be entrusted with wide powers).

Subcommittees: Research, Survey of Proposals, Finance, Supervision. The Commission must always have a representative of the United States and Great Britain.
Duties: To provide work on a world scale for all peoples, on great international projects such as building waterpower stations, international canals, irrigation schemes, Channel Tunnel, bridges of La Plata, Danube, and the Bosphorus.
Organization of production in order of importance: building industry, shipbuilding, agriculture and transport. Industrial quotas fixed quarterly; disposal of goods through a Central Marketing Board.

TERRITORIAL CHANGES:
Northern, Southern Germany, Austria, the Rhineland and Alsace-Lorraine to be separate member states under the Commonwealth. Similar status may be granted to Ukraine, Macedonia, Flanders, Basque country, and Croatia.
Nations may retain their *colonies* but they are to be exploited for the benefit of the whole Commonwealth.

MISCELLANEOUS:
The seat of the Commonwealth and headquarters of the Continental Bank should be in Switzerland, Holland, or Belgium.
Official languages: English, German, and French; French alone may later be found necessary to speed up Parliamentary debate and for army efficiency.

AUTHOR:
R. W. G. Mackay (Australian).

PROFESSION:
Attorney.

TITLE OF PLAN:
Peace Aims and the New Order — Being a Revised and Popular Edition of "Federal Europe" outlining the Case for European Federation Together with a Draft Constitution of a United States of Europe.

DATE: 1941.

PUBLISHER:
Michael Joseph Ltd., London.

TYPE:
FEDERAL. Modeled on Australian Constitution.
NAME: United States of Europe.

MEMBERSHIP:
REGIONAL: All nations of Western Europe (*without Russia*), also British Dominions if they decide to enter Union and all their colonial possessions, except India, (to be given independence and allowed to join an Asiatic Federation).

ORGANS OF GOVERNMENT:
LEGISLATIVE: Unicameral *Parliament:* Elected for four years; meets twice a year; directly chosen by men and women over twenty-one years of age. One member for every 250,000 population. At least five members for each original member nation; aboriginal natives and colonial populations not to be counted in apportionment.
Members of Parliament: At least twenty-one years of age; three years' residence within nation in which elected.
Decisions: By majority vote.
Quorum: One-third of Parliament.

EXECUTIVE OR ADMINISTRATIVE:

President: (First President to be named in the Constitution) Commander-in-chief of naval, military, and air forces.

Federal Council: Members chosen by Parliament; advises President.

Permanent Colonial Commission: Nine members appointed by President in Council; supervises President's administration of colonial territories; reports to Parliament; makes recommendations.

JUDICIAL:

Supreme Court: Chief Justice and at least six Justices (exact number determined by Parliament) appointed for life (unless removed on charge of misbehavior or incapacity) by President in Council.

Inferior Courts: To be created by Parliament.

Original Jurisdiction (Supreme Court): In disputes over treaties with other countries; between nations or residents of several nations, national minorities; interpretation of Constitution; laws of Parliament; colonial matters. Parliament can confer additional original jurisdiction.

Appellate Jurisdiction: Over other federal courts; over the court of any member nation.

TRANSFERS OF JURISDICTION FROM MEMBER NATIONS TO THE UNION:

Exclusive Jurisdiction: Relations with other nations; creation and admission of new nations; military, naval, and air defense of Federation; control of forces to maintain laws of Federation; administration and regulation of postal, telegraphic, telephone, broadcasting, television, quarantine and public health services; census and statistics; weights and measures; naturalization and aliens; immigration and emigration; custom duties, currency and coinage; banking and incorporation of banks.

Concurrent Jurisdiction: Taxation and various economic matters; insurance; control of corporations; transportation; industrial matters; social services; administration of law. Questions of jurisdiction to be given widest possible interpretation in favor of Federation.

Federation assumes the debts of the nations.

RESTRICTIONS ON THE UNION:
Laws reducing representation of a nation in Parliament must be approved by majority of electors in nation.

DEMOCRATIC RIGHTS:
Changes affecting federal franchise or extending Parliament beyond four years must be approved by majority of electors in majority of nations.

METHODS OF ENFORCEMENT:

Toward Non-Member Nations: Army, navy, and air force to be used in case of hostilities.

Toward Member Nations: When a law of a nation is inconsistent with law of the Federation, that of the Federation prevails; all obligations or agreements between nations inconsistent with Federal Constitution are abrogated; every nation to be protected against invasion, and, on application of national Executive Government, against domestic violence; constitution of each nation to continue as at establishment of Federation until altered in accordance with national constitutional procedure.

Toward Individuals: Automatic citizenship in Federation of all residents of the Federation and of the nations; equal civil and political rights irrespective of race, language, or religion; detention and punishment by individual nations of persons accused and convicted of violating laws of the Federation.

IMMEDIATE STEPS:
Includes provisions for territorial changes and liquidation of war:

Provisions of Treaty Concluding Hostilities (after Allied victory):
1. *An International Commission* with equal representation of all Western European nations with American and Russian collaboration, to supervise transition between armistice and signing of Peace Treaty.
2. After lapse of six to twelve months, meeting of Peace Conference with all European countries represented, including Russia, Japan, and United States on equal terms.

3. No dictated peace; no vindictiveness; no reparations; no indemnities; no economic or political exploitation of defeated.
4. Germany and Allies to withdraw from territories occupied after January 1, 1933.
5. All nations of Western Europe, including neutrals, to decide their own form of government.
6. Establishment of a democratic Federation with common government directly elected.
7. Transfer of all colonies of Western European nations to the Federation to be administered for welfare of natives and to be admitted as soon as possible as member nations of Federation.

Nucleus to establish Federation: Britain, France, Italy, Germany, and others who choose to join.

PREREQUISITES TO PEACE:
Allied victory with generosity to Axis people who have also been victims of international causes of war; provision of equality and freedom; no reparations; no indemnities.

RATIFICATION:
Ratification of Treaty by nations to constitute a United States of Europe. *Appointment of Treaty Commission:* One member from each original ratifying nation. *Duties:* Provide for election of first Parliament of Federation through universal adult suffrage; compulsory voting; proportional representation with single transferable vote; adequate system of registration of electors; decentralized electoral system with constituencies of similar size.
Following meeting of first Parliament, Treaty Commission ceases to function.

AMENDMENT:
By majority vote of Parliament and submission within two years to vote of world electorate, unless passed by three-fourths majority of Parliament.

MISCELLANEOUS:
Seat of Government: Vienna or other place provided by Parliament.
Official languages: English, French, German.

AUTHOR:
SIR GEORGE YOUNG (English).

PROFESSION:
Diplomat and Political Scientist.

TITLE OF PLAN:
Federation and Freedom — or Plan the Peace to Win the War.

DATE: 1941.

PUBLISHER:
Oxford University Press, London.

TYPE:
FEDERAL: Union of Free Federated Europe; based on Constitution of Switzerland with elements from those of the German and Spanish republican constitutions; and some economic features taken from the Constitution of Portugal.

MEMBERSHIP:
REGIONAL: European Union (assumes that eventually there will be other regional unions with the League of Nations keeping peace between continents); would include U.S.S.R.

Preliminary Conditions: Nations with populations of more than ten million must reconstitute themselves into federal unions with each member state having less than ten and more than two million population. Nations with populations of less than five million must federate with other nations and join the European Union as part of a federation.

Nations Excluded: (Until they approve and apply a *Declaration of Rights*): Spain, Italy, Hungary, Greece, the Balkans.
Dominions to join the League of Nations.

ORGANS OF GOVERNMENT:
LEGISLATIVE: Bicameral *Congress: Union Council; Union Parliament*.
Union Council: Two members appointed by each national Parliament.
Union Parliament: One member for each million population; direct election by single transferable proportional vote; universal suffrage.

Central Economic Council: Members chosen by occupational groups; prepares all economic and social measures in cooperation with the Social and Economic Committees of Congress.

ADMINISTRATIVE AND JUDICIAL ORGANS:
Not specified.

TRANSFERS OF JURISDICTION FROM MEMBER NATIONS TO THE UNION:
The European Union assumes entire responsibility for the internal affairs of Europe, assuring each nation equal rights, equal responsibilities, and equal restriction of all armies, navies, and air forces.
Assumes debts of member nations, including Germany's and Italy's (with deductions for property looted by them).
Controls all forms of communication and transportation including one river or ocean port in each nation and through traffic to it.
Controls commerce, currency, credit, capital; combats depressions by pump-priming.
Supervises utilities, employers' federations, trade unions, producers' or consumers' cooperatives, etc.
Administers dependencies.
Nations may secede from their national federations and exclude or expel persons or products if dangerous to nation's social system, but Union may retaliate in kind.

IMMEDIATE STEPS:
Britain should plan postwar reconstruction securing support of the United States, Russia, and the governments-in-exile; the reconstruction program should be such as to be acceptable to a minority of the enemy and a majority of the neutrals to increase the chances of winning the war and shortening its duration.
A Constituent Congress will have to frame the European Constitution.

PREREQUISITES TO PEACE:
". . . no peace could be permanent, however carefully it had been prepared by us as victors, unless it was also such as we should have been prepared ourselves to accept if vanquished."

LIQUIDATION OF THE WAR:
Establishment of an International Commission on Rectification of Frontiers, Reparations, Repatriations, etc.

TERRITORIAL CHANGES:
Geneva becomes capital of the European Union; the seat of the League of Nations is to be moved out of Europe or made extraterritorial.
Poland must become a federal union; Denmark and Norway must form a Scandinavian Federation; Czechs, Slovaks, Sudetens, a Bohemian Federation; Baltic nations must federate, possibly with Sweden, Holland, Belgium, and Switzerland.

France is to be reconstituted into the *French Federation* consisting of the following state divisions: *Northern* — Capital, Rouen; *Southern* — Capital, Marseilles; *Eastern* — Capital, Lyons; *Western* — Capital, Bordeaux; *Central* — Capital, Orleans; *Brittany* — Capital, Rennes; Paris and the Ile de France become a metropolitan canton.

Germany is to be reconstituted into the *German Federation* consisting of the following state divisions: *Saxony* — Capital, Dresden; *Bavaria* — Capital, Munich; *Austria* — Capital, Vienna; *Swabia* — Capital, Stuttgart; *Rhenania* — Capital, Cologne; *Westphalia* — Capital, Frankfort; *Hanover* — Capital, Hanover; *Silesia* — Capital, Breslau; *Berlin* and the Federal District; *Prussia* — Capital, Potsdam (Parts of Prussia are to be divided between Saxony, Westphalia, Hanover, and Silesia).

England is to be reconstituted into the *British Federation* consisting of the following state divisions: *Greater London* plus surrounding area and City of Westminster to be the Federal District; *South England* — Capital, Reading. Ports: Bristol, Southampton, Thames. *Central England* — Capital, Birmingham. Ports at Immingham, the Thames, and Birkenhead. *Northern England:* Lancashire and Yorkshire — Capital, Manchester. Ports at Middlesbrough, Hall, and Liverpool. *Border England and Ulster* — Capital, Newcastle or Belfast; *Scotland* — Capital, Edinburgh; *Wales* — Capital, Cardiff. (The British Federation would have forty-seven members in the European Union.)

India should become a member of an Asiatic Federation.

AUTHOR:
ABRAHAM WEINFELD (American).

PROFESSION:
Attorney.

TITLE OF PLAN:
Towards a United States of Europe — Proposals for a Basic Structure.

PAMPHLET

DATE: 1942.

PUBLISHER:
American Council on Public Affairs, Washington, D. C.

TYPE:
FEDERAL: Based on United States Constitution with several modifications. NAME: United States of Europe.

MEMBERSHIP:
REGIONAL: Europe without Russia or England.

ORGANS OF GOVERNMENT:
LEGISLATIVE: Bicameral *Congress: Senate; House of Representatives.*
House: Two-year term; candidate at least twenty-five years of age; seven years citizen of the United States of Europe and resident of the nation electing him; representatives apportioned according to population but not more than one for every million; each nation to have at least one representative; colonial and mandated populations not to figure in apportionment. *Electorate:* Citizens over twenty-one years of age; three months resident in district where they vote.

Exclusive powers: Originates revenue bills; sole power of impeachment.

Senate: Six-year term; one-third of Senate renewed every two years; candidate at least thirty years old; nine years citizen of United States of Europe and resident of nation where chosen; direct election as for representatives.

Exclusive power: To try impeachments.

Congress to assemble at least once a year; members of Cabinet may participate in meetings of Congress and of Committees. National legislatures to direct time, place, and manner of elections, but Congress may make or alter regulations.

EXECUTIVE OR ADMINISTRATIVE:
President: Four-year term; elected by majority of votes cast in United States of Europe, provided he obtains majority in each nation; if no candidate has a majority, the House and Senate in joint session by majority vote elect one of the two candidates receiving the highest votes.
Duties: Commander-in-chief of army, navy, and air force; grants reprieves and pardons; negotiates treaties with consent of Senate; appoints ambassadors, judges, and other officers with consent of Senate.

Vice-President: Elected by the same method.

Prime Minister and *Heads of Departments:* As provided by Congress. (Congress may create additional administrative bodies authorized to exercise legislative, executive, and judicial powers, subject to appeal to the courts.)

JUDICIAL:
Supreme Court; Supreme Administrative Courts and inferior courts established by Congress; justices hold office during good behavior; appointed by President with consent of Senate.

Jurisdiction: Over cases under the Constitution, laws of the United States of Europe, treaties, controversies to which United States of Europe is party; controversies between two or more nations, between a nation and citizen of another nation; between citizens of different nations, etc.

TRANSFERS OF JURISDICTION FROM MEMBER NATIONS TO THE UNION:
Exclusive Jurisdiction:
  Declare war; maintain army, navy, and air force.
  Levy and collect uniform taxes throughout United States of Europe.

Exclusive jurisdiction over federal district and other federal property secured by purchase.
Regulate commerce with foreign nations and between the member nations.
Regulate postal, telegraph, telephone, radio, television, and similar services.
Regulate naturalization, aliens, immigration, extradition, and interstate migration.
Regulate money, coinage, and legal tender.
Admit new nations into the Union.
Administer all colonies and mandates with object of encouraging self-government and admission as nations into the Union; residents to be consulted on interim legislation and administration.
Protect each nation against invasion, and on request of executive, against domestic violence.

Concurrent Jurisdiction: (With federal law supreme in case of conflicts with national law.)
Regulate banking, bankruptcy and insolvency, bills of exchange, promissory notes, weights and measures, copyrights, patents, marriage, divorce, guardianship, conditions of labor, and social legislation.
Authorize organization of corporations, and regulate those engaged in interstate commerce.
Own or operate, or own *and* operate farms, mines, factories, means of transportation and communication, banks, insurance systems, stores.
Expropriate by uniform legislation and with proper compensation lands, houses of business.
Integrate categories of private enterprise.
Conciliate and arbitrate industrial disputes.

RESTRICTIONS ON NATIONS:
No nation may enter into any treaty, alliance or confederation; maintain a militia or grant any title of nobility.
No nation may levy import or export duties without consent of Congress except whatever is necessary to carry out its inspection laws; all such laws subject to revision and control of Congress.
No nation may engage in war unless actually invaded or in imminent danger of invasion.

DEMOCRATIC RIGHTS:

Neither Congress nor legislative authority of any nation may pass laws establishing a religion or prohibiting free exercise of religion, abridging freedom of speech or of listening to others; freedom of the press or of reading; freedom of assembly and petition. They shall provide security against unreasonable searches and seizures; right to speedy and public trial in criminal prosecutions; compensation for private property taken for public use. Excessive bail not to be required; no ex-post-facto laws or laws imposing punishment without a judicial trial to be passed; no discrimination on account of nationality, race, religion, or sex.

Every citizen entitled to opportunity to work, and to fair payment for work; unemployment insurance; medical treatment; old-age pensions; freedom to organize in unions of own choice.

IMMEDIATE STEPS:

Establishment of a *European Organization Committee:* Each nation appoints two members to the Committee and pays their salaries and expenses; same representation for governments-in-exile; nations unrepresented either by de-facto or exile governments may be represented by a committee; should several committees claim to be representative, the European Organization Committee decides by majority vote which is most representative; functioning governments are to lend money to the national committees and exiled governments to enable them to function; amounts to be repaid by the future governments.

Each member of the EOC has one vote; EOC appoints following subcommittees:

Census Committee: Two representatives of each nation plus experts and advisers. Takes census of all persons in the United States of Europe territory; ascertains their nationality.

Boundaries Committee (same rules of organization): Draws boundaries between nations irrespective of trade or military considerations. Nations are to cede necessary territories to one another within two years of their first legislative meeting following ratification of federal constitution. In case of failure to do so, Boundaries Committee empowered to sue nation before Supreme Court of United States of Europe.

Constitution Drafting Committee (same rules of organization): Approves draft constitution by two-thirds vote; calls ratifying conventions in the states.

Congress Organization Committee (same rules of organization): Divides nations into congressional districts; calls for election of representatives and senators to Congress.

TERRITORIAL CHANGES:
Federal administration of colonies and mandates of member nations.

RATIFICATION:
By majority vote of conventions in two-thirds of the nations and at least two-thirds of the votes of all nations in favor of ratification.

AMENDMENT:
By majority of votes in each House, and ratification by legislatures or conventions in two-thirds of the nations, whichever method prescribed by Congress; if ratification is by conventions, method of election of delegates to be prescribed by Congress.

AUTHOR:
RICHARD N. COUDENHOVE-KALERGI (Austrian-born; French citizen).

PROFESSION:
Writer and organizer.

TITLE:
Crusade for Pan-Europe.

DATE: 1943.

PUBLISHER:
G. P. Putnam's Sons, New York.

TYPE:
FEDERAL: Based on Swiss Constitution. NAME: United States of Europe.

MEMBERSHIP:

REGIONAL: All European nations between Portugal and Poland; Turkey and Egypt may be included if they wish to join; European neutrals in the present war may remain outside in the beginning if they wish to protect their higher standard of living; Russia excluded because of her size and totalitarian system.

RELATIONSHIP TO WORLD COMMONWEALTH:

European Federation: To be united with other regional federations such as the British Commonwealth, the Pan-American Federation, a Far East Federation, and the Soviet Union under a *Commonwealth of the World* with a *permanent council* of regional delegates, retaining the League of Nations Secretariat, the Permanent Court of International Justice, the International Labor Organization, and the International Institute of Intellectual Cooperation. *Duties:* Mediation, arbitration; limitation of armaments; intervention on request of any regional federation to preserve internal order, but non-intervention in case of civil war; permanent consultation and mutual assistance against aggressors determined by Court. London to be capital of World Commonwealth. *Enforcement:* United States air supremacy assuring American control of the skies to prevent intercontinental wars and to protect World Commonwealth.

In case one regional federation is attacked by another, all other regional federations, united under Commonwealth of the World, to defend the victim if the aggressor refuses mediation by Supreme Council of World Commonwealth. Permanent Court to determine the aggressor.

ORGANS OF GOVERNMENT OF THE UNITED STATES OF EUROPE:

LEGISLATIVE: Bicameral: *House of Representatives; Senate.*

House of Representatives: Representation to be based on population; representatives to be chosen through general election.

Senate: Two Senators from each member nation, preferably the prime minister and foreign secretary of each member nation.

EXECUTIVE OR ADMINISTRATIVE:

Executive Board: Seven members; elected by House and Senate (no two may be of the same nationality); different chairman to be chosen

Charts of Plans to Unite Nations Since 1914

each year; each member of Board to head one of following executive departments: *Foreign Affairs; Army; Finance; Commerce; Interior; Justice; Transport.*

European Army: Small, professional, highly mechanized force recruited from member nations with none having more recruits than ten per cent of the total force; European Army to be of equal strength with Soviet Army (to prevent Europe from being at Russia's mercy). *Commander-in-chief:* Preferably a high-ranking Swiss officer to be named for specified term by federal government. Additional compulsory training of all European men in local or regional militias on Swiss model to assist European army in case of invasion, but not for intervention against Europe's neighbors (militia to have no mechanized equipment).

JUDICIAL:
Supreme Court: Elected by House and Senate.
Federal Courts of Appeal: Jurisdiction — on appeal by individuals in case of infringement of Bill of Rights by their national governments.

TRANSFERS OF JURISDICTION FROM MEMBER NATIONS TO UNITED STATES OF EUROPE:
To control armament industry, public utilities, continental railway system, civil aviation, monetary system, and electric power.
To disarm all member nations.
To establish European Bill of Rights assuring all persons political, linguistic, religious, and social rights.
To control all large European trusts established and owned by Nazi Germany.
To administer disputed areas such as the Sudeten, Danzig, Fiume, Carpatho-Russia, Macedonia, Transylvania if satisfactory settlements cannot be made; to protect all citizens of such areas against oppression.
To establish a single federal language, preferably English, in addition to each national language.

RESTRICTIONS ON UNITED STATES OF EUROPE:
Pledge to *Britain* (as part of price for British consent to establishment of European Federation): not to build warships, submarines, or bombing planes.

United States, Britain, and *Soviet Union* entitled to interfere in all major issues of European Federation that may endanger their future such as domination of Federation by Germany.

NATIONS RETAIN:
Right to republican or constitutional monarchical form of government.
Right to national languages, dialects, traditions, and constitutions.

NATIONS UNDERTAKE:
To grant their peoples a Bill of Rights and to respect its provisions.

DEMOCRATIC RIGHTS:
Equal suffrage in federal elections for men and women.
Right of minorities to use own language.

METHODS OF ENFORCEMENT:
Toward individuals: Enforcement of federal court decisions.

Toward Member Nations: Use of European Army to prevent aggression, domination, or secession. Pledge by *Britain, Russia,* and the *United States* to assist European Federation with air and naval forces if Federation is invaded.

IMMEDIATE STEPS:
Pledge by United Nations to call a *European Constitutional Assembly* immediately on cessation of hostilities.
Immediate establishment of *Supreme Council* of Commonwealth of World by prominent leaders of the United States, Britain, the Soviet Union, France, and China with one Indian of high moral authority to act as trustee for India, and an Arab delegate to represent the Near East. France to act provisionally as trustee for Europe, the United States for Pan-America, China for the Far East, and Great Britain for her Empire.

PREREQUISITES TO PEACE:
United Nations victory.

LIQUIDATION OF THE WAR:
Preliminary peace treaty should determine boundaries of Germany and Italy, and set up procedure for election of delegates to European Constitutional Assembly.

United Nations to appoint High Commissioner, preferably an American, to act as trustee of United Europe, taking charge of administration and reconstruction of all liberated and reoccupied Europe; heads of European national governments to be members of High Commissioner's advisory board.

Duties: To take charge of whole economic and financial machine taken over from Germany; to organize direct or indirect elections (under supervision and control of army of occupation) for the Constitutional Assembly with one delegate for every million inhabitants.

Constitutional Assembly: To determine whether European Federation is to be established. If delegates decide against it, Assembly to be dissolved, various European nations to be reestablished and traditional peace conference organized.

If Assembly decides in favor of European Federation, Assembly is to draft a federal constitution, elect an *Executive Board* to act as an *Emergency Government* for Europe with national governments reestablished under federal control.

Emergency Government to take over authority of High Commissioner on reconstruction, disputes between European nations, and negotiation of treaties with non-European nations. During first few years federal civil service to be made up chiefly of Swiss nationals.

Large estates to be broken up in Germany, Poland, Spain, Hungary, etc., and distributed among landless farmers who are to be encouraged to develop cooperative farming. Nazi criminals to be punished. German Junker aristocracy to be deprived of economic and political influence by drastic land reform.

TERRITORIAL CHANGES:
Germany to be changed into a federal state; within it Prussia to be divided into three states centered around Cologne, Hamburg, and Berlin. Federal capital of Germany to be transferred to Frankfort. Germany to give up Austria, Memel, and Sudeten area.
African colonies to remain under present national administration but treated as one large economic unit regardless of political affiliation.
Establishment of autonomous colony in East Africa for resettlement of Eastern European Jews if Palestine is inadequate.

AUTHOR:
Dr. Leo Dub (American).

PROFESSION:
Physician.

TITLE OF PLAN:
The Unitary State — Continent of Europe and Its Culture States.
A Solution of the European Peace Problem.

DATE: 1943.

PAMPHLET

PUBLISHED BY:
The author in Boston, Massachusetts.

ORGANIZATIONAL BACKING:
United Nations Committee, Boston, Massachusetts.

TYPE:
UNIFIED STATE allowing for full cultural autonomy of member nations.
NAME: Unitary State Continent of Europe (USCE).

MEMBERSHIP:
REGIONAL: Continental Europe without England or Russia.

ORGANS OF GOVERNMENT:
LEGISLATIVE: Bicameral *European Central Parliament*.
  First Chamber: One representative, directly elected, from each country (Europe to be divided into 100 countries, each with a population of 3,500,000).
  Second Chamber: Equal number of delegates from each European Culture State.
  Legislation must pass both Chambers.

EXECUTIVE OR ADMINISTRATIVE:
  European State President.
  Secretaries for Common European Affairs.

Ten *Territorial Officials.*
One Hundred *Country Officers.*
One Thousand *Provincial Officers.*
Ten Thousand *District Officers.*
European Police.

JUDICIAL: Courts.

TRANSFERS OF JURISDICTION FROM MEMBER NATIONS TO THE UNITARY STATE:
To introduce artificial language *Continental* composed of 1,000 commonly used words, phonetically written, without idioms, using Latin and Germanic roots of Basic English.
To protect life, health, property, political and religious rights, and the right to work.
To regulate production, distribution, the monetary system, customs, postal service, traffic, railways, telephone, telegraph, standardization of education.

CULTURE GROUPS RETAIN:
Right to establish separate Culture States.
Right to monarchical or republican forms.
Right to retain own cultural institutions, education, language, art, literature, religion, charitable institutions, cultural relations.
Individuals may choose the Culture State to which they wish to belong.

TERRITORIAL CHANGES:
Europe to be divided as follows:
Ten *Territories* each with a population of thirty-five million.
One Hundred *Countries* each with a population of 3,500,000.
One Thousand *Provinces* each with a population of 350,000.
Ten Thousand *Districts* each with a population of 35,000.
The ten *Territories* are to have the following names:
North, Elbe, Rhine, West, Southwest, South, Southeast, Danube, Middle and East, East.
Switzerland is to be the administrative headquarters of the Unitary State.

AUTHOR:
The British Government.

TITLE:
The Declaration of Union (offer of Union to France by the British Government).

DATE: June 16, 1940.

SOURCE:
London Times, June 18, 1940.

TYPE:
Practically a unified state. **NAME:** Franco-British Union.

MEMBERSHIP:
REGIONAL: United Kingdom, French Republic.

ORGANS OF GOVERNMENT:
LEGISLATIVE: The two Parliaments to be formally associated.

EXECUTIVE OR ADMINISTRATIVE:
  A Single War Cabinet.
  Joint organs of defense, foreign, financial, and economic policies.

JUDICIAL:
  None specified.

TRANSFERS OF JURISDICTION FROM MEMBER NATIONS TO THE UNION:
Interchangeable citizenship for subjects of the two countries.
Direction of all land, sea, and air forces placed under Single War Cabinet.
Repair of war damage within their territories from joint resources.

MISCELLANEOUS:
The object of this offer of Union was to encourage the French Government to continue its resistance against Germany. It was not accepted.

AUTHOR:
GREEK NATIONAL GROUP.

TITLE OF PLAN:
Balkan Union. Reply to the Questionnaire on the Balkan Union, 1931.

PUBLISHED IN:
Balkan Union — A Road to Peace in Southeastern Europe, by Theodore I. Geshkoff, 1940, Columbia University Press, New York.

TYPE:
FEDERAL. NAME: Balkan Union under the League of Nations.

MEMBERSHIP:
SUBREGIONAL — Members: Albania, Bulgaria, Greece, Roumania, Yugoslavia, Turkey.

ORGANS OF GOVERNMENT:
LEGISLATIVE: Unicameral *Assembly:* Representation in proportion to population; number of votes of largest nations not to exceed three times the number of votes of the smallest nations; no nation to have less than ten representatives; election methods prescribed by Union. *Decisions:* By absolute majority of votes. Unanimity to modify treaty constituting Union.

Method of Election: Representatives to be elected partly by the national legislatures; the rest by members of municipal and departmental councils, universities, and by the most representative agricultural, labor, commercial, and industrial organizations in each country.

Powers: Legislates on own or Council's initiative, laws having obligatory force in territory of the Union; or makes recommendations having force only after adoption by legislative branch of each country; may order popular referenda on questions of general importance. Laws voted by Assembly subject to Council veto.

EXECUTIVE OR ADMINISTRATIVE:
Council: Consists of delegates of governments of member nations; all nations have equal number of votes; presided over by delegates of

each member nation in turn; President of *Assembly* may be present and express advisory opinions.

Duties: Calls Assembly into ordinary session once a year; into extraordinary session on request of one-third of Assembly members; approves or vetoes laws passed by Assembly; publishes laws in official *Union Journal*; coordinates policies of member nations.

Names *Executive Committee* to meet in case of emergency.

Administrative Departments:
1. Balkan Board of Highways, Communications, Posts, Telegraphs, Telephones, etc.
2. Balkan Board of Hygiene, Labor, and Social Policy.
3. Committee on Minorities.
4. Secretariat-General of the Council: personnel to be engaged from among nationals of all member nations; responsible to Council or to the Executive Committee which appoints them.

JUDICIAL:

Supreme Court of the Union: Chief Justice may be nominated by the Permanent Court of International Justice.

Jurisdiction: To settle legal disputes between member nations; to investigate or impeach high administrative officials of the Union for offenses in service; to give advisory opinions on request of Council or member nations regarding conformity of national laws to Union laws.

TRANSFERS OF JURISDICTION FROM MEMBER NATIONS TO THE UNION:

Declare war and conclude peace; disarmament of member nations.
Establish a monetary system.
Establish supreme Board of Highways and Communications.
Unify posts, telegraphs, telephones.
Establish customs union among member nations.
Conclude treaties of commerce.
Unify measures of public hygiene, protection of labor, social policy, and agricultural produce.
The Union may levy a very small tax and establish fixed dues, equal or not, to be paid by each nation as determined by the Council.
Obligations under the League of Nations Covenant remain in force.

Union may provide common representation in the League and in foreign nations by special or permanent delegations appointed by the Council.

Member nations are prohibited from negotiating treaties of alliance with other nations; other treaties may be negotiated if not contrary to Treaty establishing the Union, nor directed against its security.

Territorial changes between member nations subject to consent of all parties concerned.

NATIONS UNDERTAKE:
To submit all disputes to mediation by the Council, subject to appeal to the Assembly and final appeal to a special tribunal.
To defend the Union and each member nation in event of attack whether by a member or a foreign nation.
To teach at least one Balkan language in their schools other than their own.

DEMOCRATIC RIGHTS:
Guaranteed by Union laws to nationals of member nations in Union territory:
1. Equality of treatment with nationals of each nation.
2. Admission and freedom of travel.
3. Freedom of religion, language, nationality, and press.
4. Right of domicile for trade, and freedom of economic activity.

METHODS OF ENFORCEMENT:
Joint military action by member nations in the event of aggression against the Union or a member nation by another member nation or by a foreign nation.
(The Union does not seem to be provided with military force of its own. — EDITORS.)

RATIFICATION:
Of Treaty constituting the Balkan Union by national governments.

MISCELLANEOUS:
Seat of the Union: Istanbul or Salonika.
Official language: French.

AUTHORS:
MINISTERS OF THE KINGDOMS OF GREECE AND YUGOSLAVIA.

TITLE:
Constitution of a Balkan Union (between the Kingdom of Greece and the Kingdom of Yugoslavia).

DATE: January 15, 1942.

SOURCE:
Inter-Allied Review, June 15, 1942.

TYPE:
CONFEDERATION. NAME: Balkan Union.

MEMBERSHIP:
REGIONAL: Greece and Yugoslavia; other Balkan states whose governments are freely and legally constituted may join.

ORGANS OF GOVERNMENT:
LEGISLATIVE: Presidents of national ministerial councils (cabinets) to meet, whenever circumstances require, to discuss questions of general interest to the Union.

Regular meetings between parliamentary delegations of member nations to exchange views on questions of common interest submitted to them by competent organs. (Compare with organization of Dual Monarchy, p. 397.)

EXECUTIVE OR ADMINISTRATIVE:
Political Organ: Regular meetings of Ministers for Foreign Affairs.
Commission on Intellectual Cooperation.
Commission on Coordination and Public Opinion: To coordinate work of member nations.

Economic and Financial Organ: Two delegates from each member government competent in economic and financial matters.

Permanent Military Organ: Common General Staff of National Armies headed by chiefs of member governments or their representatives.
Army and Aviation Bureau.
Navy Bureau.

Permanent Bureau: With Political, Economic, Financial, and Military Sections; serves as Secretariat of Union organs; prepares material for them; studies and reports on problems of political, economic, financial, and military cooperation of Union members; supervises application of decisions.

JUDICIAL:
None specified.

TRANSFERS OF JURISDICTION FROM MEMBER NATIONS TO THE UNION:
To coordinate foreign policy of member nations.
To consult at all times when member nations' vital interests are menaced.
To prepare arbitration and conciliation agreements between member nations.
To coordinate foreign commerce policies, customs duties, organization of customs union.
To develop a common economic plan.
To improve communication and transportation between members and trade in transit.
To prepare draft agreement establishing a Balkan monetary union.
To adopt common plan of defense, armaments; to defend European frontiers of member nations.

RATIFICATION:
Union established on exchange of instruments of ratification.

MISCELLANEOUS:
Original text in French.

AUTHORS:
THE GOVERNMENTS OF POLAND AND CZECHOSLOVAKIA.

TITLE:
Confederation of Poland and Czechoslovakia.

DATE: January 25, 1942.

SOURCE:
Inter-Allied Review, June 15, 1942.

TYPE:
CONFEDERATE.

MEMBERSHIP:
REGIONAL: Poland and Czechoslovakia; other nations with which their vital interests are linked may join.

ORGANS OF GOVERNMENT:
Common General Staff to prepare defense measures; in time of war: unified supreme command.
Other common organs to ensure common policy.

TRANSFERS OF JURISDICTION FROM MEMBER NATIONS TO THE CONFEDERATION:
To assure common policy on foreign affairs, defense, economic and financial matters, social questions, transport, posts, telegraphs.
To coordinate foreign trade policies and customs duties so as to form a customs union.
To assure permanent parity between currencies of member nations.
To coordinate taxation measures.
To develop and administer means of transportation and communication; uniform postal and telecommunication rates throughout Confederation.
To coordinate social policies.
To cooperate in educational and cultural matters.
To eliminate passport and visa restrictions on passenger traffic between member nations.
To regulate rights of free domicile and exercise of gainful occupation by citizens of member nations throughout Confederation.
To regulate mutual recognition by member nations of school and professional diplomas, documents, court sentences, legal aid and execution of court judgments.

NATIONS UNDERTAKE:
To defray expenses of common administrative organs.
To guarantee their citizens freedom of conscience, person, learning,

speech, writing, organization, and association; equality before the law; eligibility to all national offices; independent courts; control of national governments by freely elected representative bodies.

AUTHOR:
KAZYS PAKSTAS (Lithuanian).

PROFESSION:
University Professor.

TITLE OF PLAN:
The Baltoscandian Confederation.

PAMPHLET

DATE: March, 1942.

PUBLISHED BY:
Lithuanian Cultural Institute, Chicago, Illinois.

TYPE:
CONFEDERATE: Constitution to be modeled on Constitutions of United States, Switzerland, and British Commonwealth.

MEMBERSHIP:
REGIONAL: Sweden, Lithuania, Denmark, Finland, Norway, Latvia, Esthonia. (Eastern Prussia: see territorial changes.—EDITORS.)

ORGANS OF GOVERNMENT:
LEGISLATIVE: Bicameral — *Congress; Senate.*
  Congress: One representative for each 100,000 inhabitants (total 241).
  Senate: Each member nation ten Senators (total seventy).

EXECUTIVE OR ADMINISTRATIVE:
  Swedish King to assume title of *Emperor of Baltoscandia;* if republican pattern is followed, recommends Swiss method of executive board, or giving each outstanding national, religious, and political group the opportunity to head the government.

Ministries: Foreign Relations, Defense, Communications, Finance.
General Staff and one leader who is appointed only in time of emergency.

Judicial:
None suggested.

TRANSFERS OF JURISDICTION FROM MEMBER NATIONS TO THE CONFEDERATION:
Gradual lowering of duties on interstate commerce.
Jurisdiction over most important lines of communication affecting international relations within the Confederation.
Monetary units to have same price and value; distinctive names could be retained by each country.
Common control over duties and custom-houses.
Each nation may retain its own legations and consulates.
Official languages: English and Swedish.

METHODS OF ENFORCEMENT:
Greatest emphasis to be laid on the need for common defense against aggression and to keep the Baltic free and open.
Effective separation of Germany from Russia, allowing Germany to protect herself against dangers from Asia.
Cooperation with Central European federated group of Poland and Czechoslovakia.
Cooperation with Anglo-American Alliance through the establishment of naval and air bases on Baltic Islands off the coast of Denmark and Esthonia.

IMMEDIATE STEPS:
Sweden, being the largest and most central country of Baltoscandia, with Stockholm the likeliest capital, must first approve the plan and take the organizing initiative. Approval of American and British political leaders is also needed.

TERRITORIAL CHANGES:
Eastern Prussia is to become a part of Baltoscandia with complete self-government, and recognized as an autonomous unit of the Confederation.

AUTHOR:
Dr. S. R. Chow (Chinese).

PROFESSION:
Professor of International Relations at National Wuhan University.

TITLE:
A Permanent Order for the Pacific.

DATE: December, 1942.

PUBLISHER:
Institute of Pacific Relations (China Council).

TYPE:
CONFEDERATE. NAME: Pacific Association of Nations.

MEMBERSHIP:
REGIONAL: China, Soviet Russia, India, United States, Canada, Australia, New Zealand, Philippines, Great Britain, Netherlands, Korea; Japan and Thailand may become members when the original member nations are satisfied they will fulfill their duties; new members may be admitted by two-thirds vote of original members.

ORGANS OF GOVERNMENT:
LEGISLATIVE: *General Conference:* Member nations to be represented by delegations to be fixed according to area, population, economic resources, and other political or cultural factors; to meet annually and in extraordinary session on request of majority of member nations or on request of Pacific Council. *Decisions:* By two-thirds majority. *Duties:* To discuss problems and decide policies of general interest to region and controversial issues between member nations.

EXECUTIVE OR ADMINISTRATIVE:
Pacific Council: One-year term; five members elected by General Conference, each member nation nominating one candidate; not more than one of same nationality eligible to Council. *Decisions:* By two-thirds majority. *Duties:* To see that General Conference decisions are carried out by appropriate agency; to take necessary emergency action

during recess of General Conference; to report regularly to General Conference. Pacific Council responsible to General Conference for discharge of its duties.

International Military Staff: Appointed by General Conference.
Duties: To command international force; to formulate and execute military sanctions under authority of General Conference or of Pacific Council.

Permanent Secretariat: Appointed by Pacific Council with approval of General Conference; directed by both bodies. *Duties:* To serve as research and information center on economic, social, and other problems of the region.

JUDICIAL:
Pacific Court: Five-year term; five to seven Judges elected by General Conference; not more than one Judge may be of the same nationality; elected from list of jurists recommended in equal number by each member nation. *Jurisdiction:* Over all legal (non-political) disputes; matters referred to it by parties concerned or by General Conference or Pacific Council.
(The Pacific Court may be abolished if a World Court is established.)

TRANSFERS OF JURISDICTION FROM MEMBER NATIONS TO THE ASSOCIATION:

(Expense of maintaining Pacific Association to be divided among member nations in proportion to number of representatives allotted to each in the General Conference.)

To avert war by exercising joint influence.

To take joint preventive measures.

To help victim nation in case of war; to enforce sanctions against the aggressor.

To adopt regional plan for armament reduction and limitation.

To supervise and control administration of colonies and dependencies.

NATIONS UNDERTAKE:

To bind themselves in pacts of non-aggression, arbitration, and mutual assistance.

To submit disputes to arbitration, judicial decision, or conciliation.

To meet acts of war against a member nation by immediate collective economic or military sanctions.
To contribute a definite quota to the international military force.

NATIONS RETAIN:
Right to present any proposal or grievance to Association for discussion and investigation.

METHODS OF ENFORCEMENT:
International military force to be stationed permanently in strategic posts and held in readiness to move anywhere within region in case of emergency.
Military and economic sanctions in event of war.

IMMEDIATE STEPS:
Pacific Association of Nations should be set up immediately at end of war.

MISCELLANEOUS:
If a world organization is established, the Pacific Association should be subordinated to it. The world organization should have final jurisdiction over: access to key raw materials, problems of national and racial freedom, and sanctions against aggressors.

AUTHOR:
John Van Ess (American).

PROFESSION:
Missionary.

TITLE OF PLAN:
Meet the Arab.

DATE: 1943.
   (First printed in *The Palestine Post,* August 2, 1937.)

PUBLISHER:
The John Day Co., New York.

TYPE:
FEDERAL. NAME: The United States of the Near East.

MEMBERSHIP:
REGIONAL: Five States: Lebanon, Syria, Jebel Druze, Israiliyeh (to be composed of Judea and the south country to the Gulf of Aqaba thus creating the Jewish half of Palestine), Urduniyah (the rest of Palestine and Transjordan).

ORGANS OF GOVERNMENT:
The structure of the federal government to be patterned after that of the United States of America.

TRANSFERS OF JURISDICTION FROM MEMBER NATIONS TO THE FEDERATION:
Control and administration of posts, telegraph, communications, currency, defense, foreign affairs, courts, general health.
Organization of federal education for federal service with compulsory instruction in Arabic, Hebrew, and English.
Cooperation with other regions of Near East through common defense staff; coordinated foreign policy, especially on economic cooperation with rest of the world.

STATES RETAIN:
Their autonomy, the collection and expenditure of local revenue, public order, administration of justice, sanitation and health measures, irrigation, and education.

METHODS OF ENFORCEMENT:
Britain and the United States to guarantee peace in the Near East to enable the national governments to spend their revenues on constructive enterprises instead of on unnecessary military establishments.

IMMEDIATE STEPS:
Consent and cooperation of France would have to precede establishment of Federation.

LIQUIDATION OF THE WAR:
War settlement must enable refugee Jews to return to their homes in

Poland, Germany, and Roumania. Jews in Palestine would probably limit immigration into their part of it voluntarily.

TERRITORIAL CHANGES:
District of Jerusalem to be federal capital.

MISCELLANEOUS:
The author suggests the following measures in order to create a better balanced economy in the Near East: The establishment of plants to process oil by-products in Iraq, Bahrein, and Saudi Arabia to be financed partly by the foreign-owned parent concerns, partly by the native workers. The irrigation of Iraq by impounding the flood waters of the Euphrates within existing natural basins and building of transverse canals over the whole land. The annual floods would be controlled, the marshes dried, the land populated by Bedouins engaged in sheep-raising. Wool from Iraq and cotton from Egypt could be sent to Palestine for processing.

Great Britain may acquire air bases within the Federation by treaty.

PART III

THEORETICAL PLANS

CHARTS OF PLANS TO UNITE NATIONS SINCE 1914

D. IDEOLOGICAL

"The basic principles of international morality, taking full account of the necessity of creating confederations of States having similar aims, must be restored after the war, in the course of which they have been trampled under foot, and the principles of morality must form the basis of the future peace. This peace should provide ways and means of giving territorial, strategic and economic security to states like Poland, which are exposed to the danger of German aggression."
  WLADYSLAW RACKIEWICZ, Poland; London, September 1, 1942.

"For my part, I therefore say definitely that I am not prepared to take risks again with either Germany, Italy or Japan. I have no faith in the promises of their statesmen nor in the smooth assurances of their apologists. There is only one security for mankind in respect of all of them, to ensure that they are totally disarmed and in no position ever to try their strength again. Then indeed peace may have its chance. After the bitter lessons which we have learned, we must insist upon the fullest precautions."   ANTHONY EDEN, April 1, 1943.

"As the provisions of the four-nation declaration are carried in effect, there will no longer be need for spheres of influence, for alliances, for balance of power or any other of the special arrangements through which, in the unhappy past, the nations strove to safeguard their security or to promote their interests."
  CORDELL HULL, Washington, D. C., November 18, 1943.

IDEOLOGICAL PLANS

STREIT first proposed union between fifteen democracies. Since the outbreak of war he advocates union with the British Commonwealth and all its non-self-governing possessions. He follows the American Constitution to a large extent, but suggests a Board of Five with a Premier and Cabinet as the executive. He believes a Provisional Union should be set up during the war, with power to negotiate armistice and peace terms with the Axis nations.

Crichton Clarke limits membership in the Union to nations with written constitutions providing for representative, republican government.

A plan for a *Federation of Free Peoples* drafted by Grenville Clark is similar to Streit's original proposal for a nuclear union of democracies, except that Clark proposes *confederate* instead of federal structure. He adds three Latin American nations to Streit's list of democracies. At the author's request, this plan is not included here.

Alguy bars a great number of nations from membership in his Confederate Peace Union until democratic reconstruction has taken place within them. The countries to be disarmed by the victorious democracies, in addition to the Axis nations, include Poland, Spain, and Turkey.

King-Hall advocates an Anglo-American alliance. He would have the American President and the King of England decide when aggression has occurred and use a Joint Anglo-American Fleet and Air Force to compel the aggressor nation to withdraw to its own borders.

Kelland adds a series of four-nation defensive and offensive alliances to a permanent Anglo-American alliance. A militarily impregnable United States is his final hope for safety should the various alliances disintegrate.

AUTHOR:
CRICHTON CLARKE (American).

PROFESSION:
Attorney.

TITLE OF PLAN:
World Constitution for United Nations of the World.

MANUSCRIPT

DATE: 1934 (?)

TYPE:
FEDERAL. Modeled after United States Constitution.
Short title: UNOW. NAME: United Nations.

MEMBERSHIP:
Limited to nations who qualify by having a *written constitution* providing for a representative, republican form of government with administrative subdivisions conforming to the same economic, financial, and military limitations as the States of the United States of America.

ORGANS OF GOVERNMENT:
LEGISLATIVE: Unicameral.
World Congress: Six-year term; sessions at least once in three years; one delegate for every two million population, elected by the people; delegates at least thirty years old; citizens for seven years of nations represented; two-thirds vote expels a member, overrides President's veto.

EXECUTIVE OR ADMINISTRATIVE:
President and *Vice-President:* Elected by World Congress and may be recalled by it; at least thirty years old and citizens of a constituent nation.

Duties of President: Commissions all officers, nominates Justices of Supreme Court with two-thirds concurring vote of Congress; Commander-in-chief of armed forces; on request of Congress may appoint inferior officials; grants pardons and reprieves except in cases of impeachment; may recommend, or veto legislation. (Allowed ninety-day period in which to sign or veto.)

JUDICIAL:
World Supreme Court: Justices appointed by President with two-thirds concurrence of Congress; hold office during good behavior.

Jurisdiction: Original jurisdiction in all cases to which a nation is party; appellate jurisdiction in all others.

Inferior Courts to be established by Congress.

TRANSFERS OF JURISDICTION FROM MEMBER NATIONS TO THE UNITED NATIONS:
Constitution and laws of United Nations are supreme.

Guarantees each constituent nation republican form of government, protection against invasion, and, on request of nation, against domestic violence.

Congress has authority: To levy and collect taxes, borrow money, provide for general safety, regulate commerce among member nations, coin international money, grant patent rights; prescribe uniform method for organizing, arming, and disciplining of naval, air, and reserve militias of constituent nations and exercise general supervision over them; to take over and administer mandates of member nations to fit them for self-government; may authorize merging of nations; may grade them according to their living standards as basis for establishing maximum taxes assessed by member nations on imports.

NATIONS RETAIN:
Right to prohibit importation of specified articles after adequate notice to World Congress.

Merger or partition of nations can occur only with consent of their legislatures and World Congress.

Control of migration and travel by citizens of other member nations unless all member nations come to agreements regarding uniform migration, travel, naturalization, and navigation regulations.

AMENDMENT:
By two-thirds vote of Congress; or Constitutional Convention called on request of two-thirds of the legislatures of the member nations and ratification by three-fourths of the legislatures or by conventions in three-fourths of the member nations.

AUTHOR:
CLARENCE K. STREIT (American).

PROFESSION:
Journalist.

TITLE OF PLAN:
1. Union Now: A Proposal for a Federal Union of the Leading Democracies.
2. Union Now with Britain.

DATE:
1. 1939.   2. 1941.

PUBLISHER:
Harper & Brothers, New York.

ORGANIZATIONAL BACKING:
Federal Union, Inc., Washington, D. C.

TYPE:
FEDERAL: Based on United States Constitution. NAME: Union of the Free.

MEMBERSHIP:
IDEOLOGICAL and linguistic.

Member Nations:
1. *According to Union Now* — Australia, Belgium, Canada, Denmark, Finland, France, Ireland, Netherlands, New Zealand, Norway, Sweden, Switzerland, Union of South Africa, United Kingdom, United States.
2. *According to Union Now With Britain* — Australia, Canada, Ireland, New Zealand, the Union of South Africa, the United Kingdom, the United States, together with all their non-self-governing possessions.

ORGANS OF GOVERNMENT:
LEGISLATIVE: Bicameral *Congress: House of Deputies; Senate.*
House of Deputies: Three-year term; one Deputy for each million

of population; each nation to have at least one; Deputies at least twenty-five years old; directly elected by citizens.

Senate: Eight-year term; two from each nation of less than twenty-five million population; two more for each additional twenty-five million; Senators to be at least thirty years old; ten years resident in nation electing them; directly elected at large; half of Senate renewed every four years.

Reapportionment according to census to be taken every ten years. Bills, resolutions, orders must pass both houses by majority vote; two-thirds vote necessary to repass legislation vetoed by executive board.

EXECUTIVE OR ADMINISTRATIVE:
Board of Five; Premier; Cabinet.

Board: Three members elected directly by citizens; one elected by Senate; one by House; five-year terms; terms to expire one at a time in odd-numbered years; Board members must be at least thirty-five years old. Each President for one year by rotation. *Decisions:* By majority vote.

Duties: Commander-in-chief of Union forces; commissions Union officers; appoints ambassadors, ministers, consuls; negotiates treaties with consent of Premier and Congress; appoints justices of High Court and lower Union Courts with advice and consent of Senate; recommends measures for consideration of Congress; convenes extraordinary sessions of Congress; may dissolve either House and order new elections.

Premier: Appointed by Board; exercises executive powers delegated to it by Board, with help of a *Cabinet* of his own choosing, until he loses confidence of the House or Senate; the Board then appoints another Premier.

JUDICIAL:
High Court: Not less than eleven judges; appointed for life.

Jurisdiction: Over all cases arising under Constitution, laws of the Union, and treaties made by it; cases affecting ambassadors, ministers, consuls; controversies between two or more nations; between a nation and citizens of another nation; between citizens of different nations; between a nation, its citizens and foreign nations or persons.

Inferior Courts established by Congress.

TRANSFERS OF JURISDICTION FROM MEMBER NATIONS TO THE UNION:
>Levy and collect income and other taxes, uniform throughout the Union. Grant Union citizenship; admit new nations into the Union.
>Treat with foreign governments.
>Raise, maintain, control land, sea, and air forces.
>Make war and peace.
>Regulate commerce among member nations and with foreign nations.
>Coin and issue money.
>Fix standard of weights and measures.
>Operate or control interstate communications services.
>Govern Union District and other federal property.

NATIONS RETAIN:
>Right to maintain a militia and police force but may not engage in war unless invaded or in imminent danger.
>Right to guarantee their people greater democratic rights than enumerated in Union Constitution.
>Powers not given to the Union to be reserved to the nations or to the people.

DEMOCRATIC RIGHTS:
>Freedom of speech, press, and conscience.
>Freedom of person, dwelling, communication; security against unreasonable searches and seizures.
>Freedom from ex-post-facto laws, excessive bail or fines, cruel and unusual punishments.
>All citizens twenty-one years of age, born or naturalized in the *self-governing* nations of the Union are citizens and have right to vote; persons living in *non-self-governing* territories of the Union to have all rights of citizens except right to vote.

METHODS OF ENFORCEMENT:

Towards Non-Member Nations: Treats with foreign governments; Congress makes war and peace.

Towards Member Nations: Defends them against invasion; protects each nation against domestic violence on application of national legislature or executive.
>Union laws operate directly on the individual.

Charts of Plans to Unite Nations Since 1914

IMMEDIATE STEPS:
Joint Declaration and Resolution by United States Congress authorizing the President to invite the democracies of the British Commonwealth to unite in a Provisional Federal Union, setting up an Inter-Continental Congress, and Executive and Judicial organs, with power over war, peace, foreign affairs, currency, trade, and communications; power to tax and borrow, enforce its laws on individuals, and settle disputes between member nations.

PREREQUISITES TO PEACE:
Offer by the Provisional Union to negotiate armistice and peace terms with the Axis nations on the following conditions: no indemnities, reparations, occupations, annexations; arbitration of disputes on details. Axis may retain prewar system of government with armed forces intact.

TERRITORIAL CHANGES:
Colonies and mandates of member nations become territories of the Union without upsetting the existing administration. These "politically inexperienced" populations to be prepared for membership in the Union as soon as "prudent experiment justifies."

RATIFICATION:
1. *As provided in Union Now:* Ratification by ten democracies, or by France, the United Kingdom, and the United States.
2. *As provided in Union Now with Britain:*
   (a) The *Provisional Union* to be established "on acceptance by the United States and the United Kingdom or Canada."
   (b) Ratification of the *permanent* Constitution of the Union by the people of the United States and of the United Kingdom, or of the United States and Canada.

AMENDMENT:
Proposals made by two-thirds majority of the House and Senate with approval of three-fifths of the Board, or by two-thirds majority of either House or Senate and unanimous approval of Board, or by special constituent assembly, or by petition of one-fourth the voters in one-half the nations.

MISCELLANEOUS:
Senators and representatives to the first *Congress* of the *Provisional Union* to be chosen by the national legislative bodies from a list nominated by the chief executives.

AUTHOR:
WALTER A. LEACH (American).

TITLE OF PLAN:
A New Structure.

DATE: 1942.

PUBLISHED:
By the author, Lincoln, Nebraska.

TYPE:
FEDERAL.

MEMBERSHIP:
IDEOLOGICAL: Open to all nations which adopt a Bill of Rights guaranteeing self-government and individual freedom.

ORGANS OF GOVERNMENT:
LEGISLATIVE: *Congress:* No details given.

EXECUTIVE OR ADMINISTRATIVE:
General Improvements Commission: Establishes a universal language; proposes amounts to be taxed from member nations; exercises right of eminent domain.

Rules Commission: Draws up International Code of Rules.

Military Commission: Recruits army from all member nations in proportion to their male population capable of military service; establishes unified command; selects personnel; determines size of forces in relation to possible opponents; protects members against aggression; enforces judgments of the Court.

Migration and Colonization Commission: Supervises population shifts and similar federal projects.

JUDICIAL:
Supreme Tribunal and Federal Courts: Whatever number of justices needed for efficiency.
Jurisdiction: International civil and criminal cases and administration of justice. Nations responsible for enforcing court judgments against their own nationals.

TRANSFERS OF JURISDICTION FROM MEMBER NATIONS TO THE FEDERATION:
Basic and only law: "No social body or individual nation shall injure or violate the justly established rights of any other social body or individual." All *decisions* of Congress derive from it, such as taxation of member nations; issuance of currency; administration of colonies. Nations must surrender for trial any individual offending against international law.

NATIONS RETAIN:
Right of secession within thirty days of passage of any amendment abridging freedom of the nation or of its citizens, if it can prove that its withdrawal will not cause injustice to the federation, its members, or citizens.

METHODS OF ENFORCEMENT:
Towards Member Nations and Non-Member Nations: Armed force.
Towards Individuals: Courts; and enforcement of decisions by the nations.

TERRITORIAL CHANGES:
Colonies of member nations are transferred to federal administration.

AMENDMENT:
Of the *Constitution* by four-fifths vote of the total membership of Congress.
Of the *Bill of Rights* by nine-tenths vote of all the members of the federation.

MISCELLANEOUS:
Money can be collected by the federation from individuals only in satisfaction of a court judgment.

AUTHOR:
JEREMIAH S. ALGUY (Czechoslovak).

PROFESSION:
International Lawyer.

TITLE OF PLAN:
Permanent World Peace.

DATE: 1943.

PUBLISHER:
Standard Publishing Co., New York.

TYPE:
CONFEDERATE. Based on League of Nations Covenant. NAME: Peace Union.

MEMBERSHIP:
IDEOLOGICAL: Self-governing states, dominions and colonies, which give satisfactory guarantees to observe the Covenant, may be admitted to membership if the United States, the British Empire, and the U.S.S.R. agree, plus two-thirds of the other members.

States which are not to be admitted immediately: Turkey, Albania, Bulgaria, Poland, Roumania, Hungary, Spain, and Portugal (author more hopeful of democratic reconstruction in these states); Afghanistan, Thailand, Iran, Iraq, Saudi-Arabia, Egypt, Ethiopia, Liberia. (Germany, Italy, and Japan are not mentioned at all, but are barred by implication.)

ORGANS OF GOVERNMENT:
LEGISLATIVE: Unicameral *Assembly:* Each nation one to three representatives and only one vote; delegations vote as a unit; two-thirds

vote required in general; majority vote for decisions on procedure and appointment of committees; votes of nations involved in a breach of the Covenant are not to be counted in any vote on such a breach.

EXECUTIVE OR ADMINISTRATIVE:
Secretary-General: Appointed by the Assembly.
Secretariat: Appointed by Secretary-General with Assembly approval. All positions open equally to men and women.

JUDICIAL:
Peace Tribunal: Judges elected for life by Assembly irrespective of nationality; judges having the nationality of the disputants may not sit in on case; a judge may be dismissed for cause by unanimous vote of his fellow judges.

Jurisdiction (compulsory): Any question referred to it by Assembly; all cases involving international law, treaties, colonies, possessions; nature and extent of reparations for breaches of international obligations; any question of jurisdiction is decided by the Court; parties to cases brought before the Tribunal must be member or non-member nations, legal representatives of autonomous minorities, colonies, and — by permission of the Tribunal — international organizations.

Powers: Fixes period within which nations must comply with its decisions; decides on inflicting sanctions in the event of non-compliance.

General Sanctions Office: Determines nature of sanctions, reparations, and contributions to the Blockade Fund; final decision up to Tribunal.

Code of Justice: Based on international law, custom, general law recognized by nations, judicial decisions, and teachings of most highly qualified jurists of the various nations.

TRANSFERS OF JURISDICTION FROM MEMBER NATIONS TO THE UNION:
Assembly may advise reconsideration of treaties; abrogate treaties inconsistent with the Covenant; administer nations which have relapsed into barbarism; protect rights of all nations to equal commercial treatment in the colonies; protect freedom of natives.

NATIONS UNDERTAKE:
To submit all disputes between them to arbitration, judicial settlement, or inquiry by the Assembly; not to resort to war; to carry out decisions of the Assembly; to cooperate in sanctions against any nation refusing to submit its case to settlement or refusing to comply with the decision, or engaging in war; to help any nation cooperating in sanctions, whether it is a member or not; to establish a Blockade Fund of two billion dollars; to support the Peace Union through fixed contributions and special assessments; to register all treaties with the Secretariat; to make no treaties inconsistent with the Covenant.

Non-members of the Peace Union are to be invited to sign a *Treaty of Competence and Sanctions* (terms undefined by the author); if they refuse, members of the Union are to coerce them into signing.

NATIONS RETAIN:
Complete independence except for submitting to decisions of the Assembly; right to secede upon two years' notice if all obligations fulfilled and Treaty of Competence and Sanctions signed within one month.

METHODS OF ENFORCEMENT:
General Sanctions Office on orders of Tribunal or Assembly carries out sanctions operating on nations; simultaneous application of sanctions obligatory on all nations. Sanctions may include:

1. Total severance of all trade, financial, and personal relations with recalcitrant nation or its citizens by all nations whether members of the Peace Union or not.
2. Application of sanctions against nations refusing to cooperate in disciplining the recalcitrant nation.
3. Expulsion from the Union by two-thirds vote of the Assembly plus agreement of the United States, British Empire, and U.S.S.R.

LIQUIDATION OF THE WAR:
Occupation and *administration* by American, British, Russian, Dutch, Belgian, Danish, Norwegian, Greek, Yugoslav, and Free French troops of territories, railways, public utilities, and factories of Axis Powers; destruction of all goods useful to arms production.

Disarmament of Axis Powers, Poland, Spain, Turkey, Syria, Egypt, Transjordan, Iraq, Iran, Saudi-Arabia and other Arab states.

Arrest of all individuals offending against laws and customs of war in lands occupied since March, 1939; individuals to be sentenced by Allied Military Tribunals before conclusion of Peace Treaty. *But Allies are not to be bound by the Hague Convention and Annex on Laws and Customs of War in administration of occupied lands.*

International Criminal Courts: To try all racist crimes committed before and during the war; deportation of those found guilty to distant, little-populated, guarded islands; sentence of "Civic Degradation" for those acquiescing in racist crimes to entail loss of vote and eligibility to office with confiscation of property to benefit *General Indemnification Fund* for the victims.

Aid resettlement of dispossessed populations; plan enormous social relief works.

TERRITORIAL CHANGES:
Creation of a Jewish State.

AMENDMENT:
By unanimous agreement of all member nations present in the Assembly; proposal must be on the agenda six months prior to meeting.

MISCELLANEOUS:
Member nations undertake to respect and protect equal rights of all *civilized* human beings, especially racial, religious, and linguistic minorities, and to grant the usual rights of autonomy if requested.

AUTHOR:
STEPHEN KING-HALL (English).

PROFESSION:
Writer.

TITLE:
Total Victory.

DATE: 1942.

PUBLISHER:
Harcourt, Brace & Co., New York.

TYPE AND MEMBERSHIP:
1. Alliance: Anglo-American.
2. Economic League — International.

ORGANS OF GOVERNMENT:
LEGISLATIVE: None.

EXECUTIVE OR ADMINISTRATIVE:
Joint British American Fleet and Air Force to be known as *The Peace Force:* Navy — three times as strong as next largest fleet, twice as strong as any combination of three other fleets; air force — four times as strong as next largest air force, twice as strong as any combination of two other air forces. Eighty per cent of personnel British and American; twenty per cent foreigners eligible for ten-year enlistments. Forces stationed on all territories under sovereignty of Britain and United States.
Duties: Whenever the President and the King declare that a nation has committed aggression, the Peace Force is to wage war against the aggressor nation until its forces are withdrawn to its own borders. Other nations to be invited to cooperate with military and economic sanctions.

JUDICIAL:
President and King to act as *mediators* in any dispute between nations if requested to do so.
American and British Governments to pledge *never to take initiative* in resorting to armed force against other nations but to refer all disputes to *arbitration*.

TRANSFERS OF JURISDICTION FROM MEMBER NATIONS TO THE ECONOMIC LEAGUE:
To initiate large-scale international public works cutting across national frontiers.
To undertake economic development of Central Africa.
To establish free trade in all colonial possessions.
To provide international administration of certain ports.

NATIONS UNDERTAKE:
To set up large reserves of raw materials inside frontiers of non-colonial powers (that they may not be at undue disadvantage in case of war).

METHODS OF ENFORCEMENT:
Anglo-American military action to prevent aggression.

IMMEDIATE STEPS:
Issuance of Anglo-American Proclamation to Mankind valid for ten years and renewable for five; to be published in all languages and broadcast from all British and American stations every six months.

PREREQUISITES TO PEACE:
British and American Governments to call on German people to demand recall of all German forces from occupied territories; German frontiers to be those existing previous to Munich settlement; reestablishment of governments in occupied countries as conditions of armistice on sea, land, and air. Negotiation of questions of Polish Corridor, Danzig, and the Sudeten, and relations between Austria and Germany. Britain and the United States to maintain armed forces they consider necessary for their security.

AUTHOR:
CLARENCE BUDINGTON KELLAND (American).

PROFESSION:
Writer.

TITLE:
The Zones of Safety.

DATE: August 25, 1943.

PUBLISHED BY:
National Republican Club, New York.

TYPE:
Multiple Alliance.

FUNCTION OF MEMBERSHIP IN THE PROPOSED ALLIANCES:
1. Trusteeship by Russia, Great Britain, United States, China.
2. Offensive and Defensive Alliance between Russia, Great Britain, United States, China.
3. Permanent Defensive Alliance between United States and Great Britain.
4. Entente (understanding or agreement) of North and South American Nations.
5. Military impregnability of United States.

No organs of government specified.
No transfers of jurisdiction.

"The United States remains independent, individual, a separate and distinct nation until the end of time."

METHODS OF ENFORCEMENT:
Offensive and defensive alliance of Russia, Great Britain, United States, and China against any nation threatening the peace.
Permanent defensive alliance between United States and Great Britain to act as one in case of attack by any nation or combination of nations.
Military and economic entente of Western Hemisphere standing as one against any invasion of American soil.
Impregnable United States able to stand alone with five-ocean navy, air force, standing army, nation ringed with defenses.

PREREQUISITES TO PEACE:
Unconditional surrender of Axis nations.

LIQUIDATION OF THE WAR:
Russia, Great Britain, United States, and China as trustees to administer indefinitely territories, people, and economy of defeated and bankrupt nations:

1. Set up local government.
2. Police territories to prevent violence and riot.

3. Restore order and aid in rehabilitation by sustaining local government.
4. Protect private property, safety, and civil rights.
5. Assist nations to set up the kind of government each selects.
6. Conserve assets of each nation so that nations can be released from the trusteeship as going concerns.
7. Restore France as first-class power as soon as possible and admit her to trusteeship.
8. Establish *International Commission* to study structure of Europe and of the world to suggest concrete plan to eliminate causes of war; suggest redistribution of territories; assure access to raw materials; bring about abatement of national hatreds; solve problems of language and race.

Trusteeship to continue until Commission evolves just set of peace specifications or until problems have solved themselves. Then final treaties are to be negotiated, the Commission discharged, and the trusteeship terminated.

TERRITORIAL CHANGES:
The United States is to acquire by negotiation, purchase, or force:
1. Islands in Pacific for naval bases, flying fields, fortresses.
2. Dakar and Casablanca.
3. Permanent naval and air bases on Iceland and Greenland.
4. Enlarged base on Bermuda.
5. Islands of Caribbean Sea.
6. Secure cession of territories to United States or to South American nations of land still owned in Western Hemisphere by European nations.

PART III

THEORETICAL PLANS

CHARTS OF PLANS TO UNITE NATIONS SINCE 1914

E. Court Plans
ADVISORY DISARMAMENT CONFERENCE
INTERNATIONAL AIR FORCE

"At the end of this war we must either throw the full weight of American influence to the support of an international order based on law, or we must outstrip the world in naval and air, and perhaps in military force. No reservation to a treaty can let us have our cake and eat it too."
ROBERT H. JACKSON, Indianapolis, October 2, 1941.

... "The Soviet Government considers it necessary that any one of the leaders of fascist Germany who in the course of the war already has fallen into the hands of authorities of states fighting against Hitlerite Germany be brought to trial without delay before a special international tribunal and punished with all the severity of criminal law."
VYACHESLAFF MOLOTOV, Moscow, October 14, 1942.

... "I think myself, being a warm partisan of the whole conception of international justice, it would be most unwise to treat a court, however independent, as specially qualified to solve what are really political problems."
VISCOUNT SIMON, Great Britain; London, August 5, 1942.

ADVISORY DISARMAMENT CONFERENCE
INTERNATIONAL AIR FORCE

WHILE many writers urge the establishment of some kind of world court, with power to make and enforce political decisions, few of them work out their proposals in detail.

Dyruff's plan for a *Court of Arbitration and Justice,* and Sells' plan for a *World Tribunal* are drafted with considerable care. Both would equip the Court with military force to compel observance of its decisions. Dyruff, seeking a method to end the first phase of the World War (1915) without military victory, worked out a detailed schedule for separate war-time and peace-time organization of the Court. He assigned representation to both belligerent groups and to all neutrals in a manner calculated to prevent either belligerent from having a preponderant voice in the Court's decisions settling the issues of the war. Armed forces at the disposal of the Court were to be contributed permanently by the member nations. The Court was to have authority to punish both nations and individuals for violation of its decrees. While all nations and individuals were to break all contact with a nation being disciplined by the Court, the Court itself was to supply the recalcitrant nation with food and other necessities.

Sells' plan also provided for a permanent grant of armed forces to the Tribunal and suggested an interesting method of financing the Court to make it independent of the supporting nations within twenty-five years.

Both plans actually endow the Court with *legislative* functions, for it is empowered to make and enforce what are really political and not judicial decisions.

De Baer's draft of a *United Nations Criminal Court for the Trial of Persons Accused of War Crimes* is in Part III-B, The United Nations.

World judicial bodies already in existence are described in other sections: the *Permanent Court of Arbitration* in Part IV; the *Permanent Court of International Justice* in Part V.

The American Unofficial Committee on Disarmament, under the chairmanship of Dr. Shotwell, proposed an autonomous, permanent Disarmament Conference. It would utilize both the League Council and the Permanent Court of International Justice to assist in enforcing obligations assumed by the nations under the proposed Treaty.

Proposals for an international armed force are presented in considerable detail in many of the charted plans. The New Commonwealth Institute is one of its most persistent advocates. The suggested *International Air Force,* under the direction of a Board of Control, High Command, and Judicial Board, was drafted before the present war and conceived as limited at first to Europe.

AUTHOR:
H. Francis Dyruff (American).

PROFESSION:
Attorney.

TITLE OF PLAN:
A Suggested Basis upon Which to Form an International Court of Arbitration with a View to Ending the Present War in Europe, and to Prevent in Future All Similar Conflicts. (Together with a suggested basis of representation at the outset, and also for normal times after the present conflict has been arbitrated and settled.)

Submitted to the Ford Neutral Conference for Continuous Mediation.

MANUSCRIPT

DATE: January, 1915.

TYPE:
Court provided with military force.

MEMBERSHIP:
About twenty-five nations: the belligerents and neutrals of the first World War.

ORGANS OF GOVERNMENT:
International Court of Arbitration and Justice: Each representative on the Court to have one vote; salary and expenses of representatives paid

Charts of Plans to Unite Nations Since 1914

by nations represented; representatives must be second generation native-born citizens of nation they represent; sixty per cent from each nation must be recognized lawyers. *Decisions:* By sixty per cent vote of the total membership; amendment of Court's rules and laws only by seventy-five per cent vote of total membership. (Until Court adopts own rules, it is to be governed as far as practicable by rules in use in United States Senate.) *Presiding Justice:* To be elected by membership; rules on admission or non-admission of evidence, subject to appeal to vote of Court whenever requested by a member.

Seat of the Court: A neutral place in the Western Hemisphere selected by it; land to be purchased providing absolute control and permanent sovereignty of surrounding territory and waters for one hundred miles in all directions.

Member nations and number of representatives on Court:

Nation	Preliminary Representation		Permanent Representation
ALLIES:			
England	3		10
France	3		10
Greece	1	Allies 16 votes	2
Russia	3		10
Japan	2		5
Belgium	2		5
Serbia	1		2
Roumania	1		2
ENTENTE:			
Germany	7		10
Austria-Hungary	6	Entente 16 votes	10
Turkey	2		5
Bulgaria	1		2
INTERESTED SEMI-NEUTRALS:			
Italy	3	Semi-neutrals 4 votes	10
Portugal	1		5

PROXIMATE NEUTRALS:

Norway	2		5
Sweden	2	Proximate neutrals	5
Holland	2	12 votes	5
Denmark	2		5
Spain	2		10
Switzerland	2		5

AMERICAN NEUTRALS:

Brazil	6		5
Argentina	3	American neutrals	2
Chile	3	35 votes	2
Bolivia	3		2
United States	20		10

Total 83

Total Votes of Preliminary Court: 83; *Votes necessary to block any decision:* 34.

Method of Appointment: Depending on the number of representatives allotted each nation, representatives to be appointed by the following national bodies in the order given: the lower legislative body; the upper legislative body; the Cabinet, the Ruler or President and Cabinet; the Ruler or President. (In the United States a certain number of the representatives to be elected by the Governors of the several states by majority vote.)

TRANSFERS OF JURISDICTION FROM MEMBER NATIONS TO THE PRELIMINARY COURT:

Full power to arbitrate, hear, and determine all questions, claims, or controversies that arise out of the European conflict, and to enforce its decrees.

Full power to pass upon and enforce its decrees as to the rights, claims, requests for damages of all neutral nations (or of their citizens, made through their executive departments).

RESTRICTION:

May not award any European or American territory to any nation not contiguous to the territory awarded.

SUPPORT:
Specific sums assessed each member nation by the Court payable yearly in advance. Court may levy special assessments to cover deficits.

PERMANENT COURT:
Power to prescribe rules of future admission of nations to membership, except that every rule adopted on membership must be by vote of seventy-five per cent of the total membership.

When invoked by member nation involved in war with non-member nations, Court has right to act as if all nations involved were members of the Court. But nations may not become members of the Court (after its permanent organization) during the time matters in which they are involved are before the Court.

NATIONS UNDERTAKE:
Each member nation to contribute permanently twenty per cent of its total armed forces of every category (land, naval, and air) fully equipped and manned (except that the armed forces contributed by a nation against whom a decree is to be enforced are to be disarmed and interned for the period of enforcement).

METHODS OF ENFORCEMENT:
Towards Member and Non-Member Nations: Whenever the Court declares its intention to proceed against any nation or nations for disobedience of its decrees, no nation or citizen of any nation may furnish the disobedient nation with any supplies whatsoever. The Court to have full power to punish *both nations and individuals* who break this provision. *But it is the duty of the Court to supply food and other necessities to the peaceful, civilian population of the disobedient nation.*

IMMEDIATE STEPS:
Upon ratification of the Articles establishing the Court, there shall be an *immediate declaration of a truce;* nations entitled to representation to select their representatives.

Court to convene immediately, decide on regular place of meeting, assess member nations their quota of money and armed forces of all categories to be placed at its disposal.

All belligerent nations to return as far as possible to normal conditions, *holding occupied territory until Court's final decision,* but withdrawing all armed forces except garrisons. Thereafter any acts of war to be punished by the Court.

RATIFICATION:
By signing of Articles by Austria-Hungary, France, Germany, Great Britain, Holland, Italy, Russia, and the United States.

MISCELLANEOUS:
The author sought the support of statesmen with the power to bring about acceptance of this plan, rather than popular support. He sent out thousands of copies to the heads of governments, cabinet ministers, legislators, educators all over the world.

AUTHOR:
ELIJAH W. SELLS (American).

PROFESSION:
Certified Public Accountant.

TITLE OF PLAN:
A Plan for International Peace.

PAMPHLET

DATE: 1915.
(In 1924 included in the author's "The Natural Business Year and Thirteen Other Themes.")

TYPE:
Tribunal provided with military force.

MEMBERSHIP:
Worldwide: About fifty-nine nations and their dependencies.

ORGANS OF GOVERNMENT:
Congress of the Peace Tribunal: About seventy-five members.

1 representative from each nation with 25 million or less population.
2 representatives from each nation with 25 to 100 million population.
3 representatives from each nation with 100 to 250 million population.
4 representatives from each nation with population over 250 million.

Representatives appointed or elected by every nation for one-year terms, subject to reelection for three consecutive years; after lapse of one year again eligible for election or appointment.

Powers: Authority to settle differences between nations; to enforce decisions after due notice given; power to suppress hostilities between nations and compel them to submit differences to Tribunal.

Appoints three departments from its own members:

Judiciary; Civil Commission; Armament Commission.
May remove member of any department on proper charges.

Judiciary: Hears arguments and adjudicates all international disputes; compels appearance of disputants; members of the Court representing nations involved as disputants, not to participate in the case.

Civil Commission: Chairman, Secretary, Treasurer, Comptroller.
Duties: Administers civil affairs of Tribunal. *Decisions:* By majority vote.

Armament Commission: Directs military measures imposed by Tribunal; organizes two general staffs of nine members each (no two members to be from the same nation); one staff for land, the other, for naval operations. *Decisions:* By majority vote.
If the decision to go to war against a nation has to be made, the Civil and Armament Commissions to meet in joint session, with the Chairman of the Civil Commission presiding. Members of the offending nations not to participate. *Decisions:* By majority vote.

TRANSFERS OF JURISDICTION FROM MEMBER NATIONS TO THE TRIBUNAL:
Nations to transfer all warships and equipment to the Tribunal; discontinue navy yards and similar establishments except those necessary to supply Tribunal; reduction of all armies to fifty per cent of size in peace time; armed forces not to exceed one-twentieth of one per cent of nation's population; similar reduction in production of military equipment.

364   Theoretical Plans

Nations appropriate for twenty-five years for support of Tribunal one-third of average annual expenditures for army and navy for previous five years; amounts to be paid to Treasurer of Tribunal. Tribunal to spend only fifty per cent of receipts each year; surplus to be invested in bonds of member nations until the interest yield supports the Tribunal without further contributions from the nations.

AUTHOR:
AMERICAN UNOFFICIAL COMMITTEE ON DISARMAMENT; Chairman, JAMES T. SHOTWELL (American).

PROFESSION (of Chairman):
Professor of History, Director Carnegie Endowment for International Peace.

TITLE OF PLAN:
Draft Treaty of Disarmament and Security from *On the Rim of the Abyss*.

DATE: 1924 and 1936.

PUBLISHER:
The Macmillan Co., New York.

TYPE:
CONFEDERATE special conference. NAME: Draft Treaty of Disarmament and Security.

MEMBERSHIP:
UNIVERSAL: Members and non-members of the League of Nations may ratify the Treaty.

ORGANS OF GOVERNMENT:
LEGISLATIVE: *Permanent Advisory Conference Upon Disarmament:* Sessions once in three years. *Duties:* To codify international law relating to preparation for and acts of aggression; to publish periodic reports on armaments of member nations; to advise member nations on measures to be taken to carry out purposes of Treaty; to prepare

Charts of Plans to Unite Nations Since 1914   365

supplementary treaties establishing demilitarized zones and to promote disarmament and peace; to advise Permanent Court of International Justice on Court's request.

Permanent Technical Committee: To advise Permanent Court of International Justice on technical questions on Court's request.

EXECUTIVE OR ADMINISTRATIVE:

Council of the League of Nations (See: p. 421): *Duties:* To determine on request of a member nation whether a signatory nation has exceeded its armament limitation, whether its military or other preparations cause fear of aggression or may lead to hostilities. *Jurisdiction:* If Council decides danger of aggression exists, member nations may carry out provisions of existing mutual-assistance pacts. If Council finds no danger of aggression, member nations are under no obligation to render assistance, but nation which continues to feel itself menaced, despite Council's decision, may freely prepare its own defense, subject to limitations of treaties in force and obligation to notify Council of its intentions.

Commission of Inquiry: Acting under direction of Council. *Duties:* To make official examinations and reports on national military, naval, and air programs with the right of investigation within territory of member nations.

JUDICIAL:

Permanent Court of International Justice (See: p. 422): To determine on complaint of a member nation whether aggression has been committed; to determine whether international law has been violated by acts of aggression or preparation for them even if war does not result.

Court to have *compulsory jurisdiction* over any dispute arising under this Treaty with the right to determine whether it has jurisdiction and whether its decrees have been carried out.

TRANSFERS OF JURISDICTION FROM SIGNATORY NATIONS TO THE CONFERENCE, LEAGUE COUNCIL, AND COURT:
To codify international law relating to aggression.
To publish reports on armaments of signatory nations.
To prepare supplementary treaties.
To determine whether aggression has been committed.

NATIONS UNDERTAKE:
   Not to engage in aggressive war.
   To limit or reduce their armaments to the point needed to maintain peace and national security.
   To study the possibilities of future bilateral or multilateral reduction of armaments.
   To assist Commission of Inquiry on Armament in its work.
   To submit charges of violation of this Treaty to the Permanent Court of International Justice and to accept its decision on fulfillment or violation of Treaty.
   To support the Permanent Advisory Conference Upon Disarmament in proportion to national military budgets.

NATIONS RETAIN:
   Right to negotiate bilateral and multilateral mutual assistance and defense treaties consistent with this Treaty.
   Right to withdraw from Conference after one year's notice to Secretary General of League.
   Right to use force for purposes of defense or for protection of human life.
   Right to determine measures breaking off commercial, financial, and personal intercourse with an aggressor nation and its nationals, and use of military force against the aggressor according to their own interests and obligations.

METHODS OF ENFORCEMENT:

Aggression to Constitute: Use of military force by land, sea, or air against another nation (except during a state of war, in defense, or to protect human life); and refusal to submit to jurisdiction of Court within four days of charge of violation of Treaty.

Mandatory Enforcement: Signatory nations to withdraw privileges, protection, rights, and immunities granted under international or national law or treaty in their territories or on the high seas to commercial, financial, and property interests of signatory nation or its citizens judged an aggressor by the Court.

Voluntary Enforcement: Signatory nations may take additional measures to end commercial, financial, and personal intercourse with aggressor and its nationals, as well as military action.

Nation adjudged an aggressor by Court to be liable to pay full indemnity to other signatory nations for all damages resulting from its aggression.

RATIFICATION:
In Europe: By five nations including France, Great Britain, and Italy.
In Asia: By two nations including Japan.
In North America: By the United States of America.
In Central America and the West Indies: By one West Indian and two Central American nations.
In South America: By four nations, one of them Argentina, Brazil, or Chile.
In Africa and Oceania*: By two nations.

MISCELLANEOUS:
In March, 1919, Dr. Shotwell suggested to the Paris Peace Conference an amendment to the League Covenant providing for *associate status* for nations not members of the League to enable them to participate in periodic conferences dealing with specific matters of international interest. His proposal was not accepted.

* Lands of the Central Pacific Ocean including Melanesia, Polynesia, Australia, New Zealand, and the Malay Archipelago.

AUTHOR:
MILITARY RESEARCH COMMITTEE OF THE NEW COMMONWEALTH INSTITUTE (English).

TITLE OF PLAN:
Air Force for the Peace Front.

PAMPHLET

DATE: 1939.

PUBLISHER:
The Peace Book Co., London.

Theoretical Plans

ORGANIZATIONAL BAC┄┄┄:
The New Commonwealth, London.

TYPE:
International Air Force.
  NAMES: International Strategic Reserve. International Force.

MEMBERSHIP:
Probably limited to Europe in the beginning.

ORGANS OF GOVERNMENT:
LEGISLATIVE: *Board of Control:* One delegate from each member nation with full power to act. *Decisions:* By majority vote.
  Duties: To confirm appointments; validate regulations; pass budget; control funds.

EXECUTIVE OR ADMINISTRATIVE:
The High Command: To be recruited in the beginning from trained officers of member nations. *Duties:* Directs Air Force.

Supply Corporation: Established by Board of Control. *Duties:* To supply Air Force; may engage in production of supplies or secure them from manufacturing firms of all nations. Empowered to sue and to represent the Air Force in suits brought against it.

Design Department: To prepare designs of aircraft and to place contracts.

Research Department. Inspection Department. Intelligence Service.

┄┄┄ *Schools:* Candidates free to choose short-term service or ┄┄┄ent with pe┄┄┄ ghts, marriage allowances, and other ┄┄┄. Voluntary ┄┄┄ents with safeguard against disproportionate enlistment f┄┄┄ one nation. Permission to enlist to be ┄n by national gov┄ents releasing candidates from national ┄ilitary service. *Privileges:* Possession of special international passright of citizenship in any member nation. Candidates to be ┄een the ages of eighteen to thirty.

┄┄ *Board:* Two-year term; four members, two to be renewed each ┄ear. First four members appointed by first four member nations in

To secure and maintain equitable treatment of commerce of all League members.
To endeavor to take steps for prevention and control of disease.
To encourage and promote voluntary national Red Cross organizations to improve health, prevent disease, and mitigate suffering.

NATIONS RETAIN:
Right to withdraw from League after two years' notice provided all international obligations have been fulfilled at time of withdrawal.
Right to request meeting of Council in case of aggression or danger of aggression.
Right to call attention of Assembly or Council to matters affecting international relations, threatening peace, or good understanding between nations.
Right to continue treaties of arbitration and regional understandings like the Monroe Doctrine.

METHODS OF ENFORCEMENT:
Towards Member Nations: Disputes between member nations not settled by arbitration may be submitted to Council by either party to the dispute. Statements of both sides to be published by the Council together with terms of settlement brought about by Council. (Disputes found to arise out of matters within national jurisdiction of either party excepted.)
If dispute is not settled, Council by unanimous or majority vote to publish facts of dispute and its recommendations for settlement.
If Council report is unanimous: member nations *agree not to go to war with nation complying with Council's recommendations. If Council report is not unanimous:* member nations to decide their own course of action.
Disputes referred by Council to decision of Assembly require vote of all representatives of nations on Council and majority vote of representatives of other member nations, parties to the dispute excepted.
If a member nation resorts to war in disregard of arbitral award or Council's recommendations, or before expiration of time limit set for inquiry, all other member nations to break all trade, financial relations, and intercourse with warring nation. *Council to recommend to the governments concerned* size of military and naval forces to be contributed to protect covenants.

Towards Non-Member Nations: In disputes between League member and non-member or between two non-members, non-member to be invited to join League for settlement of dispute by arbitration or by Council. If membership refused and war waged on League member, sanctions and military action to be applied.

If both nations are non-members and refuse temporary League membership, Council may try to prevent hostilities and settle dispute.

IMMEDIATE STEPS:

President of *Commission on the Formation of a League of Nations* of the Peace Conference to invite seven Powers including two neutrals to name representatives to a Committee with the following duties:

1. To prepare plans for organization of the League.
2. To prepare plans for establishment of seat of League.
3. To prepare agenda for first Assembly meeting.

Committee to report to first Council and Assembly.

RATIFICATION:

By original members listed in Annex to Covenant: By signing Treaty of Peace.

By neutral nations invited to accede without reservation: By depositing a *Declaration of Accession* with the League Secretariat two months after Covenant comes into force.

Other self-governing nations, dominions, and colonies may become members by two-thirds vote of the Assembly.

AMENDMENT:

Ratification by governments of nations represented on the Council and by majority of governments represented on the Assembly.

Amendments binding on nations ratifying them; those dissenting cease to be League members.

TITLE:
The International Labor Organization.

DATE: 1919.

SOURCE:
The United States in the International Labor Organization by Ethel M. Johnson, Washington Branch of I. L. O., Washington, D. C., 1939.

TYPE:
CONFEDERATE specialized agency.

MEMBERSHIP:
Fifty-four Nations.

ORGANS OF GOVERNMENT:

LEGISLATIVE: *International Labor Conference:* Four delegates from each member nation: Two representing the government; one representing principal association of employers; one representing principal association of labor. Annual sessions. *Conventions* adopted by two-thirds vote; then submitted to member governments for ratification; ratified conventions registered with League of Nations. *Recommendations* made by majority vote — suggest enactment of national legislation and regulation. *Duties:* To discuss proposals for draft conventions; to recommend national legislative action.

EXECUTIVE OR ADMINISTRATIVE:

Governing Body: Thirty-two members — Eight represent governments of the chief industrial nations; eight elected by Conference for three-year term; eight elected by employer delegates to Conference; eight elected by worker delegates to Conference. Sessions four times a year, usually in Geneva, occasionally in some other country. *Duties:* Elects Director; formulates general policies for Office; prepares agenda for International Labor Conference.

International Labor Office: Permanent secretariat of Governing Body and of International Labor Conference; personnel about 400 representing about forty nationalities. Official languages: French and English. *Duties:* To prepare material for use of Governing Body, International Labor Conference, and committees; execute their decisions; collect and disseminate current information on labor, economic, and industrial problems, regulation of hours of employment, methods of wage payment, technological causes of unemployment, problems of migratory labor, industrial technology and safety, social insurance systems, scientific management; publish economic and technical periodicals, bulletins, analysis of labor laws.

Correspondence Committees: Advisory groups whose members do not meet but are consulted by Office for information and advice.

Permanent Technical Committees, such as Permanent Agricultural Committee to advise Conference on agricultural labor; International Public Works Committee to provide continuous exchange of information and experience on advance planning of public works to reduce depressions and prevent unemployment.

Preliminary Technical Conferences: To advise Governing Body on matters to come before Conference.

JUDICIAL:
Commission of Inquiry: Nominated by member nations, except those directly concerned in the complaint. *Jurisdiction:* Over complaints of non-observance of conventions brought by employers' organizations or member nations. Publication of findings and recommendations.

As a last resort, member's non-compliance may be brought before the Permanent Court of International Justice.

OBJECTIVES OF THE INTERNATIONAL LABOR ORGANIZATION:

Right of association of employed and employers.
Payment of adequate wages to maintain a reasonable standard of life.
Adoption of eight-hour day and forty-eight-hour week.
Weekly rest of at least twenty-four hours.
Abolition of child labor; limitation on work of young persons to permit continuation of education and proper physical development.
Men and women to receive equal pay for work of equal value.
Equitable economic treatment of all workers lawfully resident within a country.
Provision of national system of inspection with women participating to ensure enforcement of laws and regulations protecting employed.

NATIONS UNDERTAKE:

To pay expenses of International Labor Organization in proportion to their size and industrial importance.

Charts of Confederate & Federal Constitutions

To implement ratified conventions by enacting legislation.

To submit annual report to International Labor Office on measures taken to implement conventions.

To submit draft conventions to their appropriate legislative authority within twelve and at most eighteen months after adoption by International Labor Conference.

Nations may request technical assistance on labor legislation and labor-law administration, and borrow experts of International Labor Office.

MISCELLANEOUS:

The International Labor Conference adopted sixty-seven conventions by June, 1939, dealing with fifty-nine subjects such as minimum age for employment of children, regulation of hours of work, weekly rest periods, employment on public works, unemployment, social insurance, industrial accidents, occupational diseases, etc.

TITLE:
Constitution of the Argentine Republic.

DATE: September 25, 1860.

SOURCE:
The Federal System of the Argentine Republic by L. S. Rowe, Carnegie Institution of Washington, 1921.

TYPE:
FEDERAL. NAMES USED:
  The United Provinces of the Rio de La Plata.
  The Argentine Republic.
  The Argentine Confederation.
  The Argentine Nation (to be used in enactment and approval of laws).

MEMBERSHIP:
Fourteen Provinces; one Federal District; ten Federal Territories.

ORGANS OF GOVERNMENT:
LEGISLATIVE: Bicameral *Congress: House of Deputies; House of Senators.*

House of Deputies: Four-year term; eligible for reelection; half the membership renewed every two years; one Deputy for every 33,000 inhabitants or fraction of not less than 16,500. Deputies must be at least twenty-five years old; native or naturalized four years; resident of province two years before election; election regulated by Congress (first direct election under the Constitution was regulated by the provincial legislatures). Vacancies to be filled by election of a new Deputy. *Exclusive Powers:* To initiate legislation on taxation, recruiting of troops; to impeach, before the Senate, the President, the Vice-President, Ministers, Justices of the Supreme Court, and Judges of the inferior courts for misconduct or crime in office or for ordinary offenses by two-thirds vote of Deputies present.

Senate: Nine-year term; Senators may be reelected indefinitely; elected by plurality vote of the provincial legislatures (two Senators for the Federal District elected in the same manner as the President); Senators must be at least thirty years old; citizens six years with annual income of 2,000 pesos or equivalent amount of capital; native or two years resident in the province electing them; one-third of the Senate renewed every three years. Vacancies must be filled immediately by the provincial legislature.

Vice-President: President of the Senate; may vote only in case of tie; Senate may elect President Pro Tempore in Vice-President's absence.

Exclusive Rights of Senate: To try persons impeached by the House of Deputies (when President is tried, President of Supreme Court presides over Senate); two-thirds vote of members present required for conviction; may authorize President to declare state of siege in case of foreign invasion.

Miscellaneous: Laws may originate in either House introduced by the members or by the Executive; no member of a religious order may be elected to Congress; a provincial governor may not represent his province during his term of office; each House may request information and explanations from the Ministers.

EXECUTIVE OR ADMINISTRATIVE:

President of the Argentine Nation: Six-year term; may not be reelected for term immediately following; must be native-born, or if born on foreign soil, the son of a native citizen; must be Roman Catholic and have all other qualifications for Senator.

Charts of Confederate & Federal Constitutions

Method of Election of President and Vice-President: The Federal District and each of the provinces elect by direct vote an Electoral College of twice their representation in Congress; Electors to have qualifications for Deputies, and elected in the same manner; Deputies, Senators, officials of the Federal Government ineligible.

Four months before President's term expires, Electors meet in their respective capitals and vote by separate signed ballot for President and Vice-President. Two lists made of persons voted for President and those voted for Vice-President; one set of lists sent to President of the provincial legislature; other set to the President of the Senate. Lists opened before joint session of Congress; those receiving an absolute majority of the votes for President and Vice-President are elected; if none receives such majority, Congress by majority vote elects the President and Vice-President from the two candidates with the highest votes; at least three-fourths of all members of Congress must be present.

Duties of the President: Enforces and executes the laws of the nation; appoints, with advice of Senate, Justices of the Supreme Court and of the inferior federal courts; with advice of Senate appoints and removes diplomatic officials; appoints and removes ministers of state, officials of the department, consular agents, and government employees not otherwise appointed. Selects bishops for the cathedrals from three names proposed by the Senate; with advice of the Supreme Court may grant or refuse passage to decrees of the councils, bulls, briefs, and rescripts of the Vatican, but grant or refusal must be enacted into law if they contain provisions of a general or permanent character. Opens and may extend regular sessions of Congress; convenes extraordinary sessions; reports to Congress on state of the nation, on reforms promised by the Constitution; makes recommendations; negotiates and signs treaties of peace, commerce, navigation, alliances, boundaries, concordat, neutrality; receives ministers and ambassadors. Commander-in-chief of all land and naval forces; declares war with approval of Congress; may declare state of siege with consent of the Senate in one or more places in case of foreign invasion. If internal trouble occurs during a recess of Congress, President may alone declare state of siege suspending constitutional guarantees, but he may not condemn anyone or inflict punishments; may merely arrest or exile individuals from one part of the country to another if they refuse to leave national territory entirely; may fill vacancies requiring Senate consent during recess of Congress, but such appointments expire at close of next session.

President may not leave the national capital without permission of Congress unless grave necessity demands it during recess.

Secretaries of State: Eight; head the executive departments; appointed and removable by the President; must countersign all Presidential acts; report to Congress on opening of each session on state of nation and work of each department; may attend sessions of Congress and participate in debate but not vote; may not become Senators or Deputies unless they have first resigned their office.

JUDICIAL:

Supreme Court of Justice: Justices appointed by President with advice of Senate; hold office during good behavior; must be lawyers with eight years' practice in national courts and have qualifications required for Senators.

Jurisdiction: In cases concerning foreign ambassadors, ministers, and consuls; cases to which a province is party, or its citizens and a foreign state; controversies to which nation is party or between citizens of different provinces.

Inferior Courts: Established by Congress.

TRANSFERS OF JURISDICTION FROM MEMBER PROVINCES TO THE REPUBLIC:

To declare war and make peace.

To fix the strength of the armed forces; call out the militia of the provinces to help execute the laws, suppress insurrection, and repel invasion.

To guarantee to each province enjoyment and exercise of its institutions; to intervene in the provincial territory to guarantee republican forms of government and to repel foreign invasion; and, when requested by the provincial authorities, to maintain them in power or to reestablish them if deposed by sedition or by invasion from another province.

To admit new provinces into the nation; but no new province may be formed from the territory of another, nor two or more provinces

Charts of Confederate & Federal Constitutions

formed into one without consent of the legislatures concerned and Congress.

To settle the national boundaries and fix those of the provinces.

To establish freedom of commerce and movement of goods throughout the nation.

To levy import and export duties and direct taxes; to borrow money.

To operate the postal service.

To encourage European immigration; Congress may not restrict, limit, or obstruct by taxation the entrance of foreigners coming to cultivate the soil, engage in industry, or introduce and teach arts and sciences.

To regulate conditions of naturalization and citizenship.

To promote establishment of trial by jury.

To provide for use and disposition of national lands.

To establish a Federal Bank with branches in the provinces.

To regulate navigation of rivers; to establish or abolish customs houses.

To coin money, regulate its value, and that of foreign currency.

To establish uniform system of weights and measures.

To enact civil, commercial, penal, and mining codes without encroaching on local jurisdiction.

To regulate commerce with foreign nations and among the provinces.

The constitution, national laws, and treaties are the supreme law of the land.

RESTRICTIONS ON THE PROVINCES:

Provincial constitutions must be republican, representative, and provide for administration of justice and primary instruction.

Extradition of criminals obligatory for all provinces.

DEMOCRATIC RIGHTS:

Citizens of each province to enjoy rights, privileges, immunities of citizens of the other provinces.

Right to work, engage in industry, commerce; freedom of movement, press, association, religion, teaching and study; and right to petition the authorities.

Freedom from slavery; slaves entering the national territory become free; their owners to be compensated according to law.

Equality before the law, for taxation and all public burdens.

Private property may not be confiscated for crime nor requisitions made by any armed force; condemnation of property for public purpose to be authorized by law and indemnity paid.

Death penalty for political offenses, torture, and whipping abolished. No ex post facto laws.

Trial by jury for ordinary crimes in the province where committed. Right to fair trial under established law and before the regular courts; security against arrest except on a warrant from proper authority; inviolability of private correspondence and papers except in circumstances determined by law.

Aliens to enjoy all civil rights of citizens; may not be compelled to become citizens or forced to pay extraordinary taxes; naturalization after two years' consecutive residence (or less for services rendered the Republic); naturalized citizens free to render or to refuse military service during ten years following their naturalization.

Rights and guarantees naturally derived from principles of the sovereignty of the people and of the republican form of government are retained by the people even if not enumerated.

RESTRICTIONS:

Every Argentine citizen obliged to bear arms in defense of the country and constitution (naturalized citizens excepted for ten-year period).

The Federal Government supports the Roman Catholic religion. (The object of this custom, surviving from colonial times, was to curb the power of the Church in political affairs.—Editors.)

METHODS OF ENFORCEMENT:

Hostilities on the part of one province against another shall be considered an act of civil war to be suppressed by the Federal Government.

Governors of the provinces are also agents of the Federal Government for the enforcement of the Constitution and the national laws.

AMENDMENT:

Need for amendment of Constitution must be declared by Congress by two-thirds vote, but the amendment itself must be made by Convention called for the purpose as prescribed by Congress.

Charts of Confederate & Federal Constitutions

MISCELLANEOUS:
Since June 4, 1943, the Argentine Republic is ruled by a small group of officers who overthrew the government of Acting President Ramon S. Castillo. Technically the Constitution is still in effect, but actually there is no Congress.

TITLE:
Constitution of the United States of America.

DATE:
March 4, 1789, with amendments.

SOURCE:
Documents Illustrative of the Formation of the Union of the American States, Government Printing Office, Washington, 1927.

TYPE:
FEDERAL. NAME: United States of America.

MEMBERSHIP:
Forty-eight States; one Federal District; two Federal Territories; eight Dependencies.

ORGANS OF GOVERNMENT:
LEGISLATIVE: Bicameral *Congress: Senate; House of Representatives.*

Senate: Ninety-six members, six-year term; two Senators from each State; direct election by persons qualified to vote for the most numerous branch of the State Legislatures; one-third of the Senate renewed every two years. *Qualifications:* At least thirty years old; nine years a citizen; inhabitant of the State from which elected. Vacancies may be filled by special election or by temporary appointment by the State Executive. *Presiding Officer:* The Vice-President of the United States; votes only in case of tie. *Duties:* Approves or rejects by two-thirds vote treaties negotiated by the President; consents to Presidential appointment of ambassadors, judges, and other federal officials. Has sole power to try impeachments. When the President is tried, the Chief Justice of the Supreme Court presides.

House of Representatives: 435 members, two-year term; representatives apportioned according to population; direct election by persons qualified to vote for the most numerous branch of the State Legislatures. Chooses Speaker and other officers. *Duties:* Sole power of impeachment by two-thirds vote of those present; revenue legislation must originate in House. *Qualifications:* At least twenty-five years old; seven years a citizen; inhabitant of the State represented.

Congress meets in January of each year; each House judge of election and qualification of its own members. *Quorum:* A majority of the members of each House. Each body determines its own procedure; may expel a member by two-thirds vote; two-thirds vote of both Houses required to override Presidential veto. No person holding any other office under the United States may be a member of either House.

EXECUTIVE OR ADMINISTRATIVE:

President and Vice-President: Four-year term; native-born; at least thirty-five years old; fourteen years resident in United States.

Method of Election: Election of the President and Vice-President by an Electoral College, as prescribed in the Constitution, is no longer applied in practice; candidates for President and Vice-President are nominated by the political parties; each party in the State also nominates electors equal in number to the State's representation in Congress; the popular vote for the parties' candidates for President and Vice-President determines which slate of electors wins in the State; the affirmation of the popular vote by the Electoral College survives as a custom.

Duties of President: Commander-in-chief of the army and navy, and of State militias when in the actual service of the United States; grants reprieves and pardons; negotiates treaties with advice and consent of Senate; appoints, with consent of Senate, ambassadors, public ministers, and consuls; judges of the Supreme Court and other officers not otherwise appointed; may fill vacancies when Senate is recessed until the next session (In practice, the President appoints the heads of the executive departments who form his Cabinet and are responsible only to him.—EDITORS); reports to Congress on state of Union; recommends measures to Congress; may convene extraordinary sessions of Congress; receives foreign ambassadors and other public ministers; sees that the laws are faithfully executed; commissions federal officers;

Charts of Confederate & Federal Constitutions 437

approves or vetoes legislation within ten working days, otherwise it becomes law without his signature.

Vice-President: Presides over the Senate; assumes presidency in the event of President's death, resignation, or other inability to discharge his duties.

President, Vice-President and all civil officers of the United States may be removed from office on impeachment and conviction for treason, bribery, or other high crimes and misdemeanors.

Judicial:

Supreme Court: Nine Justices; appointed by President with consent of Senate; one of them serves as Chief Justice.

Federal District Courts, and inferior courts established by Congress.
Jurisdiction: Over all cases arising under the Constitution, laws of the United States, and treaties; cases affecting ambassadors, public ministers, and consuls; admiralty and maritime jurisdiction; cases to which the United States is party; between two or more States; between citizens of the same State claiming lands under grant from different States; between citizens of a State and foreign states, citizens, or subjects.

TRANSFERS OF JURISDICTION FROM MEMBER STATES TO THE UNION:

The Constitution and federal laws are the supreme law of the land; judges in all States are bound by them, provisions in State Constitutions and laws notwithstanding.

Levy and collect uniform taxes, duties, and taxes on income.

Borrow money.

Provide for the general welfare.

Regulate commerce with foreign nations and between the States.

Provide for the common defense; raise and support armies; provide and maintain a navy; regulate the organization, arming, and discipline of state militias, calling on them to help execute the laws of the Union, suppress insurrections, repel invasions.

Declare war; conclude peace.

Provide uniform currency, regulate its value and that of foreign exchange.

Take the census.

Fix standard of weights and measures; provide patents and copyrights.
Govern the federal district, territories, and properties.
Admit new states into the Union.
Guarantee every State a republican form of government.
Protect States from invasion, and, on application of their Legislature or Executive, from domestic violence.

RESTRICTIONS ON THE FEDERAL GOVERNMENT:
No export duty may be levied on articles from any State.
No preference may be given to the ports of one State over those of another.

STATES RETAIN:
Powers not delegated to the Federal Government nor prohibited to States are reserved to the States respectively or to the people.
Right to appoint officers of the militia and to train it according to regulations prescribed by Congress.
States may not be deprived of territory or joined with other States without the consent of the respective legislatures as well as of Congress.

OBLIGATIONS AND RESTRICTIONS ON THE STATES:
Full faith and credit shall be given in each State to the public acts, records, and judicial proceedings of every other State.
Citizens of each State entitled to privileges and immunities of citizens in every other State.
Extradition of persons charged with treason or crime.
States may not enter into treaty, alliance, or confederation, coin money, pass retroactive laws, levy import and export duties except when necessary to execute State inspection laws, subject to revision and control of Congress.
No State may keep troops or warships or engage in war unless actually invaded or in imminent danger.
No State may abridge the privileges or immunities of citizens of the United States, nor deprive any person of life, liberty, or property without due process of law, nor deny any person within its jurisdiction equal protection of the laws.

When the right to vote in federal or State elections is denied by a State to any of its citizens over twenty-one years of age for any reason, except participation in rebellion or other crime, the representation of such State in Congress is to be reduced proportionately.

DEMOCRATIC RIGHTS AND RESTRICTIONS ON THE FEDERAL GOVERNMENT:

Freedom of religion, speech, and press; right of peaceful assembly; right of petition for redress of grievances.

No religious test shall be required as qualification to any office under the United States.

Security against unreasonable searches and seizures.

No one may be deprived of life, liberty, or property without due process of law; no one may be compelled to be a witness against himself, nor twice to be put in jeopardy for the same offense.

Private property may not be taken for public use without just compensation.

Right to speedy and public trial by jury in criminal prosecutions, to information as to nature of the accusation, to be confronted with witnesses, to obtain witnesses in his favor, to be defended by counsel.

Security against excessive bail and fine, and against cruel and unusual punishments.

Privilege of writ of habeas corpus may not be suspended unless public safety requires it in case of rebellion or invasion.

Retroactive laws forbidden.

Slavery and involuntary servitude, except as punishment for crime after legal conviction, forbidden.

Right of citizens to vote may not be denied on account of sex, race, color, or previous condition of servitude.

AMENDMENT:

May be proposed by two-thirds vote of both Houses of Congress, or by special convention called by Congress on request of the Legislatures of two-thirds of the States; ratification by Legislatures in three-fourths of the States or by conventions in three-fourths of them, whichever method is prescribed by Congress. However, no State may be deprived of equal representation in the Senate without its consent.

TITLE:
Constitution of the United States of Brazil.

DATE:
Decreed by the President, November 10, 1937.
(First Federal Constitution adopted in 1891.)

SOURCE:
International Conciliation, January, 1939, No. 346, Carnegie Endowment for International Peace, New York.

TYPE:
FEDERAL. NAME: United States of Brazil.

MEMBERSHIP:
Twenty States; one Federal District; one National Territory.

ORGANS OF GOVERNMENT:
LEGISLATIVE: Bicameral *National Parliament: Chamber of Deputies; Federal Council;* in addition *National Economic Council; and the President.*

Chamber of Deputies: Four-year terms; three to ten Deputies from each State in proportion to population; elected by Councilors of the Municipal Chambers and ten citizens elected at the time of the Municipal elections. *Duties:* Enacts tax and other laws which tend to increase expenditure; determines strength of land and sea forces; may decree intervention to administer a State if necessary to assure republican presidential government, constitutional rights, or solvency; may impeach President by two-thirds vote for attempts against existence of Union, the Constitution, free exercise of political power, proper employment of public funds, execution of judicial decisions, and for "crimes of responsibility" as defined by law. Time limit of forty-five days to consider the Budget, and an additional fifteen days to consider amendments of Federal Council.

Federal Council: Six-year term; one representative from each State elected by State Legislative Assemblies; State Governor may veto Assembly's nominee but two-thirds vote of *all* members of Assembly

Charts of Plans to Unite Nations Since 1914   369

alphabetical order from among their own judges. *Duties:* To determine together with High Command whether aggression has taken place requiring suppression by the Air Force. Minority of two members of Judicial Board may appeal to Board of Control which must meet immediately and decide by majority vote whether aggression has occurred.

TRANSFERS OF JURISDICTION FROM MEMBER NATIONS TO THE INTERNATIONAL AIR FORCE:
International Air Force to have twice the strength of the strongest national air force in offensive and defensive planes; to receive annual contributions from member nations equal to proportion of their annual resources or of their war budgets; to have extraterritorial air bases in each member nation's territory.

NATIONS UNDERTAKE:
To assure Air Force freedom of movement *in peace time.*
To permit Air Force to fly by most direct route *in time of war* at minimum ceiling of 10,000 feet, with the right to refuel and reequip in member nations' territory without committing them to belligerency. (Refusal of these privileges by member or non-member nations to be interpreted as siding with aggressor.)

METHODS OF ENFORCEMENT:
For failure to pay dues to Air Force: Loss of protection.
For use of national armed forces for other than defensive purposes, or for organizing armed rebellion in foreign territory: Punitive action by Air Force until offending nation sues for armistice and its at disposal of High Command.

MISCELLANEOUS:
Spanish suggested as official language Air Force.

PART III

THEORETICAL PLANS

CHARTS OF PLANS TO UNITE NATIONS SINCE 1914

F. SAMPLES OF WORLD PUBLIC WORKS PROJECTS

"Our ultimate objective can be simply stated: It is to build for ourselves, for all men, a world in which each individual human being shall have the opportunity to live out his life in peace; to work productively, earning at least enough for his actual needs, and those of his family; to associate with the friends of his choice; to think and worship freely; and to die secure in the knowledge that his children, and their children, shall have the same opportunities."

FRANKLIN D. ROOSEVELT, Washington, June 7, 1943.

... "You who suffered so deeply in the long depression years know that we must move on a great social offensive if we are to win the war completely. Antifascism is not a short-term military job. It was bred in poverty and unemployment. To crush Fascism at its roots, we must crush depression. We must solemnly resolve that in the future we will not tolerate the economic evils which breed poverty and war."

JOHN G. WINANT, Durham, England, June 6, 1942.

"We must look to the future, not to the past. Out of the ruins of the old, we must build new institutions for the service of humanity. The foundations of our postwar world must be firm enough and permanent enough to insure the production of more and better things, more and better services, greater leisure, greater security, greater opportunity for a full and useful life for all — not for a few."

WALTER NASH, New Zealand; Charlottesville, Va., July 11, 1942.

... "I am looking ahead to the day when the Iowa farmer can drive his own car to Buenos Aires — when the Oklahoma oil man can go by air to Chungking and there hire an auto to drive himself into India and finally west to Moscow and Paris. . . . The future of the world holds a promise greater than the past has ever shown us. The future is not a fixed thing. It is not predestined. We have only to bestir ourselves in order to realize our dreams. For we have the lands, the forests, the mines and the people. We have in our hands the tools of science, gigantic in their power, miraculously swift in their accomplishment. We can control floods, make the desert bloom, house a nation in comfort, conquer poverty, and stamp out most disease. We know we can do these things if we will to do them."

HENRY A. WALLACE, New York, November 17, 1943.

SAMPLES OF WORLD PUBLIC WORKS PROJECTS

The prospect of worldwide unemployment, on a scale of hitherto unimagined magnitude, is our most formidable postwar problem.

It is expected that after the war the work of reconstruction, the supplying of tools, and of consumption goods will absorb considerable numbers of former war workers, millions of demobilized soldiers, and other unemployed, for several years. Most authorities, however, agree that public-works projects should be drawn up and ready to absorb all who will be unemployed when these extraordinary demands cease. Many local, state, and national governments are already drafting blueprints for immediate postwar use.

But unemployment is a world problem, and its solution will depend on a well-coordinated, worldwide program of public works. We therefore include two examples of interesting long-range international projects. Both seek to absorb all possible types of unemployed for many decades.

Sörgel's plan, presented in several volumes in great technical detail, is constantly being perfected in collaboration with other German, Swiss, and French engineers. It involves an ambitious electrification program, lowering of the Mediterranean, soil reclamation, and irrigation of the Sahara Desert. Sörgel's object is not only to provide work, but also new land on which to settle surplus populations.

De Boer proposes a unified worldwide road, rail, sea, and air transport system, coordinated wherever possible and serviced with oceangoing ferryboats and helicopter service to economize on unnecessary loading and unloading of freight.

Both plans ignore national boundaries, disregard military considerations, and seek to unite diverse peoples in common constructive undertakings.

AUTHOR:
Herman Sörgel (German).
With the cooperation of many German, Austrian, and Swiss engineers.

PROFESSION:
Engineer.

TITLE OF PLAN:
Atlantropa.

DATE: 1932.

PUBLISHER:
Fretz & Wasmuth A. G., Zurich, Switzerland.
Piloty & Loehle, München, Germany.

TYPE:
ENGINEERING PROJECT to occupy Europe's 12 million unemployed, bringing about the unification of Europe and Africa through lowering of the Mediterranean and irrigation of the Sahara Desert.

MEMBERSHIP:
Europe, including Russia and England. NAME: Atlantropa Union.

ORGANIZATIONAL MACHINERY:
   A. *Technical Departments:*
      1. *The Natural Sciences:* Geophysics, Geography, Surveying, Oceanography, Meteorology, Hydrodynamics, Chemistry, Salt Extraction, Hygiene, Nutrition.

      2. *Construction:* Deep-sea and underwater construction; Locks and Dams; Harbors, Canals; Electrotechnics; Building of Fortifications.

      3. *Traffic:* Air, Land, Water Transport; Uniform Customs; Distribution of Electric Power.

   B. *Economic Departments:* Planning; Labor; Statistics; Uniform Weights and Measures; Financing; Colonizing and Cultivation; Irrigation.

   C. *Political Departments:*
      1. *Diplomatic:* Atlantropa Union; Diplomatic Representation in Asia and America; International Law; International Chambers of Commerce.

      2. *Naval Affairs:* Navigation; Naval Bases; Harbors; Naval Disarmament; Protection of Shipping.

3. *Territorial Department:* Division of Territory; Political Boundaries; Population Problems; Minorities; Natural and Language Boundaries; Administration; Organization; Neutral Union District.

THE PROJECT:
Seeks to reclaim three and one-half million square kilometers of land through lowering of the Mediterranean, and irrigation of North Africa; and the ultimate production of two hundred million horsepower of electrical energy by means of hydroelectric dams constructed at Gibraltar, Tunis, Messina, the mouth of the Nile, Gallipoli, across the Adriatic, at the mouth of the Rhone, the mouth of the Ebro.

In thus controlling the flow of water into the Mediterranean, the water level could be reduced 165 cm. yearly (the actual normal evaporation rate of the Mediterranean). The principal dams would be at Gibraltar and at Gallipoli (at the Dardanelles), shutting off the chief source of water flowing into the Mediterranean.

IMMEDIATE STEPS:
The education of European public opinion to support the project. (The author and his associates have been doing this since 1929, when the plan was first published under the title *Panropa*. They have arranged numerous exhibits and have been adding constantly to the technical details and actual specifications that would be involved.)

MISCELLANEOUS:
The 1938 edition of this plan, *Die Drei Grossen A: Amerika, Atlantropa, Asien* (The Three Great A's: America, Atlantropa, Asia), envisions Greater Germany and the Italian Empire as the pillars of Atlantropa, and has been mentioned several times as one of the typical geopolitical plans of the Nazis. Although the plan predates Hitlerism by many years, and the author has constantly stressed the need of popular support, he has always had a strong racial bias and proposed this plan as one way to prevent mixing of the black and white races (by leaving the menial work to the African people with the whites doing the directing).

The plan, however, is important because of its potentiality as a worldwide public-works project, capable of absorbing millions of unemployed for decades. As a regional project it would be dangerous, but as a world project, safeguarding the rights of the African people, it should have great potential value.—EDITORS.

AUTHOR:
SACO DE BOER (American).

PROFESSION:
Architect.

TITLE OF PLAN:
Planning the Peace — A World Road System.

DATE: 1937.

MANUSCRIPT

TYPE:
ENGINEERING PROJECT establishing a system of world roads, railroads, steamship and air lines for postwar reconstruction.

EXTENT:
Europe-Asia-Africa System.

ORGANS OF ADMINISTRATION:
The World Road System is to be the property of all the peoples of the world. It is to be managed by a Commission, representing all the nations, and Subcommissions located in each nation.

REQUIREMENTS:
Standardized World Rail Lines that do not interfere with existing local lines; coordination of timetables; connections with major points of the World Road System; train-carrying ferry ships to avoid loading and unloading.

World Road System: Standardized road signs and engineering; by-passing of cities to avoid acquisition of expensive land; ocean-going

Charts of Plans to Unite Nations Since 1914 377

ferryboats. Maps available in at least two languages: that of the country traversed, one in the common international language.

World Air Lines: Through-flight lines to follow the rail and highway, and even ship lanes.

Combined rail signals, air beacons, highway signs in one set of signal towers; worldwide radio connections; emergency landing fields for planes in arterial right-of-way; all telegraph wires to be placed underground; helicopter service from terminals to post-offices, large hotels, office buildings.

Terminals: Wherever possible, airport, railroad, harbor, and highway terminals should be combined.

FINANCING:

Half the construction funds to be raised by ten per cent tax on travel returns on gasoline, railroad, water transportation, hotels, sales of automobiles.

Half to be paid by individual nations; nations unable to pay their share to receive gold loan from United States Treasury with which to pay workers standard minimum rates.

Conditions which may be set on such gold loans are: Use of simplified English to be taught as world language in the schools in addition to the national language; freeing of the educational systems from nationalistic histories and political creeds.

The System should then become self-supporting, maintenance costs to be paid out of transit activities.

SUGGESTED ROUTES:

1. London-Paris-Rome-Sicily to Tunis; or Taranto to Alexandria and Egypt with ferry service over the Mediterranean, up the Nile along the East African coastline to Zambesi and the Cape.

2. Paris to Gibraltar along the West coastline of Africa to the Gold Coast and Dakar, southward to the Congo and the Cape.

3. London-Rotterdam-Berlin-Warsaw-Moscow-Peking; then north by water over the Bering Sea; or over the Aleutians to Alaska, to Chicago and to points beyond.

4. Berlin-Baghdad, via Vienna, Budapest, the Balkan cities to Turkey, to Gulf of Persia, Indies, Bombay, Calcutta, Singapore, Malay

Peninsula, Sumatra, Java; by ferry connection to Australia and New Zealand; by water to Hawaiian Islands, San Francisco, Panama Canal and New York, to Santiago de Chile and Buenos Aires, then over the Atlantic to Ireland and London.

IMMEDIATE STEPS:
Earliest possible preparation of the engineering plans.
Wide publicity to enable every person to understand the plans for his district.
National governments to acquire lands for right-of-way and provide priority for construction.
The agreement to finance the project to be included in the peace settlement.

MISCELLANEOUS:
De Boer believes that such a daring program of reconstruction and new construction would solve the problems of adjustment and unemployment all over the world as well as in the United States. He says that highway engineers estimate that in the United States alone, present highway transportation provides work for ten per cent of all employables.

PART IV

PRACTICAL ATTEMPTS

EVOLUTIONARY STAGES TOWARD A GOVERNED WORLD
1375 B.C. TO 1918

"Agesilaos reached the Arkadian town of Eutaia, and found in it only old men, women, and children. Every male of the military age had gone to attend the Arkadian Constituent Assembly, and to take his share in the formation of the Arkadian Federal Constitution."
E. A. FREEMAN: *History of Federal Government*, 1863.

"Let us only hope that the dream of world federation may have less the character of the Delian Confederacy. . . . The tragic motivation of that historical drama was that the heroine, Athens, democratic and brilliant and arrogant, loved freedom for herself, but could not understand the equally passionate love of freedom of the other Greek cities."
LIN YUTANG: *Between Tears and Laughter*,
The John Day Co., New York, 1943.

AMENOPHIS IV (also known as **Ikhnaton**):
(Egypt) 1375-? to 1358-? B.C.

His mother Thil, and his wife, Nephretite, persuaded him to withdraw all his troops from the conquered lands, leaving only his ambassadors to represent him. All the states had autonomy, Amenophis retaining only advisory control. The federation lasted until his death, when his son-in-law's efforts to maintain it were defeated by the priests and generals.

BOEOTIAN LEAGUE:
(Greece) 776 to 171 B.C.

Thebes was the capital and dominated the League, choosing two Magistrates while all the other cities chose one each. The Magistrates served as supreme military commanders and general administrators. Rivalry with Sparta was a frequent source of war. The League passed through several periods until its final dissolution, when the member cities placed themselves under Roman protection.

THE PELOPONNESIAN LEAGUE:
(Greece) 550 to 371 B.C.

The League, organized for defense against external aggression, was a loose confederation whose members had complete autonomy in their internal affairs. Sparta was the founder and leading member. The Spartan Assembly had to consent before the other members of the League could be called together to decide on joint military action. Sparta held the military command of the League and could demand that each member supply troops and equipment up to two-thirds of its armed strength.

THE THESSALIAN LEAGUE:
(Greece) 511 to 344 B.C.

The first union of Thessalian cities was achieved under a monarchy. Later a *Federal Council* was developed composed of delegates of the cities. The *Tagus* (or General) was elected by a majority of the states to command the military forces. Subject tribes were forced to pay tribute and furnish contingents to the League, but had no voice in its affairs. In 344, the League itself became a dependency of Macedonia.

THE CONFEDERACY OF DELOS:
(GREECE) 477 to 454 B.C.

The Confederacy was organized for common defense to prevent discord between members, and to suppress piracy in the Eastern Mediterranean. It functioned through an assembly, the *Synod* at Delos, meeting periodically. Each member had one vote. The Synod arbitrated disputes between members, appropriated money, and decided on military action. *Athens* was the *executive*, collecting quotas of ships, soldiers, and money from the members according to their resources. Members could not secede from the Confederacy, and two attempts at secession were defeated by arms. The Confederation changed into an empire when Athens began to supply more and more of the military forces, concentrating them within the city, and wielding despotic power.

AETOLIAN LEAGUE:
(GREECE) 426 to 189 B.C.

The League was a Union of districts instead of cities, functioning through an *Assembly of Citizens,* meeting once a year to elect the *Magistrates,* make peace and war, commission and receive ambassadors. It also elected the *Senate* which carried on affairs of state between meetings of the Assembly, brought general measures before it, and often acted in the name of the League without first consulting the Assembly. Also elected by the Assembly were the Federal General, and the Commander of Cavalry.

The Federal General was President of the Assembly, commanded the armies of the League, negotiated with foreign powers, and summoned extraordinary meetings of the Assembly. He was forbidden to express his opinion on questions of peace and war in order not to inflame the Assembly with his warlike harangues.

By means of conquest the League expanded its territories. Some of the conquered lands, however, were admitted into the League on terms of equality, while others were held as dependencies or conquered provinces.

After becoming a dependent ally of Rome, the League was finally dismembered.

ARKADIAN UNION:
(GREECE) 370 to 330 B.C.

The Union was founded by Lykomedes of Mantineia. The capital city, Megalopolis, was formed out of a union of several small villages to prevent jealousy among the cities or domination by any one of them. The Federal Assembly, called the *Ten Thousand,* was open to every citizen of an Arkadian city who wished to attend. The Assembly decided on war and peace, received ambassadors from other Greek states, maintained a standing army, and sat in judgment on political offenders. The *Senate, Federal Magistrates,* and the *Federal General* were chosen by lot to conduct the affairs of the Union between meetings of the Assembly. The Union became allied to Macedon because of its opposition to Sparta, and soon after lost its independent status.

ACHAIAN LEAGUE:
(GREECE) 274 to 145 B.C.

Functioned through a *Popular Assembly* which all citizens, at least thirty years of age, could attend, with the privilege to speak, and participate in the decisions. The Assembly, meeting twice a year, had the sole right to commission ambassadors; decide war and peace, and make alliances; provide uniform coinage, weights, and measures. The meetings were held every six months in a different city, and lasted about three days. The Assembly could admit new cities to the League on terms of equality. The permanent *Federal Magistrates* or Ministers carried on the affairs of the League between meetings of the Assembly, and placed proposals before it. The *President* or *General* of the League was the military leader in time of war. He held office for one year, and could not be reelected until the lapse of one year. The cities were assessed sums for the support of the federal garrisons. In all other matters, the cities had complete autonomy. Rome defeated the League, destroyed its federal constitution, Assembly, and Magistracies, and isolated each city.

LYKIAN LEAGUE:
(GREECE) 168 B.C. to 50 A.D.

A Federal Union of twenty-three cities, meeting in *Assembly* in a different city each time. All male citizens had the right to attend the Assembly and speak, but before the vote was taken, the citizens of each town met separately to make their decision. The large cities had three votes; smaller ones, two; and the rest, one. (This is considered to be the first recorded instance of an attempt to apportion votes by population.—EDITORS.) Taxes and other obligations were assumed in the same proportion. When the League became a Roman dependency, it lost its power over questions of war, peace, and alliance; but in all other matters, it preserved its autonomy, and its own laws.

THE ROMAN EMPIRE:
27 B.C. to 476 A.D.

Rome conquered most of the then civilized world in Europe, Asia, and Africa. The subject lands were ruled from Rome as member provinces, permitted to retain local autonomy, especially in religious and cultural matters. Rome built roads, aqueducts, bridges, canals, irrigation systems; enlarged the harbors; drained swamps; introduced uniform systems of taxation, and Roman law throughout the Empire.

In 395 A.D. it was divided into the Western and Eastern Empires. After 410 A.D., the Western Empire was invaded by various Germanic tribes, lost its distant provinces, and the city of Rome itself was subjugated by the Visigoths. The Eastern Empire maintained its unity until the capture of Constantinople by the Turks in 1453.

Roman law has continued as the basis of most European legal systems to the present day. Latin was the universal language throughout the Middle Ages.

HOLY ROMAN EMPIRE:
800 to 1806

The Holy Roman Empire was an unsuccessful attempt to recreate in territorial extent and political stability the Western Roman Empire, destroyed by the Germanic invasions. The more powerful German Kings sought additional prestige through coronation as Emperor by the Pope in Rome. The Popes, for their part, sought to extend their influence and power over the Emperors. Thus, while the stated objective of the so-called Holy Roman Emperors was to defend the

Catholic Church against heresy and disobedience they were engaged in frequent political rivalry as well as war with the Popes.

At one time the Empire included in an uneasy and discordant alliance Germany, Austria, Italy, France, Denmark, Poland, Bohemia, Moravia, and Hungary; but for the most part it was *limited to German-inhabited territories.* In fact, in many European histories it is called the *Holy Roman Empire of the German Nation* (German: Heiliges Römisches Reich Deutscher Nation; Latin: Sacrum Imperium Romanum Nationis Germanicae).

The Emperors were elected by the more powerful German Princes and Archbishops. The number of *Electors* varied between seven, eight, and nine. The privilege came to be hereditary.

The authority of the earlier Emperors was limited by the armed forces at their disposal. After 1648 (Treaty of Westphalia), the Imperial authority consisted of hardly more than granting titles of nobility. The German lands, divided into hundreds of rival states, were dominated by the more powerful princes who formed alliances within and without the Empire until it was officially abolished by Napoleon in 1806. In 1815, the Congress of Vienna attempted to reorganize the relations among the German states by creating the German Confederation.

THE LOMBARD LEAGUES:
(ITALY) 1093 to 1250

The Leagues were loose confederations organized from time to time to resist efforts of the German Emperors to bring the cities of the Lombard Plain under their control. The confederations functioned through a congress *Rectores Societatis Lombardiæ,* which met irregularly.

At one time as many as thirty-six cities were allied to prevent the Imperial armies from entering Italy and to maintain a common army supported by contingents and contributions from each city in proportion to its resources. The cities were pledged not to negotiate a truce or peace without common consent, and to submit their disputes for settlement by the League. Deputies from each city met as *Rectors* and decided all matters affecting general security.

At the height of their unity and strength, the cities cooperated in rebuilding Milan, destroyed by one of the Emperors, and built a new city, Alessandria, at a strategically desirable spot. Various cities contributed settlers to populate it.

With the encouragement and support of the Popes, the Leagues succeeded in securing many concessions from the Emperors, including recognition of their right to determine questions of war and peace, erection of fortifications, and jurisdiction in civil and criminal matters.

The Leagues frequently attacked neighboring cities to force them into alliance or to prevent their negotiating independently with the Emperors. Increased rivalry among the members, internal factional struggles, and the rise of despotic governments within the cities led to the final decline of the confederations.

THE RHENISH CONFEDERATIONS:
(GERMANY) 1254 to 1813

Among the numerous leagues and confederations, organized by various German cities and states for defense against hostile princes and to safeguard common economic interests, those of the Rhine Valley were the most persistently revived. Their representatives generally met in assemblies to decide on military quotas to be provided by each member. Disputes among them were to be submitted to arbitration.

Under Napoleon's leadership, sixteen Princes of Southern and Western Germany, who separated from the Holy Roman (German) Empire in 1806, established the *Confederated States of the Rhine*. The Confederation was to function through a *Diet* composed of a *College of Kings* and a *College of Princes*. Napoleon was proclaimed the *Protector of the Confederation* which was allied with France. They were mutually pledged to engage in all continental wars in which either was involved. Armed quotas to be contributed by each member were specified in the Treaty establishing the Confederation. Napoleon forced compliance with these military provisions but the other articles of union were never put into practice. The more powerful Princes began to withdraw when they saw their independence menaced by France, and with Napoleon's defeat, the Confederation was dissolved in 1813.

THE SWISS CONFEDERATION:
1291

Organized to resist Habsburg domination. The original members were the cantons of Schwyz, Uri, and Unterwalden. They were pledged to aid and defend each other "with our lives and property within and and without our boundaries each at his own expense against every enemy who shall attempt to molest us." Differences were to be decided by the wisest men appointed by each canton. Members of the Confederation refusing to abide by their decision were to be compelled to do so by the others.

In 1351, Zurich and Lucerne were added to the membership and a firm and perpetual union was established. The pledge of mutual assistance was strengthened by providing that there was to be no "evasion or delay" in sending aid. If a distant march or long campaign were contemplated, a *Congress* of representatives of the cantons was to meet to decide on measures. The cantons retained their previous alliances and the right to form new ones but these had to be consistent with obligations to the Confederation.

Some of the other cantons were first admitted as associates or subject territories. By 1474 the Habsburgs relinquished their feudal powers, and the Treaty of Westphalia (1648) recognized the cantons' independence.

In alliance with the Rhine cities and other neighboring lands the Confederation took part in several wars. There were also frequent disputes among the Confederates: at one time Zurich called on Austrian aid against Schwyz, and religious disputes divided them until religious equality was finally granted to each parish.

Under the influence of the French Revolution *The Helvetic Republic* was established in 1798 with a *Great Council, Senate,* and *Five Directors;* its capital Lucerne. Partly as a result of French domination together with the fact that the Constitution did not really satisfy the cantons, the *Swiss Diet* annulled it in 1813. A new Constitution was adopted in 1815, abolishing subject territories and class privileges. The autonomy of the twenty-two cantons was recognized, and the Congress of Vienna (1815) affirmed Switzerland's neutrality.

Suppression of monasteries in one of the Protestant cantons caused a brief civil war, when seven of the Roman Catholic cantons organized the *Sonderbund,* and sought redress by armed rebellion. They were defeated in 1845.

A federal constitution was adopted in 1848, providing for a *Council* of two *Deputies* from each of the twenty-two cantons, a *National Council* of elected *Deputies,* and a *Court* of eleven members. French, German, and Italian became the official languages. The Constitution established toleration of all Christian denominations; however, members of religious orders were forbidden to enter the Confederation. In 1874, the Constitution was revised and is still functioning.

THE HANSEATIC LEAGUE:
(GERMANY) 1367 to 1648

The League was organized for economic collaboration by a number of German cities under the leadership of Lübeck. It functioned through an assembly of instructed delegates, the *Bundestag* or *Hansetag.* Decisions were by majority vote. At times as many as a hundred and sixty-four cities belonged to the League although not all joined in every enterprise. Expenses were divided among the cities in proportion to their resources.

The Hansetag negotiated alliances and waged numerous wars. It secured important trading privileges for its members and maintained a trade monopoly in Northern Europe.

Lübeck shaped the policies of the League but only those cities which agreed to her proposals were bound to participate in common ventures. However, member cities which did not take part in League undertakings were penalized by depriving their merchants of Hanseatic privileges and protection.

Gradually the inland cities lost interest in overseas trade and withdrew from the League. The more important harbor cities began to compete with one another and broke away from Lübeck's leadership. After 1684, only Lübeck, Bremen, and Hamburg retained the name and traditions of the Hanseatic League.

THE GREAT PEACE CONFEDERACY OF THE IROQUOIS:
(New York State) 1457

The "Great Immutable Law," or Constitution of the Five Nations, adopted by the Iroquois, contained the following preamble: "I,

Dekanawideh, and the confederate lords now uproot the tallest pine tree and into the cavity thereby made we cast all weapons of war. Into the depths of the earth, down into the deep underearth currents of water flowing into unknown regions, we cast all weapons of strife. We bury them from sight forever and plant again the tree. Thus shall all Great Peace be established and hostilities shall no longer be known between the Five Nations, but only peace to a united people."

Foreign nations were to be invited to join the Great Peace and to be persuaded by reason. Three successive councils were to extend this invitation anew. But if the foreign nations did not yield to persuasion and reason the Confederacy was to engage in an emergency war of compulsion.

The Civil Chiefs of the Confederacy were nominated, and, if incompetent, deposed by the noblest women of the tribe. The nominations were confirmed by popular councils in which both men and women took part.

The Constitution could be amended in the light of changing conditions.

THE UNION OF UTRECHT:
1579

Union of the Principality of Guelders, County of Zutphen, counties and lands of Holland, Zeeland, Utrecht, and Frisia to drive out the Spaniards and their following, and to withdraw from the Holy Roman Empire. The Provinces sent representatives to meet in Utrecht to discuss current affairs of the Union. Decisions were by majority vote and were binding also on provinces unable to send representatives. Changes in the articles of Union could be made only by the common advice and consent of the allies. The Articles provided for uniform coinage, taxation, and religious freedom. "Good law and justice" were to be administered to natives and foreigners alike to avoid offending foreign powers. Duties and taxes levied by the cities and provinces were to apply equally to all members of the confederation. Disputes between any two provinces were to be settled by the other members; disputes involving all the provinces were to be decided by the Lords Stadtholders of the provinces.

The provinces were bound to help each other in the event of any "forceful act" inflicted on any of them by the King of Spain, and to help one another against other aggressors on decision of all the members of the Union.

THE NEW ENGLAND CONFEDERATION OR THE UNITED COLONIES OF NEW ENGLAND:
1643

The English colonies of Massachusetts, Plymouth, Connecticut, New Haven and the plantations connected with them established a "firm and perpetual league of friendship and amity" for protection against Indian attacks. The Confederation was "to hear, examine, weigh and determine all affairs of war, or peace, leagues, aides, charges, and numbers of men for war, division of spoils or whatsoever is gotten by conquest . . . to frame and establish civil agreements and orders, preserve peace among themselves and bring about speedy passage of justice . . ." and to admit new members.

Each of the four colonies appointed two *commissioners* with full powers to meet annually or as often as necessary. The commissioners had to be church members. They chose a president from among their own number, but he had no greater powers than the others. Decisions required the approval of at least six of the eight commissioners. If at least six did not agree, the matter had to be referred to the General Courts (assemblies) of the four Confederates.

If a Confederate colony was invaded, all the other members were bound to send help in the following proportion: Massachusetts, one hundred men; the others, forty-five men each. If the commissioners decided that the invasion was unprovoked, expenditures for defense were apportioned among the Confederates. If, however, the commissioners found that the invasion had been provoked, the invaded member had to bear the expenses of the war alone and also recompense the invader.

The Confederates were pledged to return runaway servants and fugitive criminals.

In 1648, the General Court of Massachusetts asked to be granted five commissioners instead of only two because the contributions of Massachusetts in men and money were so much greater than that of the other Confederates. The commissioners of the other colonies refused to agree to this change.

The reluctance of Massachusetts to become involved in war by decision of the commissioners of the other colonies culminated in her refusal to engage in conflict against the New Netherlands. She based her refusal on the argument that the commissioners were never granted the power to determine the justice of an offensive war except by unanimous consent.

THE ALBANY CONGRESS:
1754

After the New England Confederation, this was the most important attempt to bring about a union of American colonies. The Congress was called by several of the colonial governors, who, fearing that war with France was imminent, hoped through the Congress to strengthen friendly relations with the Six Indian Nations (the Iroquois), to consider unified methods of defense, and to evolve some plan of union.

Seven colonies sent delegates: Massachusetts, New Hampshire, Connecticut, Rhode Island, New York, Pennsylvania, and Maryland.

Benjamin Franklin, one of the Pennsylvania delegates, was the most enthusiastic supporter of union, and served on the committee which reported the plan endorsed by the Congress.

The union proposed in the Albany Plan was to be established by Act of the British Parliament. A *President-General* was to be appointed by the English King, and a *Grand Council* of representatives elected by the colonial assemblies for three-year terms. Each colony was to send from two to seven delegates according to its proportionate share of the common revenues. The Grand Council was to meet annually, or, in case of emergency, it could be convened by the President-General on request of at least seven members of the Council. The Grand Council could not be dissolved or its sessions extended without its consent. Twenty-five members representing a majority of the colonies were necessary for a quorum. Legislation passed by the Grand Council required the consent of the President-General, who, with the Council's advice, had authority to negotiate with the Indians, regulate trade with them, nominate all military officers, declare war, and make peace. All civil officers were to be nominated by the Grand Council with consent of the President-General.

The Grand Council was to have authority to levy taxes, to purchase lands, to establish new settlements, to regulate and govern them until given separate government by royal decree.

Upon the death of the President-General, the Speaker of the Grand Council was to succeed him, pending a new appointment by the King. Laws passed by the Grand Council were to be in harmony with English laws, and any legislation could be disapproved within three years by the King in Council.

While most of the colonial governors favored this plan in the belief that some kind of union would be better than none in the event of hostilities with France, the colonial assemblies opposed it as giving too much power to the President-General and to the Grand Council. The English Government rejected the plan on the ground that it invested the colonies with too much power.

It is interesting to note how much this plan for colonial union resembles the federal organization granted much later to Canada, Australia, and the Union of South Africa.

Features proposed in the Albany Plan were not incorporated in the Articles of Confederation, but appear in the federal constitution of 1787.

UNITED STATES OF AMERICA:
1778

The Union was organized under the *Articles of Confederation* as the United States of America for common defense in the war of independence from England. The member states were: New Hampshire, Massachusetts, Rhode Island, Connecticut, New York, New Jersey, Pennsylvania, Delaware, Maryland, Virginia, North Carolina, South Carolina, and Georgia.

The Articles established a *Congress* to which each state could send from two to seven members for three-year terms. Each state had one

Evolutionary Stages Toward a Governed World

vote. Congress decided on war and peace, commissioned and received ambassadors; negotiated treaties, except commercial ones.

Congress was also the last resort on appeal in all disputes and differences between states on petition from state governments. The disputing states each named three commissioners to constitute a *Court*. If they could not agree, Congress nominated three persons from each state, with seven to nine commissioners drawn by lot. The commissioners or judges decided the controversy by majority vote. If either party to the dispute refused to submit to the authority of the Court or to appear to defend its cause, the Court nevertheless pronounced final judgment and transmitted the records of the case to Congress for preservation "for the security of the parties concerned." (The Articles of Confederation provided no enforcement operating on member states.—EDITORS.)

Between sessions of Congress, a *Committee of the States,* consisting of one delegate from each state, was appointed to manage the general affairs of the United States.

The Confederation was supported by quotas of money and troops requisitioned from the member states. All important decisions such as making war and peace, negotiating treaties and alliances, appropriating money, had to have the consent of at least nine states in Congress. Changes in the fundamental Articles had to be ratified by the legislature of each state.

Ratification of the Constitution of 1789 changed the Confederation into the first complete federal union of modern times, with the laws of the federal government operating directly on the individual citizen in all matters assigned to federal jurisdiction.

CONGRESS OF VIENNA:
June, 1815

General Treaty liquidating the Napoleonic Wars (ratified June 9, by the Emperor of Austria, Kingdom of France, Kingdom of Great Britain, Prince Regent of Portugal, King of Prussia, Emperor of Russia, King of Sweden) provided for the following: Poland was divided between Russia, Prussia, Austria; Cracow was declared a free city and neutral; general amnesty to all Poles; free navigation of rivers and free commerce in the ports.

Parts of the *Kingdom of Saxony* added to Prussia; arrangement guaranteed by Austria, Russia, Great Britain, and France.

King of England became King of *Hanover* instead of Elector of the Holy Roman Empire.

German Confederation established. United Provinces of Netherlands and Belgium formed into *Kingdom of Netherlands. Swiss Confederation* recognized and its neutrality reaffirmed.

HOLY ALLIANCE:
September, 1815

Initiated by Alexander I of Russia. Members: Russia, Austria, and Prussia. The rulers pledged that they would apply justice, Christian charity, and peace to international relations. England refused to participate. (For further details see Czar Alexander I in Part II, p. 59.)

QUADRUPLE ALLIANCE:
1815 to 1818

Members: Russia, Austria, Prussia, and England.

Object: To exclude Napoleon and his family from the French throne, to maintain the political and territorial settlement of the Congress of Vienna, and to renew meetings of the Congress. In 1818, with the admission of France, it became the Concert of Europe.

CONCERT OF EUROPE:
September, 1818, to October, 1820

Members: Russia, Austria, Prussia, England, and France.

Object: To maintain peace in Europe and legitimate governments in power.

When the three-year allied occupation of France expired and she had paid all reparations, the Quadruple Alliance, established in 1815, became the Concert of Europe, with the admission of France to equal membership. The Concert broke up in 1820 on the issue of intervention to suppress revolutions in Spain, Portugal, and Naples. Austria and Russia favored intervention, but England opposed it.

Evolutionary Stages Toward a Governed World

GERMAN CONFEDERATION:
1815 to 1866

Established by the Congress of Vienna to guarantee the internal and external safety, independence, and territorial integrity of each German state. Each member pledged to abide by the *Articles of Union* establishing the Confederation and was assured equal rights, autonomy, and independence. The Confederation had full authority to declare war and conclude peace.

The Confederation functioned through an *Assembly* of representatives of each state appointed by the rulers, with Austria presiding. The Assembly had thirty-eight members with sixty-nine votes divided among them. Most decisions in the Assembly by two-thirds vote, except changes in the Articles of Confederation and in religious matters, which required unanimity.

The *Council* represented the larger states: Austria, Prussia, Bavaria, Saxony, Hanover, Württemberg, Baden, Kurhessen, Duchy of Hesse, Denmark, and Netherlands. Each had one vote, while the other twenty-seven states had altogether six votes. Decisions were by majority vote.

Disputes between members were to be decided by the Assembly, with final appeal to an Austregal Court.

The first meeting of the Confederation was in September, 1815. After war between Austria and Prussia in 1866, Austria was expelled from the Confederation.

Bismarck reorganized the Confederation, and in 1871 succeeded in bringing all the German states together under the federal constitution which established the Empire. Since 1933, Germany has been a unified state.

INTERNATIONAL LEGISLATION, ADMINISTRATIVE UNIONS, AND TECHNICAL CONFERENCES:
1864

Organized, functioning world government, to provide continuous legislation on a world scale, is foreshadowed by a number of technical conferences and specialized administrative unions. These developed largely through the efforts of specialists who found their work seriously hampered by lack of accurate information, uniform regulation, supervision, and administration.

Modern international legislation dates from the *International Telegraphic Conference* held in Paris in 1864. Ten years later (1874), the General Postal Union, renamed in 1878 the *Universal Postal Union*, was established at Berne, Switzerland with twenty-two member nations. With a worldwide membership, it is now the most widely known and successful administrative union in existence, serving as a model for many later technical administrations. National membership is acquired by ratification of the Postal Convention and contribution to the expenses of its maintenance. Dues are apportioned according to seven classifications. The Union's *Permanent Bureau* is located at Berne. A *Congress*, meeting every five years, revises the postal regulations and establishes new ones subject to national ratification.

Numerous other agreements and conventions, with varying national participation, regulate a large number of technical, humanitarian, economic, and cultural matters, such as: sanitation, labor, dangerous drugs, white and African slavery, agriculture, aviation, commerce, weights and measures, copyrights, customs, fisheries, navigation, maritime law; protection of submarine cables, wireless, radio; exchange of scientific and literary publications, and of official documents. Enforcement of these conventions is most often left to the national governments, but frequently a central bureau is established to collect information, organize periodic conferences, and serve as a clearing house for the participating governments. Examples of other such unions or bureaus are the International Institute of Agriculture, the International Office of Public Health, the Metric Union, the International Bureau of Exchanges, the International Labor Organization, the North Atlantic Ice Patrol.

Official government delegates also attend numerous international technical and professional conferences, congresses, and meetings, such as those of the International Geodetic Association and the International Prison Congress.

The Covenant of the League of Nations provided for coordination under the League of these administrative and technical bodies, but as the League did not acquire universal membership, these bureaus retained their separate existence, organization, and financing by member nations while cooperating with the League to avoid duplication of effort.

THE DUAL MONARCHY — AUSTRIA-HUNGARY:
1867 to October, 1918

The Dual Monarchy of Austria-Hungary was established in 1867 under the *Ausgleich* (Settlement). Since 1526, the Habsburg Emperors of Austria were also Kings of Hungary. In 1849, under the revolutionary leadership of Louis Kossuth, Hungary was declared a Republic. Austria, assisted by Russian armies, defeated the Hungarians in their war of independence, instituted a reign of terror, and treated the country as a conquered province. In 1866, after her own defeat by Prussia, Austria, anxious to placate Hungary and to end the country's passive resistance to her absolutist rule, negotiated the *Ausgleich* with Hungarian leaders. Hungary's constitutional, legal, and administrative autonomy was restored and the Dual Monarchy was established. In 1918, after defeat in the World War, the Dual Monarchy was dissolved. Austria became a Republic, but annexed by Germany in 1938. Hungary continued as a monarchy ruled by a Regent.

From 1867 to 1918, the two nations maintained separate Parliaments and Cabinets for internal affairs. The *Ausgleich* provided for joint diplomatic representation, customs legislation, interchangeable currency, regulation of railway lines, administration of the occupied territories of Bosnia-Herzegovina, and military defense (except the voting of contingents, the regulation of military service, disposition and maintenance of the army). The budget for these common services was determined by uniform legislation submitted separately to the Austrian *Reichsrat* and to the Hungarian *Parliament*. Each nation's quota of the joint expenditures was voted from time to time by the two Parliaments on the recommendation of the Parliamentary *Delegations*. Hungary contributed about one-third of the expenses and Austria, two-thirds. Both countries, however, contributed equally to the support of the Imperial-Royal Family.

Each country's Parliament appointed sixty delegates annually. The

Delegations met alternately in Vienna and in Budapest. Each *Delegation* elected its own *President* and *Vice-President* and other officers from among its own membership. The Delegations sat separately, and the *Joint Ministries* had to submit proposals relating to common affairs to each Delegation.

If three written attempts to secure agreement between the Delegations, sitting separately, failed, either Delegation could propose that the matter be resolved in joint session; then the other Delegation could not reject such an arrangement. In joint sessions of the Delegations it was determined by lot which of the two Presidents was to preside.

Thirty members constituted a quorum and decisions were by majority vote of those present. In joint sessions each Delegation had to have an equal number of members. If one delegation had more members present, those in excess could not vote. Only members of the respective legislative bodies could be members of the Delegations, which communicated with each other in their own language, with certified translations attached in the language of the other. If the two Parliaments could not agree on the proportion of the common expenditure to be paid by each country, the Emperor fixed the proportion, but only for one year.

Impeachment proceedings, in cases of violation of the agreement on the conduct of joint affairs, could be initiated by either Delegation but had to be resolved by both to be legally effective. Each Delegation could then name twenty-four judges from its own country, twelve of whom could be eliminated by the other Delegation. The *accused* could eliminate twelve from the remaining twenty-four, but an equal number had to be eliminated from each country. The remaining *Judges* formed the *Court* trying the impeachment.

There was no dual citizenship. Austrians were citizens of Austria; Hungarians, citizens of Hungary.

INTER-PARLIAMENTARY UNION:
1889
    Organized by Randal Cremer (English) and Frederic Passy (French) as an association of members of the national legislative bodies of the

Evolutionary Stages Toward a Governed World

world. The first meeting was held in Paris in 1889. The Union meets annually or every second year in different capitals except in time of war. International problems such as arbitration, treaties, reduction of armaments, customs duties, passport regulations, health, and finance are discussed. Although the Union is without authority it wielded a certain amount of influence in some countries. The meeting of 1894 led to the Permanent Court of Arbitration at The Hague, and that of 1904 in St. Louis led to the second Hague Conference of 1907. The Union functions through the *Inter-Parliamentary Council*, composed of two members from each national parliamentary group; the *Executive Committee* composed of five members from five national groups elected by the Conference. The Executive Committee directs the *Inter-Parliamentary Bureau*.

ARBITRATION TREATIES:
1889 to 1914

Great faith in arbitration to prevent war was characteristic of this period. In 1889 the *First Pan-American Conference* recommended *compulsory arbitration* in all cases except those endangering national independence, but this recommendation was never acted upon, with the exception of the arbitration treaty between Argentina and Chile which, without exception, covered all cases.

After 1907, Secretary of State Elihu Root negotiated arbitration treaties between the United States and about twenty-five nations. These treaties, however, excluded from arbitration questions involving vital interests, independence, and honor.

Between 1913 and 1914, Secretary of State William Jennings Bryan negotiated treaties between the United States and thirty other countries, pledging them to refrain from hostilities pending investigation and report by *Permanent Commissions for Investigation and Report*. The treaties covered all disputes not settled by diplomacy. The United States Senate ratified twenty-nine of these treaties.

The *Permanent Commission* was to have five members: one from each disputing nation; one chosen by each disputing nation from a nation not involved; one chosen by common agreement between the two nations.

The Permanent Commissions were to be established four months after ratification of each treaty by the governments negotiating it. Disputes not settled between nations by diplomacy were to be referred to the Commission, but it could also act on its own initiative and request the cooperation of the governments concerned in its investigation. Within one year the Commission's report was to be presented to the governments, which then were free to act on or ignore the report. Pending investigation, the governments undertook not to increase their military and naval armaments, unless danger from a third power compelled them to do so.

These bilateral treaties were negotiated for five-year periods but were to remain in force until twelve months after notice was given by one of the contracting governments to terminate the treaty.

THE HAGUE CONFERENCES:
1899 and 1907

The First Hague Conference (1899) was called by Czar Nicholas II. Twenty-six nations met at The Hague. Every nation was represented on each committee with an equal vote both in committee and in plenary sessions. The Conference appointed Commissions on *Armament and Weapons, Usages of War,* and *Arbitration.*

The Second Hague Conference (1907) was suggested by President Theodore Roosevelt upon request of the Inter-Parliamentary Union. This time forty-four nations were represented. Commissions were appointed to study and make recommendations on *Arbitration, War on Land, War on Sea, Maritime Law, Petitions and Editing.*

The two Conferences sought to humanize war by regulating the practices of land and sea warfare and limiting the types of armaments to be used. The Conference of 1899 adopted a detailed code of warfare on land. This was revised in 1907. The rights and duties of neutrals were clarified. *The Hague Convention for the Pacific Settlement of International Disputes,* drafted by the first Conference and revised by the second, recommended the offer of *good offices, mediation,* an *International Commission of Inquiry,* and *International Arbitration* as methods of preventing war.

The Second Hague Conference adopted thirteen conventions dealing with the conduct of war, recommending peaceful settlement of disputes, and prohibiting forcible collection of contract debts. Each convention had an important reservation providing that none was binding on any belligerent unless all belligerents had ratified it. Since none of the conventions, at the outbreak of World War I, had been ratified by the belligerents, they were consequently ignored by the warring nations.

One concrete result of the First Hague Conference (1899) was the establishment of the *Permanent Court of Arbitration* at The Hague (see p. 402). The Second Hague Conference (1907) urged a supplementary *International Court of Arbitral Justice* to meet annually, and an *International Prize Court,* but they were not established.

PAN-AMERICAN UNION:
1890

Established in 1890 as a result of the first Pan-American Congress held in Washington the previous year, it was first called the Bureau of American Republics and received its present name in 1910. Twenty-one American nations are represented. Only Canada and the Guianas in the Western Hemisphere are not members. Objects of the Union are: the arbitration of all disputes between member nations, establishment and maintenance of friendly commercial relations, collection and distribution of commercial data and information, and the preservation of peace. Headquarters of the Union are in Washington, D. C.

The *Governing Board* of the Union is made up of the ambassadors and ministers of the American republics accredited to the United States. The Secretary of State of the United States is ex-officio chairman. Since 1923, any American nation without an accredited minister to the United States may appoint a special representative to the Pan-American Union. The *Director General* of the Union is elected by the Governing Board and is the executive of the Union. The Union is supported by quota contributions from each member nation assessed in proportion to population.

Conferences are held about every five years (the eighth Conference was held at Lima, Peru, in December, 1938). Since the outbreak of war, there have been special meetings of the Ministers of Foreign Affairs of the American Republics to consider coordinated measures of defense for the Hemisphere and for cushioning the economic effects of the war on the American nations.

Pan-American Conferences have adopted numerous resolutions, recommendations, agreements, and conventions. These require the ratification and implementation of the member nations before they go into effect. There are no central administrative or enforcement agencies. The Pan-American Union acts as a clearing house and depository of treaties, conventions, and agreements ratified by the American nations, and prepares agendas and other technical details for the various conferences and meetings.

Previous conferences have dealt with such subjects as the unification of commercial and civil law, codification of international law, women's rights, conservation, immigration, labor migration, and the desirability of establishing an Inter-American Court of International Justice.

Numerous special technical conferences have been held on recommendation of the Pan-American Conferences. Among these have been the Special Pan-American Conference on Housing, the Inter-American Radio Conference, and the Pan-American Sanitary Conference.

Conventions adopted by the Conferences, and open for the ratification of member governments, deal with copyrights, the building of a Pan-American Highway, commercial aviation, provisional administration of colonies and possessions in the Americas owned by European nations, and the establishment of an Inter-American Bank.

THE PERMANENT COURT OF ARBITRATION: 1901

The Court consists of a Panel of 130 judges of highest reputation and proved ability in questions of international law. Each member nation nominates from one to four judges. The same person may be nominated by more than one nation. Judges are nominated for six-year terms, and may be reappointed. They function at the seat of the Court (The Hague) only when chosen by a party to an arbitration case and receive compensation only when on active service. Nations requesting arbitration choose two judges each from the Panel, one of them not of their own nationality. The four judges or arbitrators then together choose the Umpire from the Panel.

Disputes submitted to the Court are of a judicial character or concern

Evolutionary Stages Toward a Governed World

the interpretation of existing treaties. Most arbitration treaties exclude questions involving *vital interests, independence,* and *honor.* Each nation is free to define these for itself. Numerous cases of minor importance presented to the Court were successfully arbitrated and the awards carried out by the nations involved.

CENTRAL AMERICAN COURT OF JUSTICE:
1908 to 1918

Established by Treaty for a ten-year period; it was not renewed. Its seat was first at Cartago, then at San José, Costa Rica. *Members: Guatemala, El Salvador, Honduras, Nicaragua, Costa Rica.* The legislature of each of the five states elected one judge for a five-year term; judges could be replaced before expiration of their term of office only in case of resignation, incapacity, or death.

The Court exercised jurisdiction in controversies between signatory states, between a citizen of a signatory state and the government of another signatory, and between a signatory and a foreign nation. *Decisions:* One of the decisions of the Court averted war involving Honduras, El Salvador, and Guatemala.

The Court decided against Nicaragua and the United States in a dispute brought by Costa Rica and El Salvador over rights to the San Juan River and the Gulf of Fonseca, ceded by Nicaragua to the United States. The United States and Nicaragua both refused to accept the Court's decision. (Some authorities place the responsibility for failure to renew the treaty on the influence of the United States. Others explain her indifference to the Court as due to the United States having been engaged in World War I at the time. Others oppose Regional Courts on the ground that they may hinder the functioning of a World Court.—EDITORS.)

THE HAGUE CONGRESS OF WOMEN; THE FORD NEUTRAL CONFERENCE FOR CONTINUOUS MEDIATION; AND THE INTERNATIONAL COMMITTEE FOR IMMEDIATE MEDIATION:
1915 to 1916

These *popular* attempts to end war by peaceful means through continuous mediation are unique in history because of their democratic character and initiation by women. They are still among the most controversial events of the first phase of World War I. The *Hague Congress of Women* was called in February, 1915, by Dutch, English, and German woman suffrage leaders to decide on a peaceful method of stopping the war and to plan the international organization of nations. Approximately 2,400 women from about twenty belligerent and neutral nations were present at the four-day Congress. Hundreds of others were prevented from attending by their governments or were stopped at the frontiers.

The major achievement of the Congress was the acceptance of a plan to organize a *Neutral Conference for Continuous Mediation* to bring about the earliest possible cessation of hostilities by:

1. Submitting to all belligerents simultaneously reasonable proposals as a basis of peace.

2. Inviting suggestions for settlement from each of the belligerent nations on the basis of the proposals submitted.

Principles of a just and permanent peace were drafted by the Congress providing for:

1. Non-recognition of conquest; no transfer of territory without the consent of the men and women residing in it.

2. Autonomy and a democratic parliament not to be refused to any people.

3. Agreement by governments to refer future international disputes to arbitration and conciliation.

4. Agreement by governments to unite in social, moral, and economic pressure on any country resorting to war instead of to arbitration or conciliation.

5. Secret treaties to be void; ratification of future treaties to require the consent of each national legislature.

6. Representatives of the people to take part in the peace conference with women included among them.

7. Establishment of a *Permanent International Court of Justice* to

settle differences over the interpretation of treaties and of international law.

8. Establishment of a *Permanent International Conference*, holding regular meetings, to settle differences arising from economic competition, expanding commerce, increased population, and social and political changes; to safeguard rights of weaker nations and of primitive peoples; to formulate and enforce principles of justice and equity.

9. Development of an *International Federation*.

The Congress organized the *International Committee of Women for Permanent Peace* (later named the Women's International League for Peace and Freedom) and appointed two *Delegations* to carry its resolutions to the various governments and to discuss with them its plan for a Neutral Conference for Continuous Mediation. The *Delegation* sent to the *belligerent* governments was made up of women from neutral countries, the Netherlands and Italy, with Jane Addams of the United States at its head. Their task was to persuade the belligerent governments to accept mediation by a group of neutral nations. The *Delegation* to the *neutral* governments was made up of women from belligerent as well as neutral nations with Rosika Schwimmer of Hungary as its head and the other members from Great Britain, the Netherlands, and the United States. Their objective was to persuade the neutral governments to organize a Neutral Conference for Continuous Mediation.

The Delegations met with extraordinary success — they consulted with all the responsible governments, many of whom received them more than once. The belligerent governments admitted that a neutral conference for mediation would be acceptable to them, and the European neutral governments declared themselves ready to act.

The two Delegations then met in the United States, issued a joint report, and tried to secure the cooperation of President Wilson to call the Neutral Conference or at least to cooperate with it if called by the two European neutral governments who had expressed their willingness to initiate such a Conference. President Wilson refused, and the Delegations, fearing that without the cooperation of the United States — the world's most powerful neutral nation — an official conference could not be organized, proceeded to seek the establishment of an unofficial popular conference of neutrals to initiate mediation.

Henry Ford, impressed by the Delegations' documentary evidence, agreed to finance the establishment and work of such a neutral conference. He chartered the *Oscar II* to transport a peace pilgrimage of Americans to Europe as a dramatic gesture preceding the Conference. This peace pilgrimage, merely incidental to the serious aim of the Conference, was labeled the *Peace Ship* and was deliberately used by the press as an object of ridicule. The distorted publicity accorded the *Peace Ship* discredited the work of the Conference and overshadowed it in the mind of the American public.

The Ford Neutral Conference for Continuous Mediation was officially opened February 10, 1916, in Stockholm, Sweden, with three to five delegates elected by the peace organizations of six neutral countries: Denmark, the Netherlands, Norway, Sweden, Switzerland, and the United States. The Conference elected its *Chairman, Vice-Chairmen,* and *General Secretary.* With the aid of experts and in utter disregard of the military situation, the Conference was to draft tentative proposals to end the war and to reorganize the world to prevent future wars. Delegations of at least two members each were to carry these proposals *simultaneously* to all belligerent governments for acceptance or suggestions for changes. The Delegations were then to return to Conference headquarters to revise their proposals for simultaneous resubmission to the belligerents, until terms acceptable to all nations permitted the declaration of an armistice and the calling of a general peace conference.

Although the Ford Neutral Conference became a target of organized ridicule in the United States, it was taken most seriously in Europe and had great popular support in both neutral and belligerent countries. Members of parliaments and university professors were among the distinguished persons elected as delegates to the Neutral Conference.

The combined pressure of Ford's closest intimates and several American and Dutch delegates prevented the Conference from becoming an active agent of mediation and turned it into a mere study organization. This did not interest Ford, who had organized the Conference for peace action, and he withdrew his financial support.

The Ford Neutral Conference cost about $400,000, estimated to be less than one per cent of the cost of a single battleship.

In May, 1916, the members of the Conference, who remained loyal to the original plan of continuous mediation, joined to form a new organization — *The International Committee for Immediate Mediation* (1916) which immediately started mediating action according to the original plan, but lack of funds proved too great an obstacle for its continuance.

PART V

PRACTICAL ATTEMPTS

CHARTS OF CONFEDERATE AND FEDERAL CONSTITUTIONS

Constitution of the German Empire, 1871
Covenant of the League of Nations, 1919
Constitution of the International Labor Organization, 1919

American Constitutions

The Argentine Republic
The United States of America
The United States of Brazil
The United States of Mexico
The United States of Venezuela

British Constitutions

The Structure of the British Empire
The Commonwealth of Australia
The Dominion of Canada
The Union of South Africa

European Constitutions

The Swiss Confederation
The Union of Soviet Socialist Republics

"Cos, everywhere you go, you 'ear everyone saying as it carn't be done.
"What cannot?"
"Sayin' as nothin' carn't. Look at 'em up in the 'Ouse o' Commons. Prime Ministers and Arch-deacons and Lord 'Igh Sekkertries, and whatnot. A bloke's on'y got ter get up an' say, 'Wot abaht doin' so-an'-so?' — and the Prime Minister says, 'Carn't be done!' An' all them Lord 'Igh Sekkertries opens their beaks and says, 'Carn't be done!' An' then all the other blokes opens their beaks like a lot of 'ens on a pole, an' says, 'Carn't be done!' An' ten to one it's bein' done all the time. . . . And, arter everyone's been doin' wotever it is for ten years, up 'ops one of the Lord 'Igh Sekkertries and says, 'I b'leeve it could be done.' An' the Prime Minister says, 'I b'leeve it could!' And all the other blokes opens their beaks and says, 'I b'leeve so!' And, two years later they passes a law sayin' it's gotter be done, an' they makes the Lord 'Igh Sekkertry a peer or a juke or something."

From: "At the New Bull and Bush" by HERBERT DE HAMEL in LORD DAVIES' *The New Commonwealth*, April, 1935.

"The importance of Germany is independent from her temporary military or political power; therefore, without her being admitted, a true 'League of Nations' cannot be spoken of. What the treaty of peace proposes to establish is rather a continuance of the inimical coalition not deserving the name of 'League of Nations.' The inner structure, too, does not realize the true League of Nations. Instead of the dreamt of holy alliance of the nations, there reappears in it the fatal idea of the holy alliance of 1815, the belief as though it were possible to secure to the world a peace from above by way of diplomatic conferences with diplomatic organs. We miss technical proper authorities with impartial tribunals beside the select committee controlled by the Great Powers, which may submit the whole civilized world to its control at the expense of the independence and equality of rights of the smaller states. The maintenance of the old political system with its tricks and rivalries based on force is thus not rendered impossible!"

Protest of the GERMAN DELEGATION to the Versailles Peace Conference, May 19, 1919.

From: *The Drafting of the Covenant*, Vol. I, by DAVID HUNTER MILLER, G. P. Putnam's Sons, New York, 1928.

"I almost despair of seeing a favorable issue to the proceedings of our convention, and do therefore repent having had any agency in the business. The men, who oppose a strong and energetic government, are in my opinion narrow-minded politicians, or are under the influence of local views. The apprehension expressed by them, that the *people* will not accede to the form proposed, is the *ostensible*, not the *real* cause of opposition. But, admitting that the present sentiment is as they prognosticate, the proper question ought nevertheless to be, Is it, or is it not, the best form that such a country as this can adopt? If it be the best, recommend it, and it will assuredly obtain maugre opposition."

        Letter of GEORGE WASHINGTON to ALEXANDER HAMILTON, from Philadelphia, Summer of 1787.
From: KENNETH B. UMBREIT's *Founding Fathers,* Harper and Bros., New York, 1941.

CONFEDERATE AND FEDERAL CONSTITUTIONS

IN STUDYING constitutions it is important to keep in mind that they often combine aspirations for the future with compromises in the present; that there may be a wide gap between what is written and practiced; and that unwritten factors have developed through usage.

It is interesing to compare the chart of the Covenant of the League of Nations with that of the Constitution of the German Empire of 1871 and with the German Confederation of 1815 (See p. 395). While the German Constitution of 1871 is basically federal, its confederate features are the dominant position of Prussia, especially in military matters, her veto prerogative, and the important reservations of some of the other states. Although Germany did not participate in the drafting of the League Covenant, the organization and veto powers of the Council strongly resemble these German precedents.

Many plans suggest the creation of numerous economic bodies in addition to the existing International Labor Organization, with similar employer and labor representation besides that of governments. The International Labor Organization has no enforcement authority of its own.

The Constitution of the United States of America, one of the oldest, shortest, and most simply written, has greatly affected the structure of most of the documents included in this section. Its influence is especially seen in the other American constitutions. The great compromise in representation of large and small states as worked out in the structure of the Senate and House of Representatives and the exercise of parallel authority between the States and the Federal Government, each operating on the individual, have been applied repeatedly in various sections of the world where sovereign groups have sought to organize their peaceful coexistence.

The Argentine and Brazilian Constitutions are technically, although not actually, in effect. Since the revolt of June 4, 1943, the Argentine Republic is ruled by a small group of army officers. There is no Congress. The Brazilian Constitution has been decreed, but the nation is ruled under conditions defined in that document for a state of emergency. The President's term is extended until the Constitution has been approved by plebiscite, for which, however, no date has yet been set by him. On the other hand, to guard against such forcible seizures of power, the

Mexican Constitution provides that the fundamental law cannot be abrogated even though its observance is prevented by rebellion. Its force is to be restored as soon as the people regain their liberties.

The Argentine Constitution, contrary to that of the United States of America, provides also for representation of the Federal District and empowers the Federal Government to suppress hostilities between provinces.

Drafted to end party dissension, the threat of class warfare, and the infiltration of communism, the Constitution of Brazil seeks to establish government along the corporative lines of Italian fascism. The powers of Congress are greatly limited. Legislation is mostly in the hands of the President and the Economic Council. Members of both Houses are indirectly elected. Only in the event of disagreement between Congress and the President over amendments to the Constitution or election of a new President are decisions to be made by vote of all citizens over eighteen. The federal powers in economic matters are detailed at great length. Outstanding among the guarantees of individual rights is the provision that no distinction is to be made between Brazilians on account of color or race. Children born in or out of wedlock have equal rights and the Government recognizes its obligation to maintain and educate offspring of indigent parents. On the other hand, restrictions on individual freedom include censorship, forbidding of strikes and lockouts, prohibition of divorce, and the imposition of death sentences for attempts to change the political or social order established by the Constitution.

The Mexican and Venezuelan Constitutions strengthen the right of petition by adding the duty of the official addressed to give the petitioner the requested information. The Mexican and Swiss Constitutions place strong curbs on religious activity of a political nature while permitting religious freedom exercised under state supervision. Labor and social welfare guarantees occupy an important place in the Mexican Constitution.

Most of the federal constitutions in the American group forbid the reelection of the President for consecutive terms.

The Constitution of Venezuela prohibits capital punishment. It authorizes the Federal Supreme Court to present an annual memorial to Congress suggesting reforms through legislation. Significantly, the Constitution also provides that troops are to be confined to their barracks on election days. Communist and anarchist doctrines and war propaganda are forbidden.

Departing from the usual federal procedure, the provinces have *unequal* representation in the Canadian Senate. Senators are appointed for life by the Governor-General; to qualify they must possess a certain amount of property. An important provision grants pensions to provincial officials who could not be absorbed by the Federal Government or given work of equal rank when provincial functions were transferred to the Dominion of Canada. To avoid ambiguity, powers not specifically enumerated in the Constitution as retained by the provinces, are delegated to the Union. The Australian Constitution, on the other hand, leaves residuary powers with the provinces. Australia provides for compulsory voting with penalties for failure to discharge this duty.

Easiest to amend is the South African Constitution with the requirement of a two-thirds vote of the total number of members of both Houses in joint session.

In both Australia and South Africa participation in political affairs is restricted to persons of European descent; the large native populations (with a minor exception in South Africa) possess no political rights.

Next to the Constitution of the United States of America, that of the Swiss Confederation is most often adapted by peace planners. One of its significant features is the absence of a single executive. The Federal Council of seven members is elected in joint session by the Federal Assembly. No two members of the Council may be from the same canton. Each of the seven Council members directs one of the Federal Departments. Two of their number are elected President and Vice-President of the Confederation annually, but this additional office confers no further authority. In the Council of States where the cantons are equally represented, each canton determines for itself whether its deputies are elected or appointed and furnishes their salaries. Unique in regional federations, the cantons do not authorize the Federal Government to maintain a standing army; nor may the cantons keep permanent troops above three hundred men in addition to their police.

The Soviet Constitution stresses primarily the preservation of cultural autonomy of the member republics, retaining for the Federal Government complete direction of the national economy especially in the heavy industries. Labor and social rights are enumerated at length including equal rights of men and women. The Constitution forbids discrimination on grounds of racial or national origin. A provision shared with the British Commonwealth of Nations permits secession by the member republics.

TITLE:
Constitution of the German Empire.

DATE: April 16, 1871 to 1918.

SOURCE:
Modern Constitutions by Walter F. Dodd, University of Chicago Press, 1909.

TYPE:
FEDERAL with certain confederate features.
NAMES: German Empire, Confederation, Eternal Alliance.

MEMBERSHIP:
Twenty-two member states; three Hanseatic cities.

ORGANS OF GOVERNMENT:
LEGISLATIVE: Bicameral: *Bundesrat; Reichstag.*
Bundesrat (Council of States): Representatives of member states; total fifty-eight votes divided as follows:

Prussia	17 votes
Bavaria	6
Saxony	4
Württemberg	4
Baden	3
Hesse	3
Mecklenburg-Schwerin	2
Brunswick	2
Seventeen other States	1 each

Each member state could appoint as many delegates as it had votes; but votes of each state had to be cast as a unit. *Decisions:* By majority

Charts of Confederate & Federal Constitutions 417

vote; in case of tie, Prussia's vote to decide*; votes not represented or uninstructed not to be counted*; Imperial Chancellor to preside at sessions.

Permanent Committees on:

- Army and Fortifications.
- Marine Affairs.
- Customs Duties and Taxes.
- Commerce and Trade.
- Railroads, Posts, Telegraphs.
- Judicial Affairs.
- Accounts.

At least four states to be represented on each committee: *Prussia to be represented on all of them; Bavaria to have permanent seat on Committee on Army and Fortifications*;* other members of military and naval committees appointed by Emperor; members of other committees elected by Bundesrat; committees formed anew at each session; members eligible for reelection.

Committee on Foreign Affairs: Bavaria to preside; composed of plenipotentiaries of Bavaria, Saxony, Württemberg, and of two other states elected annually by Bundesrat.*

Duties of Bundesrat: To provide administrative regulations necessary for execution of imperial laws; to prepare legislation to be submitted to the Reichstag, and to act on resolutions received from the Reichstag; legislation not of concern to the whole empire to be voted on only by states concerned.*

Rights: Members of Bundesrat may appear before Reichstag to present views of their respective state governments; Bundesrat may be convened by Emperor without Reichstag for preparation of business; must be convened on demand of one-third of members.

Reichstag: Five-year term; delegates chosen by general direct election and secret ballot apportioned according to population; men over twenty-five eligible to vote for and to be elected delegates. Proceedings public. *Decisions:* By majority of total membership. May be dissolved by resolution of Bundesrat and consent of Emperor, but new elections must be held within sixty days; new Reichstag convened within ninety days; may not be adjourned for more than thirty days nor more than once in the same session without its consent; elects

* These are Confederate features.

own President, Vice-President, and secretaries; determines own procedure.

(Until 1906 delegates received no salary; in that year legislation provided they were entitled to free transportation on German railways during sessions and to 3,000 marks annually; lack of compensation would naturally restrict eligibility to the well-to-do.—EDITORS.)

EXECUTIVE OR ADMINISTRATIVE:

King of Prussia: President of empire with title of *German Emperor*. *Duties:* To represent empire abroad; to declare war with consent of Bundesrat; to conclude peace; to negotiate alliances; to conclude treaties with approval of Bundesrat and Reichstag; to accredit and receive ambassadors; to open and adjourn both chambers; to prepare and publish laws and supervise their execution; to issue decrees and ordinances countersigned by the Imperial Chancellor; to appoint and dismiss officials; to declare martial law within any part of the empire if public security is threatened; to exercise supreme command of the navy.

The Imperial Chancellor: Appointed by Emperor; presides over Bundesrat; countersigns imperial decrees and ordinances.

JUDICIAL:

Until altered by imperial legislation, existing jurisdiction of state courts continued.

Disputes between states not of a judicial nature to be adjusted by Bundesrat on request of either party.

Right of appeal to Bundesrat by individuals for relief from restriction or denial of justice in violation of a state constitution.

Offenses against the empire which if committed against one of the states would be considered high treason to be tried in *Superior Court of Appeals* of the three free Hanseatic cities at Lübeck; no appeal from its decision.

TRANSFERS OF JURISDICTION FROM MEMBER STATES TO THE CONFEDERATION:

Laws of the empire under the constitution take precedence over those of the states.

To provide common citizenship and protection.

To regulate freedom of migration, domicile and settlement, citizenship, passports, trade, industry, insurance.
To levy customs duties, and taxes on domestic salt and tobacco, brandy, beer, sugar and sugar products.
To regulate weights and measures; coinage; currency.
To provide general banking regulations.
To grant patents and copyrights.
To protect German navigation and trade abroad.
To establish common consular representation.
To regulate, construct, and administer the railways and waterways for commerce and defense.
To regulate the posts and telegraphs.
To contract loans in case of extraordinary need.
To establish principles of civil and criminal law and judicial procedure.
To determine military and naval affairs.
To establish laws regarding the press and right of association.
To regulate reciprocal execution of civil judicial sentences, authentication of public documents.
To compel the states to carry out their constitutional duties.

STATES RETAIN:
Administration and collection of customs and consumption taxes but supervised by imperial officers; quarterly net revenue to be transferred to Imperial Treasury.
Right to propose resolutions and motions for deliberation of Bundesrat.
Right to appoint minor officers of respective military contingents and to employ all troops stationed within their territories for police purposes.

Bavaria reserves matters relating to domicile and settlement; colonization and emigration to foreign countries; railway regulations, other than those in interest of defense, not to apply to her.*

Bavaria and *Württemberg* retain control of administration and rates on internal postal and telegraphic communication and with neighboring foreign states.*

Bavaria, *Württemberg*, and *Baden* reserve taxation of brandy and beer.*
Cities of *Bremen* and *Hamburg* to remain free ports outside the common customs frontier until they request admission.*

* These are Confederate features.

INDIVIDUAL RIGHTS:
Subjects or citizens of each state to be treated as natives in every other state.
No German may be limited in his right of residence, business activities, eligibility to public office, acquisition of real estate, right of citizenship, and right to equal protection of the laws by any state of the Confederation.

RESTRICTIONS ON INDIVIDUAL RIGHTS:
Compulsory military service according to the Prussian system.

METHODS OF ENFORCEMENT:
If the states of the Confederation do not fulfill their constitutional duties, Bundesrat to determine form of compulsion to be carried out by Emperor.

AMENDMENT:
Fourteen votes against an amendment sufficient to defeat it. (Prussia having seventeen votes could alone defeat any amendment.—EDITORS.)
Provisions of the Constitution securing certain rights to the states may not be amended without consent of the states affected.

TITLE:
The Covenant of the League of Nations.

DATE:
April 28, 1919 (as adopted by the Peace Conference in Paris).

SOURCE:
Documents Regarding the Peace Conference, International Conciliation, June, 1919, No. 139, American Association for International Conciliation, New York.

Instruments Relating to the Permanent Court of International Justice, International Conciliation, March, 1943, No. 388, Carnegie Endowment for International Peace, New York.

Charts of Confederate & Federal Constitutions 421

TYPE:
CONFEDERATE. NAME: League of Nations.

MEMBERSHIP:
Nations listed as prospective Original Members in Annex to Treaty of Peace as its signatories (only the victorious Allied nations): United States of America, Belgium, Bolivia, Brazil, British Empire (Canada, Australia, South Africa, New Zealand, India), China, Cuba, Czechoslovakia, Ecuador, France, Greece, Guatemala, Haiti, Hedjaz (Saudi-Arabia), Honduras, Italy, Japan, Liberia, Nicaragua, Panama, Peru, Poland, Portugal, Roumania, Serbia (Yugoslavia), Siam (Thailand), Uruguay.

Neutral Nations invited to accede to the Covenant: Argentine Republic, Chile, Colombia, Denmark, Netherlands, Norway, Paraguay, Persia (Iran), El Salvador, Spain, Sweden, Switzerland, Venezuela.
(About sixty-three nations have been members of the League at one time or another; its membership, September, 1943, was about forty-five, of whom only about six paid their dues fully, and thirteen others made partial payment.)

ORGANS OF GOVERNMENT:
LEGISLATIVE: Bicameral — *Assembly; Council.*

Assembly: Not more than three representatives from each member nation; each member nation one vote (unit vote); to meet at stated intervals, and as needed. *Duties:* May deal with any matter within League jurisdiction or affecting world peace.

Council: One representative and one vote for each nation represented on Council: United States, British Empire (the representative of the British Empire was appointed by the United Kingdom Government), France, Italy, Japan, and four other nations selected by the Assembly from time to time; League members not represented on Council to be invited to send a representative to attend Council meetings on matters affecting their special interests; Council to meet at least once a year. *Decisions* (in both bodies): By unanimous agreement of all nations represented at the meeting; majority vote sufficient on matters of procedure, and appointment of investigating committees.

EXECUTIVE OR ADMINISTRATIVE:
Council: Exercises limited executive functions.

Secretariat; Secretary General; Secretaries; Staff.
First Secretary General named in Annex to Covenant; succeeding Secretaries General appointed by Council with majority approval of Assembly.
Secretaries and Staff appointed by Secretary General with approval of Council; positions open equally to men and women.

Permanent Commission to advise Council on reduction of armaments and military and naval questions.

Permanent Commission to receive and examine Annual Reports on administration of Mandates.

International Bureaus and *Commissions* already existing or to be established to be placed under League direction.

JUDICIAL:
Diplomacy.
Hague Court of Arbitration; Special Arbitration Tribunals.

Permanent Court of International Justice (World Court): Nine-year term; fifteen judges *nominated by* national groups in the Permanent Court of Arbitration; *elected by* majority vote of *Assembly* and *Council;* judges may be reelected. *Quorum:* Nine judges. Court elects own *President* and *Vice-President* for three-year terms; may be reelected. Salary fixed by Assembly on suggestion of Council. Court in permanent session except for vacations. *Decisions:* By majority of judges present; in case of tie, President casts deciding vote; Court's judgment final and without appeal; application for revision possible on presentation of new facts. Court's decisions have no binding force except between the parties concerned.

Registrar and *Deputy-Registrar:* Seven-year term; nominated by members of Court and elected by Court by secret ballot and majority vote. *Duties:* In charge of archives, accounts, and all administrative work of Court.

Jurisdiction of Court (only nations may bring cases before Court): Over cases referred to it by nations and over all matters provided for in treaties and conventions in force. *Optional Clause:* Nations *may recognize compulsory jurisdiction* of Court unconditionally, or for a limited time, or on condition that certain other nations grant similar recognition in following cases: the interpretation of a treaty;

Charts of Confederate & Federal Constitutions

any question of international law; any breach of international obligation, and amount of reparations for it. If Court's jurisdiction over a dispute is questioned, the Court to decide whether it has jurisdiction or not. In cases brought before it, Court to apply: international conventions recognized by contesting nations; international custom; general principles of law recognized by civilized nations; judicial decisions and teachings of most highly qualified jurists of the various nations.

If contesting nations agree, the Court may decide a case *ex aequo et bono* (according to its discretion of what is just and good).

Nations not members of the League of Nations may become members of the Court. Fifty-one nations have ratified the Protocol establishing the Court.

TRANSFERS OF JURISDICTION FROM MEMBER NATIONS TO THE LEAGUE:
Buildings and other property occupied by League to be inviolable.
Expenses of Secretariat to be allocated among member nations in the proportion decided by the Assembly.
National representatives accredited to League and League officials to enjoy diplomatic privileges and immunities.

To formulate plans for consideration and action of member governments for armament reduction to lowest point consistent with national safety and for enforcement by common action of international obligations (subject to recommendation and revision at least every ten years); armament limitation accepted by national governments may not be exceeded without Council's consent.

To advise national governments how evil effects of private armament manufacture may be prevented with due regard to armament needs of nations unable to manufacture own armaments.

To advise member governments how to fulfill their obligations in case of aggression, threat, or danger of aggression against a member nation.

To propose steps to be taken if member government fails to carry out arbitral award.

To collect and distribute relevant information on matters of international interest regulated by general conventions, but not under control of an international bureau or commission.

To expel member nation violating League Covenant.

All treaties and international engagements of member governments must be registered with League Secretariat to be binding.

May advise reconsideration of treaties that have become inapplicable or dangerous to world peace.

NATIONS UNDERTAKE:

To give effective guarantees of sincere intention to observe their international obligations and accept regulations prescribed by League regarding armaments, military, and naval forces.

To exchange full and frank information as to national armaments, military and naval programs, and industrial adaptability to war manufacture.

To respect and preserve against external aggression the territorial integrity and political independence of all League members.

To submit disputes to arbitration or to inquiry by League Council; to agree not to go to war until three months after arbitral award or report of Council.

To agree to carry out arbitral awards; not to go to war against a member government complying with arbitral award.

To agree to abrogation of obligations inconsistent with League Covenant and not to enter into any new ones.

To support one another in case of financial and economic sanctions in defense of League Covenant to minimize loss and inconvenience.

To afford passage through their territories of forces of League members cooperating to protect the Covenant.

To administer as Mandates colonial possessions of defeated nations guaranteeing freedom of conscience, commercial equality for all League members; prohibition of slave trade, arms and liquor traffic, military or naval fortifications, or military training of natives except for police and defense purposes.

To render annual reports to Council on Mandate administration.

To endeavor to secure (subject to international conventions in existence or to be agreed on) and maintain fair and humane conditions of labor; and to establish and maintain the necessary international organization for the purpose (International Labor Organization).

To entrust League with execution of agreements on White Slave and dangerous drug traffic; trade in armament with certain countries.

To secure and maintain freedom of transit and communication.

Charts of Confederate & Federal Constitutions 441

may override him. President of Union nominates ten additional members.

Qualifications: Native-born citizens at least thirty-five years old. *Those elected by the State Assemblies:* Must be registered voters; must have held office under the Union or the State for at least four years. *Those nominated by the President:* Must have distinguished themselves in some branch of national production or culture.
Duties: Ratifies treaties, conventions, agreements on international and interstate commerce, port regulations, coastwise navigation. Legislates for the Federal District and Territories. Approves presidential appointments to the Supreme Federal Tribunal, Tribunal of Accounts, and of regular diplomatic representatives. Approves agreements between the States. Elects Provisional President if office of President becomes vacant. If Provisional President cannot assume office within a day, President of Federal Council serves temporarily. Tries President after impeachment by Chamber of Deputies. Indicts and tries Judges of Supreme Federal Tribunal for "crimes of responsibility." Its consent required before concessions of more than 10,000 hectares of land can be made. Time limit of twenty-five days to consider the Budget. *Presiding Officer:* A Minister of State appointed by the President.

Parliament — Quorum: Absolute majority of members. *Decisions:* By majority vote; two-thirds vote overrides President's veto. Meets annually on May 3 for four months. Vacancies filled by supplementary elections; President fills vacancies of his nominees on Federal Council. Both Houses elect their officers and committees, determine procedure, establish their own internal police forces; may expel a member by majority vote; may summon Ministers of State to explain matters within their jurisdiction. If neither Chamber finishes consideration of the Budget within the allotted time, it stands as presented by the Administrative Department.

Restrictions on Parliament: One-third of members of either Chamber necessary to introduce legislation; laws affecting national economy must be submitted to National Economic Council before Parliament may discuss them; laws initiated by President and favorably reported by National Economic Council may be read only once in each Chamber and accepted or rejected; no amendments permitted;

President may at any time withdraw these laws and amend them, consulting National Economic Council only if substantial changes are made. Parliament's consent not needed for measures decreed during a state of emergency or war declared by the President. Parliament cannot suspend a state of emergency or war. At end of state of emergency or war, if Parliament does not approve of measures taken by President during that period, he may dissolve Parliament, and order new elections. President may detain members of either Chamber if it delays its consent twelve hours or refuses to suspend immunities of those involved in any conspiracy against the security of the State, its citizens, or established institutions.

National Economic Council: Equal number of employers' and employees' representatives chosen by professional associations and syndicates recognized by law; President appoints three additional members to each section of the Council: industry and crafts, agriculture, commerce, transportation, credit; President may permit Cabinet members, Directors of Ministries, representatives of State Governments, of associations and syndicates to participate in meetings of committees and sections of the Council when matters of special interest to them are considered; Council organizes own technical and expert staff.

Duties: To promote corporative organization of national economy; to report on all matters related to national production; to investigate conditions of labor, agriculture, industry, commerce, transportation, and credit in order to increase and coordinate national production; to draft legislation dealing with economic matters; must approve matters within its jurisdiction before President can issue decree-laws.

EXECUTIVE OR ADMINISTRATIVE:

President: Six-year term; elected by an Electoral College composed as follows: twenty-five electors in proportion to each State's population elected by the Municipal Chambers; fifty electors, equally divided between employers' and employees' associations elected by National Economic Council; twenty-five electors elected by Chamber of Deputies; twenty-five by Federal Council. Members of Parliament or of State Assemblies ineligible. Organized ninety days before expiration of President's term; meets in capital twenty days before expiration of term. Candidate chosen by Electoral College is elected *if President does not nominate a candidate.* If he nominates a candidate, the choice between the two is made by direct, universal suffrage of men and women over eighteen. President's term of office prolonged until his successor is inaugurated.

Qualifications for President: Native-born; at least thirty-five years old. *Duties:* Sanctions, promulgates, and publishes laws; convenes and adjourns Parliament; may veto legislation within thirty working days; issues decree-laws during recess or dissolution of Parliament on matters within Union jurisdiction, and at all times in relation to the armed forces, organization of the government, or when authorized by Parliament. *Decree-laws may not involve amendments to the Constitution, electoral legislation, the budget, taxation, institution of monopolies, currency, public loans, or alienation or mortgage of Union property.* May alter items in the budget as long as lump sums voted by Parliament are not exceeded.

Conducts foreign affairs; negotiates international conventions and treaties subject to approval of Federal Council; declares war with Parliamentary authorization — in case of invasion, without it; makes peace. Supreme commander of armed forces; decrees their mobilization.

Appoints Ministers of State, Attorney General, Mayor of Federal District; with approval of Federal Council, appoints Ministers of Justice; may nominate Presidental candidate. Determines provisional execution of laws pending approval of Parliament.

Dictatorial Powers: May decree *state of emergency* for whole or part of nation in case of foreign menace, imminence of internal disturbance, or conspiracy to disturb the public peace; may decree *a state of war* whenever he considers use of armed force necessary; during a state of war, President may suspend any part of the Constitution; laws passed during a state of emergency or war may not be brought before the Courts. During *state of emergency*, President limited to following measures: detention or banishment of citizens to other parts of nation; censorship of correspondence, all written and oral communications; may suspend right to organize public meetings; may authorize searches and seizures.

Ministers of State: Appointed by President; native-born; over twenty-five years old. *Duties:* To endorse Presidential acts; not responsible to Parliament or the Courts for advice given to President.

Administrative Department: Organized by Presidential decree.
  Duties: To study all government departments to determine changes in the interests of economy and efficiency; organization of budget; organization of working relations between departments and the public. Draws up yearly budget estimates. Supervises carrying out of budget.

National Security Council: Composed of Ministers of State and Chief of Staff of armed forces. President presides. *Duties:* To study all questions relating to national security; to hear all appeals for concessions of land or establishment of industries and means of communication in territory 150 kilometers within the frontier.

JUDICIAL:
Supreme Federal Tribunal; Supreme Military Tribunal; Tribunal of Accounts; Tribunals of Appeal.

Supreme Federal Tribunal: Eleven Justices (may be increased to sixteen on request of Justices) nominated by President with approval of Federal Council. *Qualifications:* Native-born; of outstanding legal knowledge and integrity; thirty-five to fifty-eight years old.
  Jurisdiction: To indict and judge Justices of the Supreme Tribunal, Ministers of State, Justices of State Tribunals of Appeal, of the Federal District, of the Territories, of the Tribunal of Accounts, ambassadors and ministers. Disputes between the Union and the States; between the States. Disputes as to jurisdiction between Tribunals. Extradition of criminals demanded by other countries. Confirms foreign sentences. Judges ordinary appeals in cases in which the Union is interested, or special appeals when decisions are against a treaty or Federal law; when constitutionality of a law is in question, or a local law or act of local government; when final decisions of State Tribunals of Appeal and the Supreme Federal Tribunal give differing interpretations of the same Federal law.

Supreme Military Tribunal: Tries military offenses; may include civilians committing offenses against nation's external security or its military institutions.

Tribunal of Accounts: Members nominated by President with approval of Federal Council. *Duties:* Administers the budget; checks accounts rendered by those responsible for public funds and properties, and legality of contracts made by Union.

Charts of Confederate & Federal Constitutions

Tribunals of Appeal: In the States, the Federal District, and the Territories. Candidates for the lower courts must take competitive examinations; promotion by seniority and merit.

Jurisdiction: All cases not specifically under jurisdiction of Supreme Federal Tribunal.

Rights of all Justices: Life tenure which may be terminated only by sentence of two-thirds of active Justices of Tribunal immediately superior, or by resignation or retirement. Retirement compulsory at sixty-eight, and for proved physical disability; retirement optional after thirty years' service, on full pay. Salary may not be reduced but is taxable. Justices even though retired may not exercise any other public function.

Attorney General: Appointed by President; same qualification as for Justice of the Supreme Federal Tribunal; heads Federal Public Ministry which functions in connection with Supreme Federal Tribunal. May represent Treasury in debt-collection cases.

TRANSFERS OF JURISDICTION FROM MEMBER STATES TO THE UNION:
Federal law nullifies conflicting State legislation.
Admit new territories.
Conduct foreign affairs; declare war, make peace; provide for defense.
Authorize production and supervise commerce in all war materials.
Control, exploit, grant concessions in telegraph services, radio, railways crossing State lines, air traffic.
May transform a State into a Territory, if State fails for three years to collect sufficient revenues to meet its expenses, until its financial capacity is reestablished.
May create Federal Territories out of parts of States in the interest of national defense.
Levy customs; regulate foreign and interstate commerce.
Determine basis and scope of national education.
Regulate naturalization and immigration (may not exceed two per cent of each nation's residents in Brazil during past fifty years).
Provide uniform regulation whenever public well-being and order demand it.
Regulate monopolies and nationalization of industries.
Control federal property, mines, metallurgy, hydraulic power,

RESTRICTIONS ON INDIVIDUAL RIGHTS:
  Compulsory military service.
  Naturalization may be revoked by due process for political or social activity harmful to the national interest or for accepting commissions or employment from a foreign government without permission of President.
  Death sentence permissible for attempts with help or subsidy of a foreign state or organization of international character to change the political or social order established by the Constitution.
  Censorship of press, theater, cinemas, and radio for peace, order, and public safety.
  Meetings contrary to public morals and good usage may be prevented.
  Strikes and lockouts prohibited.
  Only native-born Brazilians may manage newspapers.
  Only Brazilians may own and operate certain businesses.
  Liberal professions open only to native-born or naturalized citizens who have done their military service in Brazil.
  Divorce prohibited.

METHODS OF ENFORCEMENT:
  President may nominate an "interventor" to administer any State to prevent imminent invasion by another State or a foreign country; to reestablish order in a State; or on petition from the Supreme Federal Tribunal to insure execution of Federal laws and sentences.

AMENDMENT:
  When an amendment is brought before Parliament on the initiative of the President, it must be voted on *en bloc* by majority vote of the Chamber of Deputies and of the Federal Council without any change.
  When an amendment is brought before Parliament on the initiative of the Chamber of Deputies, it must be approved by majority vote of both Houses of Parliament.
  If the President's amendment is rejected, or Parliament, despite the President's opposition, approves the amendment initiated by the Chamber of Deputies, the President may decide within thirty days which amendment to submit to a national plebiscite. The amendment becomes a part of the Constitution if the plebiscite is favorable.

Charts of Confederate & Federal Constitutions

Tribunals of Appeal: In the States, the Federal District, and the Territories. Candidates for the lower courts must take competitive examinations; promotion by seniority and merit.

Jurisdiction: All cases not specifically under jurisdiction of Supreme Federal Tribunal.

Rights of all Justices: Life tenure which may be terminated only by sentence of two-thirds of active Justices of Tribunal immediately superior, or by resignation or retirement. Retirement compulsory at sixty-eight, and for proved physical disability; retirement optional after thirty years' service, on full pay. Salary may not be reduced but is taxable. Justices even though retired may not exercise any other public function.

Attorney General: Appointed by President; same qualification as for Justice of the Supreme Federal Tribunal; heads Federal Public Ministry which functions in connection with Supreme Federal Tribunal. May represent Treasury in debt-collection cases.

TRANSFERS OF JURISDICTION FROM MEMBER STATES TO THE UNION:
Federal law nullifies conflicting State legislation.
Admit new territories.
Conduct foreign affairs; declare war, make peace; provide for defense.
Authorize production and supervise commerce in all war materials.
Control, exploit, grant concessions in telegraph services, radio, railways crossing State lines, air traffic.
May transform a State into a Territory, if State fails for three years to collect sufficient revenues to meet its expenses, until its financial capacity is reestablished.
May create Federal Territories out of parts of States in the interest of national defense.
Levy customs; regulate foreign and interstate commerce.
Determine basis and scope of national education.
Regulate naturalization and immigration (may not exceed two per cent of each nation's residents in Brazil during past fifty years).
Provide uniform regulation whenever public well-being and order demand it.
Regulate monopolies and nationalization of industries.
Control federal property, mines, metallurgy, hydraulic power,

water rights, forests, hunting, and fishing as to exploitation, nationalization, and industrial use.
Unify and standardize electrical establishments, installations, safety measures, high-tension lines crossing State lines.
Establish civil, commercial, aerial, labor, penal, and judiciary codes.
Regulate insurance, theaters, cinemas, cooperatives, savings institutions, currency, credit, exchange, banking.
Control copyrights, press, meeting and association, civil status, registration.
Regulate electoral matters affecting the Union, States, and Municipalities.
Organize and train State police forces and use them as army reserves.

STATES RETAIN:
Right to decree their own Constitutions and laws; may exercise all rights not expressly or implicitly denied by the Constitution of the Union.
Right to make agreements among themselves subject to approval of Federal Government.
Organization of State Judiciary; filling of State offices.
With approval of Federal Government, State Assemblies may legislate on matters specially delegated to them, and on the following matters to meet local needs if no Federal law exists or until it does: subsoil resources, mining, metallurgy, water and hydrolectric power, forests, hunting, fishing, radio communications, public relief, hygiene, sanitariums, clinics, health resorts, medicinal springs.
Establish extra-judicial bodies for conciliation and arbitration.
Protect plants and herds against disease.
Regulate agricultural credit and farmers' cooperatives.
Tax all territorial, except urban property, sales and consignments, exportation of State-produced merchandise up to ten per cent of its value, industries and professions, State services (States may create other forms of taxation but there must be no double taxation).
Regulate vocational apprentice schools created by industry and economic syndicates.

RESTRICTIONS ON THE UNION, THE STATES, THE MUNICIPALITIES:
Federal taxes must be uniform.
No customs barriers or traffic restrictions may be established.

None may establish or subsidize religious cults, or hinder their exercise.
No Federal, State, or Municipal authority may refuse to give full credit to the documents of the others.

OBLIGATION:
Reciprocal extradition of criminals.

INDIVIDUAL RIGHTS:
No distinction between native-born Brazilians may be made.
No person may be kept in prison without due process of law.
Limited right of writ of habeas corpus.
Defendants assured a hearing and right to defense by counsel.
No Brazilian may be extradited to a foreign country.
No retroactive laws may be passed.
No life sentences permitted; but death sentences for certain crimes are permissible.
Newspapers libeling or defaming a citizen must print freely his reply, defense, or correction; the responsible editor subject to prison, and the newspaper, to fine; anonymity prohibited.

LABOR AND SOCIAL WELFARE:
Large families to be granted aid according to need.
Indigent parents entitled to government aid and protection for maintenance and education of their children.
Children born in or out of wedlock have equal rights.
Right to education in public institutions of all grades according to individual ability, aptitude, and vocational tendency.
Right of workers to minimum wages; eight hours work (law may increase it); extra pay for night work; weekly rest on Sundays and other holidays when possible; unemployment compensation; annual vacations with pay after a year's continuous service; medical assistance and hygienic protection to women workers during pregnancy.
Old age, life, and accident insurance.
Squatter's right of any Brazilian continuously occupying and working ten hectares or less of land; entitled to legal ownership through a declaratory judgment.
Right of Indians to possession of lands on which they are located; but these may not be sold.

RESTRICTIONS ON INDIVIDUAL RIGHTS:

Compulsory military service.

Naturalization may be revoked by due process for political or social activity harmful to the national interest or for accepting commissions or employment from a foreign government without permission of President.

Death sentence permissible for attempts with help or subsidy of a foreign state or organization of international character to change the political or social order established by the Constitution.

Censorship of press, theater, cinemas, and radio for peace, order, and public safety.

Meetings contrary to public morals and good usage may be prevented.

Strikes and lockouts prohibited.

Only native-born Brazilians may manage newspapers.

Only Brazilians may own and operate certain businesses.

Liberal professions open only to native-born or naturalized citizens who have done their military service in Brazil.

Divorce prohibited.

METHODS OF ENFORCEMENT:

President may nominate an "interventor" to administer any State to prevent imminent invasion by another State or a foreign country; to reestablish order in a State; or on petition from the Supreme Federal Tribunal to insure execution of Federal laws and sentences.

AMENDMENT:

When an amendment is brought before Parliament on the initiative of the President, it must be voted on *en bloc* by majority vote of the Chamber of Deputies and of the Federal Council without any change.

When an amendment is brought before Parliament on the initiative of the Chamber of Deputies, it must be approved by majority vote of both Houses of Parliament.

If the President's amendment is rejected, or Parliament, despite the President's opposition, approves the amendment initiated by the Chamber of Deputies, the President may decide within thirty days which amendment to submit to a national plebiscite. The amendment becomes a part of the Constitution if the plebiscite is favorable.

RATIFICATION:
This Constitution comes into effect on the date decreed by the President and it is to be submitted to a national plebiscite in the form decreed by him. President's term of office is prolonged until the result of the plebiscite is known. At this writing (February, 1944), the plebiscite has not yet been held nor a date set for it. Brazil is governed under conditions prescribed for a *state of emergency*. There is no *National Parliament*.

MISCELLANEOUS:
According to the Preamble this Constitution was decreed by President Getulio Vargas to end party dissensions, the threat of class warfare, and the infiltration of communism. The President cannot be his own nominee to succeed himself.

TITLE:
Constitution of the United States of Mexico.

DATE:
1917, with amendments to January 8, 1943.

SOURCE:
English translation issued by *Asociación de Empresas Industriales y Comerciales*, Mexico, D. F. (mimeographed).

TYPE:
FEDERAL. NAME: United States of Mexico.

MEMBERSHIP:
Twenty-eight States; the Federal District; three Territories; and adjacent islands in both oceans.

ORGANS OF GOVERNMENT:
LEGISLATIVE: Bicameral *Congress: Chamber of Deputies; Senate*.
Chamber of Deputies: Three-year terms; one deputy and one alternate for every 150,000 population or fraction exceeding 75,000; no state to have less than two deputies and no territory less than one; direct

election by citizens over twenty-one, or over eighteen if married; candidates must be at least twenty-five years old; native-born; residents of state or territory electing them at least six months before election. *Disqualification: Candidates* may not be in active army service, command police corps, or rural constabulary (in the election district) for at least ninety days before election; Ministers or Secretaries of the Executive Departments of State, Justices of the Supreme Court, Secretaries of State Governments, magistrates, federal and state judges must resign ninety days before election to qualify as candidates; no ministers of religion may be candidates.

Quorum: More than one-half the total membership.

Exclusive Powers: Sits as Electoral College to elect the President; approves the annual budget; supervises Comptroller of the Treasury; appoints officers and staff of Treasury; acts as Grand Jury to determine if charges warrant impeachment; impeaches high officials before Senate; approves or disapproves appointment of federal justices.

Senate: Six-year term; two Senators and two Alternates from each State; two from the Federal District; direct election; same qualifications as for Deputies, except that Senators must be at least thirty-five years old.

Quorum: Two-thirds of Senators.

Exclusive Powers: Approves treaties and conventions with foreign powers; confirms nominations of diplomatic and consular officers; high treasury, army, and navy officers; authorizes President to send troops beyond national borders; permits passage of foreign troops through national territory; permits presence of foreign fleets in Mexican waters for more than a month; decides on intervention within a State in case its constitutional government breaks down; appoints by two-thirds vote a Provisional Governor to call for new elections; adjusts political disputes within a State on appeal from any branch of the State government; approves nominations of Supreme Court Justices.

Senators and Deputies may not be reelected for terms immediately following, but their Alternates may be elected. In the absence of a quorum, the Alternates are summoned; if none appear within thirty days, new elections must be held.

Sessions: Begin first day of September of each year; may not last beyond December 31 of the same year.

The Permanent Committee: Twenty-nine members: Fifteen Deputies;

Charts of Confederate & Federal Constitutions

fourteen Senators; appointed by each House on day of adjournment. *Duties:* To call extraordinary sessions of Congress or only of one House, specifying matters to be dealt with; approve appointment of federal judges; administer oath of office; grant leaves of absence to federal justices and to the President of the Republic; appoint an Acting President for such period (not in excess of thirty days).

EXECUTIVE OR ADMINISTRATIVE:

President: Six-year term; not eligible for reelection; must be second-generation native-born; over thirty-five; resident in nation for year preceding election. *Disqualification:* Must not belong to any ecclesiastical order or be a clergyman; must have left active army service six months prior to election and must have resigned federal administrative office or State or Territorial Governorship six months before election; must not have served as Substitute or Provisional President.

Duties: Executes laws enacted by Congress; appoints and removes Secretaries of Executive Departments, Federal Attorney General, Governors of Federal District and Federal Territories; appoints, with approval of Senate, diplomatic and consular officers; high army, navy, and Treasury officers; directs land and sea forces and National Guard; declares war on resolution of Congress; conducts diplomatic negotiations; negotiates treaties to be ratified by Congress; nominates federal officers and judges.

Executive Departments: Established by Congress; Secretaries must be native-born; at least thirty years old. *Duties:* Sign Presidential regulations, decrees, and orders; report to Congress at each regular session on work of the Departments.

Board of General Health: Directly under the President; in case of serious illness or epidemics, assumes full executive powers; its rulings must be obeyed by all other administrative authorities.

JUDICIAL:
Supreme Court; Circuit and District Courts.

Supreme Court of Justice of the Nation: Six-year term; twenty-one Judges nominated by President; approved by Senate and House; Judges must be native-born; over thirty-five but not over sixty-five years old; law graduates; resident in nation five years before appointment; Court elects one of its members Chief Justice each year; subject to reelection. Supreme Court may sit together or divide into four Courts of five Judges each.

Exclusive Jurisdiction of Supreme Court: Over controversies between two or more States; between one or more States and the Federal Government; all cases to which the Federal Government is party; controversies over constitutionality of the powers of different branches of the State Governments; questions of jurisdiction between the Federal Government and the States; between courts of one State and those of another.

Circuit and District Judges: Appointed by Supreme Court; may name auxiliary Circuit and District Judges to expedite business and special commissions to investigate violations of individual rights, subversion of popular will; Circuit and District Courts supervised by Supreme Court Justices.

Jurisdiction of Federal Courts: Violations of individual rights. Federal laws or acts limiting or encroaching on the sovereignty of the States; State laws or acts invading the sphere of federal authority; civil or criminal controversies over enforcement of federal laws or treaties; controversies between a State and one or more citizens of another State; cases involving diplomatic and consular officers.

Attorney General: Same qualifications as for Justice of the Supreme Court; appointed by President and removable by him. *Duties:* Legal adviser of Government; prosecutes all offenses against the Federal Government.

TRANSFERS OF JURISDICTION FROM MEMBER STATES TO THE UNION:
To admit new states or territories into the Union.
To form new states within existing ones under certain conditions.
To determine boundaries of member states.
To protect the states against invasion and external violence; and against insurrection on request of State legislature or Executive when legislature not in session.
To govern the Federal District and the territories.
To levy taxes to meet budget expenditures.
To prevent restrictions on interstate commerce.

Charts of Confederate & Federal Constitutions

To legislate on hydrocarbides, mining, electric power, commerce, credit institutions, cinema industry, labor.

To declare war and make peace.

To raise and maintain the army and navy; regulate its organization and service; regulate organization, armament, and discipline of the National Guard.

To enact laws on nationality, status of aliens, citizenship, naturalization, colonization, emigration, immigration, and public health.

To regulate means of communication, post roads, postoffices; use of waters under federal jurisdiction.

To issue money, regulate its value, and that of foreign currencies; adopt general system of weights and measures.

To define crimes and offenses against the nation; grant pardons.

To establish, organize and maintain rural, elementary, high, secondary, and professional schools; schools of scientific research, fine arts, technical training, agricultural and mining schools, arts and crafts schools, museums, libraries, observatories, etc; to divide the cost between the Federal Government, the states, and the municipalities.

To tax foreign commerce, utilization and exploitation of natural resources, credit institutions, insurance companies, public services, electric power, gasoline and petroleum byproducts, forest exploitation; proceeds of some of these taxes to be divided between the states and territories.

To regulate utilization of natural resources, to conserve them, to insure more equitable distribution of public wealth.

To expropriate private property for reasons of public utility on payment of indemnity.

The Federal and State legislatures, respectively, may fix the maximum area of individual or corporate rural property and provide for division of excess lands.

STATES RETAIN:
Sole power to determine maximum number of ministers of religious creeds according to needs of each locality.

RESTRICTIONS ON STATES:
Must adopt popular, representative, republican form of government; State governors must be native-born, directly elected for six-year terms, ineligible for reelection; deputies in State legislatures

must be in proportion to population, ineligible for reelection for term immediately following. *Municipalities* within states must have directly elected town councils and mayors; source of revenues fixed by State legislatures, funds administered by municipalities.

May not enter into alliances, treaties, coalitions with other states or with foreign powers; nor issue money; nor levy taxes on persons or property passing through their territory; nor prohibit or tax entry or withdrawal of domestic or foreign merchandise; nor contract loans with foreign governments; nor maintain permanent troops or warships or make war on any foreign power except in case of invasion or imminent peril.

Must extradite fugitives from justice from other states or foreign countries; must publish and enforce federal laws; give full faith and credit to public acts, records, judicial proceedings of other states.

DEMOCRATIC RIGHTS:

Slavery forbidden; slaves entering from abroad are free and entitled to protection of the laws.

No treaty shall authorize extradition of political offenders or offenders of the common order who have been slaves in the country where the offense was committed.

Primary education obligatory and must be provided free by the State.

Freedom of expression, writing, and publishing; no law or authority may establish censorship, require bond from authors or printers or restrict liberty of printing.

Right of peaceful petition in political matters by citizens to public officials and employees; every petition to be answered in writing by the official addressed informing petitioner of decision taken.

Right of peaceful assembly and association; but only citizens may assemble to take part in national political affairs.

Freedom of movement within the nation.

No retroactive laws.

No person may be deprived of life, liberty, property, possessions, or rights without proper court trial.

Security against molestation of person, family, domicile, papers or possessions except on written order of a competent authority, stating legal grounds for action taken.

Security against arrest unless on a specific charge, accusation, or

Charts of Confederate & Federal Constitutions

complaint for a specific offense, punishable by imprisonment if supported by credible evidence issued by competent judicial authority. None may be imprisoned for purely civil debts; judicial costs in the administration of justice prohibited.

Detention without formal order of commitment may not exceed three days.

Right to release on bail, speedy and public trial by jury, and adequate defense in criminal cases; detention may not exceed maximum penalty for offense charged; period of detention to be figured as part of prison term imposed.

Unusual corporal punishments or unusual and overwhelming penalties, and capital punishment for political offenses forbidden. Freedom of religious choice and practice, but public worship must be confined within places under governmental supervision; Congress may not establish or forbid any religion.

RESTRICTION ON THE ABOVE RIGHTS:
In case of invasion, grave disturbances of public peace, or other emergency, the President, with concurrence of the Ministers and approval of Congress or its Permanent Committee, may suspend by general decree, for a limited time, any of the guarantees of individual rights. If Congress is recessed it must be convened immediately to grant these powers.

LABOR AND SOCIAL WELFARE:
(Enforcement divided between State and Federal Governments.) Eight hours maximum day work; seven hours maximum night work. Overtime one-hundred per cent above pay for ordinary work; women and children under sixteen may not engage in overtime work, unhealthy and dangerous occupations, night work in factories, or in commercial establishments after ten P. M.; children between twelve and sixteen may not work more than six hours a day; one day's rest for every six days' work.

Protection of women workers during and after pregnancy.

Equal pay for equal work regardless of sex or nationality.

Minimum wage (exempt from attachments, or deductions) must be sufficient according to prevailing regional conditions to satisfy worker's normal needs, education, and position as head of family.

Participation in profits by workers in agricultural, commercial, manufacturing, and mining enterprises.

Both workers and employees have right to form syndicates, unions, professional associations for defense of their respective interests.

RESTRICTIONS ON DEMOCRATIC RIGHTS:

Education to be socialistic, excluding religious doctrine, fanaticism, and prejudice; no religious body, minister of any creed may intervene or support financially primary, secondary, and normal schools. Private schools must conform to these restrictions.

Monastic orders may not be established.

Only native-born Mexicans may be ministers of any religious creed. Ministers of religion may not criticize the fundamental laws, the authorities, or the government; they have no vote, nor may they assemble for political purposes.

No publication of a religious character may comment on national political affairs or give information on acts of the authorities.

Political associations may not indicate religious affiliation in their names; political assemblies may not be held in places of public worship.

No minister of any religious creed may inherit personally or as trustee real property used by any association for religious propaganda or for religious or charitable purposes; nor inherit anything from anyone to whom he is not related by blood within the fourth degree.

All real property held by the churches, irrespective of creed, shall revert to the nation, as well as places of public worship.

Public or private charitable institutions, those for scientific research, diffusion of knowledge, mutual aid societies may not be under the patronage, direction, administration, charge, or supervision of religious orders, institutions, or of religious ministers, or their followers.

No trial by jury shall be granted for violation of the foregoing provisions.

Compulsory military service.

OBLIGATIONS OF CITIZENS:

Jury service; service in municipal and other public elective offices; services in connection with elections are obligatory and without remuneration.

METHODS OF ENFORCEMENT:
Enforcement of laws operates on individuals through the courts, public prosecutors, municipal, state, and federal agencies.
The Federal Government may intervene to suppress insurrection on request of the State legislature, or the executive when the legislature is not in session.

AMENDMENT:
By two-thirds vote of members of Congress and approval of majority of State legislatures.

MISCELLANEOUS:
The Constitution shall not lose force even though its observance is interrupted by rebellion; its force is restored as soon as the people have regained their liberties.

TITLE:
Constitution of the United States of Venezuela.

DATE:
July 16, 1936. 127th year of Independence; 78th year of the Federation.

SOURCE:
Translation from the original Spanish text by Filippus Mosèsco (in manuscript).

TYPE:
FEDERAL.

MEMBERSHIP:
Twenty States; one Federal District; two Federal Territories; Dependencies (the Venezuelan Islands). The capital city, Caracas, has autonomy in its economic and administrative management.

ORGANS OF GOVERNMENT:
LEGISLATIVE: Bicameral *Congress: Senate; Chamber of Deputies;* four-year term for both; half the membership renewed every two years.

Senate: Two Senators and two Substitutes elected by each State legislature from outside its own membership; Senators must be native-born; over thirty years old; resident in the state three years prior to election.

Chamber of Deputies: Municipal Councils of each State meeting in convention in the State capital elect one Deputy and one Substitute for each 30,000 population and one additional Deputy for fraction over 15,000. Deputies must be native-born; at least twenty-five years old; three years' resident prior to elections in the State, Federal District, or territories they are to represent. In the territories, uncivilized natives are not to be counted for purposes of representation.

Sessions: Annually, to last ninety days; cannot be extended. President may call extraordinary sessions but only those matters may be considered for which Congress was convened.

Quorum for first session: Two-thirds of the members; if there are less, those present can compel the attendance of absentees.

Quorum at other sessions: Absolute majority of the elected members. Members continue to have immunity thirty days after sessions.

Joint Sessions: For purposes of nomination and election; to take cognizance of the President's resignation; to examine the President's annual message; to examine reports, accounts, petitions of Cabinet Ministers; to receive new states into the Union.

Congress may censure Cabinet Ministers but they are removable by the President only if the Supreme Court declares legal grounds exist to bring them to trial.

Duties: To legislate on all matters within federal jurisdiction, to approve or reject peace treaties negotiated by the Executive, to declare war; to name committees of investigation to whom Federal, State, and municipal administrations and courts must submit information and documents.

Legislation must be initiated by at least three members of either Chamber. The Executive may initiate legislation through one of the Cabinet Ministers.

EXECUTIVE OR ADMINISTRATIVE:

President: Five-year term; native-born; at least thirty years old (clergymen ineligible); cannot be reelected for the term immediately following; elected by joint session of Congress; previous President continues as Acting President until the President-Elect takes oath of office before Congress or Supreme Court. The President may appoint a Cabinet Minister to serve as temporary executive; if office of President becomes permanently vacant, Congress must be called into extraordinary session to elect a new President; if there is no Acting Federal Executive, and no Cabinet Minister has been appointed, the Cabinet by majority vote can elect a Minister to act as President until the new President-Elect assumes office.

Duties: To name and remove Ministers of the Cabinet; to command the armed forces directly or through designated persons; to conduct war, to receive foreign ambassadors and diplomats; to appoint the Governor of the Federal District; to administer the Federal territories and dependencies; to publish the Federal laws in the *Official Gazette*; to administer the laws; to declare war when decreed by Congress; to conduct diplomatic negotiations; to reorganize states dominated by rebel forces whose own governors participate in the rebellion; to use the Federal forces to terminate armed conflict between two states when President's offer of mediation has failed; to grant amnesties; to report annually to Congress.

Cabinet Ministers: Heads of the Departments created by Congress; Ministers must be native-born; at least thirty years old (clergymen ineligible). *Duties:* Countersign Presidential decrees belonging to their respective departments; share responsibility with President in matters on which they voted in the affirmative; report on work of the Departments to Congress; Minister of the Treasury presents draft budget to Congress within first thirty days of the regular session; Ministers may speak in Congress and must give it information when requested; responsible under criminal and civil law for any illegal acts.

Attorney General: Five-year term; native-born lawyer, at least thirty years old; elected by Congress together with five substitutes who fill vacancies in the office of Attorney General in the order of their election. *Duties:* Supervises proper application of the laws in the Federal tribunals, those of the states, and of the municipalities; gives advisory opinions when requested by Congress, the President, Cabinet Ministers, or the Federal Supreme Court; prefers charges against Federal employees for misconduct in office; acts as prosecutor before the

Federal Supreme Court; represents the federation in all suits to which it is a party.

National Economic Council: Composed of representatives of producers, consumers, labor, capital, and the professions; President determines function and organization.

JUDICIAL:
Federal Supreme Court: Five-year term; seven members; must be native-born; over thirty years old; members of the bar; on expiration of term, they continue in office if not replaced; seven Judges and seven Substitutes elected by Congress by majority vote.
Jurisdiction: To try impeachment of the President, Cabinet Ministers, the Attorney General, the Governor of the Federal District, members of the Federal Supreme Court, Governors of the Federal Territories, and the presidents of the states in accordance with State laws; to try civil and criminal cases against foreign diplomatic agents in conformity with international law, and national diplomatic agents in case of impeachment or misconduct in office; to decide controversies between officials of various states; between two or more states; between the states and the Federal District; to decide conflicts of jurisdiction between branches of the Federal Government; between the branches of State Governments; between the states and the Federal Government.
The Federal Supreme Court may nullify Federal, State, or municipal laws in conflict with the Constitution; Federal legislative and executive acts which violate rights reserved to the states or which threaten their autonomy; may decide disputes between the Federation and individuals.
Once a year the Court is to present a Memorial to Congress reporting on its work and indicating reforms that should be introduced by legislation.

TRANSFERS OF JURISDICTION FROM MEMBER STATES TO THE UNION:
To conduct foreign affairs.
To protect the general interest and maintain public peace.
To regulate commerce, trademarks, copyrights, industrial rights, weights and measures, banking, credit institutions, social welfare, sanitation, conservation, development of agriculture and stock-raising,

Charts of Confederate & Federal Constitutions

development and exploitation of natural resources, labor, public registration, elections; immigration, admission, naturalization, and expulsion of foreigners.

To regulate all matters pertaining to the army, navy, and to military aviation.

To regulate public instruction and the national census.

To provide uniform currency and coinage.

To regulate transportation by land, air, sea, river, lake, and in the ports.

To levy export and import duties.

To administer posts, telegraph, telephone, wireless; to open and maintain national highways.

To organize and govern the Federal District, territories and dependencies, and admit new states.

To regulate and dispose of the salt-pits, pearl oyster beds, mines, uncultivated lands and their products.

To organize public works (without limiting the rights of the states and municipalities in this respect).

To encourage European immigration.

STATES RETAIN:

Sovereignty not specifically granted to the Federation nor prohibited to them.

Twenty per cent of the annual national tax income is divided among the states in proportion to population.

Two or more states may unite to form a single state, but their right to return to their former autonomy is reserved.

OBLIGATIONS AND RESTRICTIONS ON THE STATES:

States may not secede from the Union or make alliances or solicit foreign protection; they may not cede any portion of their territory.

They undertake to defend themselves and the Federation.

The Government of the Federation and of the states must be republican, federal, democratic, elective, representative, responsible and alternative (the President may not be reelected). States to be divided into districts; municipalities within the districts to have full autonomy in economic and administrative matters.

They must draft their constitutions and laws in conformity with the

Federal Constitution; and must elect municipal councils and legislative assemblies in conformity with the Federal election laws.

States and municipalities may maintain only police and prison guards; they must pledge to carry out the Constitution, laws, decrees, orders, and resolutions of the Federal Government.

Verdicts of State Tribunals subject to review by Federal Supreme Court.

States may not impose customs duties on imports and exports or on merchandise in transit.

States and municipalities must render full faith to the public acts and judicial proceedings of the Federal authorities, the other states, the Federal District; are bound to carry them out and to cooperate with the Federal Government when called on.

States may not declare or wage war; they must maintain strict neutrality in any dissensions between other states unless called upon for service by the Federal Government.

States and municipalities may not negotiate foreign loans.

In all public acts and official documents of the Federation, the states, the Federal District, the Federal Territories, Federal Dependencies, and municipalities, mention must be made along with the calendar date of the date of Independence, April 19, 1810; and the date of the Federation, February 20, 1859.

DEMOCRATIC RIGHTS:

Inviolability of life; capital punishment may not be established.

Forcible recruiting for military service forbidden.

Slavery ended; slaves entering Federal territory are automatically free.

Freedom of thought expressed by word, press, or writing except those which cause injury, defamation, or instigate violation of the laws.

Freedom of travel and change of residence.

Freedom to work and to establish industries; no industry may be granted a monopoly.

Right of peaceful assembly.

Right to petition public officials and to have the petition answered.

Religious liberty under Federal inspection of all cults with final appeal to the Ecclesiastical Bureau.

Security against arrest for ordinary debts not arising from criminal offenses; against arrest and imprisonment except on warrant and for an offense meriting imprisonment; against being held incommunicado; in criminal cases none may be compelled to testify against himself, consort, or near relatives; sentences may not be for longer than twenty years.

Equal protection of the laws to all throughout the national territory.

Private property may be expropriated for public or social use only through regular proceedings and compensation; but property may be confiscated in retaliation in time of international war, and, when decided by majority vote of Congress and approved by two-thirds of the State legislatures, for restoration to the National Treasury of sums illegally taken by high public officials.

Troops are to be confined to their barracks on election days.

RIGHTS OF LABOR:
At least one day of rest in every work week.
Vacations with pay.

RESTRICTIONS ON INDIVIDUAL RIGHTS:
Anonymous communications, war propaganda, advocacy of communist or anarchist doctrines forbidden. Those propagating either to be considered traitors and punished, if nationals, by expulsion from six months to one year; if foreigners, indefinitely.

Suffrage *limited to men* over twenty-one years of age who know how to read and write and have not been deprived of their political rights through penal punishment.

In case of international war, civil war, epidemics, or events threatening the security of the nation, its institutions, or form of government, the President with the Cabinet may restrict or suspend by decree certain civil rights, except those protecting life, freedom from slavery, and security against unusual punishment. The decree must give reasons for such restriction, enumerate the rights suspended, and name the territory to which it applies.

METHODS OF ENFORCEMENT:
Enforcement through the courts operating on individuals.
Use of Federal armed forces to terminate armed conflict between two states when mediation by the Federal President has failed; to reorganize states dominated by rebel forces when the president of the state also participates in the rebellion.

AMENDMENT:
By majority vote of Congress and ratification by two-thirds of the State legislatures.

The Constitution may be changed in whole or in part when solicited by three-fourths of the State legislatures.

THE STRUCTURE OF THE BRITISH EMPIRE

The *British Empire* includes the *British Commonwealth of Nations* consisting of the United Kingdom of Great Britain and Northern Ireland, Australia, Canada, the Union of South Africa, New Zealand, the Irish Free State, and Newfoundland; the various self-governing colonies; the Crown colonies; India, and other non-self-governing territories. The British Empire rules 500,000,000 human beings of various races under diverse arrangements and forms of government. Some colonies are self-governing to the extent that there is a native majority in the legislature, but certain powers such as defense and foreign affairs are reserved to the British Parliament. Other colonies have limited self-government with restricted native representation in the legislatures. Many are administered entirely by a British Governor and British officials directly under the Colonial Office of the United Kingdom. The *Protectorates* are governed by native rulers who have transferred some of their sovereignty, especially over military and foreign affairs, to the British Government. In addition, there are *Condominiums* where the British Empire shares governmental functions with other nations. The Empire also rules over *Mandates* assigned to it by the League of Nations.

The *British Commonwealth of Nations*, consisting of the United Kingdom of Great Britain and Northern Ireland, and its former colonies, now the Dominion of Canada, the Commonwealth of Australia, the Dominion of New Zealand, the Union of South Africa, the Irish Free State (Eire), and Newfoundland, developed gradually from close centralized control exercised by the Parliament of the United Kingdom into a loose union of sovereign nations united by common allegiance to the Crown.* The Governor-General of each Dominion is appointed by the King with the advice and consent of the *Dominion* Government instead of the Parliament of the *United Kingdom.** The Governor-General in each Dominion is no longer the agent of the *English Parliament* in the Dominions, but, like the King, is merely the *titular* head of the Dominion Government. Government in the Dominions is modeled after the English

* The Irish Free State (Eire) does not swear allegiance to the Crown and does not receive a Governor-General. The President, directly elected for a seven-year term, discharges duties assigned in the other Dominions to the Governor-General.

Parliamentary system under the political leadership of a Prime Minister who forms his *Cabinet* and has to have the confidence of the lower house of Parliament. The Statute of Westminster (1931) affirmed the full sovereign status of the Dominions in their internal and external affairs.

The British Commonwealth has no central organization. It functions through conferences held from time to time to discuss problems of interest to the Empire and the Dominions. Resolutions, recommendations, and agreements negotiated through these conferences come into effect in the Dominions only when enacted by their respective Parliaments.

Three of the Dominions — the Dominion of Canada, the Commonwealth of Australia, and the Union of South Africa — have *federal* constitutions which we present in chart form. These constitutions are of added interest because various complex institutions, established before the Union, had to be adapted. Duality of language in Canada and South Africa was a problem met by official recognition and use of both languages. The transitional measures so recently effected in order to create a Federal Government from separate colonial governments contain valuable suggestions for the *imminent transition to orderly world government.*

The Federal Union of *Canada*, formed in 1867, shortly after the American Civil War, seeking to avoid similar conflicts between its provinces and the Federal Government, retained all powers not specifically delegated to the provinces. On the other hand, in *Australia*, united in 1901, the states retain all powers not specifically granted to the Commonwealth. Still another version of federalism was applied by the Constitution of the *Union of South Africa*, which created practically a unified State, granting all powers, except a few unimportant ones, to the Union Government.

TITLE:
An Act to constitute the Commonwealth of Australia.

DATE:
January 1, 1901, with amendments to 1938.

SOURCE:
Official Yearbook of the Commonwealth of Australia, 1940.

Charts of Confederate & Federal Constitutions

TYPE:
FEDERAL. NAME: Commonwealth of Australia.

MEMBERSHIP:
Six States; one Federal District; four Territories; two Mandates.

ORGANS OF GOVERNMENT:
LEGISLATIVE: Bicameral *Parliament: Senate; House of Representatives.*

Senate: Six-year term; six from each State by direct election; one-half the Senate renewed every three years; President of the Senate elected by the Senators from their own members; he may vote at all times; in case of a tie the decision is in the negative. *Quorum:* One-third of the whole number of Senators. *Decisions:* By majority vote. Qualifications same as for Representatives.

House of Representatives: Three-year term; direct election; representation in proportion to population; each State entitled to at least five representatives. *Qualifications:* At least twenty-one years old; entitled to vote for members of the House of Representatives; three years resident in the Commonwealth; native-born or naturalized five years; House elects its own Speaker; he may not vote except in case of a tie. *Quorum:* One-third of the whole number of members. *Decisions:* By majority vote. Vacancies filled by elections.
Exclusive Rights: Appropriation and tax legislation may originate only in the House and may not be amended by the Senate. Purpose of legislation appropriating revenue must be recommended by the Governor-General before it can be passed.

Both Houses: Qualifications of electors determined by Parliament, but no person having the right to vote for the more numerous House of the State legislature may be deprived of the right to elect members to the Commonwealth Parliament.

Joint Sessions: If legislation passed by the House and rejected by the Senate, after three months is repassed by the House and again rejected by the Senate, the Governor-General may dissolve both Houses; if the newly elected House again passes the legislation and the Senate rejects it, the Governor-General may convene a joint session which may enact the legislation by majority vote of the members present.

New elections must be called ten days after Parliament is dissolved; the House of Representatives may not be dissolved six months before its term would anyway expire.

EXECUTIVE OR ADMINISTRATIVE:

Governor-General: Appointed by the King; Commander-in-chief of naval and military forces; salary paid by the Commonwealth as determined by Parliament; convenes, dissolves, prorogues Parliament; appoints administrative officers and others as provided by the Constitution.

Federal Executive Council: Executive Councilors appointed by Governor-General and removable by him. *Duties:* To advise Governor-General as to government of the Commonwealth and appointment of officers. (The Governor-General-in-Council means the Governor-General acting with the advice of the Executive Council.)

Ministers of State: Eleven; appointed by Governor-General to administer the Departments of State; may not hold office longer than three months if not members of either House of Parliament. Members of Federal Executive Council.

Inter-State Commission: Seven-year term; appointed by Governor-General-in-Council; removable by him for incapacity or misbehavior on request of both Houses of Parliament; salaries fixed by Parliament. *Duties:* To adjudicate and administer provisions of the Constitution and laws of the Commonwealth relating to trade and commerce.

JUDICIAL:

High Court of Australia: Chief Justice and not less than two Justices as prescribed by Parliament; other federal courts created by Parliament or existing courts invested with federal jurisdiction; Justices appointed by Governor-General-in-Council; removable for misbehavior or incapacity on request of Parliament.

Jurisdiction: Over disputes arising under any treaty; affecting consuls or representatives of other countries; to which the Commonwealth is party; between States; between residents of different States; between a State and residents of another State; over injunctions sought against an officer of the Commonwealth; appeals from decrees, judgments, orders, and sentences of other federal courts or of the State Supreme Courts; of the Inter-State Commission on questions of law.

Parliament may confer additional jurisdiction over disputes arising under the Constitution, laws of Parliament, admiralty and maritime jurisdiction.

Trial by jury for offenses against Commonwealth law.

TRANSFERS OF JURISDICTION FROM MEMBER STATES TO THE COMMONWEALTH:

Trade and commerce with other countries and among the States.
Uniform taxation.
Uniform export and production bounties.
Loans on credit of Commonwealth.
Postal, telegraph, telephone, and similar services.
Naval and military forces of the Commonwealth and of the States.
Currency, coinage, banking; weights and measures.
Census and statistics; copyrights, patents, trademarks.
Lighthouses, lightships, beacons, buoys.
Immigration, emigration, naturalization, aliens.
Special legislation dealing with the people of any race other than native tribes (such as Australian white immigration policy).
Foreign affairs.
Marriage, divorce, parental rights, custody, and guardianship.
Invalid and old-age pensions.
Conciliation, arbitration, and settlement of industrial disputes extending beyond State limits.
Control of railways for naval and military transport.
Acquisition of State railways, railway construction and extension with consent of the State concerned.
Admit or establish new States; alter boundaries of a State with consent of the State Parliament and majority vote of the electors of the State.
Uniform customs and excise duties.
Assume State public debts.
Protect the States against invasion and on request of the State Executive against domestic violence.
Administer the Federal District, Federal Territories, and Dependencies.

RESTRICTIONS ON THE COMMONWEALTH:
The Commonwealth may not establish a religion, impose any religious observance, or prohibit the free exercise of any religion, or set up a religious test for qualification for public office under the Commonwealth.

RESTRICTIONS ON THE STATES:
Each State must give full faith and credit to the laws, public acts, records and judicial proceedings of every other State.
Persons resident in one State may not be subjected to discrimination in other States.

STATES RETAIN:
Their Constitutions as existing at the establishment of the Commonwealth, until altered in accordance with the State Constitutions; in case of conflict with State law, Commonwealth law is supreme.
All powers not transferred to the Commonwealth nor forbidden to the States.
Levy of export and import duties in amounts necessary to execute State inspection laws, but such inspection laws may be annulled by the Commonwealth.
Reasonable use of waters and rivers for conservation and irrigation.
Grant of subsidy for mining gold, silver, or other metals; subsidize, with consent of the Commonwealth Parliament, the production or export of goods.

AMENDMENT:
Approval by absolute majority of each House of Parliament and submission to approval of electors of each State as prescribed by Parliament.
If the two Houses cannot agree on the proposed amendment, the Governor-General may submit it to the decision of the electors in each State.

MISCELLANEOUS:
Voting for Commonwealth elections has been *compulsory* since 1925.
Aboriginal natives may not be counted as part of the population of the Commonwealth or the States for purposes of representation.

TITLE:
British North America Act.

DATE:
1867, with amendments to 1940.

SOURCE:
British North America Act and Amendments 1867 to 1927.
  J. O. Patenaude, Printer to the King's Most Excellent Majesty, Ottawa, 1938.

TYPE:
FEDERAL. NAME: Dominion of Canada.

MEMBERSHIP:
Nine Provinces; two Federal Territories.

ORGANS OF GOVERNMENT:
LEGISLATIVE: Bicameral *Parliament of Canada: the Senate; the House of Commons.*

Senate: Ninety-six Senators appointed *for life* by the Governor-General as follows:

2 Provinces	24 each.
2 Provinces	10 each.
4 Provinces	6 each.
1 Province	4

Qualifications: Native-born or naturalized; at least thirty years old; resident of the Province to be represented; owner of $4,000 property above debts and liabilities.

Disqualification: A Senator ceases to be a member of the Senate if he fails to attend two consecutive sessions of Parliament, if he loses his property or residence qualification, if he becomes bankrupt or insolvent, is accused of treason, is convicted of a felony or other crime, or declares allegiance to a foreign power. Senate determines qualifications of members and declares vacancies.

Quorum: Fifteen; *Speaker* appointed from members of Senate by

Governor-General and removable by him; Speaker entitled to vote at all times; in case of tie the vote is negative. *Decisions:* By majority vote.

House of Commons: Five-year term; members elected according to population in each Province; representation determined according to the following method: Quebec is always to have sixty-five members; the number of members allotted the other Provinces is determined by the proportion of Quebec's representatives to its population; the resulting number of persons per representative becomes the basis of representation in the other Provinces. Representation may not be decreased unless the decrease in population is greater than five per cent.

Qualifications: Of members of the House of Commons and of those voting for them to be the same as for the Provincial Legislative Assemblies until otherwise prescribed by Parliament.
Speaker elected by the House from its own members; he votes only in case of a tie. *Quorum:* Twenty. *Decisions:* By majority vote; appropriation and tax legislation must originate in the House but purpose must have been recommended by the Governor-General.
Parliament must meet at least once a year.

EXECUTIVE OR ADMINISTRATIVE:

Governor-General: Appointed by the King; Commander-in-chief of the armed forces; salary determined by Parliament; convenes Parliament and may dissolve House of Commons and call new elections; appoints Judges of the Superior, District, and County Courts in each Province.

Privy Council: Ministers of the Departments appointed by the Governor-General and removable by him. (The Prime Minister must have the confidence of the House of Commons and forms the Cabinet.)
Duties: To advise the Governor-General and to consent to functions to be performed by the Governor-General-in-Council.

JUDICIAL:
General Court of Appeal: As established by Parliament.

Superior, District, Admiralty, and *County Courts:* Judges appointed by Governor-General; salaries fixed by Parliament.
Judges of the Superior Courts hold office during good behavior but are removable by the Governor-General on request of Parliament.

TRANSFERS OF JURISDICTION FROM MEMBER PROVINCES TO THE UNION:

All powers not assigned exclusively to the Provinces are reserved to the Union; Provincial laws in conflict with Acts of Parliament are void.

Eminent domain, regulation of trade and commerce, unemployment insurance, taxation and borrowing, public debt and property, currency, coinage, banking.

Navigation, shipping, quarantine, beacons, buoys, lighthouses, maintenance of marine hospitals, ships, ferries, canals, railways, postal service, telegraph, works connecting two Provinces or extending beyond the limits of a Province; works situated within a Province but declared by Parliament to be for the general welfare; fisheries.

Military and naval affairs.

Statistics, weights and measures, patents, copyrights; census every ten years (in two Provinces every five years).

Admission of new territory; establishment of Provinces; Indian affairs.

Naturalization and aliens, marriage and divorce, criminal law.

PROVINCES RETAIN:

Levy of taxes for Provincial needs and borrow money on credit of Province.

Appointment, payment, and tenure of Provincial officers.

Management and sale of public lands, timber, and wood.

Provincial prisons, hospitals, asylums, charities, charitable institutions, municipal institutions.

Licensing of various business enterprises, local works, incorporation of companies operating within the Province.

Property, civil rights.

Agriculture and immigration when not in conflict with Acts of Parliament.

Administration of justice, organization, and maintenance of civil and criminal courts, and civil procedure within the Province.

Lands, mines, minerals, royalties held at the time the Union was established.

Provincial land and property may not be taxed; boundaries may be changed only by consent of the Provincial legislatures concerned.

Education, except that the rights of the Protestant and Roman Catholic minorities in educational matters may not be abridged.

May amend their own constitutions.

Receive annual grants between $100,000 and $240,000 for expenses of Provincial Government from the Government of Canada according to population.

RESTRICTIONS ON THE PROVINCES:
Lieutenant-Governor of each Province appointed by Governor-General-in-Council for five-year term; removable for cause; salary fixed by Parliament. (Otherwise, Provincial Governments are organized along Parliamentary lines similar to that of the Government of Canada. However, the legislatures of all the Provinces, except Quebec, are unicameral.)

AMENDMENT:
By address of the Parliament of Canada to the Parliament of the United Kingdom.

MISCELLANEOUS:
English or French may be used in any court, debates in Parliament and Legislative Assemblies; records, acts, and journals must be kept and published in both languages.

At the establishment of the Union when functions discharged by the separate Provincial Governments were transferred to the Union, the Provincial officials involved were also transferred; those that could not be absorbed or given work of equal rank were pensioned.

TITLE:
An Act to Constitute the Union of South Africa.

DATE:
September 20, 1909; in effect May 31, 1910 (with later amendments).

SOURCE:
Select Constitutions of the World by B. Shiva Rao.
Madras Law Journal Press, 1934.

TYPE:
FEDERAL: (The Constitution of the Union of South Africa grants such extensive powers to the Federal Government that the Provinces are

Charts of Confederate & Federal Constitutions

practically its administrative subdivisions, and some authorities consider the Union in reality a unified State. It is of special interest because of the close unification achieved so soon after a bitter war among the Provinces and with England [the Boer War — October, 1899 to May, 1902].—EDITORS.)

MEMBERSHIP:

Four Provinces; Union administers Southwest Africa under a Mandate from the League of Nations since December, 1920.

ORGANS OF GOVERNMENT:

LEGISLATIVE: Bicameral *Parliament: Senate; House of Assembly.*

Senate: Ten-year term; eight Senators nominated by the Governor-General-in-Council; eight Senators elected by each Provincial Assembly in joint session. *Qualifications:* At least thirty years old; British subject of European descent; qualified to be a registered voter for election of members to the House of Assembly; five years' residence in the Union; Senators elected by the Provincial Legislatures must possess immovable property of at least 500 pounds (above mortgages). *Quorum:* Twelve Senators. *Decisions:* By majority vote.

President of the Senate: Chosen by the Senators from their own members. Deputy President chosen to preside in President's absence. President votes only in case of a tie.

House of Assembly: Five-year term; elected by direct vote of white men and women of European descent in proportion to population as determined by census every five years, except registered voters in the Cape of Good Hope may not be disqualified because of race or color alone; voters must be at least twenty-one years old; those on active service in the armed forces may not vote.

Candidates to the House of Assembly must be registered voters; five years' residence within the Union; British subjects of European descent. *Quorum:* Thirty members. *Decisions:* By majority vote. *Speaker* chosen by the House from its own members; votes only in case of a tie.

Disqualification for Membership in Both Houses: Conviction for crime of a year's imprisonment or more (unless five years elapsed since expiration of term); insolvency; if declared of unsound mind by

Court; holding office under the Union, except Ministers of State, pensioners, or retired or part-time members of the armed forces.

Miscellaneous: Appropriation bills must originate in the House of Assembly and may not be amended by the Senate; appropriation and revenue bills may be introduced only after purpose recommended by the Governor-General. If the two Houses cannot agree on any proposed legislation during two sessions, the Governor-General may convene a joint session and legislation passes by majority vote of the two Houses sitting together. If the Senate fails to pass appropriation and revenue bills, the joint session may be convened during the same session.

EXECUTIVE OR ADMINISTRATIVE:

Governor-General: Appointed by the King; his salary may not be reduced during his term of office; Commander-in-chief of the armed forces.
Summons, prorogues, or dissolves Parliament; convenes joint sessions.

Executive Council: Members chosen by the Governor-General to advise him. (Governor-General-in-Council refers to the Governor-General acting with the advice of the Executive Council.)

Duties of Governor-General-in-Council: Appoints and removes officers of the Union unless otherwise provided; sets uniform date of election; appoints and removes Provincial administrators; fixes salaries of members of the Provincial councils and executive committees; passes on ordinances of the Provincial councils; appoints judges of the Supreme Court and of the Appeals Court.

Ministers of State: Eleven; members of the Executive Council; three months after appointment by Governor-General must become members of either House of Parliament. Administer the Departments of State. Ministers may sit in either House but may vote only in the one of which they are members.

Harbor and Railway Board: Five-year term; three commissioners appointed by Governor-General-in-Council; a Minister of State to be chairman; commissioners may be reappointed and may be dismissed for cause before expiration of their term; salaries fixed by Parliament. *Duties:* To control and manage the railways, ports, and harbors of the Union.

JUDICIAL:

Supreme Court of South Africa: The Chief Justice; four Judges of Appeal; four Provincial divisions of the Supreme Court; local divisions of the Supreme Court called Superior Courts.

Jurisdiction of local and Provincial divisions of the Supreme Court: Suits to which the Union Government is party; suits over the validity of Provincial ordinances; local divisions to have jurisdiction as to the validity of elections to the House of Assembly and the Provincial councils.

Final appeal to the Appellate Division of the Supreme Court: Judgments or orders of the Appellate Division to have full force and effect throughout the Union. Civil and criminal cases may be appealed to the Appellate Division only by its permission.

Judges appointed by Governor-General-in-Council; salaries determined by Parliament; may be removed from office only on request of both Houses of Parliament for misbehavior or incapacity. Parliament may reduce the number of Judges in any division of the Supreme Court (except the Appellate Division) by not filling vacancies.

THE PROVINCES:

EXECUTIVE: *Administrator of the Province:* Five-year term; appointed by Governor-General-in-Council; removable by him for cause; preference to be given to person resident in the province; salary determined by Parliament.

Auditor of Accounts: Appointed by Governor-General-in-Council and removable by him for cause; salary determined by Governor-General-in-Council and approved by Parliament.

Duties: To examine and audit accounts of the Province to which he is assigned subject to regulations prescribed by Governor-General-in-Council approved by Parliament; must countersign all money payments authorized by the Administrator.

LEGISLATIVE: *Provincial Councils:* Three-year term; each Provincial Council to have as many members as it sends to the House of Assembly; but no Provincial Council to have less than twenty-five; qualifications of candidates and electors same as for House of Assembly. Sessions at least once a year convened by Administrator.

Councils elect their own chairmen; determine own rules of procedure but these may be disapproved by the Governor-General-in-Council. Salaries of Councilors determined by Governor-General-in-Council.

Each Provincial Council at its first meeting, from its own members or outside, elects the *Provincial Executive Committee:* Three-year term; four members. Administrator serves as Chairman; salaries determined by Provincial Council with approval of Governor-General-in-Council. Vacancies filled by the Provincial Council if in session, by the Executive Committee if it is not, pending an election by the Council. The Administrator and members of the Executive Committee who are not members of the Provincial Council may participate in Council sessions but may not vote.
Decisions: By majority vote; in case of tie, the Administrator casts the deciding vote.
In matters over which the Provincial Councils have neither delegated nor reserved powers, the Administrator may act without the Executive Committee when required to do so by the Governor-General-in-Council.

Ordinances passed by the Provincial Council must be presented to the Governor-General-in-Council for his assent; within one month he must declare whether he assents or withholds his assent, or whether he reserves it for further consideration. Ordinances of the Provincial Councils have effect only if not in conflict with any Act of Parliament. Provincial Councils may recommend enactment of laws by Parliament on matters beyond their jurisdiction.

TRANSFERS OF JURISDICTION FROM MEMBER PROVINCES TO THE UNION:
Full power to make laws for the peace, order, and good government of the Union.
Control and administration of native affairs and matters affecting Asiatics throughout the Union and formerly vested in the Governors of the Colonies.
All rights and obligations under conventions or agreements which were binding on any of the Colonies before the establishment of the Union.
Alter boundaries of the Provinces; form new Provinces out of those

in the Union; divide a Province into two or more Provinces on request of the Provincial Councils concerned.

Admit new territories into the Union if transferred by the Parliament of the United Kingdom.

Administer railways and harbors; regulate public traffic.

Assume all Colonial debts and liabilities and all financial assets of the Colonies.

Take over the Crown lands, public works, and all Colonial property throughout the Union, and all rights of the Colonies.

Assume all rights to mines and minerals as well as their disposal vested in the Colonies at the establishment of the Union.

Determine financial relations between the Union and the Provinces and grant necessary sums to the Provinces for the proper discharge of services and duties assigned to them.

PROVINCES RETAIN:
(Subject to assent of the Governor-General-in-Council and the Union Parliament.)

Right of direct taxation within the Province.
Negotiation of loans on the credit of the Province.
Education, other than higher education.
Agriculture.
Right to establish, maintain, and manage hospitals and charitable institutions.
Local works and undertakings.
Roads and bridges, other than those connecting Provinces.
Markets and pounds (cattle or animal pens).
Fish and game preservation.
Enforcement of Provincial ordinances.
Matters local to the Province.
Matters delegated by Parliament.

AMENDMENT:
By two-thirds vote of the total number of members of both Houses in joint session.

MISCELLANEOUS:
Official languages: Dutch and English; records, proceedings, judgments, journal of Parliament must be published in both languages.

Pretoria is the seat of the Union Government.
Capetown is the seat of the Union Parliament.
Basutoland, the Bechuanaland Protectorate, and Swaziland are administered by a High Commissioner not for the Union of South Africa but directly for the United Kingdom.

TITLE:
The Federal Constitution of the Swiss Confederation.

DATE:
May 29, 1874 (based on the Constitution of 1848), with amendments to 1931.

SOURCE:
Source Book on European Governments by William E. Rappard and others. D. van Nostrand Co., New York, 1937.

TYPE:
FEDERAL. (A limited *federation* although the original name Swiss *Confederation* is retained.)

MEMBERSHIP:
Twenty-two sovereign cantons.

ORGANS OF GOVERNMENT:
LEGISLATIVE: Bicameral *Federal Assembly: The National Council; The Council of States.*

The National Council: Four-year term; one Delegate for every 22,000 population or fraction above 11,000; each canton (and those divided into half cantons) at least one; direct proportional representation, each canton or half canton making one constituency. Every (male) Swiss over twenty years old, not deprived of active citizenship by his canton, eligible to vote. (But federal legislation may prescribe uniform regulations.) Clergymen ineligible for election. Delegates' salaries paid by the Federal Treasury.

The Council of States: Forty-four Delegates; two from each canton;

Charts of Confederate & Federal Constitutions

popularly elected in most of the cantons but appointed in some; cantons determine mode of election and whether the terms are one, two, three, or four years. Delegates' salaries paid by the cantons.

Both Houses elect their own President and Vice-President for each ordinary and extraordinary session from among their own members; Delegates of the same canton may not serve as President or Vice-President during the following session.

Sessions: Once a year; extraordinary sessions called by Federal Council on demand of one-fourth of the members of the National Council or of five cantons. *Quorum:* Absolute majority of total number of members of each House. *Decisions:* By absolute majority of the members voting in each House. Consent of both Houses necessary to enact federal laws, decrees, and ordinances. Legislation may be initiated by members of either House and by the cantons through correspondence.

Joint sessions to elect Federal Council, Federal Tribunal, Chancellor of the Confederation, the Commander-in-chief of the Federal Army; to grant amnesties and pardons; to decide conflicts of competence. During joint sessions, President of the National Council presides; decisions by majority of both Councils voting together.

The Federal Assembly deals with all matters transferred to Confederation and not assigned to the other federal branches.

EXECUTIVE OR ADMINISTRATIVE:

Federal Council: Four-year term; seven members; elected by joint session of the Federal Assembly, selected from Swiss citizens eligible to the National Council; not more than one member may be chosen from the same canton; subject to reelection after every election of the National Council; vacancies filled for remainder of the term at the first session of the next Federal Assembly. Members of the Council may hold no other office nor continue their profession during their term of office. *President* of the Confederation and *Vice-President* of the Federal Council elected for one year by the Federal Assembly from the members of the Federal Council. The retiring President may not be elected President or Vice-President the following year.

Quorum: At least four members; members of the Federal Council may participate in discussion and make proposals in both Houses of the Federal Assembly, but may not vote.

Duties: The Federal Council is the supreme executive authority of the Confederation; each member heads one of the Executive Departments; reports to the Federal Assembly on its administration at each ordinary session and submits special reports when requested; presents draft laws and ordinances to the Assembly. In case of emergency, when the Federal Assembly is not in session, raises needed troops, but must summon the Federal Assembly if the troops exceed 2,000 men and if they are under arms over three weeks.

Federal Chancery (or Secretariat): Headed by *Chancellor of the Confederation;* four-year term; elected by Federal Assembly; serves both Federal Assembly and Federal Council; supervised by Federal Council.

JUDICIAL:

Federal Tribunal: Members and deputy members elected by Federal Assembly, providing for representation of the three official languages of the Confederation: German, French, and Italian. Organization of the Federal Tribunal and its sections, number of members, term of office, and salary determined by Federal Assembly; Swiss citizens eligible to the Federal Council, eligible to the Federal Tribunal. Tribunal organizes its own chancery and appoints personnel.

Jurisdiction: Over disputes of civil law between the Confederation and the cantons; between the Confederation or the cantons and public corporations or private individuals when they are plaintiffs and when federal legislation determines that the dispute is important; between cantons; concerning statelessness and questions of citizenship between the different cantons. Over conflicts of jurisdiction between the Federal and cantonal authorities; conflicts on public law between cantons; over violations of rights of citizens; violations of intercantonal agreements and treaties affecting individuals. The Federal Tribunal may decide other disputes submitted to it by the parties concerned as provided by federal legislation. Additional jurisdiction may be granted by federal legislation.

The Federal Tribunal *assisted by a jury* has jurisdiction over criminal matters such as treason against the Confederation, revolt or violence against Federal authorities, crimes and offenses against international law, crimes and offenses occasioning federal armed intervention, charges against Federal officials.

Charts of Confederate & Federal Constitutions

Federal Administrative Tribunal: Jurisdiction over federal disputes referred to it; applies disciplinary measures as prescribed by federal legislation; determines cantonal administrative conflicts if jurisdiction granted by the cantons and approved by the Federal Assembly.

TRANSFERS OF JURISDICTION FROM MEMBER CANTONS TO THE CONFEDERATION:

To guarantee the cantons their territory, their sovereignty, their constitutions, the liberty and constitutional rights of their citizens, and the rights and prerogatives conferred on the authorities by the people.

To declare war and make peace; conclude alliances and treaties with foreign states, especially customs and commercial treaties.

To issue currency; fix system of weights and measures.

To manufacture and sell gunpowder (monopoly of the Confederation).

To levy customs duties at the Swiss frontiers.

To operate the postal and telegraph systems.

To levy contributions on the cantons in proportion to their wealth and taxable resources.

To receive half the gross yield of the military exemption tax levied by the cantons and to prescribe a uniform tax due from those exempted.

To legislate on foreigners entering and leaving the country and their sojourn and establishment within it; application of these regulations by the cantons subject to appeal to the Confederation; to expel foreigners jeopardizing internal or external security of Switzerland.

To regulate organization, instruction, and armament of the armed forces, but the cantons are entrusted with execution of the military laws under federal supervision and are responsible for supply and upkeep of equipment to be repaid by the Confederation.

To order and subsidize public works of interest to the nation or a considerable part of it; may prohibit public works prejudicial to the military interests of the Confederation.

To maintain stores of grain; to encourage its cultivation.

To supervise conservation measures.

To utilize hydraulic resources: may grant concessions when the cantons concerned cannot agree; taxes and dues paid for use of hydraulic power belong to the cantons concerned.

To regulate export of hydroelectric power.

To construct and operate railroads.
To regulate fisheries and hunting.
To establish and subsidize institutions of higher learning.
To subsidize cantons to help them carry out their obligation to provide compulsory free primary instruction open to adherents of all creeds.
To regulate child labor in factories; hours of labor of adults; protection against unsanitary and dangerous industries.
To supervise emigration agencies and insurance companies.
To introduce accident, sickness, old-age and survival insurance, compulsory on all or on certain classes of citizens.
To supervise roads and bridges; to regulate air traffic.
To regulate acquisition and loss of Federal citizenship.
To regulate extradition of accused persons from one canton to another; extradition for political and press offenses not compulsory.

RESTRICTIONS ON THE FEDERAL GOVERNMENT:
The Confederation may not maintain a standing army.
All vital necessities and materials necessary for industry and agriculture to be taxed as little as possible.
Export duties to be moderate.
Federal laws, international treaties concluded for an indefinite period or for more than fifteen years, Federal ordinances, when of general importance but not urgent, must be submitted for approval or rejection by the people if 30,000 voters or eight cantons so demand.

RESTRICTIONS ON THE CANTONS:
Cantonal constitutions must contain nothing contrary to the provisions of the Federal Constitution; they must provide for representative or democratic* forms of government and for the exercise of political rights; the constitutions must have been accepted by the people and must provide for amendment on demand of an absolute majority of the citizens.
Special alliances and political treaties between cantons forbidden.
The cantons may not, without Federal consent, maintain permanent troops of more than 300 men in addition to police.

* Direct application of the legislative power by assemblies of citizens instead of through their elected representatives.

CANTONS RETAIN:
All rights not delegated to the Federal authority.

To conclude legislative and administrative conventions among themselves if the Federal authorities approve; if approved, the cantons may call on the Federal authorities for cooperation in executing them.

In exceptional cases the cantons may conclude treaties with foreign states on matters of public economy, neighborhood, and police relations but these may not infringe on the rights of the Confederation or the other cantons; cantons may correspond directly with the subordinate authorities and agents of the foreign states on these matters.

To enact regulations to prevent abuse of the freedom of the press but these must be approved by the Federal Council.

To determine composition of cantonal armed contingents, nominate and promote officers, subject to instructions of the Confederation.

To organize, direct, and supervise the primary schools.

DEMOCRATIC RIGHTS:
Freedom of conscience and belief; but religious opinion frees none from performance of a civic duty.

Freedom of press; but the Confederation can prevent abuse of the Confederation or its authorities.

Freedom of lawful association.

Right of petition guaranteed.

No extraordinary tribunals may be established.

Imprisonment for debt abolished.

All corporal punishments forbidden.

Political offenses may not be punished by death.

RESTRICTIONS ON DEMOCRATIC RIGHTS:
Compulsory military service (militia); each soldier receives his first arms, equipment, and uniform free of charge; these remain in his possession under Federal regulations.

Order of Jesuits and affiliated societies may not be received in any part of Switzerland, and their members may not engage in activity in churches and schools. This prohibition may be extended to other religious orders whose activities are dangerous to the State or endanger peace between religious creeds.

Establishment of new convents or religious orders, or reestablishment of those suppressed, is forbidden.

METHODS OF ENFORCEMENT:
> The government of any canton *threatened from without* may call on the help of the other cantons, immediately informing the Federal Government; the cantons are obliged to help at the expense of the Confederation.
>
> In case of *internal troubles or threat from another canton,* the Federal Government must be informed; in case of emergency, the threatened cantonal government may call on other cantons for help or if unable to do so, the Federal Government may intervene to guarantee the cantonal territory, its constitution, the liberty and constitutional rights of its citizens and the rights and prerogatives of the authorities; the Federal Government is obliged to intervene if the disturbances endanger national security.
>
> Expenses must be borne by the canton calling for assistance unless otherwise determined by the Federal Assembly.
>
> The cantons must grant free passage to troops which come immediately under Federal command.

REVISION OF THE CONSTITUTION:

Total Revision: When one House of the Federal Assembly decides on total revision and the other House does not agree, or when 50,000 qualified voters demand total revision, the question is submitted to a vote of the people. If the majority vote for total revision, the Federal Assembly is instructed to prepare the revision for submission to the people.

Partial Revision: By popular initiative when requested by 50,000 qualified voters, stated in general terms or in a drafted proposal. This proposal, whether approved by the Federal Assembly or not (it may submit a counterproposal), and the draft for total revision come into force when accepted by a majority of the citizens voting and a majority of the cantons. The cantonal vote to be determined by the popular vote in each canton.

TITLE:
Constitution of the Union of Soviet Socialist Republics.

DATE: 1938, amended to 1940.

Charts of Confederate & Federal Constitutions

SOURCE:
State Publishing House of Political Literature (English translation printed in the Soviet Union).

TYPE:
FEDERAL. NAME: Union of Soviet Socialist Republics.

MEMBERSHIP:
Eleven Union Republics; in 1940, the Constitution was amended to add five Republics made up of Lithuania, Latvia, Esthonia, Moldavia, and former Finnish territory.

Within the *Union Republics* there may be the following political subdivisions: *Autonomous Republics, Territories, Regions, Autonomous Regions,* areas, districts, cities, rural localities.

ORGANS OF GOVERNMENT:
LEGISLATIVE: Bicameral *Supreme Soviet: The Soviet of the Union; The Soviet of Nationalities:* Both have four-year terms.

The Soviet of the Union: One Deputy for every 300,000 population. *The Soviet of Nationalities:* Twenty-five Deputies from each Union Republic; eleven from each Autonomous Republic; five from each Autonomous Region; one from each national area.

Both chambers elected by all citizens over eighteen irrespective of race, nationality, religion, educational or residential qualifications, social origin, property status, or past activities (except insane persons and those convicted whose sentences include loss of electoral rights); candidates nominated by Communist Party organizations, trade unions, cooperatives, youth organizations, and cultural societies.
(However, according to Article 126: The Communist Party . . . "is the leading core of all organizations of the working people, both public and state." Membership is confined to the "most active and politically most conscious citizens in the ranks of the working class . . ." For an understanding of the stringent membership regulations, see the Constitution of the Communist Party in *Source Book on European Governments* by William E. Rappard and others. D. van Nostrand Co., New York, 1937.—EDITORS.)
Both chambers have equal rights and the right to initiate legislation.

Sessions: Twice a year convened by the Presidium of the Supreme Soviet; special sessions convened by the Presidium at its discretion or on demand of one of the Union Republics.

Duties: Exercises exclusive legislative power; in joint session elects or appoints the other branches of the Union government.

Executive or Administrative:

Presidium of the Supreme Soviet: One President; eleven Vice-Presidents; one Secretary; twenty-four members; elected by the Supreme Soviet and responsible to it. *Duties:* Convenes Supreme Soviet; interprets laws of the USSR in operation; issues decrees; dissolves Supreme Soviet; conducts referendums; annuls decisions and orders of the Council of People's Commissars of the USSR and of the People's Commissars of the Union Republics; appoints and dismisses People's Commissars on recommendation of Chairman of Council of People's Commissars, subject to confirmation by Supreme Soviet; exercises right of pardon; appoints and removes higher command of armed forces; proclaims state of war between sessions of Supreme Soviet; orders mobilization; ratifies international treaties; appoints and recalls ministers; proclaims martial law.

Council of People's Commissars: The Chairman, the Vice-Chairmen, the Chairman of the State Planning Commission, the Chairman of the Soviet Control Commission, the People's Commissars of the USSR, the Chairman of the Committee on Arts, the Chairman of the Committee on Higher Education, the Chairman of the Board of the State Bank.

The Council of People's Commissars is responsible to the Supreme Soviet when it is in session and to the Presidium between sessions.

Duties:

Coordinates and directs work of Federal and State People's Commissariats and of other economic and cultural institutions.

Adopts measures to carry out the national economic plan and State budget.

Maintains public order.

Fixes quota for armed forces and directs their organization and development.

Sets up Special Committees and Central Administrations.

May *suspend* decisions and orders of the Councils of People's Commissars of the Union Republics and *annul* orders and instructions of the individual People's Commissars of the USSR.

The People's Commissars of the USSR: Direct the administrative departments which are federal in scope, called the *All-Union People's Commissariats,* such as:
Defense, Navy, Heavy Industry, Defense Industry, Machine-Building Industry, Foreign Affairs, Foreign Trade, Railways, Post, Telegraph, Telephones, Water Transport, Agricultural Stocks.

JUDICIAL:

Supreme Court of USSR: Five-year term; elected by Supreme Soviet; supervises activities of all judicial organs of the USSR and of the member Union Republics.

Special Courts: Five-year term; elected by Supreme Soviet.

Supreme Courts of Member Union Republics, Autonomous Republics elected for five-year terms by the respective Supreme Soviets of the Republics.

People's Courts: Three-year term; elected by direct equal suffrage and secret ballot of citizens of the various districts.

Procurator of the USSR: Seven-year term; appointed by Supreme Soviet.
Duties: Appoints for five-year terms the Procurators of the Union and Autonomous Republics, Autonomous Regions and Territories; exercises supreme supervisory power over strict execution of the laws by People's Commissariats, institutions subordinate to them, and by public servants and citizens of the USSR.

THE REPUBLICS:

The Union Republics and the Autonomous Republics: Organs of government patterned after those of the USSR with the Supreme Soviets elected by universal, direct, equal suffrage and secret ballot.

The Union-Republican People's Commissariats have jurisdiction over the following administrative departments: Food Industry, Light Industry, Timber Industry, Agriculture, State Grain and Livestock Farms, Finance, Trade, Internal Affairs, Justice, Public Health.

In Territories, Regions, Autonomous Regions, areas, districts, cities, and rural localities, the functions of local government are carried out by the *Soviets of Working People's Deputies:* Two-year terms; elected by the working people.

Executive Committees: Chairman, Vice-Chairman, Secretary, and Members; elected by Soviets of Working People's Deputies; discharge local administrative functions.

TRANSFERS OF JURISDICTION FROM MEMBER REPUBLICS TO THE UNION:

To conduct international relations; conclude and ratify treaties with foreign nations.
To declare war and make peace.
To admit new Republics into the USSR.
To supervise observance of the Federal Constitution.
To insure that Union-Republican Constitutions conform to the Federal Constitution.
To confirm boundaries between Union Republics and the formation of new Territories, Regions, and Autonomous Republics within the Union Republics.
To organize defense and to direct the armed forces.
To conduct foreign trade on the basis of State monopoly.
To establish national economic plans.
To approve the Federal budget and the taxes and revenues which go to the Federal, Republican, and local budgets.
To administer Federal banks; industrial, agricultural, and trading enterprises.
To administer transport and communications.
To direct the monetary and credit system.
To organize State insurance; to raise and grant loans.
To establish basic principles in education and public health.
To organize uniform system of national economic statistics.
To establish principles of labor legislation.
To determine the judicial system, judicial procedure, criminal and civil codes.
To regulate Federal citizenship and the rights of foreigners.
To issue Federal acts of amnesty.

Federal law prevails in case of conflict between Union-Republican laws and Federal laws.

Laws passed by the Supreme Soviet of the USSR to be published in the languages of the Union Republics.

UNION REPUBLICS RETAIN:
Right to secede from the USSR.

RIGHTS OF CITIZENS:
Right to be defended by counsel; to use own language in court and right to services of an interpreter.
Equality of citizens irrespective of nationality or race in economic, State, cultural, social, and political life; direct or indirect restriction of rights on account of race or nationality, advocacy of racial or national exclusiveness, or hatred and contempt punishable by law.
Right to work and payment in accordance with the quantity and quality of work performed.
Right to rest and leisure; vacations with pay; maintenance in old age, in case of sickness, loss of capacity to work, free medical service.
Universal, compulsory elementary education; free higher education; State aid to students in universities and colleges; free vocational, technical, and agricultural training.
Equality of women with men in economic, State, cultural, social, and political life; maternity leave with full pay.
Separation of State and school from the church; freedom of religious worship and of antireligious propaganda.
Freedom of speech, press, assembly; association in public organizations such as trade unions, cooperatives; youth, sport, and defense organizations; cultural, technical, and scientific societies.
Security against arrest except by court decision or sanction of a Procurator.

RESTRICTIONS ON DEMOCRATIC RIGHTS:
Compulsory military service.
Monopoly of political activity by the Communist Party.

AMENDMENT:
By two-thirds vote of each chamber of the Supreme Soviet.

BASIC CONSTITUTIONAL CHANGES

ON FEBRUARY 1, 1944, the Supreme Soviet of the Union of Soviet Socialist Republics amended the Federal Constitution, transforming the present Federal Departments of Foreign Affairs and Defense from All-Union to Union-Republican People's Commissariats and returning to the member Union Republics a *direct share* in the following Federal powers:

1. The right to enter into direct relations with foreign nations, to conclude agreements, and to exchange diplomatic and consular representatives with them.
2. The right to organize Union-Republican military units.

These changes actually provide for *concurrent jurisdiction* over foreign affairs and defense by the Soviet Union and the Union Republics. It is important to realize that, according to the Constitution, the Federal Government not only retains "representation of the Union in international relations, conclusion and ratification of treaties with foreign States" but now, by the amendment, also assumes the right to establish "the general character of the relations of the Union Republic with foreign States."

In the same way, while Federal direction of all matters relating to defense is retained, the amendment confers the additional power to establish "the directing principles of the organization of military formations of the Union Republics."

It must be kept in mind that the Presidium of the Supreme Soviet and the Council of People's Commissars of the Union continue to have the power *to coordinate and to annul* decisions of all Union-Republican Commissars. Moreover, the Communist Party remains "the leading core of all organizations of the working people, both public and state," and is *the government* in both the Union and the Union Republics.

These amendments may be mere wartime political maneuvers. Nevertheless, they mark a unique departure in the constitutional development of federations. Hitherto federal organization has tended toward increasing centralization. This would be the first time that a federation has attempted to decentralize toward more confederate organization by sharing jurisdiction with its member states in such all-important fields as foreign relations and defense.—EDITORS.

DEFINITIONS OF TECHNICAL TERMS USED IN THIS BOOK

Absolute majority: A vote by a majority of the total number of members (whether all are present and voting, or not). For instance, with fifty members in the legislature, a minimum of twenty-six favorable votes would be necessary to pass any law.

Aggression: Unprovoked invasion of a country or other initial act of armed hostility. (Committees of the League of Nations have tried for twenty years to define aggression without being able to agree on a satisfactory definition — EDITORS.)

Alliance: An agreement between two or more nations stating the terms of joint action in the event certain circumstances occur. The usual purpose of an alliance is joint military support by all in case of armed attack by an outside nation against any member signing the agreement.

Arbitration: The settlement of disputes between states, associations, or individuals by judges of their choice or by arbitration courts, selected by the interested parties in a manner usually regulated by prior agreement.

Armistice: A temporary cessation of hostilities by agreement — a truce for preparation of peace negotiations.

Belligerent: A nation at war.

Bicameral: Two branches or Houses in the legislative body.

Bilateral: An agreement or treaty between two nations affecting them equally.

British Commonwealth: Includes the United Kingdom of Great Britain and Northern Ireland, and all the self-governing dominions: Canada, Union of South Africa, Australia, New Zealand, the Irish Free State (Eire), and Newfoundland.

Definitions of Technical Terms

British Empire: Includes Great Britain and Northern Ireland, all the self-governing dominions; all the Crown Colonies, India, and other non-self-governing areas.

Cabinet: The heads of government departments — Internal Affairs, Justice, Education, Commerce, Agriculture, Foreign Affairs, Army, Navy and others — form the Cabinet. In parliamentary systems the Prime Minister, himself a member of Parliament, heads the Cabinet. The Cabinet is selected by the Prime Minister from elected members of Parliament, and is responsible to him and to Parliament. Each department has a political Undersecretary, an elected member of Parliament, who, in the absence of the Minister from sessions of Parliament, takes his place in answering questions regarding the conduct of the department. Each department also has an Undersecretary with only administrative duties who is a permanent civil servant. In the United States the Cabinet officers are not elected representatives. The President selects them, and the Cabinet is responsible to him.

Cartel (used internationally; in the United States, trust or monopoly): An agreement controlling the commercial policy of firms or corporations operated independently. The object is to divide markets, maintain prices, and to prevent overproduction of raw materials and manufactured articles.

Concession: Grant by a government of land or property, or the right to use them for specified purposes.

Condominium: Joint dominion or ownership. Two or more nations share the government of the same territory.

Confederation: A government of limited powers, formed by two or more nations, generally dependent on member nations for financial support and enforcement of its decisions. The central deliberative body is composed of representatives of the national governments. In forming the Confederation, nations may bind themselves to follow the decisions of the central body in whatever limited powers they have delegated to that body. But without direct means of enforcement and taxing power, the Confederation is usually ineffective unless at least

Definitions of Technical Terms

the more powerful member nations decide to assist it. Many modifications of confederate organization are possible, some of them bordering closely on federal structure. In general, however, whenever the preponderance of authority and means of enforcement in matters supposedly delegated to the supranational organization is in reality retained by the nations, especially by the more powerful ones, the organization remains confederate rather than federal in character.

Congress: A formal assembly of delegates, or a national legislature.

Constituency: The district represented by an elected official. Constituents are the voters of the representative's district.

Constitution: The fundamental organic law or principles of government of a nation, state, society, or other organized body of men, embodied in written documents, or implied in institutions and customs as, for instance, in England.

Consultative: Advisory.

Contingents: A nation's share, proportion, or quota of troops.

Conventions: Agreements between governments having the effect of law on nations ratifying them. Enforcement is left to the respective nations.

Corporative State: The State is supreme over all economic and social groups within the nation. Governmental control is exerted through a hierarchic structure of State-organized corporations of employers' federations and labor syndicates grouped according to occupation. No strikes or lockouts are permitted. Disputes between employers and labor must be settled by arbitration or by State-appointed magistrates. The State intervenes in the processes of production whenever political interests are at stake or private enterprise is unable to function effectively.

Customs Union: An agreement between two or more nations to exchange goods without quota restrictions, export, or import duties, thus establishing a free-trade area for the member nations.

De facto government: A government which is in effective control but not recognized by all nations.

Diet: In some countries the name of the legislative assembly.

Diplomacy: Conduct of negotiations between governments by appointed and instructed representatives.

Dumping: Selling quantities of goods abroad cheaper than in the home market, or even under the actual cost of production.

Embargo: Prohibition by a government of trade in certain articles or of all trade with another nation.

Eminent Domain: Right of a government to take over private property for public use for reasonable compensation.

Equity: Used with Tribunal means that the administration of justice should take into consideration principles of equality and fairness in addition to common and statute law.

Ex-officio: A given office entitles the holder to participate in other specified departments, councils, commissions, or government agencies, usually without the right to vote.

Ex post facto law: A law affecting or providing punishment for acts committed before its passage, which were not offenses under law before the act was passed. A retroactive law.

Extraterritorial: A specified area exempt from the jurisdiction of the nation in which it is located.

Federal: See Federation.

Federation: A federation is formed when two or more states or nations permanently transfer to the central government control over essentially common interests, such as defense, commerce, and currency, with the federating nations, or their people, retaining all other powers. In a federation the government generally levies its own taxes, and

Definitions of Technical Terms

the citizens usually have direct representation in the federal government. Federal enforcement agencies can operate directly on individuals in all matters under federal jurisdiction.

Full faith and credit: The aim of this clause is to provide for recognition in all states of the public acts, records, and judicial proceedings of every state. For instance, marriages performed in one state are to be considered legal in all states.

Habeas Corpus: The right of a person, either imprisoned or detained in another's custody, to be brought into court so that the lawfulness of his detention may be investigated.

Ideological: Based on similarity of ideas or theories of government.

Impeachment: To charge a public official before a competent tribunal with misbehavior in office.

Initiative, referendum, and recall: Methods of popular control over legislation. The initiative is a device by which a given percentage of voters may introduce or enact legislation. The referendum is a direct vote of the people, for or against laws either proposed or enacted by the legislature. Recall is the procedure by which the electorate is able to remove a public official from office.

International law: Body of rules arising from custom, agreements, and treaties applied by and to nations in their international intercourse. At present, these rules depend upon nations for their enforcement. Some of the plans propose that international law be formulated regularly by a world legislature and enforced under its authority.

Interstate or interregional: Relations *between* states or regions.

Intrastate or intraregional: Matters of concern *within* the state or region. Internal affairs.

Joint session: Meeting together of two or more governmental bodies; for instance, both legislative chambers meeting as one.

Jurisdiction: The authority of a court to hear and decide cases, or of a government to control and to make laws. Jurisdiction may be limited to specific matters, or it may be absolute.

Concurrent Jurisdiction: Authority exercised jointly by separate legislative, administrative, or judicial bodies.

Kollegium: Used in some of the Old Plans for *Congress.*

League: A league is formed between two or more nations to accomplish common purposes. It may be an alliance without joint administrative organs or a confederation with a central administrative body of very limited authority.

Majority: The greater number of votes of those present and voting even if only one more than half.

Mandate: As used by the League of Nations characterizes colonial or dependent territories, transferred temporarily by the League to member nations which were commissioned to set up responsible governments safeguarding the welfare of native populations. Mandates were placed into A, B, C classifications according to their stage of development.

Mediation: The effort to reconcile conflicts between two or more nations by one or several nations — either impartial or equally friendly to both sides.

Ministers:

    1. *Political:* Elected Members of Parliament, selected by the Prime Minister or Premier to head governmental departments, responsible to him and to Parliament. Together with the Prime Minister or Premier, they form the Cabinet in parliamentary systems of government.

    2. *Diplomatic:* Ministers appointed by governments to head their legations abroad to conduct diplomatic business. Smaller nations are generally represented by legations instead of embassies and they also receive legations from the large countries. The functions, rights, and duties of ministers and ambassadors are the same.

National (of a country): Means the same thing as a citizen of a country.

Definitions of Technical Terms

Parliament: Name of the legislative body in many countries.

Plebiscite: Vote of the people on questions submitted for their adoption or rejection — usually concerning their choice of nationality.

Plenary sessions: Full meeting of the whole membership of legislatures, conferences, or assemblies.

Plenipotentiary: A person given full power to transact any business for his government, often conferred temporarily on diplomatic agents.

President, King, or Governor in Council: The President, King, or Governor acting with the advice of his Council.

Prime Minister or Premier: The responsible head of the executive and administrative branches of the government. He must be an elected Member of Parliament, designated by the King or chief executive. If the party disapproves of the person chosen Prime Minister, no party member would consent to serve in his Cabinet, thus forcing appointment of someone more acceptable to the party in power.

Prize Court: A court having jurisdiction over captures at sea in time of war.

Proportional Representation (P. R.) with a single transferable vote: Proportional representation is a method of voting to secure representation for minorities in elected bodies. There are several systems but practically all of them are based on election of candidates at large, from wide areas rather than from separate wards or districts. The single transferable vote is also called the Hare system. Under it, the voter indicates his preferences among the various candidates by marking his first choice and his succeeding choices. Its advocates claim it secures the representation of groups in proportion to their numbers, gives the voters complete freedom of choice, and protects the ballot against manipulation by parties.

Provisional government: Temporary government. Provisional government may be official or unofficial. (Examples: the temporary governments of Holland, Norway, and others — governments-in-exile — are officially recognized by many nations; the unofficial provisional Czech government set up by Thomas G. Masaryk in Pittsburgh during World War I was recognized at the end of the war.)

Definitions of Technical Terms

Quorum: A fixed proportion of the full membership of any governmental body which must be present for the legal carrying on of business.

Ratify: To approve formally.

Regional: Limited to nations within a certain area. The units of the region may be contiguous (touching) or may be grouped around a body of water.

Sanctions: Coercive economic, military, or other measures to prevent or to punish violations of international agreements by nations.

Secession: Withdrawal by a nation or state from membership in a political organization.

Secretariat: Administrative staff under a responsible public official, usually a Secretary-General, to assist him in carrying out his duties.

Sovereignty: Independent, unlimited political authority or jurisdiction. In the charts we have used transfers of jurisdiction instead of transfers of sovereignty.

Staggered Term: Arrangements whereby terms of elective or appointive office expire at different times in order to provide continuity of experience in governmental bodies.

Subregional: A smaller regional group within a more inclusive body.

Supranational: Above nations or national interests.

Tribunal: A court, or forum of justice.

Unicameral: Only one chamber or House in the legislative body.

Unit vote:
1. All national delegates, each having a vote, must vote the same way on every issue.
2. A whole national delegation, irrespective of numbers, has together only one vote.

Union: Two or more nations united under one government whose form they determine.

United Kingdom: Includes England, Scotland, Wales, Northern Ireland, Isle of Man, and Channel Islands.

Universal: Every nation may join — worldwide, global, all-inclusive.

INDEX

INDEX

Abend, Hallett 6
Achaian League 383
Addams, Jane 405
Administration
 by neutrals 89
 See: Organs of Government
Administrative Powers
 See: Organs of Government (Executive) under individual charts
Advisory Council on Italy . . . 243
Aetolian League 382
Afghanistan 153, 211, 346
Africa 13, 33, 35, 38, 53, 63, 81, 140, 154, 168
 267, 271, 317, 367, 374, 375, 376, 377, 384, 396
Agesilaos 380
Aggression 18, 22, 37, 41, 115, 175, 369, 391
 accessory 199
 advocated 35, 47, 76
 defined 19, 260, 366, 493
 German 236, 237
 international control 156
 mineral control 26
 nations defended 205
 Poland 24
 prevention 189, 200
 punished 93
 raw materials 26
 regional areas 189
 renounced 230, 238
 suppression 7, 176
 Soviet Union 24
Air Force
 Anglo-American . . . 337, 350
 regional 275
Air Traffic 161
 European control 296
Alaska 377
Albania 142, 184, 211, 219, 277, 279, 289
 321, 346
Albany Congress 391
Alberoni, Giulio 38
Algeria . . . 142, 154, 184, 282
Alguy, Jeremiah S. . . . 337, 346
Aliens
 civil rights 434
 legal rights 389
Alliance 4, 5, 19, 27, 42, 47, 50, 52, 74
 Anglo-American . . 328, 337, 350
 Anglo-Saxon 81
 cantons retain 387
 counter-alliances 18
 defensive . . . 32, 236, 337, 352

Alliance — continued
 defined 493
 disadvantages 19
 ended 51
 enforcement 22
 German Princes 385
 Great Powers 394
 Holy 60
 instability 18
 Lippmann 6
 military 266, 268
 no popular control 18
 offensive 337, 352
 prohibited . . . 56, 105, 182, 311
 unnecessary 336
Allied
 cooperation 3
 food control 13
 raw material control 13
 shipping control 13
 victory 12
Allies . . . 221, 242, 244, 305, 359
Alsace-Lorraine 287, 301
Amendment
 Alguy 349
 American Constitution (U.S.) . . 439
 Argentine Constitution . . . 434
 Australian Constitution . . . 470
 Bordwell 148
 Brazilian Constitution . . . 448
 Brewer 128
 Canadian Constitution . . . 474
 Clarke 339
 Corliss 157
 German Constitution (1871) . . 420
 Harris 96
 Jennings 297
 Johnson 166
 Keen 197
 Leach 345
 League Covenant 426
 Mackay 305
 Mexican Constitution . . . 457
 Minor 106
 Newfang 136
 Rosser 173
 Rudd 226
 South African Constitution . . 479
 Soviet Constitution . . 491-492
 Speers 177
 Streit 343
 Swiss Constitution 486

Amendment — continued
United Nations Relief and Rehabilitation Administration 250-251
Venezuelan Constitution 464
Walton 125
Weinfeld 313
Amenophis IV
See: Ikhnaton
America . . 13, 14, 24, 41, 53, 63, 72, 74
See also: United States of America, Constitution (United States of America)
American Civil War 70, 466
American Constitutions
See: Constitutions (Argentine, United States of America, Brazil, Mexico, Venezuela)
American Unofficial Committee on Disarmament 357, 364
Andorra 298
Angell, Norman 8
Anglo-American Agreement . 232-235
Anglo-Egyptian Sudan 153
Anglo-Russian Treaty . . 236-239, 268
Angola 211
Anhalt 185, 283
Anonymous (1745) 38
Anonymous (1782) 47
Anonymous (1787) 48
Anonymous (1800) 56
Anonymous (1808) 61
Anonymous (1814) 66
Anonymous (1826) 72
Anonymous (1916) 277, 279
Appointment
See: Organs of Government (Executive) under individual charts
Apportionment
See: Organs of Government (Legislative) under individual charts
Arabs . . . 142, 169, 184, 211, 316, 349
Arbitration 31, 32, 56, 78, 79, 80, 109, 117
205, 386, 393, 400, 404
  advocated 399
  Balkan 325
  compulsory 37, 281, 399
  defined 493
  European 288
  industrial disputes 311
  international disputes 299, 314, 330, 350
  jurisdiction 402
  League Covenant 425
  Pan-American 401
  procedure 402
  reservations 403
  trade differences 131
  treaties 399
  World War I 357

Argentine Republic 11, 154, 270, 360, 399
421, 429
See also: Constitution (Argentine)
Aristotle 11
Arkadian Union 383
Armament
  controlled 115
  conversion 111, 131, 271
  equal limitation 307
  European control 315
  European licensing 296
  federal monopoly 278
  government manufacture 483
  international control 19, 135, 161, 219, 285
  international inspection 19, 93, 139, 189
199, 258
  international licensing . . 114, 128, 134
  international manufacture . 182, 285
  international monopoly . 204, 205, 206
  international regulation . 93, 200, 280
  international supervision . 219, 280
  investigation 365
  limitation 45, 49, 78, 134, 192, 196, 330
365, 400
  manufacture suspended . . 110, 111
  monopoly of democracies . . 199, 202
  national manufacture prohibited . 172
  postwar regulation 240
  prevention 175
  quota reduction 363
  reduction 50, 51, 61, 122, 135, 196, 273, 330
366, 399
  reports 365
  restrictions 124
  scrapping 111
  world government monopoly . . . 118
Armed Contingents 43, 397
  Greek 381, 382
Armistice . . 89, 286, 351, 361-362
  defined 493
  equal representation 165
  equal terms 165
  joint 232
  simultaneous 406
  three-year 176
Army
  abolished 53
Articles of Confederation . . 392, 393
Asia 14, 35, 38, 52, 63, 81, 140, 154, 168, 181
225, 262, 267, 270, 271, 276, 285, 328, 367, 376
384, 478
Asia Minor 281
Athens 380, 382
Atlantic Charter . 230-231, 232, 246, 259
Atrocities
  German 242

Index

Authority Granted International Unions
See: Transfers of Jurisdiction
Autonomy 404
  cultural 51, 319
  Egypt 381
  Greece 381, 383
  Hungary 397
Ausgleich 397
Australasia 154
Australia, Commonwealth of   11, 63, 154
168, 173, 182, 225, 231, 270, 279, 295, 329, 340
          367, 378, 392, 421, 465, 466, 493
See also: Constitution (Australia), British Commonwealth
Austria   20, 39, 47, 50, 60, 64, 70, 75, 78, 120
152, 153, 211, 219, 241, 242, 277, 282, 283, 289
301, 308, 317, 351, 385, 393, 394, 395, 397, 398
Austria-Hungary   279, 282, 359, 362, 397
Aviation (civil)
  federal monopoly 200
Axis   12, 18, 133, 159, 160, 174, 200, 201, 202
208, 209, 221, 226, 239, 252, 253, 255, 256, 265
        274, 277, 305, 337, 343, 348, 349, 352
  disarmed 176
  training period 159
Azores 166

Baden 185, 283, 395, 416, 419
Bahrein 333
Bain, Leslie Balogh 140
Balance of Power 39, 40
  advocated 61
  unnecessary 336
Balkan States 142, 306
Ball-Hill-Burton-Hatch Resolution . 7
Bank for International Settlements, 293, 294
Bartholdt, Richard 81
Basic English 319
Basque country 301
Basutoland 480
Bavaria 151, 185, 283, 308, 395, 416, 417, 419
Bech, Joseph
  quoted 275
Bechuanaland Protectorate . . . 480
Belgian Congo 207, 211
Belgium 36, 76, 79, 128, 154, 207, 211, 219
225, 231, 243, 269, 279, 289, 295, 301, 308, 340
                       359, 395, 421
Bellers, John 36
Benes, Eduard
  quoted 275
Bentham, Jeremy 51
Bermuda 166, 229, 353
Berne 62
Bessarabia 211, 283

Bill of Duties
  international 174
Bill of Rights . 51, 96, 129, 163, 315, 344
  international . . . 166, 174, 206, 259
  provided 157
See also: Rights, Democratic and Individual Rights
Bingham, Alfred M. 289
Birth Control 119
  international legislation 109
Bismarck 395
Bloch, Jean de 80
Blockade 128
  except food 357
  neutral 58
Blood, sweat, and tears 3
Boeotian League 381
Boer War 79, 81, 475
Bohemia 31, 282, 385
Boissy-d'Anglas 52
Bok Peace Award 9
Bolivar, Simon 73
Bolivia 153, 360, 421
Bordwell, Percy 143
Bosnia 142, 397
Bosphorus 135, 281, 301
Boundaries
  abolished 51
  linguistic 67
See also: Territorial Changes
Boycott 76, 262
  advocated 196
  neutral 58
Brailsford, H. N. 8
Brazil, United States of . . 11, 154, 360
                         421, 440
See also: Constitution (Brazil)
Bremen 388, 419
Brewer, William C. 89, 125
Briand, Aristide 287
British Commonwealth of Nations 14, 152
162, 184, 210, 212, 218, 220, 225, 261, 272, 277
278, 292, 302, 315, 337, 343, 416, 465, 466, 493
  structure 465-466
See also: British Empire, England, Great Britain, United Kingdom
British Constitutions
See: Constitution (Australia, Canada, Union of South Africa)
British Crown Colonies . . 184, 465, 494
British Empire 133, 194, 213, 227, 229, 267
268, 269, 273, 279, 346, 348, 350, 351, 421, 465
                             494
  structure 465-466
See also: British Commonwealth, England, Great Britain, United Kingdom
British Government 320

Index

British Guiana 401
British Northwest African Colonies . 211
Brunswick 185, 283, 416
Bryan, William Jennings 399
Bukovina 283
Bulgaria   142, 153, 184, 202, 211, 219, 277
                 279, 289, 321, 346, 359
Bureau of American Republics . . 401
Burma 142, 154, 168, 202, 271
Burritt, Elihu 77
Byng, Edward J. 148

Cairo Conference 244
Campaign for World Government 107, 112
Campanella 34
Canada, Dominion of   11, 79, 120, 154, 168
182, 225, 231, 270, 279, 295, 329, 340, 343, 392
                 401, 421, 465, 466, 471, 493
See also: Constitution (Canada), British
   Commonwealth
Canadian Experts 229
Can't be Done 10, 411, 412
Cantor, S. J. 120
Capital Punishment
   for political activity 448
   prohibited 414, 462
   for war crimes 255
Caribbean Islands 168 353
Cartel
   defined 494
   European control 288, 315
   international control . . . 132, 294
   international supervision . . 152
   prohibited 171, 285
Castillo, Ramon S. 435
Catholic (Roman) . 387, 430, 434, 473
   official religion 73
Catholic Church 72, 385
Censorship
   Brazil 448
Central Africa 151
Central America 367
Central American Court of Justice . 403
Chagny, Count de Paoli 69
Channel Tunnel 301
Chiang, Kai-Shek 244
   quoted 228
Children
   See: Minors
Chile 153, 360, 399, 421
China   6, 13, 33, 97, 128, 148, 154, 162, 168
181, 182, 183, 184, 189, 190, 199, 202, 207, 211
212, 219, 221, 225, 228, 229, 231, 239, 244, 247
260, 261, 267, 268, 269, 271, 272, 273, 278, 316
                 329, 352, 421
Chinese Communists 269

Chinese Nationalist Party 269
Chow, S. R. 329
Christian   31, 37, 42, 47, 49, 60, 388, 394
   princes 8, 32, 34, 35, 42
Christianity 72, 81
Church and State
   separation 55, 112, 492
Churchill, Winston   230, 231, 242, 244
                         245, 277
   quoted 187, 227, 276
Citizenship
   European 291
   federal 200
   See also: World Citizenship
Civil Service
   international 271
Civil War
   federal suppression 434
   international intervention . . 76
   Swiss 387
Clark, Grenville 337
Clarke, Crichton 337
Clootz, Baron de (Jean Baptiste du Val-de-
   Grâce) 51
Collaboration
   pledged 245
Collective Security 236, 237
Colombia 154, 421
Colonies   6, 14, 26, 40, 76, 144, 149, 151, 156
                 174, 184, 185
   British described 465
   emancipation 51, 157
   equal access 285
   European administration . 303, 305, 311
   federal administration 343
   federal control 199
   German 182
   ill-treatment 207
   international administration   16, 71, 99
   101, 110, 112, 134-136, 141, 159, 162, 168
        206, 221, 263, 269, 285, 290, 345
   international inspection . . . 258
   international policy 259
   international supervision . 191, 209, 281
                 290, 293, 296
   Italian 182
   join World State 157
   just division 41
   literacy 16
   national administration . . 196, 317
   national control 301
   national trusteeship 258
   Pan-American administration . 402
   plebiscite 160, 281
   regional pooling 209, 210-211
   regional supervision 330
   self-government 92, 110, 141, 159, 263, 269

Index

Comenius, Johann Amos (Komensky) 35
Commerce
  European regulation 297
  international regulation   21, 76, 104, 118
                140, 145, 164, 179, 339
  neutral boycott 58
Commission to Study the Organization of Peace 257
Common Man
  concern over war 8
Communication
  European control 303, 307
  European regulation . . . 297, 311
  international administration . . . 205
  international control . . . 108–109
  international regulation . . 192, 265
  international supervision . . . 128
Communist
  ideological union 14
Communist Doctrines
  forbidden 415
Communist Party . . . 487, 491, 492
Compulsory Military Service
See: Conscription
Concert of Europe 81, 394
Condominium
  British described 466
  defined 494
Condorcet, Marquis de (Marie Jean Antoine Nicolas Caritat) . . . 48
Confederacy of Delos . . . 380, 382
Confederate
  plans 4
  structure discussed 19
  world organization 8
Confederation   4, 11, 13, 19, 27, 44, 53, 64
    69, 70, 72, 73, 74, 75, 382, 389, 394
  analyzed by U. S. Convention . 10
  Czech-Polish 13, 277
  defined 494
  democracies 337
  disadvantages 19
  enforcement 22
  Greek 381
  Greek-Yugoslav 13, 277
  ideological 346
  Iroquois 388
  Italian cities 385
  national violations 18
  New England 390
  organs 18
  regional   203, 210, 211, 222, 272, 275, 288
                327, 329, 335
  Rhenish 386
  structure 18
  subregional 324, 326
  Swiss 387, 388

Confederation — continued
  Union of Utrecht 389
  United States 392
Conference
  diplomatic 13
  secret 18
Congo 153, 377
Congress of Panama (1826) . . . 73
Congress, United States of America 16, 81
                156, 180, 343
  resolutions 6
See also: Constitution (United States of America)
Congress of Vienna 385, 387, 393, 394, 395
Connally Resolution 6
Connecticut 390, 391, 392
  convention 25
Conquest
  non-recognition 404
Conscription 3, 12, 485
  abolished 300
  Argentine 434
  Brazil 448
  international advocated . . . 171
  Mexico 456
  Soviet 491
Considérant, Victor 75
Constitution
  Argentine 413, 414, 429-435
  Arkadia 380
  aspirations 413
  Australia . . 90, 302, 415, 466-470
  Brazil 413, 414, 440-449
  British Commonwealth 327, 416, 465-466
  Canada . . 90, 415, 466, 471-474
  compromises 413
  confederate 421, 426
  Europe 52, 277, 286
  See also: Constitution (Swiss Confederation, Soviet Union)
  federal   11, 416, 429, 435, 440, 449, 457, 466
                471, 480, 487
  German Confederation . . 21, 413
  German Empire . 21, 413, 416-420
  German Republic 306
  international 10
  Iroquois (Five Nations) . . . 388
  Mexico 414, 449-457
  as peace proposal 277, 286
  Portugal 306
  Spanish Republic 306
  Swiss Confederation 57, 125, 279, 284, 313
       327, 387, 388, 414, 415, 480-486
    division of authority 415
    influence 415
    no standing army 415
    structure 415

Constitution — continued
  temporarily ineffective 413
  Union of South Africa 415, 466, 474-480
  Union of Soviet Socialist Republics 184
            290, 415, 416, 486-492
    basic amendment 492
    centralized economy 415
    cultural autonomy 415
    secession permitted 416
  United States of America 10, 21, 24, 89
    94, 96, 125, 129, 137, 144, 148, 151, 152, 153
    156, 157, 177, 180, 184, 309, 327, 332, 337
        338, 340, 393, 413, 415, 435-439
    compromises 413
    division of authority 413
    drafters 10
    enforcement on individual . . 413
    influence 413
    unwritten features 413
  Venezuela 414, 457-464
  written 11
Constitutional Convention . . . 89
  advocated 162
  Arkadian 380
  European 293, 307, 316, 317
  international 7, 54, 55, 147, 150, 214, 226
  national 209, 270
  regional 270
  United States of America . . 2, 10, 24
  Journal 24
Consultation
  diplomatic 240
Conventions
  economic 12
    amendment 13
    ratification 12
  labor 427
Corliss, John B. Jr. 153
Corregidor 159
Costa Rica 231, 403
Coudenhove-Kalergi, Richard N. . 313
Council on Foreign Relations . . . 7
Council for Universal Peace and Security
                169
Courland 36, 283
Covenant of League of Nations
See: League of Nations
Cremer, Randal 398
Crimea 169
Criminal Court
  international . . . 109, 251-256, 349
Croatia 142, 301
Crozier, Alfred Owen 89, 90
Crucé, Eméric 33
Cuba 153, 231, 421
Culbertson, Ely 190, 203

Currency
  European control 307
  international 96, 109, 118, 121, 134, 155
        171, 294, 339, 342, 345
  international regulation . . . 145
  international standards . . . 114
  national stabilized 258
Customs Union
  defined 495
  international 136
Czar Alexander I 59, 60, 394
Czar Alexander III 78
Czar Nicholas II 80, 400
Czar Paul 58, 78
Czechoslovakia 13, 20, 24, 120, 142, 211
  219, 231, 243, 275, 277, 289, 293, 308, 325, 326
             328, 421, 500
  partitioned 24
Czech-Polish Governments . . . 325

Dalmatia 142, 283
Dante 31
Danubian Club of London . . . 277
Danzig 298, 315, 351
Dardanelles . 135, 168, 221, 281, 375
De Baer, Marcel 251, 357
De Boer, Saco 373, 376, 378
Declaration on Austria . . . 241-242
Declaration on Iran 245-246
Declaration on Italy 240-241
Defense
  Pan-American 402
De Gaulle, General Charles
  quoted 187
De Hamel, Herbert
  quoted 411
Dekanawideh 389
Delaware 392
Delian Confederacy 380, 382
Demilitarized Zones 365
Demobilization 168
  European 301
  gradual 165-166
  international planning 263
  internationally directed . . . 285
  neutral organization 287
  systematic 111
Democracies
  federal union 337
  united 245
Democracy 16, 404
  Greece 383, 384
  safeguards 142
Democratic and Individual Rights
  American Constitution (U.S.) . 439
  Argentine Constitution . . 433-434
  Bingham 292

Index

Democratic and Individual Rights — cont.
- Bordwell 147
- Brazilian Constitution 447
- Coudenhove-Kalergi 316
- De Baer 255
- German Constitution (1871) . . 420
- Greek National Group 323
- Johnson 165
- Mackay 304
- Mexican Constitution . . . 454-455
- Minor 106
- Rosser 172
- Soviet Constitution 491
- Stassen 265
- Streit 342
- Swiss Constitution 485
- Venezuelan Constitution . . 462-463
- Weinfeld 312
- Women's Organization for World Order 118
- Michael Young 183
- *See also:* Rights, Bill of Rights

Denmark   36, 58, 76, 78, 79, 137, 142, 153, 211, 219, 225, 243, 279, 289, 295, 308, 327, 328, 340, 360, 385, 395, 406, 421

Dictated Peace
- opposed 305

Dictatorship
- Christian 31
- presidential 413, 443

Diplomacy 400
- abolished 156
- replaced 109
- retained 243

Diplomatic Conference
- opposed 411

Disarmament . . 3, 42, 74, 75, 78, 79, 150
- advocated 63
- Axis 200, 201
- Balkan 322
- conference 293, 364
- European 299
- international supervision . . 290, 291
- punitive 12, 39, 215
- quota limitation 208, 225
- total 68
- total European . . . 297, 311, 315
- unilateral   12, 24, 231, 240, 256, 260, 263, 265, 335, 337, 349
- universal 12, 118

Discrimination
- Australia 469
- prevention 164
- prohibited 416, 491

Divorce 119
- prohibited 448

Dodd, Walter F. 416

Domination
- Athens 382
- French 386
- Thebes 381
- *See also:* Great Powers

Dominican Republic 231
Dual Monarchy — Austria-Hungary 397
Dub, Leo 318
Dubois, Pierre 31
Durand, Lieutenant Ferdinand . . 75
Dutch, Oswald 298
Dutch East Indies   142, 154, 207, 210, 211, 293
Dyruff, H. Francis 357, 358

East Prussia 142, 327, 328
Eaton, Howard O. 89
Economic Conventions
See: Conventions
Economic Interdependence . . . 41
Economic Organization
- bureaus 12
- Hanseatic 388
- international 350
- uncoordinated 12
- unions 12, 13

Ecuador 153, 421
Eden, Anthony 236, 243
- quoted 335

Education
- of Axis 215
- defeated nations 182-184
- international control . . . 164, 175
- international inspection . . . 258
- international regulation . . . 171
- international revision . . 152, 221
- international supervision . . 149, 151
- international textbook revision 108, 141
- unified international policy . . 202

Egypt   7, 154, 211, 219, 269, 279, 290, 314, 333, 346, 349, 377, 381
Eire 295
See also: Ireland, Irish Free State
Elections 9
- international
- federal regulation 22
- restrictions 22
- types 21
See: Organs of Government (Legislative, Executive) under individual charts

Ellsworth, Oliver 25
Embargo 128
Emperor Wilhelm I 78
Empire 6
- British described 465
- dissolved 156

Empire — continued
    Holy Roman 384
    liquidated 112
    Roman 384
Enforcement
    Anglo-American 332
    automatic 366
    blockade 128
    bombing 369
    coercion of states opposed . . . 24, 25
    confiscation customs duties . . 100
    defense department abolished . 89, 99
    discussed 25
    economic boycott 76
    economic sanctions . . . 193, 292
    embargo 106, 128
    expulsion 106, 135
    French policing 31
    on individuals 25, 89, 100, 109, 115, 127-
        128, 147, 156, 161, 165, 207, 361
    individuals protected 25
    legal procedure . . . 304, 316, 342
    local 25
    loss of protection 369
    military 22, 71, 74, 76, 124, 128, 193, 216
        260, 286, 292, 316, 345, 352, 357, 360
    military, naval quotas 32
    military opposed . . . 81, 89, 110
    national 25
    national rights suspended . . . 124
    by nations 323
    on nations . . . 22, 115, 156, 207, 361
    non-military 110, 122, 161
    papal excommunication 31
    public opinion 72, 74
    raw material control 26
    regional 273
    suspension 93
    tariffs 135, 136
    U. S. air supremacy 314
    voluntary 366
    voluntary compliance 71
    War 31, 32, 196
    world law 22, 110
    See also: Methods of Enforcement, Sanctions, International Army, World Army, Police
England 8, 14, 24, 32, 36, 50, 51, 58, 65, 67
    68, 69, 70, 75, 76, 80, 173, 185, 277, 290, 298
    299, 308, 309, 318, 359, 374, 391, 392, 394, 495
    500
    See also: British Commonwealth, British Empire, Great Britain, United Kingdom
Entente
    World War I 359
Erasmus 32
Esperanto 122

Esthonia . . 142, 211, 221, 289, 327, 328
Ethiopia 20, 153, 346
Europe 13, 14, 31, 33, 34, 35, 36, 37, 39, 40
    41, 42, 46, 47, 49, 52, 53, 54, 55, 59, 60, 61, 63
    65, 67, 68, 69, 70, 72, 74, 75, 78, 79, 142, 150-
    151, 154, 167, 169, 181, 220, 225, 236, 237, 238
    243, 248, 262, 267, 269, 270, 272, 275, 276, 284
    286, 287, 288, 289, 290, 295, 298, 302, 307, 308
    309, 310, 312, 316, 317, 318, 353, 358, 367, 368
        374, 376, 384, 406
European Advisory Commission . . 243
European Air Force . . . 300, 303, 310
European Army 278, 291, 296, 300, 303
        310, 315
European Bank 290, 303
European Citizenship 304
European Navy . . 291, 300, 303, 310
Executive
    See: Organs of Government (Executive) under individual charts
Executive Machinery 5, 7
Executive Powers
    See: Organs of Government (Executive) under individual charts
Expulsion 41, 64, 72, 89, 93, 126, 128, 135
    advocated 106
    Austria 395
    Japan 244
    Soviet Union 24

Fabian Society 8
Fascism
    complete destruction 240
    economic organization 414
    organizations suppressed . . . 241
    and poverty 371
Fascist
    unions 14
Federal
    authority 19
    enforcement on individuals . . 19
    international elections 22
    plans 4, 89
    structure 19, 20, 21
    union 16
    unions of democracies 21
Federal District
    Greece 383
Federal Union, Inc. 340
Federal Union, London 197
Federalism 11, 22
    adaptation 466
    See also: Federal, Federation
Federation . . . 3, 4, 11, 13, 20, 27
    African 168
    Albany Plan 391
    Asiatic . . . 168, 277, 302, 308, 314

Index

Federation — continued
  Balkan 152, 202, 283, 321, 324
  Baltic 308
  Baltic-Scandinavian 327
  Bohemian 308
  Danube 152
  defined 496
  Dutch East Indian 152
  Egypt 381
  English 308
  European 60, 64, 69, 74, 79, 80, 81, 167
  266, 277, 278, 279, 281, 282, 284, 286, 289
            294, 298, 302, 306, 309, 313
  French 308
  German 64, 308
  Greek 382, 383
  ideological 338, 340, 344
  Indonesian 266, 271
  international advocated 405
  linguistic 340
  Mongolian 168
  Near East 332
  North American 168
  old plans 35, 37, 52, 63, 64, 65, 69, 71, 75, 76
  Pan-American 314
  Pan-Arab 152
  Polish 308
  powers transferred 21
  regional   11, 167, 202, 266, 283, 295, 298
            302, 306, 309, 314, 332
  Scandinavian 308
  South American 168
  Subregional . 142, 151-152, 277, 292, 293
            301, 308, 317, 321
  universal 90, 94, 97, 102, 107, 110, 113, 116
  120, 123, 125, 129, 132, 137, 140, 144, 148
  153, 157, 160, 163, 167, 170, 173, 177, 181
Fichte, Johann Gottlieb 53
Finland   24, 142, 153, 211, 219, 279, 295
            327, 340
Five Nations (Iroquois) . . 388, 389
Flanders 301
Food Conference 229
Ford, Henry 406
Ford Neutral Conference for Continuous Mediation . . 279, 358, 403, 406, 407
Formosa 210, 211, 244, 271
Four Freedoms 83
Four-Nation Declaration . . 239-243
France   8, 24, 31, 32, 33, 36, 39, 45, 46, 47
49, 50, 51, 52, 55, 59, 62, 65, 69, 70, 75, 76, 78
128, 133, 151, 152, 154, 182, 184, 194, 207, 211
212, 219, 225, 243, 273, 277, 279, 293, 295, 305
308, 316, 320, 332, 340, 343, 353, 359, 362, 367
      385, 386, 387, 392, 393, 394, 421
Franco-Prussian War 78
Franklin, Benjamin 8, 45, 391

Free French 243, 348
Free Governments 268
Free Trade   41, 54, 55, 66, 68, 77, 108-109
            118, 136
  in colonies 350
Free Zone of Gex 162
Freedom of Commerce . . . 46, 60
Freedom of the Seas   40, 50, 54, 56, 60, 66
            67, 73, 231
  guaranteed by England 76
  guaranteed internationally . . . 114
Freedom of World Highways . . . 46
Freeman, E. A.
  quoted 380
French Committee of National Liberation
            243
French Guiana 401
French Morocco 142, 184
French Revolution . . . 47, 66, 387
French West Africa 154
Frisia 389
Fulbright Resolution 6

Gallipoli 375
Gargaz, Pierre-André . . . 8, 45, 46
General Postal Union 396
Genoese Republic 62
Georgia 392
Georgii, Eberhard Friedrich . . 62, 63
German Confederation   47, 71, 293, 385
            386, 394, 395
  See also: Rhenish Confederations
German Government . . . 189, 190, 411
Germany   12, 13, 24, 36, 38, 39, 42, 48, 64
65, 69, 79, 80, 96, 128, 129, 133, 151, 152, 154
168, 182, 183, 185, 194, 202, 206, 211, 213, 215
216, 219, 221, 225, 226, 228, 236, 237, 239, 241
242, 274, 277, 279, 282, 283, 289, 292, 293, 295
301, 305, 307, 308, 315, 316, 317, 320, 328, 333
335, 346, 351, 356, 359, 363, 375, 385, 386, 388
          395, 397, 411, 413
  international administration . . . 169
  See also: Constitution (German Empire), German Confederation, Rhenish Confederations
Geshkoff, Theodore I. 321
Gibraltar   135, 159, 168, 221, 281, 291
            375, 377
Gibson, Hugh 6
Goldin, Gullie B. 213
Gondon 60, 61
Görres, Josef 55
Goudar, Ange 41
Government
  courts 11
  evolution 11

Index

Government – continued
  personal unions 11
  popular decisions 27
  structure 18
  types 11
Great Britain 6, 148, 181, 182, 183, 189, 190
  206, 207, 225, 260, 279, 289, 291, 300, 301, 305
  315, 316, 329, 332, 333, 352, 362, 367, 393, 394
                          405, 494
See also: British Commonwealth, British
Empire, England, United Kingdom
Great Powers . . . 26, 47, 49, 52, 70
  domination 19, 20, 213, 413
  domination opposed 411
  intervention in Europe 316
  policing 273
  reservations 413
  territorial partitions 393
  trustees 352
  veto prerogative 413
Greece 13, 76, 142, 153, 184, 211, 219, 231
  243, 277, 279, 289, 306, 321, 324, 359, 421
  ancient leagues, confederations 10, 381
                          382, 383
Greek City States . . 11, 380, 382, 383
Greek National Group 321
Greek-Yugoslav Governments . . 324
Greenland 353
Griffin, Eldon 157
Grotius, Hugo 34
Groupe Interparlementaire Suédois . 9
Guatemala 231, 403, 421
Guelders 389

Habicht, Max 89, 160
Habsburgs 387, 397
Hague Conferences 80, 81, 399, 400, 401
Hague Congress of Women . 403, 404
Hague Convention for the Pacific Settlement of International Disputes . . 400
Hainan 210
Haiti 231, 421
Hamburg 388, 419
Hamilton, Alexander 24, 412
Hanover 308, 394, 395
Hanseatic Cities 21, 151, 388, 416, 418
Hanseatic League 388
Hard, William 216
Harris, Theodore 94
Harvard College 78
Hawaii 169, 378
Health
  international control 164
  international regulation . . 21, 118
  international service 108
Hedjaz 421

Henry IV 34
Herzegovina 142, 397
Hesse 185, 395, 416
Heymann, Hans 129
Hindu State 211
Hitler
  Hitlerism . . 228, 232, 237, 242, 375
Hofheim, Carl Joseph August . . 54, 55
Hohenzollern 283
Holbach, Baron Wiltrich . . . 44
Holland 65, 76, 79, 283, 360, 362, 389
See also: Netherlands, Dutch East Indies,
Union of Utrecht
Holstein 36
Holy Alliance . . . 60, 71, 394, 411
Holy Roman Empire, 384, 385, 386, 389, 394
Honduras 231, 403, 421
Honolulu 180
Hoover, Herbert 6
House of Representatives, United States of
  America 16, 413, 436
Huguenots 33
Hull, Cordell 243
  quoted 336
Human Relations
  Women's Organization for World Order
                                120
Humber, Robert Lee 6
Hungary 24, 32, 142, 154, 184, 202, 211, 219
  277, 289, 306, 317, 346, 385, 397, 398, 405
Huns 242

Iceland 167, 290, 295, 353
Ikhnaton (Amenophis IV) . . 7, 381
Illiteracy 123, 152
  education 171
  elimination 109
  free international schools . . . 155
Immediate Steps
  chart heading discussed . . . 6
  plans, practical attempts
    Anonymous (1916) 281
    Bain 142
    Bordwell 147
    Byng 150
    Cantor 122
    Chow 331
    Commission to Study the Organization
      of Peace 260
    Corliss 156
    Coudenhove-Kalergi . . . 316
    Crozier 93
    Culbertson 207-208
    De Baer 256
    De Boer 378
    Dutch 300

Index

Immediate Steps — continued
  Dyruff 361
  Goldin 214
  Griffin 159
  Habicht 162
  Heymann 132
  Joad and others 200
  King-Hall 351
  League Covenant 426
  Lloyd-Schwimmer 110
  MacIver 220-221
  Mackay 304-305
  Minor 106
  Nash 263
  Owen 139
  Paintin 115
  Pakstas 328
  Rogow 168
  Rosser 172
  Rudd 226
  Sörgel 375
  Stassen 265
  Straight 268-269
  Streit 343
  Swiss Committee 100
  Turner 180
  Van Ess 332
  Walton 124
  Weinfeld 312-313
  Weiss 278-279
  Welles 273-274
  Women's Organization for World Order 120
  George Young 307
  Michael Young 183
  Zimmermann 286
Immigration
  discriminatory 469
  equal restrictions 100
  European control 303
  European regulation . . . 311
  international regulation . . 345
  national regulation 105, 128, 156, 292, 300
                                                 339
  restrictions relaxed 175
Imperialism
  American advocated . . . 353
  Russia 75
  western 228
India 13, 33, 142, 152, 154, 168, 170, 182, 184, 189, 202, 213, 219, 220, 221, 225, 231, 261, 267, 268, 269, 270, 277, 293, 302, 308, 316, 329, 421, 465
Indians (American) 388, 389, 390, 392, 494
Individual Rights
See: Rights, Democratic and Individual Rights, Bill of Rights

Indo-China (French) 142, 152, 154, 168, 184, 207, 210, 211, 219, 271, 293
Initiative 484
Inter-Allied Committee on European Post-War Relief 248
Inter-American Bank 402
Inter-American Radio Conference . 402
International Administration . . 396
  backward nations 96-97
  China 97
  Mexico 97
  Russia 97
  defeated 96-97
  Germany 96
  See also: Organs of Government (Executive) under individual charts
International Administrative Unions 395
                                                                                      396
International Air Force . . 5, 342, 358
  proposed 259
  strength 369
  voluntary enlistment . . . 368
  See also: World Air Force
International Armed Contingents 47, 49, 50, 52, 53, 61, 72, 361
  See also: Quota Armed Force, World Army, Methods of Enforcement
International Army 5, 16, 27, 33, 42, 44, 57, 63, 67, 76, 115, 330, 331, 338, 342, 344, 363
  See also: Quota Armed Force, World Army, Methods of Enforcement
International Bureau of Exchanges . 396
International Capital 61, 68
  Aix la Chapelle 39
  Alexandria 77
  Australia 173
  Azores 125
  Basle, Switzerland 185
  Belgium 301
  Berlin 65, 185
  Canton of Zug 283
  Cologne 39
  Constantinople 77
  England 173
  Free Zone of Gex 162
  Geneva . . 39, 129, 150, 223, 308
  The Hague 129
  Hawaii 169
  Honolulu 180
  Istanbul 323
  Japan 173
  Jerusalem 70, 333
  London 185
  Madagascar 173
  Mexico 72
  Nanking 72

Index

International Capital — continued
 Netherlands 301
 New Guinea 173
 New Zealand 173
 Polynesia 63
 Rome 72, 77, 185
 Salonika 323
 Switzerland 301, 319
 Tokyo 185
 United States of America . . . 177
 Utrecht 39
 Vienna 305
 Washington, D.C. 185
International Committee for Immediate Mediation 403, 407
International Committee of Women for Permanent Peace 405
International Conference . . . 400
 permanent legislation 405
 popular mandate 122
International Court 404
 Inter-American 402
See also: Organs of Government (Judicial) under individual charts
International Court of Arbitral Justice, 401
International Geodetic Association . 396
International Institute of Agriculture, 396
International Institute of Intellectual Co-operation 314
International Labor Conference . . 427
International Labor Office 135, 198, 267
        273, 427
International Labor Organization 131, 196
217, 224, 257, 258, 293, 314, 396, 413, 424
        426-429
International Language 48, 164, 171, 173
        196
 Arabic 332
 artificial 99, 102, 122, 319
 Basic English 319
 English 102, 112, 125, 252, 301, 305, 315
     328, 332, 377, 427
 French 36, 43, 62, 102, 301, 305, 323
       325, 427
 German . . . 62, 65, 102, 301, 305
 Hebrew 332
 Latin 36, 60, 62, 384
 Spanish 369
 Swedish 328
International Law 34, 40, 42, 43 52, 59, 60
     65, 67, 70, 127, 195
 codification 77, 365
International Legislation . . 395, 396
International Navy . . . 5, 72, 342
See also: World Navy, Methods of Enforcement under individual charts
International Office of Public Health, 396

International Organization . . 6, 54
 promised 240
 structure 9
 women's initiative 404
See also: Organs of Government under individual charts
International Passport 368
International Peace Congress (Brussels)
        77
International Police Force. 127, 128, 178
      180, 189, 253
See also: Methods of Enforcement under individual charts
International Prison Congress . . . 396
International Prize Court . . . 401
International Public Works Committee .
        428
International Sea Police 191
International Technical Conferences 395
        396
International Telegraphic Conference 396
Inter-Parliamentary Union 9, 81, 198, 398
        400
Intervention
 advocated 77
 federal 434, 448, 463
 opposed 105, 394
Investigation
 international disputes 399
Iran 154, 211, 219, 244, 245, 346, 349, 421
See also: Persia
Iraq . . 153, 211, 219, 333, 346, 349
Ireland 152, 153, 279, 378
See also: Eire, Irish Free State
Irish Free State 211, 289, 340, 465, 493
See also: Eire, Ireland
Iroquois, Great Peace Confederacy of
       388, 391
Isoard, Jean Baptiste Claude . . . 65
Italian East Africa 210
Italian Somaliland 182, 184
Italy 24, 36, 65, 69, 79, 128, 133, 151, 154
169, 182, 184, 185, 194, 202, 211, 215, 219, 221
225, 240, 241, 243, 279, 289, 305, 306, 307, 316
335, 346, 359, 362, 367, 375, 385, 405, 421
See also: Axis, Fascism

Jackson Robert H.
 quoted 356
James, Edwin L. 2
Japan 6, 24, 128, 133, 151, 152, 154, 168
169, 173, 183-184, 185, 194, 202, 206, 209, 211
213, 219, 220, 221, 225, 226, 244, 270, 271, 278
287, 304, 329, 335, 346, 359, 367, 421
Java 378
Jebel Druze 332

Index

Jefferson, Thomas 45, 58
Jennings, W. Ivor 277, 294
Jewish National Home 215
Jewish State 209, 349
Jews   33, 70, 169, 184, 215, 317, 332, 333
Joad, C. E. M. 189, 197
Johnson, Ethel M. 427
Johnson, Richard Burton 163
Josephy, F. L. 189, 197
Judicial Machinery 5, 7
Judiciary, Judicial
See: Organs of Government (Judicial) under individual charts
Jurisdiction
See: Transfers of Jurisdiction under individual charts

Kaiser Wilhelm Canal 281
Kant, Immanuel 53, 54
Keen, Frank Noel 189, 194
Kelland, Clarence Budington   5, 337, 351
Kenya 182, 184
Kiel Canal 135
Kimber, C. D. 189, 197
King-Hall, Stephen 337, 349
Korea   154, 168, 210, 211, 219, 244, 271, 329
Kossuth, Louis 397
Krause, Karl Christian Friedrich . 63, 64
Kurhessen 395
Kuril Islands 210

Labor
battalions of unemployed . . . 223
compulsory 119
demobilization 75
Ladd, William 73
La Noue, François de 33
Lape, Esther Everett 9
Latin America, 182, 210, 218, 220, 225, 273, 337
Latvia 142, 211, 221, 289, 327
Leach, Walter A. 344
League 4, 11, 56, 59, 62, 386
analyzed by U. S. Convention . . 10
defensive 53
enforcement 22
Greek 381, 382, 383
See also: Type under individual charts
League to Enforce Peace 8
League of Nations   13, 16, 19, 22, 24, 162
197, 198, 199, 209, 224, 256, 267, 288, 289, 291
292, 293, 306, 321, 323, 364, 397, 411, 421, 427
493, 498
Advisory Committee on Social Questions
258
Council 115, 357, 365, 421
Covenant   8, 11, 89, 132, 189, 194, 197, 198
247, 257, 322, 346, 367, 396, 413, 420-426
governments' proposals 9

League of Nations — continued
Health Organization 258
Mandatory Commission . . . 135, 422
Opium Advisory Committee . . . 258
Secretariat 160, 314
League of Nations Association, London, 189
Lebanon 153, 184, 332
Legislation
presidential 414
See: Organs of Government (Legislative) under individual charts
Legislative Machinery 5, 7
Legislative Powers
See: Organs of Government (Legislative) under individual charts
Legislative Procedure
See: Organs of Government (Legislative) under individual charts
Lend-Lease 174
agreement text 232
colonial development 185
international reconstruction . . . 175
Liberia 184, 346 421
Liechtenstein 279, 298
Lin, Yutang
quoted 380
Lippe 185, 283
Lippmann, Walter 6
Lips, Alexander 67
Liquidation of the War
chart heading discussed 6
Hoover and Gibson 6
plans, practical attempts
Alguy 348-349
Anonymous (1916) 282
Bingham 293
Byng 150-152
Commission to Study the Organization of Peace 260
Corliss 156
Coudenhove-Kalergi 316-317
Crozier 94
Culbertson 208-209
De Baer 256
Dutch 300-301
Goldin 214-216
Griffin 159-160
Habicht 162
Joad and others 201-202
Johnson 166
Kelland 352-353
Lloyd-Schwimmer 111
MacIver 221
Nash 263
Newfang 135
Rogow 168-169
Speers 176

516 Index

Liquidation of the War — continued
Stassen 265
Straight 269-271
Swiss Committee 101
Van Ess 332-333
Welles 274
George Young 308
Michael Young 183-185
Zimmermann 287
Literacy 16, 20, 22
Lithuania . . . 142, 211, 221, 289, 327
Livonia 283
Lloyd, Lola Maverick . . . 89, 107
quoted 83
Lombard Leagues 385
Lombard Republics 62
London International Assembly . . 251
Lord Bryce 8
Lord Davies 411
Lübeck 388, 418
Lucerne 387
Luxembourg 211, 225, 231, 243, 275, 289
295, 298
Lykian League 383
Lykomedes 383

Macedonia . . . 301, 315, 381, 383
MacIver, Robert Morrison . . . 218
Mackay, R. W. G. 277, 302
Madagascar . . . 152, 153, 168, 173
Madariaga, Salvador de 8
Madison, James 24
Magellan 135
Mallinckrodt, Dr. Arnold 67
Malta 135
Manchuria . . . 20, 154, 211, 244, 271
Mandates 6, 26, 149
Australian 467
British described 465
European administration . . . 311
federal administration . . . 343
international administration 110, 112, 121
179, 180, 221, 290, 339
international supervision . . 115, 290
League Covenant 424
national administration . . . 424
self-government 112
South African 475
Marburg, Theodore 8
Marchand, P. R. 75
Marini, Antonius 32
Martinique-Guadeloupe 152
Maryland 391, 392
Masaryk, Thomas G. 500
Mason, George
quoted 24
Massachusetts 390, 391, 392

Massachusetts Peace Society . . . 69
Mead, Edwin D. 80
Mecklenburg 185, 283, 416
Mediation . 37, 39, 47, 49, 59, 74, 389, 400
advocated 70
civil war 269
commercial disputes 128
compulsory 192
defined 498
industrial disputes 128
international disputes 314
permanent office 192
popular 405, 407
women's initiative 404, 405
Melanesia 367
Membership
chart heading discussed 5
compulsory 389
discussed 13, 14
ideological 14, 16
plans, practical attempts
Alberoni 38
Alexander I 60
Alguy 346
American Constitution (U.S.) . 435
American Unofficial Committee on Disarmament 364
Anonymous (1745) 39
Anonymous (1782) 47
Anonymous (1787) 48
Anonymous (1808) 61
Anonymous (1814) 66
Anonymous (1826) . . . 72, 73
Anonymous (1916) . . . 279
Argentine Constitution . . . 429
Australian Constitution . . . 467
Bain 140
Bartholdt 81
Bellers 36
Bingham 290
Boissy-d'Anglas 52
Bolivar 73
Bordwell 144
Brazilian Constitution . . . 440
Brewer 126
Briand 288
British Government 320
Burritt 77
Byng 148
Campanella 34
Canadian Constitution . . . 471
Cantor 120
Chagny 70
Chow 329
Clarke 338
Clootz 51
Commission to Study the Organization

Index

Membership — continued
- of Peace 257
- Considérant 75
- Corliss 153
- Coudenhove-Kalergi 314
- Crozier 90
- Culbertson 203
- Czech-Polish Governments . . 326
- De Baer 251
- Dub 318
- Dutch 298
- Dyruff 358
- Gargaz 45
- Georgii 63
- German Constitution (1871) . 416
- German Government 190
- Goldin 213
- Görres 55
- Greek National Group . . . 321
- Greek-Yugoslav Governments . 324
- Griffin 158
- Habicht 160
- Hard 217
- Harris 94
- Heymann 129
- Hofheim 54
- International Labor Organization . 427
- Isoard 65
- Jennings 295
- Joad and others 197
- Johnson 163
- Kant 53
- Keen 194
- Kelland 352
- King-Hall 350
- Krause 63, 64, 65
- Ladd 73, 74
- La Noue 33
- Leach 344
- League Covenant 421
- Lips 67
- Lloyd-Schwimmer 107
- MacIver 218
- Mackay 302
- Marchand 75, 76
- Merrill 222
- Mexican Constitution . . . 449
- Minor 102
- Nägeli 57
- Nash 261
- New Commonwealth 368
- Newfang 133
- Oldenburg 78
- Owen 137
- Paine 58
- Paintin 113
- Pakstas 327

Membership — continued
- Rachel 35
- Rogow 167-168
- Rosser 170
- Rudd 224
- Saint-Germain 49
- Saint-Pierre 37, 38
- Saint-Simon 68
- Schindler 50
- Schlettwein 46, 47
- Schmidt-Phiseldek 71
- Sells 362
- Sineriz 74
- South African Constitution . 475
- Soviet Constitution . . . 487
- Speers 173-174
- Stassen 264
- Stead 80, 81
- Straight 266
- Streit 340
- Sully 34
- Swiss Committee 97
- Swiss Constitution 480
- Turner 177
- United Nations Relief and Rehabilitation Administration . . . 247
- Van Ess 332
- Venezuelan Constitution . . 457
- Von Lilienfeld 42
- Von Loen 40
- Von Palthen 42
- Walton 123
- Weinfeld 309
- Weiss 278
- Welles 272
- Women's Organization for World Order 116
- George Young 306
- Michael Young 181
- Zachariä 59
- Zimmermann 284
- regional discussed . . 13, 14, 16
- regional unions menace . . 16
- universal . . . 31, 33, 89, 396
- universal advocated . . . 14
- universal discussed . . 13, 16

Memel 317
Merrill, Robert Arthur . 190, 221
Methods of Enforcement
- chart heading discussed . . 5
- confederate 18
- on individuals 18, 19
- on nations 18
- plans, practical attempts
  - Alberoni 38
  - Alexander I 60
  - Alguy 348

Methods of Enforcement — continued
American Unofficial Committee on
  Disarmament 366-367
  Anonymous (1745) 39
  Anonymous (1782) 47
  Anonymous (1787) 49
  Anonymous (1808) 62
  Anonymous (1814) 66
  Anonymous (1916) 281
  Argentine Constitution . . . 434
  Bellers 37
  Bentham 52
  Bingham 292
  Bordwell 147
  Brazilian Constitution . . . 448
  Brewer 128
  Byng 150
  Cantor 122
  Chow 331
  Commission to Study the Organization of Peace . . . 260
  Condorcet 48
  Corliss 156
  Coudenhove-Kalergi . . . 316
  Crozier 93
  Crucé 33
  Culbertson 207
  De Baer 255
  Dutch 300
  Dyruff 361
  Fichte 53
  Gargaz 45
  Georgii 63
  German Constitution (1871) . 420
  German Government . . . 193
  Goldin 214
  Gondon 61
  Goudar 41
  Greek National Group . . . 323
  Habicht 161-162
  Hard 217
  Harris 96
  Hofheim 55
  Isoard 65
  Jennings 297
  Joad and others 200
  Johnson 165
  Keen 196
  Kelland 352
  King-Hall 351
  Ladd 74
  Leach 345
  League Covenant . . . 425-426
  Lips 67
  Lloyd-Schwimmer 110
  MacIver 220
  Mackay 304

Methods of Enforcement — continued
  Marchand 77
  Merrill 223
  Mexican Constitution . . . 457
  Minor 106
  Moser 57
  Nägeli 57
  Nash 262
  New Commonwealth . . . 369
  Newfang 135
  Owen 139
  Paintin 115
  Pakstas 328
  Penn 36
  Price 44
  Rachel 35
  Saint-Germain 49, 50
  Saint-Pierre 37
  Schindler 50
  Schlettwein 47
  Schmidt-Phiseldek . . . 71, 72
  Sineriz 74
  Speers 176
  Stassen 265
  Straight 268
  Streit 342
  Swiss Committee 100
  Swiss Constitution 486
  Turner 180
  Van Ess 332
  Venezuelan Constitution . . 463
  Von Lilienfeld 43
  Von Palthen 42
  Walton 124
  Welles 273
  Michael Young 183
  Zimmermann 286
Metric Union 396
Mexico, United States of   11, 57, 72, 97
                                         154, 168, 449
See also: Constitution (Mexico)
Migration
  international supervision . . 130, 164
  voluntary 110
Militarism
  Allied, Axis, German 12
Military Occupation . . 150, 183, 184
  France 394
See also: Liquidation of the War under individual charts
Military Research Committee of the New Commonwealth Institute . . . 367
Miller, David Hunter . . 9, 190, 411
Minor, Raleigh Colston 89
Minorities
  protected . . . 129, 193, 265, 291

Index

Minors
  education 109
  protected 9, 119
  state supervision, support . . . 46
Mobilization
  destructive 80
Mohammedan State 211
Molotov, Viacheslav Mikhailovich
  . . . . 237, 243
  quoted 356
Monaco 279, 298
Monarchy
  advocated 66
  established 183
  parliamentary advocated . . . 68, 77
  prohibited 110
Monroe Doctrine 425
Montenegro 142
Moravia 282, 385
Morocco 153, 184
Moscow Conference Declarations 239-243
Moser, Andr. 56
Mosèsco, Filippus 457
Moslems 182
Mozambique 210
Mutual Assistance 390
  pacts 365

Nägeli, Konrad 57
Naples 394
Napoleon I 55, 59, 60, 69, 385, 386, 394
Napoleon III 78
Napoleonic Wars 63, 65, 393
Nash, Philip C. 189
Nash, Walter 261
  quoted 188, 372
National, State, Provincial Rights Retained
  Alguy 348
  American Unofficial Committee on
    Disarmament 366
  Anonymous (1745) 39
  Anonymous (1916) 281
  Australian Constitution 470
  Bartholdt 81
  Bingham 292
  Bordwell 146
  Brazilian Constitution 446
  Brewer 128
  Canadian Constitution . . . 473-474
  Cantor 122
  Chow 331
  Clarke 339
  Clootz 51
  Commission to Study the Organization
    of Peace 259
  Condorcet 48
  Corliss 156

National, State, Etc. — Continued
  Coudenhove-Kalergi 316
  Crozier 93
  Culbertson 206-207
  De Baer 254
  Dub 319
  Dutch 300
  Gargaz 45
  German Constitution (1871) . . 419
  Hard 217
  Harris 96
  Johnson 164-165
  Leach 345
  League Covenant 425
  Lloyd-Schwimmer 110
  Mexican Constitution 453
  Minor 105
  Newfang 135
  Owen 139
  Paintin 115
  Rogow 168
  Rudd 226
  South African Constitution . . 479
  Soviet Constitution 491
  Speers 176
  Stassen 265
  Streit 342
  Swiss Committee 100
  Swiss Constitution 485
  Turner 180
  United Nations Relief and Rehabilitation
    Administration 250
  Van Ess 332
  Venezuelan Constitution . . . 461
  Von Lilienfeld 44
  Walton 124
  Weiss 278
  Women's Organization for World Order
    118
  Michael Young 182-183
Nations, States, Provinces Undertake
  Alexander I 59
  Alguy 348
  American Unofficial Committee on Disarmament 366
  Anonymous (1745) 40
  Anonymous (1800) 56
  Chow 330-331
  Coudenhove-Kalergi 316
  Czech-Polish Governments . 326-327
  De Baer 254
  Dyruff 361
  Greek National Group 323
  Hard 217
  Hofheim 55
  International Labor Organization, 428-429
  Keen 196

Index

Nations, States, etc. Undertake—continued
King-Hall 351
Krause 64
League Covenant . . . 424-425
New Commonwealth 369
Rosser 171
Rudd 226
Saint-Germain 50
Speers 176
Straight 268
Swiss Committee 100
United Nations Relief and Rehabilitation Administration 250
Nazi 151, 169, 317, 375
Negotiation 351
Nehru, Jawaharlal
quoted 188
Nephretite 381
Netherlands 36, 62, 128, 154, 207, 211, 219, 225, 231, 243, 269, 277, 289, 295, 297, 301, 308, 329, 340, 394, 395, 405, 406, 421, 499
See also: Holland, Dutch East Indies, Union of Utrecht
Neutral Commerce
protection 58
Neutral Conference for Continuous Mediation 404, 405
Neutral Flag 58
Neutrality
forbidden 36
maintained 56
privilege 59
reserved 289
Swiss 194, 387
Neutrals 33, 39
American 405
association 58
conduct plebiscites . . . 277, 281-282
direct international administration, 101-102
European 405, 406
initiate federation . . . 277, 286
initiative to end war 7
non-European 277
offer arbitration 277
organize elections . . . 277, 281-282
peace initiative 404
peace pressure 292
World War I 359-360
New Commonwealth . . . 358, 368
New England Confederation . 390, 391
New Guinea 173
New Hampshire 391, 392
New Haven 390
New Jersey 392
New Netherlands 391
New York 388, 391, 392
convention 24

New Yorker
quoted 2
New Zealand 153, 173, 182, 225, 231, 263, 270, 295, 329, 340, 367, 378, 421, 465, 493
Newfang, Oscar 89, 132
Newfoundland . . . 295, 465, 493
Nicaragua 231, 403, 421
Nigeria 154
Nobel, Alfred 79
Nobel Prizes 79
North Africa 290, 375
North America . . 154, 168, 352, 367
North Atlantic Ice Patrol . . . 396
North Carolina 392
Northern Ireland 500
See also: United Kingdom of Great Britain and Northern Ireland
Northern Sudan 211
Norway 142, 153, 211, 219, 225, 231, 243, 279, 281, 289, 295, 299, 308, 327, 340, 360, 406, 421, 499
Novosiltsov 59

Official Language
Dutch 466, 479
English 466, 474, 479
French 388, 474
German 388
Italian 388
Oldenburg 185
Oldenburg, Prince Elimar von . . 79
Oldenburg, Prince Peter von . 78, 79
Order of Jesuits 485
Organs of Government
chart heading discussed . . . 5
plans, practical attempts
Alberoni 38
Alguy 346-347
American Constitution (U.S.), 435-437
American Unofficial Committee on Disarmament . . . 364-365
Anonymous (1782) 47
Anonymous (1787) 48
Anonymous (1808) . . . 61, 62
Anonymous (1814) 66
Anonymous (1826) 72
Anonymous (1916) 280
Argentine Constitution . 429-432
Australian Constitution . 467-469
Bain 140-141
Bartholdt 81
Bellers 37
Bentham 52
Bingham 290-291
Bolivar 73
Bordwell 144-145

Index

Organs of Government — continued
Brazilian Constitution	440-445
Brewer	126-127
Briand	288
British Government	320
Burritt	77
Byng	149
Canadian Constitution	471-472
Cantor	120
Chow	329-330
Clarke	338-339
Clootz	51
Commission to Study the Organization of Peace	257-259
Condorcet	48
Considérant	75
Corliss	153-155
Coudenhove-Kalergi	314-315
Crozier	90-92
Culbertson	203-205
Czech-Polish Governments	326
De Baer	252-253
De Boer	376
Dub	318-319
Dutch	298-299
Dyruff	358-360
Gargaz	45, 46
Georgii	63
German Constitution (1871)	416-418
German Government	190-192
Goldin	213-214
Gondon	60, 61
Görres	55
Goudar	41
Greek National Group	321-322
Greek-Yugoslav Governments	324-325
Griffin	158-159
Habicht	160
Hard	217
Harris	94-95
Heymann	129-131
Hofheim	54, 55
Holbach	44
International Labor Organization	427-428
Isoard	65
Jennings	295-296
Joad and others	198
Johnson	163-164
Kant	53
Keen	194-195
King-Hall	350
Ladd	73, 74
Leach	344-345
League Covenant	421-423
Lips	67
Lloyd-Schwimmer	107-109

Organs of Government — continued
MacIver	218-220
Mackay	302-303
Mallinckrodt	67
Marchand	76
Merrill	222-223
Mexican Constitution	449-452
Minor	102-104
Moser	56-57
Nägeli	57
Napoleon	69
Nash	261-262
New Commonwealth	368-369
Newfang	133-134
Oldenburg	78
Owen	137-138
Paine	58
Paintin	113
Pakstas	327-328
Penn	36
Price	44
Rachel	35
Rogow	168
Rosser	170
Rudd	224-225
Saint-Germain	49, 50
Saint-Pierre	37
Saint-Simon	68
Schindler	50
Schlettwein	46
Schmidt-Phiseldek	71
Sells	362-363
Sineriz	74
South African Constitution	475-477
Soviet Constitution	487-89
Speers	174-175
Stapfer	62
Stassen	264
Straight	266-268
Streit	340-341
Sully	35
Sumner	78
Swiss Committee	97-99
Swiss Constitution	480-483
Turner	178
United Nations Relief and Rehabilitation Administration	247-249
Van Ess	332
Venezuelan Constitution	457-460
Von Lilienfeld	42, 43
Von Loen	40
Von Palthen	42
Walton	123-24
Weinfeld	309-310
Weiss	278
Welles	272-273
Willard	70

Organs of Government — *continued*
  Women's Organization . . . 116-118
  Worcester 69
  George Young 306-307
  Michael Young 181-182
  Zachariä 59
  Zimmermann 284-285
Oscar II 406
Otlet, Paul 8
Owen, Ruth Bryan 137

Pacts
  friendship 31, 32
  military 13
  war renounced 31
Paine, Thomas 58
Paintin, H. J. 113
Pakstas, Kazys 327
Palestine   70, 169, 184, 209, 211, 215, 219
                    290, 317, 332, 333
Panama 231, 421
Panama Canal 46, 135, 159, 168, 221, 378
Pan-American Conference on Housing
                                402
Pan-American Conferences . 399, 402
Pan-American Congresses 401
Pan-American Highway 402
Pan-American Sanitary Conference . 402
Pan-American Union 401, 402
Pantellaria 135
Paraguay 421
Pasadena Polytechnic Elementary School, 3
Passy, Frederic 398
Patton, George S., Jr.
  quoted 3
Peace
  aims 7
  dictated 27
  domination opposed 132
  global 6, 13
  organized 3, 4
  punitive approach 22
  ridiculed 406
  terms 7
  transition from war . . . 6, 26, 27
    Ball-Hill-Burton-Hatch Bill . . 7
    Randolph Bill 7
    Tenerowicz Bill 7
Peace Conference
  general 406
  popular participation 404
  women's participation 404
  World War I 420
Peace Plans . . . 4, 5, 7, 10, 12, 13, 27
  authors' backgrounds 8
  Axis 8
  Bok Award 9

Peace Plans — *continued*
  federal 89
  foreign 8
Peace Ship 406
Peace Treaties
  World War I 24
Peace Treaty
  creating world government . . 93
Pearl Harbor 159
Peffer, Nathaniel 6
Peloponnesian League 381
Penn, William 36
Pennsylvania 391, 392
People's Peace 4
Perim 135
Permanent Agricultural Committee . 428
Permanent Court of Arbitration   254, 291
                    357, 399, 401, 402, 422
Permanent Court of International Justice
  133-134, 195, 198, 199, 224, 254, 259, 291, 314
                322, 357, 365, 366, 422-423, 428
Persia 33, 421
  See also: Iran
Personal Union
  Austria-Hungary 397
Peru 154, 401, 421
Pescadores 244
Philippines 13, 142, 154, 168, 209, 211
                             293, 329
Piracy
  suppression 382
Planning
  economic 200, 201
  economic (Brazil) 442
  international economic . . 140, 198
  official postwar 12
  postwar 10
    directories of active organizations . 7
    World War I 12
  world economic . . . 121, 130, 298
Plebiscite
  in Axis nations 215
  defined 499
  Germany 283
  international supervision . 206
Plymouth 390
Podebrad, George 31, 32
Poland 13, 24, 36, 47, 65, 76, 142, 152, 154
  211, 213, 219, 221, 231, 243, 277, 279, 289, 293
  308, 314, 317, 325, 326, 328, 333, 335, 337, 346
                        349, 385, 393, 421
Policing
  defeated 26, 352
  liberated 26
  See also: Liquidation of the War under individual charts
Polish Corridor 351

Index

Polish Ukraine 211
Political Organization 3, 12
   required 13
See also: Organs of Government (Legislative, Executive, Judicial) under individual charts
Polynesia 81, 367
Pope Leo X 32
Popes . . . 31, 32, 33, 384, 385, 386
Portugal 36, 47, 58, 65, 76, 153, 211, 279
   289, 314, 346, 359, 393, 394, 421
Postwar Planning
See: Planning
Power Granted International Union
See: Transfers of Jurisdiction under individual charts
Prerequisites to Peace
  chart heading discussed 6
  plans, practical attempts
    Anonymous (1916) 282
    Bingham 292-293
    Byng 150
    Commission to Study the Organization of Peace 260
    Corliss 156
    Coudenhove-Kalergi 316
    Crozier 94
    Culbertson 208
    Dutch 300
    Griffin 159
    Habicht 162
    Heymann 132
    Joad and others 200-201
    Johnson 165
    Kelland 352
    King-Hall 351
    Lloyd-Schwimmer 111
    MacIver 221
    Mackay 305
    Newfang 135
    Owen 139
    Rudd 226
    Stassen 265
    Straight 269
    Streit 343
    Swiss Committee 101
    Turner 180
    George Young 307
    Michael Young 183
    Zimmermann 286
Price, Richard 44
Production
  European regulation 319
  international direction 268
  international organization . . . 301
  international regulation . . . 262

Production for Use
  agricultural 131
Proportional Representation 107, 290, 306
  advocated 107, 142
Prostitution 119
Protectorates
  British described 465
Protestant 473
Provence 45
Provisional Government
  national 201
  European 277, 278-279
   negotiate peace 279
   organize elections 279
   organizing committee . . 312-313
Provisional Union
  English-speaking 343
  negotiate armistice 343
Provisional World Government
  advocated 166, 190
  armistice condition 277
  emergency powers . . . 110-111
  official proposed 208
  organize armistice 110
  organize elections . . . 101, 112
  organize world government 110, 112
  popular initiative 26, 27
Prussia 40, 47, 50, 58, 60, 64, 70, 75, 78
  151, 185, 283, 308, 317, 393, 394, 395, 397, 413
         416, 417, 418, 420
Public Works 333
  electrification 374
  European 290-291
  European coordination . . . 288
  international 45, 46, 57, 68, 75, 76, 149
   151-152, 196, 258, 349, 350, 373, 376
  absorb demobilized 111
  support 130
  irrigation
   local 374
   national 373
  Roman 384
  state 373
  United States 271
  world road system 376
  world-wide 301, 373

Quadruple Alliance 394
Queen Elizabeth (England) . . . 35
Queen Victoria 78
Quota Armed Force 35, 37, 38, 66, 122
   128, 182, 190, 212-213, 386
  New England 390
  United States 393

Index

Rachel, Samuel 35
Rackiewicz, Wladyslaw
  quoted 335
Radio
  world government station . . . 108
Randolph, Jennings 7
Rao, B. Shiva 474
Rappard, William E. . . 480, 487
Ratification
  chart heading discussed . . . 6
  plans, practical attempts
    American Unofficial Committee on Disarmament 367
    Anonymous (1745) 39
    Anonymous (1916) 283
    Bordwell 148
    Brazilian Constitution . . . 449
    Brewer 128
    Corliss 157
    Culbertson 210
    De Baer 256
    Dyruff 362
    Greek National Group . . . 323
    Greek-Yugoslav Governments . 325
    Habicht 162
    Jennings 297
    Joad and others 202
    Johnson 166
    League Covenant 426
    Lloyd-Schwimmer 112
    Mackay 305
    Minor 106
    Rosser 172
    Rudd 226
    Speers 177
    Streit 343
    Swiss Committee 101
    United Nations Relief and Rehabilitation Administration . . . 250
    Walton 125
    Weinfeld 313
    Zimmermann 287
Raw Materials 114, 149
  access 198, 217, 331
  allocation 200
  controlled distribution . . . 21
  controlled production . . . 21
  as dues 204
  equal access . . 164, 175, 179, 230
  international control . . 164, 182
  international distribution 131, 182, 262, 267, 268
  international purchase . . 267, 268
  international supervision . . 140, 294
  reserves 351
  war-time shortage 246

Raw Materials — continued
  world control
    distribution 108-109
    production 108-109
Rearmament
  Germany 24
  secret 12, 24, 63
Reconstruction 26, 59, 101, 111, 139, 152
  agricultural 270
  Allied boards 13
  Anglo-American control . . . 300
  British-French 320
  economic 200
  European . . 285, 290-291, 300, 317
  German labor 181, 183
  immediate 165
  industrial 270
  international . . . 131, 168, 267, 268
  international administration, temporary 94
  international direction . . . 287
  international planning . . . 262
  national 263, 373
  political 200, 337
  regional 262
  world-wide 111, 373, 378
Red Cross 425
Referendum 484, 486
  world-wide 172-173
Refugee Conference 229
Refugees
  repatriation 109
  resettlement 109, 332-333
Regional Banks 130
Relief 34, 111
  Asiatic 248
  civilian 249
  emergency 164
  European 248
  food 269, 270
  immediate 166
  international 130
  international administration 229, 230, 258
  international distribution . . 262
  medical 269, 270
  national 250
  surplus foods 46
Reparations 130, 394
  financial 36, 37, 39, 41, 42, 49, 62, 193, 196, 367, 390
  individual 255
  international commission . . . 308
  opposed 221, 300, 305, 343
Representation 9
  basis 16
  compromises 16, 20

Index

Representation — continued
See also: Organs of Government (Legislative) under individual charts
Representative Government
Albany Plan 391
Belgium 389
Germany 386, 388, 395
Greece 382
Italy 385
Netherlands 389
New England 390
Switzerland 387
United States 392
German states 419
Restrictions
economic 414, 448
personal 414
political 414, 415
religious activity 456
Restrictions on Democratic and Individual Rights
Argentine Constitution . . . 434
Brazilian Constitution . . . 448
German Constitution (1871) . . 420
Mexican Constitution . . . 455, 456
Soviet Constitution 491
Speers 176
Swiss Constitution 485
Venezuelan Constitution . . . 463
Women's Organization for World Order 119
Restrictions on Nations, States, Provinces
American Constitution (U.S.) 438-439
Argentine Constitution . . . 433
Australian Constitution . . . 470
Bingham 292
Bordwell 146
Canadian Constitution . . . 474
Commission to Study the Organization of Peace 260
Corliss 156
Culbertson 206
Dutch 300
German Government 193
Mexican Constitution . . . 453-454
Minor 105
Owen 139
Paintin 115
Rosser 172
Rudd 226
Speers 176
Swiss Committee 100
Swiss Constitution 484
Venezuelan Constitution . . 461-462
Weinfeld 311
Welles 273

Restrictions on Nations, etc. — continued
Women's Organization for World Order 118
Michael Young 182
Restrictions on the Union
American Constitution (U.S.) . 439
Australian Constitution . . . 470
Bordwell 146
Brazilian Constitution . . 446-447
Coudenhove-Kalergi . . . 315-316
De Baer 254
Georgii 63
Mackay 304
Minor 104-105
Swiss Committee 99-100
Swiss Constitution 484
United Nations Relief and Rehabilitation Administration 250
Von Lilienfeld 43
Rhenish Confederations . . . 386
See also: German Confederation
Rhode Island 391, 392
Richard, Henry 79
Rights
aliens safeguarded 71
civil 71, 200, 304, 326-327, 342, 353, 420 433-434, 439, 454-455, 462-463, 485, 491
democratic 21
See also: Rights, political
economic . 9, 108, 119, 165, 172, 200, 269 312, 323, 371, 414, 420, 428, 433-434, 462-463 491
individual 53
minimum standards 259
labor 447, 455
legal 255, 312, 326-327, 342, 414, 439 462-463
neutral 58
personal 9, 66, 68, 83, 106, 118, 147, 165 172, 273, 312, 323, 326-327, 342, 349, 371 439, 454-455, 485
political 9, 71, 105, 118, 147, 165, 172 200, 269, 304, 312, 326-327, 433-434, 439 454-455
political restored 241
religious . 265, 273, 292, 323, 349, 371
social 172, 269
social welfare 447, 455
women's 119
See also: Bill of Rights, Democratic and Individual Rights
Rogow, Abe 167
Roman Catholic
See: Catholic
Roman Empire . 31, 32, 381, 382, 383, 384
Roosevelt, Franklin D. 230, 231, 242, 244 245

Roosevelt, Franklin D. — continued
  quoted 83, 227, 371
  world convention 7
Roosevelt, Theodore 400
Root, Elihu 399
Rosser, John H. 169
Rothschilds 70
Roumania 142, 154, 184, 202, 211, 219, 277
        279, 289, 321, 333, 346, 359, 421
Rousseau, Jean Jacques 38
Rowe, L. S. 429
Rudd, Herbert F. 223
Russia 8, 13, 14, 24, 34, 36, 37, 42, 43, 50
52, 58, 60, 65, 70, 75, 76, 97, 279, 282, 359, 362
                393, 394, 397
See also: Union of Soviet Socialist Republics

Saint-Pierre, Abbé de (Charles Irenée Castel) 37, 38, 44
Saintard 41
Saint-Germain, Palier de 49
Saint-Simon, Count Claude Henri de 68
Sakhalin 211
El Salvador 231, 403, 421
San Marino 279, 298
Sanctions 5, 43, 64
  defined 500
  economic 204, 207, 262, 330, 331, 348, 350
            357, 366, 404, 426
  expulsion 348
  League Covenant 426
  military 207, 262, 330, 331, 350, 426
  moral 404
  social 404
See also: Enforcement, Methods of Enforcement under individual charts
Saturday Evening Post
  quoted 2
Saudi-Arabia 333, 346, 349, 421
Saxony 47, 151, 185, 283, 308, 394, 395
                416, 417
Scandinavian States 65, 142
Schaumburg-Lippe 185
Schindler, Johann Gottfried . . . 50
Schlettwein, Johann August . . 46, 47
Schmidt-Phiseldek, Conrad Friedrich von 71
Schwimmer, Rosika . . 89, 107, 405
  quoted 83
Schwyz 387
Scotland 308, 500
Secession 55, 81, 105
  defined 500
  permitted 53, 64, 65, 122, 124, 165, 250
          256, 345, 416, 491

Secession — continued
  prohibited 382
Secret Treaties
  forbidden 52, 56
  investigated 159
  void 193, 404
Self-determination
  promised 230
Sells, Elijah W. 357, 362
Senate, Canada
  property qualification . . . 415, 471
Senate, Union of South Africa
  property qualification 475
Senate, United States of America 16, 204
             359, 399, 413, 435
  resolutions 6, 7
Senegal 152
Serbia 142, 359, 421
Shogun 152
Shogunate 151, 152
Shotwell, James T. . . 357, 364, 367
Siam 421
See also: Thailand
Siberia 281
Silesia 308
Sineriz, Juan Francisco 74
Singapore 135, 159
Slovakia 293
Slovenia 142
Smith, S. H. 58
Sonderbund 388
Soong, T. V.
  quoted 83
Sörgel, Herman 373
South Africa
See: Union of South Africa
South America 73, 77, 140, 154, 168, 352
                353, 367
South Carolina 392
Southern Rhodesia 295
Southern Sudan 211
Southwest Africa 475
Sovereignty Granted International Union 5
See also: Transfers of Jurisdiction under individual charts
Soviet Union
See: Union of Soviet Socialist Republics, Russia
Spain 32, 33, 36, 47, 58, 65, 69, 76, 154
211, 219, 279, 289, 306, 317, 337, 346, 349, 360
              389, 394, 421
Spanish Morocco 142
Sparta 381, 383
Speers, Wallace C. 173
Stalin, Joseph 242, 245
  quoted 228

Index

Stapfer, Ph. A. 62
Stassen, Harold E. 229, 263
Statement on Atrocities . . . 242-243
Statute of Westminster 466
Stead, William T. 80, 81
Steinbeck, John
   quoted 3
Stop the War
   judicial settlement 357
   neutral initiative 7
   popular efforts 79
   U. S. initiative 93
   women's initiative . . . 403-404
Straight, Michael 229, 266
Streit, Clarence K. 337, 340
Sudeten 315, 317, 351
Suez Canal   46, 57, 135, 168, 221, 281, 291
Sully, Duc de (Maximilian de Béthune) 34, 35
Sumatra 378
Sumner, Charles 77
Supranational Organization . . . 4, 5
See also: Organs of Government (Legislative, Executive, Judicial) under individual charts
Supreme Court
   legislative recommendations . . . 414
Suttner, Baroness Bertha von . . . 79
Swabia 308
Swaziland 480
Sweden   36, 58, 142, 153, 211, 219, 225, 279, 289, 295, 308, 327, 328, 340, 360, 393, 406, 421
Swedish Parliamentary Attorney General of Justice 9
Swiss Cantons 36, 152
Swiss Committee for the Preparation of the League of Nations . . . 89, 97, 284
Swiss Confederation . . . 387, 394, 480
See also: Switzerland, Constitution (Swiss)
Switzerland   50, 57, 80, 120, 153, 168, 185, 211, 219, 225, 279, 283, 289, 293, 295, 301, 308, 340, 360, 387, 396, 406, 421, 480
See also: Swiss Confederation, Constitution (Swiss)
Syria   142, 153, 184, 211, 290, 332, 349

Tariffs
   reduction 238, 294
Teheran Declaration . . . 244-245
Tenerowicz, Rudolph G. 7
Ter Meulen, Jacob 8
Territorial Changes
   chart heading discussed 6
   plans, practical attempts
     Alguy 349
     Anonymous (1916) . . . 282-283
     Bain 142

Territorial Changes — continued
   Bingham 293
   Byng 152
   Corliss 157
   Coudenhove-Kalergi 317
   Crozier 94
   Culbertson 209-211
   Dub 319
   Dutch 301
   Habicht 162
   Joad and others 202
   Kelland 353
   Leach 345
   Lloyd-Schwimmer 112
   MacIver 221
   Newfang 136
   Pakstas 328
   Rogow 169
   Schlettwein 47
   Straight 271
   Streit 343
   Swiss Committee 101
   Turner 180
   Van Ess 333
   Weinfeld 313
   George Young 308
   Michael Young 185
   Zimmermann 287
Thailand   154, 210, 211, 219, 271, 329, 346, 421
Thebes 381
Thessalian League 381
Thiers, President of France 78
Thil 381
Thuringia 185, 283
Transfers of Jurisdiction
   chart heading discussed 5
   nations unprepared 20
   plans, practical attempts
     Achaian League 383
     Aetolian League 382
     Albany Plan 392
     Alguy 347
     American Constitution (U. S.) 437-438
     American Unofficial Committee on Disarmament 365
     Anonymous (1745) . . . 39, 40
     Anonymous (1782) 47
     Anonymous (1787) 48
     Anonymous (1814) 66
     Anonymous (1826) 73
     Anonymous (1916) . . . 280-281
     Argentine Constitution . . 432-433
     Arkadian Union 383
     Australian Constitution . . . 469
     Bain 141-142
     Bellers 37

Index

Transfers of Jurisdiction — continued
Bingham	291
Boissy-d'Anglas	52
Bordwell	145
Brazilian Constitution	445-446
Brewer	127-128
Briand	288
British Government	320
Byng	150
Campanella	34
Canadian Constitution	473
Cantor	121, 122
Central American Court of Justice	403
Chagny	70
Chow	330
Clarke	339
Commission to Study the Organization of Peace	259
Confederacy of Delos	382
Considérant	75
Corliss	155
Coudenhove-Kalergi	315
Crozier	92
Crucé	33
Culbertson	205-206, 212
Czech-Polish Governments	326
De Baer	253-254
Dual Monarchy	397
Dub	319
Dutch	299
Dyruff	360-361
Gargaz	45
Georgii	63
German Confederation	395
German Constitution (1871)	418-419
German Government	192-193
Greek National Group	322-323
Greek-Yugoslav Governments	325
Griffin	159
Habicht	161
Hanseatic League	388
Hard	217
Harris	96
Heymann	131-132
Hofheim	54, 55
International Legislation	396
Jennings	296-297
Joad and others	198-200
Johnson	164
Keen	195-196
King-Hall	350
Ladd	74
Leach	345
League Covenant	423-424
Lips	67
Lloyd-Schwimmer	109-110
Lombard Leagues	385-386

Transfers of Jurisdiction — continued
MacIver	220
Mackay	303
Marchand	76, 77
Merrill	223
Mexican Constitution	452-453
Minor	104
Napoleon	69
Nash	262
New Commonwealth	369
New England Confederation	390
Newfang	134
Owen	138-139
Paintin	114
Pakstas	328
Peloponnesian League	381
Permanent Court of Arbitration	403
Price	44
Rhenish Confederations	386
Rogow	168
Rosser	171
Rudd	225-226
Saint-Germain	50
Saint-Pierre	37
Saint-Simon	68
Schlettwein	46
Schmidt-Phiseldek	71
Sells	363-364
South African Constitution	478-479
Soviet Constitution	490
Speers	175-176
Stassen	265
Straight	268
Streit	342
Sully	35
Swiss Committee	99
Swiss Confederation	387
Swiss Constitution	483-484
Thessalian League	381
Turner	179
Union of Utrecht	389
United Nations Relief and Rehabilitation Administration	249-250
United States (Articles of Confederation)	393
Van Ess	332
Venezuelan Constitution	460-461
Von Lilienfeld	43
Von Loen	40
Von Palthen	42
Walton	124
Weinfeld	310-311
Weiss	278
Welles	273
Women's Organization for World Order	118
George Young	307

Index

Transfers of Jurisdiction — continued
  Michael Young 182
  Zimmermann 285
  process discussed 19
Transition Period 150
  advocated 26, 89, 274
  five years 162
  neutral supervision 287
Transjordan 332, 349
Transportation
  international control . . . 108-109
  international regulation . . 151, 192
  war-time shortage 246
Transylvania 315
Treaties
  assistance 32
  legislative consent 404
Treaty of Westphalia . . 385, 387
Tripartite Pact 232
Truce 32, 41
Tucker, Dean 11
  quoted 10
Tunisia 142, 152, 153, 184
Turkey 34, 36, 37, 38, 42, 47, 50, 52, 76, 154
211, 213, 219, 290, 314, 321, 337, 346, 349, 359
                                                     377
Turks 8, 31, 32, 33, 70, 384
Turner, Jennie McMullin . . . 177
Twentieth Century Fund 7
Type
  chart heading discussed . . . 4
  plans, practical attempts
    Alguy 346
    American Constitution (U. S.) . 435
    American Unofficial Committee on Disarmament 364
    Anonymous (1916) 279
    Argentine Constitution . . . 429
    Australian Constitution . . . 467
    Bain 140
    Bingham 289
    Bordwell 144
    Brazilian Constitution . . . 440
    Brewer 125
    Briand 288
    British Government 320
    Byng 148
    Canadian Constitution . . . 471
    Cantor 120
    Chow 329
    Clarke 338
    Commission To Study the Organization of Peace 257
    Corliss 153
    Coudenhove-Kalergi 313
    Crozier 90
    Culbertson 203

Type — continued
  Czech-Polish Governments . . . 326
  De Baer 251
  De Boer 376
  Dub 318
  Dutch 298
  Dyruff 358
  German Constitution (1871) . . 416
  German Government 190
  Goldin 213
  Greek-National Group 321
  Greek-Yugoslav Governments . . 324
  Griffin 157
  Habicht 160
  Hard 217
  Harris 94
  Heymann 129
  International Labor Organization . 427
  Jennings 295
  Joad and others 197
  Johnson 163
  Keen 194
  Kelland 352
  King-Hall 350
  Leach 344
  League Covenant 421
  Lloyd-Schwimmer 107
  MacIver 218
  Mackay 302
  Merrill 222
  Mexican Constitution 449
  Minor 102
  Nash 261
  New Commonwealth 368
  Newfang 132
  Owen 137
  Paintin 113
  Pakstas 327
  Rogow 167
  Rosser 170
  Rudd 224
  Sells 362
  Sörgel 374
  South African Constitution . 474-475
  Soviet Constitution 487
  Speers 173
  Stassen 264
  Straight 266
  Streit 340
  Swiss Committee 97
  Swiss Constitution 480
  Turner 177
  United Nations Relief and Rehabilitation Administration 247
  Van Ess 332
  Venezuelan Constitution . . . 457
  Walton 123

Index

Type — continued
Weinfeld 309
Weiss 278
Welles 272
Willard 70
Women's Organization for World Order 116
George Young 306
Michael Young 181
Zimmermann 284

Ukraine 301
Ulster 152
Umbreit, Kenneth B. 412
Unconditional Surrender . . 256, 352
Unemployment
  European 373
  international insurance . . . 131
  solved 378
  world-wide 373
  world-wide planning . . 111, 151
Union
  counter-unions 16
  democracies 14, 197
  European 60
  global 16
  regional 320
Union for Democratic Control . 8
Union of South Africa 11, 154, 182, 225 231, 279, 295, 340, 392, 421, 465, 466, 474, 493
  member provinces described 477-478
  See also: Constitution (Union of South Africa)
Union of Soviet Socialist Republics 6, 11 128, 133, 148, 154, 162, 181, 182, 183, 189, 190 199, 202, 207, 211, 212, 213, 219, 220, 221, 225 228, 229, 231, 236, 237, 238, 239, 240, 241, 242 243, 244, 245, 246, 247, 260, 261, 267, 268, 269 270, 272, 273, 277, 290, 298, 302, 304, 306, 307 309, 314, 315, 316, 318, 328, 329, 346, 348, 352 356, 374, 486
  member republics described . 489-490
  See also: Russia, Constitution (USSR)
Union of Utrecht 389
United Kingdom of Great Britain and Northern Ireland 128, 154, 210, 230, 231 232, 233, 234, 235, 236, 237, 238, 239, 240, 241 242, 243, 245, 246, 247, 272, 295, 320, 340, 343 421, 465, 479, 480, 493, 500
  See also: British Commonwealth, British Empire, England, Great Britain
United Nations 18, 26, 89, 90, 133, 139, 140 141, 142, 144, 145, 147, 148, 150, 151, 159, 168 174, 176, 183, 200, 213, 214, 215, 216, 221, 226 228, 229, 230, 236, 238, 239, 242, 244, 245, 247 249, 250, 251, 252, 253, 254, 255, 256, 257, 259

United Nations — continued
260, 261, 262, 263, 264, 265, 266, 267, 268, 269 271, 272, 273, 274, 276, 316, 317, 357
  Agreement 231-232, 239
  Commission for the Investigation of War Crimes 251, 253
  continuing organization . . . 7
  Information Center 7
  military force 7
  provisional council 26
  Relief and Rehabilitation Administration 229-230, 246
United Nations Committee, Boston . 318
United Provinces . . 36, 50, 389, 394
United States of America 2, 6, 11, 13, 22 55, 70, 79, 128, 132, 133, 142, 147, 148, 154 162, 168, 177, 180, 181, 182, 183, 185, 189, 190 206, 207, 208, 209, 210, 211, 212, 213, 218, 220 221, 225, 229, 230, 231, 232, 233, 234, 235, 239 240, 241, 242, 243, 244, 245, 246, 247, 260, 261 267, 268, 269, 271, 272, 273, 300, 301, 304, 307 316, 329, 332, 337, 340, 343, 346, 348, 350, 351 352, 353, 360, 362, 367, 378, 393, 399, 401, 403 405, 406, 421, 435, 494
  union impossible 10
  See also: Albany Congress, America, Constitution (United States of America), New England Confederation
United States of Europe
  See: Federation, European
United States Treasury Department 229 377
Universal Postal Union 12, 193, 224, 396
Unterwalden 387
Uranium 26
Uri 387
Uruguay 153, 421
Utrecht 389

Van Brunt, Donald F. 4
  quoted 3
Van Ess, John 331
Vargas, Getulio 449
Vatican 183, 431
Venereal Disease
  compulsory registration and treatment 119
Venezuela, United States of 11, 153, 421 457
  See also: Constitution (Venezuela)
Venice 33, 36
Versailles Treaty 3, 411
Veto
  Prussia 420
  See also: Organs of Government (Executive) under individual charts

Index 531

Virginia 392
Viscount Halifax 232
Viscount Simon
  quoted 356
Visigoths 384
Von Lilienfeld 42, 44
Von Loen, Johann Michael . . . 40
Von Palthen, Johann Franz . . . 41
Voting
  compulsory 415, 470
  types 20
See also: Organs of Government (Legislative) under individual charts

Wales 308, 500
Wallace, Henry A.
  quoted 372
Walton, W. L. 122
War
  Africa 53
  America 53
  defensive 19
  humanized 400
  incitement punishable . . 109, 127, 170
  of independence 397
  intercontinental 14
  modern destructive 80
  prevention 78, 79, 406
  renunciation 78
War Crimes
  investigation 253
War Criminals
  Allied 208
  arrested 241
  Axis 208
  international trial 356
  legal punishment 266
  military tribunals 349
  punishment 37
  sentences 216, 254
  tried 243, 260
War Debts
  assumed 159
War Guilt
  impartial investigation 285
War Propaganda
  prohibited 382
Washington, George
  quoted 2, 412
Wavrinsky, Edvard 9
Weimar Republic 129
Weinfeld, Abraham 309
Weiss, José 277
Welles, Sumner . . . 229, 232, 272
Wells, H. G. 9
West Indies 367

Western Hemisphere 182, 210, 211, 267
  278, 285, 287, 293, 352, 353, 359, 401
Westphalia 308
Willard, Emma 70
Willkie, Wendell L. 6, 221
  quoted 187-188
Wilson, Woodrow 405
Winant, John G.
  quoted 371
Withdrawal
See: Secession
Wolsey, Cardinal 32
Women
  belligerent 405
  education 70
  equal rights . . . 119, 165, 416, 455
  equal political rights 388
  equality 133
  maternity care 455
  neutral 405
  peace initiative 404
Women's International League for Peace
and Freedom 112, 405
  Hungarian Section 107
  Swedish Section 107
Women's Organization for World Order
  116
Worcester, Rev. Noah 69
World Air Force, 131, 155, 182, 185, 229, 264
See also: International Air Force, Enforcement
World Army 104, 114, 131, 134, 138, 154
176, 182, 185, 219, 220, 223, 229, 262, 264, 267
  268, 276
  advocated 150, 225
  financing 206
  organization 209, 212
  powerful nations 22
  provided 171, 174, 175
  quotas 212-213
  voluntary enlistment 93
See also: International Army, Quota
Armed Force
World Bank 130, 134, 141, 155, 181, 198
  204, 206, 214
  government proposals 229
World Bill of Rights 9, 25
See also: Bill of Rights, Democratic and
Individual Rights, Rights
World Citizenship 35, 53, 59, 118, 150, 165
  172
  active 179
  basic right 109
  refugees 150
  resident 179
  restricted 104
World Constitution 111, 166, 173, 174, 177

Index

World Federation, Inc. 203
World Government 8, 10, 14, 26, 107, 132
 136, 157, 162, 172, 260, 263, 466
  armistice condition 26
  enforcement 25
  establishment 124
  federal 6
  foreshadowed 395
  legislative initiative 89
  neutral initiative 89
  popular initiative . . . 26, 110, 172
  popular unofficial initiative . . . 89
  structure 16, 18, 22
World Law 35, 59, 62
  enforcement 25, 27
  individual's relation 19, 20
See also: International Law
World Navy, 104, 131, 154, 182, 185, 229, 264
See also: International Navy, Enforcement
World Organization 4, 5, 6, 8, 9, 16, 22
 26, 59, 79, 89, 274
  confederate 8
  democratic structure 21
  membership discussed 13
World Party 163
World Police Force 3
  on individuals . . 5, 27, 164, 165, 166
  neutral units 158

World Police Force — continued
  professional 161
  voluntary 161-162
  volunteers 158
World State 153, 173
See also: Federation (universal)
World Union 33, 62
See also: Federation (universal)
World War I 4, 6, 24, 26, 90, 357, 358, 397
 403, 404, 500
World War II 4
World War III 3, 14
Württemberg 185, 283, 395, 416, 417, 419

Young, George 277, 306
Young, Michael 180
Yugoslavia 13, 142, 154, 184, 211, 219, 231
 243, 277, 289, 321, 324, 421

Zachariä, Karl Salomo 59
Zeeland 389
Zilliacus, K. 189, 197
Zimmermann, Carl . . . 277, 284
Zug, Canton of 283
Zurich 387
Zutphen 389

DARTMOUTH COLLEGE

3 3311 00817 6531